MONICA C. PARKER

The Power
of
Wonder

The Extraordinary Emotion
That Will Change the Way You
Live, Learn and Lead

HAY HOUSE

Carlsbad, California • New York City
London • Sydney • New Delhi

Published in the United States of America by:
TarcherPerigee, an imprint of Penguin Random House LLC
penguinrandomhouse.com

Published in the United Kingdom by:
Hay House UK Ltd, The Sixth Floor, Watson House,
54 Baker Street, London W1U 7BU
Tel: +44 (0)20 3927 7290; Fax: +44 (0)20 3927 7291; www.hayhouse.co.uk

Published in Australia by:
Hay House Australia Ltd, 18/36 Ralph St, Alexandria NSW 2015
Tel: (61) 2 9669 4299; Fax: (61) 2 9669 4144; www.hayhouse.com.au

Published in India by:
Hay House Publishers India, Muskaan Complex, Plot No.3, B-2,
Vasant Kunj, New Delhi 110 070
Tel: (91) 11 4176 1620; Fax: (91) 11 4176 1630; www.hayhouse.co.in

Photograph on page 282 by David Nutt. Used by permission of the author.
Book design by Shannon Nicole Plunkett

The moral rights of the author have been asserted.

The information given in this book should not be treated as a substitute for
professional medical advice; always consult a medical practitioner. Any use
of information in this book is at the reader's discretion and risk. Neither
the author nor the publisher can be held responsible for any loss, claim
or damage arising out of the use, or misuse, of the suggestions made, the
failure to take medical advice or for any material on third-party websites.

A catalogue record for this book is available from the British Library.

Tradepaper ISBN: 978-1-78817-992-8
E-book ISBN: 978-1-78817-994-2
Audiobook ISBN: 978-1-78817-993-5

Printed and bound in Great Britain by
TJ Books Limited, Padstow, Cornwall

to Julian,
the wonder of love made manifest

Contents

Part One

The Elements of Wonder

Introduction

My friend Franklin had a wicked sense of humor. Born and raised in a postage-stamp town in rural Georgia, he had the unassuming manner and warm smile of someone who could charm you out of your life savings, and you'd willingly part with it while offering to carry it to his car. He could spin a yarn in his languid julep of a voice about nothing in particular and still have you sitting on the edge of your seat waiting for the punch line. He had a particular affinity for a dirty joke, which somehow didn't seem as filthy as it should because he told it with such boyish cheek. And he always ended up laughing the hardest at his own bawdiness, equal parts naughty, proud, and embarrassed, the latter a by-product of a strict Southern Baptist upbringing. This was before Alzheimer's robbed him of his quick wit like the cruel thief it is, but, thankfully, in the ransacking, the disease missed the most precious of heirlooms—his sense of wonder.

A favorite expression of Franklin's was one he used when something made him curious or awestruck, from a new piece of whiz-bang technology to the kismet of a friend calling just when he needed to speak to them. More often than not, it was the simpler things like a strain of music or a sunrise over the lake, but on occasion, he would declare it for big aha moments, too.

He would just shake his head and say in his dewy Sandersville twang, "FM, Monica. FM."

FM stood for "f*cking magic," and this is how he saw so many of the moments that took him aback. He didn't feel the need to couch it in grand terms or even seek to understand why he felt moved. It was simply enough to mark it as remarkable. What lovely simplicity, and acute awareness, because so much of our life is f*cking magic, if only we could really see it.

And that, in many ways, is what this book is about.

What is wonder, and why do we need it?

Wonder purls its way through our lives from first cry to last gasp—moments that engage us, surprise us, take our breath away, and give us the gift of viewing the world, and our place in it, in an entirely different way. But something happens as we move from the wonder-filled days of childhood to obligation-laden days of adulthood. We become increasingly jaded. Like the sun that continues to shine on a cloudy day, wonder is still there, but we just can't seem to see it anymore. And then one day we stop looking.

Modern life is conditioning wonderproneness out of us. From an education system that curbs curiosity in pursuit of standardized test scores to a business culture that worships at the altar of the cult of overwork, we have traded wonder for the pale facsimile of electronic novelty-seeking—chasing the manufactured instead of the meaningful.

We need wonder. As a population, we are overwhelmed. The speed of information today means businesses, social campaigns, and whole governments can rise and fall, morph and meld, in only a few news cycles. Automation experts tell us that within a decade, 60 percent of our jobs will disappear or bear little resemblance to what they are today. One in four women is on antidepressants, and 90 percent of American doctor visits are for a stress-related ailment. Our device culture, while connecting us, has simultaneously cut us off from one another, and empathy levels have dropped almost 50 percent in the past twenty years. Inundated by change, distracted by choice, polarized into ever-reductive tribes, and struggling to reach equilibrium, we are living in a world of instant gratification, life hacks, and quick fixes. In short, we have been given the keys to a brave new world and can't yet reach the pedals. Wonder is the catalyst to build the social and emotional competencies we need to make us more open, more curious, more compassionate . . . more human.

Like a type of emotional DNA, wonder spirals its way through our shared human experience, imprinting itself on our lives. From artistic expression to religious faith; from the sound of music in a darkened concert hall to the charismatic timbre of a great leader; from the sunrise over the Grand Tetons to an electrical storm out the window of an airplane; from the birth of a child or a new idea to the end of a life or a feverish nightmare, wonder exists universally. Gently peeking its head around mental corners or bombastically announcing its arrival into our trembling psyches, wonder changes our perspective, our bodies, our souls, and our lives. Art, music, religion, politics, science, nature, love, fear, birth, death; each of the myriad experiences that compress to form the bedrock of human life has a golden vein of wonder running through it. Such a primal and primary element of our collective consciousness is ancient and well documented yet has only recently been defined and researched in earnest by the scientific community.

But what is it? Part of the challenge in answering that question is that wonder is often ineffable—it defies language. Wonder is both a journey and a destination. A verb and a noun. A process and an outcome. Five interlinking elements comprise the wonder cycle: *watch, wander, whittle, wow,* and *whoa* (or the psychological terms *openness, curiosity, absorption,* and the two phases of *awe*). *Watching*—being present and open—is the first step. Observe the world, taking nothing for granted, and try to see the familiar in unfamiliar ways. *Wandering* is an inquisitive cognitive stroll that allows curiosity to flourish—a meandering of the mind, and in some cases, a meandering of the body and soul, too. Then there is *whittle,* the paring down of mental aperture from broad to focused. This can be the feeling of absorption in a new idea or the purity of presence in a flow state. *Whittle* is when we are most prepared for the *expectation violation* of the *wow* moment, where our anticipation of what's next is challenged by something so vast that our mind struggles to make sense of it. And then comes the final stage, which transforms us as our psyche acclimates to this new stimulus—the *whoa*. This is the moment when we let out a long sigh and say, "OMG—mind blown." And that experience changes us, sometimes forever. We won't be rewarded with a *whoa* every time, but each element has its own benefit and beauty, offering an opportunity for discovery about ourselves and how we see and move through the world.

A quick review of the science shows a striking list of ways the five composite elements of wonder positively impact humans, not just psychologically, but physiologically and spiritually. Wonder makes us more creative and more desirous of studying the world around us. It makes us more humble, less materialistic, more generous, and better community members. People who are higher in the composite wonder elements are more likely to perform better in school and work and build healthier relationships. Wonder makes us less stressed and feel like we have more time. A very prosocial emotional experience, wonder quite simply makes us want to be better, more tolerant people. And if those aren't reasons enough to motivate us to want more wonder, the physiological benefits are particularly fascinating. Researchers have found a link between people who experience wonder and lower blood pressure, lower stress hormones, and decreased proinflammatory cytokines, the latter of which are the markers associated with a number of diseases, including cancer and cardiovascular disease. These links suggest a direct "biological pathway" between wonder and better health.

Science has so much to share about wonder, but it finds its true home in the hearts and minds of artists and philosophers. Literature and the arts are embroidered with wonder throughout so many of the stories, melodies, and images that move us. Philosophy has a rich history of inquiry into the numinous and sublime, and religion is replete with stories of wonderstruck followers like Christianity's Paul the Apostle and Hinduism's Arunja (both of whom we will meet later). In its simplest form, wonder can make us feel good. In its highest form, wonder can offer us nothing less than transcendence and a feeling of oneness with all universal life (and who wouldn't want that?).

The emotional language of wonder

Mark Twain once said rather wryly, "Man is the only animal that blushes—or needs to." Emotions are part and parcel of the human experience. From the Latin word *emovere*, meaning "moving," they are innate and complex. In his 1872 book, *The Expression of the Emotions in Man and Animals*, naturalist Charles Darwin asserted that emotions were an adaptive feature for survival and that expressions of emotions were shared across all cultures. While there are a few exceptions, Darwin was correct. For the most part, people from across the globe can identify a good number of our almost seven thousand human facial expressions.*

Emotions make us human, as does language, and the two are deeply linked. Some researchers believe that language evolved from the intimate emotional expressions exchanged between mother and child (a dynamic called *intersubjectivity*). It's likely the first words we uttered were to express emotion, and emotions and language evolved together from our innate desire to connect and be understood. Yet, even though we've been attempting to express our emotions to one another since time immemorial, we still often struggle to find a shared vocabulary for our feelings.

Emotive words are evocative, ever-changing, and while many emotions are universal, the words themselves are highly contextual and culturally nuanced. Just as the Inuit are said to have fifty words for *snow*, they also have words for which a translation doesn't exist in any other language, such as *iktsuarpok*, which is the anticipation of waiting for someone, when you are filled with such yearning that you keep going outside to check on their arrival. Some languages, and some people, have richer, more precise emotional vocabularies than others. This difference in *emotional granularity* means that while we may use the same emotive word as someone else, they could still have a different interpretation of the meaning, adding further complexity to sharing emotional experiences with one another.

Depending on which dictionary you read, *wonder* has as many as eleven definitions, as both noun and verb, including "to desire to know something" (v); "to express doubtful speculation" (v); "to be amazed" (v); "a state of curiosity" (n); "something surprising, impressive or miraculous" (n); "the feeling aroused by something surprising, impressive or miraculous" (n); "the

---

* People in remote, undeveloped areas identify certain primary emotions differently than their more modernized, urbanized neighbors.

state of being awestruck" (n). In looking at the history of the word, we can find wonder in the lexicon of both Greek (teras) and Latin (miraculum) as the word for miracle, or in the verbs to admire (admiratio), to think about (cogitatio), to consider or see (theoreo). The Germanic languages split from the Latin to create a second word, wundran, likely taken from the Old Norse undr, meaning "to surprise." University of California, Santa Barbara, professor Lisa Sideris calls wonder an "umbrella term," explaining, "If you look at some of the roots of the word wonder, one etymology traces it to words like miracle, miraculous, admiration, to smile, which is interesting. Some accounts—although, it's a little bit more speculative—suggest the German, wunder, that traces it to wound—that element of awe that can open you up in a kind of terrifying way and expose you, or make you vulnerable, but then many good things can come from that kind of vulnerability."

In Chinese, wonder is translated as 奇观, "a spectacular or wonderful sight or phenomenon," with the first character, 奇, meaning "odd, strange, rare, uncanny, surprising or wonderful," and 观 meaning "sight, view, or way of looking at things." And from about the same era in India, we find the word Adbhutā in the Sanskrit treatise on the performing arts titled the Nāṭyaśāstra. Translated as "marvelous," it was said by the author to be a "durable psychological state of astonishment," triggered by the "sight of heavenly beings or events, attainment of desired objects, entry into a superior mansion, temple, audience hall (sabhā), and sevenstoried palace, and illusory and magical acts." The Nāṭyaśāstra even gave stage notes to performing artists on what sort of face one might make to express the mysterious and enigmatic nature of Adbhutā: "Eyelashes are slightly curved at the end, eyeballs are raised in wonder, and the eyes are charmingly widened."

It's intriguing to see the similarities of wonder across languages and eras: both a noun and a verb, the same magical numinous tinge, each definition a composite of several similar but not identical elements, all sitting cheek to jowl. It makes for a rich and intricate emotional brocade, and one that can be challenging to study given its complexity.

Soft science, hard science, and why wonder is tough to study

Allow me, if you will, a short whistle-stop tour of the scientific method. To explore wonder, it's helpful to appreciate some of the challenges of studying *any* emotion. At their heart, scientists are and always have been ardent observers of the world, even before they were known as scientists. Aptly called "*natural philosophers,*" until the word *scientist* was coined in 1834 by Cambridge academic William Whewell, these individuals observed, noted, collected, collated, and connected dots to better understand the mechanics of what they saw around them. Through the years, contributions gradually evolved a framework of scientific inquiry until Renaissance scientists graduated from cataloging philosophical musings in a "cabinet of curiosities" to a more systematic approach. From this, the scientific method we all learned in middle school was born—observation, question, research, hypothesis, experiment, analysis, and conclusion. Beyond rigor, the scientific method ignited the predictive power of science, fundamentally transforming how we understand, see, and change the world.

There are different branches of science, and some fit within the structure of the scientific method more neatly than others. On one side sit the natural sciences such as biology, chemistry, and mathematics, often called the *hard sciences*. On the other side sit social sciences such as psychology, sociology, and economics, known as the *soft sciences*. Soft, except in toilet paper ads, is often intended as a pejorative, and we see this through the difference in perception, gravitas, and funding given to hard sciences and soft sciences. And as some soft sciences do naturally abut certain areas of more esoteric study, like parapsychology, they are frequently lumped together. Case in point, I once shared a taxi with one of the greatest mathematicians in the world, who was pivotal in some of the early development of the internet. We were on our way to an event at the American ambassador to Poland's residence, exchanging pleasantries about our fields of study. During our short, frosty (in more ways than one) drive, he told me in no uncertain terms that humans don't even know what they want to eat for breakfast, so they certainly aren't capable of understanding their emotional state reliably enough for it to be studied. His emphatic conclusion was that all social science, and hence my career, was rubbish. Suffice it to say, we were both happy to part ways at the end of the ride (although, in fairness, he did pick up the fare).

All of these layers—creating a shared taxonomy of emotions, cultural nuances, social science skepticism, and conflation of soft science with fringe woo—stack up to create a challenging environment in which to study wonder. And my taxi-mate had a sliver of a point. Hard sciences can practice a purer form of the scientific method (the generally accepted gold standard being a randomized controlled trial). In contrast, the soft sciences rely more heavily on self-reporting and subjective data. But the human condition isn't pure. It is messy, complex, and interwoven, and it requires the interpretation of intangibles.

The brain is the most complex network known (just the complexity itself is enough to give one a wonder headache). It contains about 171 billion cells, 86 billion of them neurons, and weighs in at only about three pounds, but just fueling that complex network of cells takes up about 25 percent of our human energy expenditure. One reason many have attached themselves so enthusiastically to the emerging field of neuroscience is because it hardens up soft sciences and helps us make sense of this bafflingly complex system. Unquestionably, this technology is a remarkable addition to psychology research and has allowed us to peer inside the brain, mapping elements of psychological response, but it has also further propagated the narrative that soft isn't as good as hard. Meaning only if we can see something or test something or prove something in the brain is it real, but if we can't, it isn't.

We can study the scientific nature of love—the evolutionary psychology behind mating or the oxytocin release from a lover's touch—but that doesn't adequately express the feeling, the human need, the elation, and the pain that accompanies the loss of love. It can't capture reveling in the mystery and marvel of love at first sight, the birth of a child, a strain of music heard in a darkened concert hall that is so beautiful and pure it brings tears to your eyes. Perhaps science can now explain what's happening in our cerebrum and cerebellum during those moments, but that shouldn't make them any less magical.

In many ways, brain science is like studying lightning bugs in a jar. How do you capture the essence of an emotion in a lab, shoved into a small metal tube with the cacophony of an fMRI scanner, or wearing the tentacled helmet of the EEG? If it seems stilted, it is, especially when trying to capture the response of something as moving as wonder. Addiction specialist and psychologist Peter Hendricks fears that in losing some of the mystery, we are losing the nuance, too. "What if we were sitting here next to each other, and you stood up and slapped me in the face? And then someone said that I was experiencing this emotion we call 'anger' because my amygdala was being activated in some way? I guess that's not necessarily wrong, but it's not the whole truth—it's reductionistic."

How do we look inside our brain, while still preserving the mystery of the mind? And what is the difference between the brain and the mind? Author and early psychonaut Thomas Henry Huxley shared his sense of this brain-mind dichotomy when he rhetorically asked, "How it is that anything so remarkable as a state of consciousness comes about as the result of irritating nervous tissue, is just as unaccountable as the appearance of the Djinn when Aladdin rubbed his lamp?"* I asked these questions of some of the people I spoke to for this book. By and large, the answers were surprisingly similar, even if some were flavored with a bit more of the mystical and others more grounded in the measurable world.

One scientist described the brain as "this wonderful conductor of a machine that just does its own thing," whereas the mind connects us to wonder, suggesting "the brain could not care less about Mount Rainier [her source of wonder], but the mind does." Another described the relationship between the two as "the difference between the kitchen and the meal." And others still became deeply metaphysical, describing the brain as "simply a receiver, like a TV set," while, in contrast, the mind acts as "the third eye" and "the field of consciousness that infuses and informs the entire cosmos and all sentient life." When I asked this question of Hendricks, in the end he demurred, concluding, "I just don't know that's a question that science can address."

Despite some differences, the general consensus among these thought leaders was some version of mind-body dualism—a belief system that dates to the Paleolithic era—meaning that the brain is the hardware, the mechanical construct, the physical, the piece of a system, and the mind is the consciousness, the interactions, the supraphysical, the whole. But if there was one

---

* A "psychonaut" is a psychedelic explorer.

caveat I heard from just about every researcher, it was this: "It's complicated." There is more to the mind than just the brain.

There is a danger that as we uncover the secrets of neuroscience, as we map our brain's analog signals pulsing pain and joy and fear, as the sum of circuitry that make us human is dissected and diagrammed, some of the more delicate filaments of our human mind's sensibilities will enervate under too much scrutiny. Lightning bugs can only be held in a Mason jar for so long before they die. And with this, the nuances of the intricate and mystifying human mind can get lost in so many Technicolor brain scans.

The Happiness Trap

Chief Happiness Officers, World Happiness Report, Happy Planet Index, Gross National Happiness (Finland had the highest last year if you're curious), and even Yale University's most popular course is about, no surprise, happiness. Happiness has some good PR. Before heading into all the benefits of wonder, it feels like we should first make the case for why wonder is even worth pursuing, as opposed to, say, arguably the world's most sought-after emotion, happiness. Throughout modern history, and with little contesting, happiness has been seen as the end goal and just reward for a life of laudable toil. The positive thinking movement, abundance theory, and any number of other self-help genres see some form of happiness as the objective.

It's an unfortunate irony, then, that in a world obsessed with happiness, people are so chronically unhappy. There are 280 million people with depression globally, and in the United States alone, 40 million people are suffering from anxiety. Americans spend over $200 billion annually treating mental illnesses, and these are the numbers pre-COVID-19, after which we have witnessed an enormous increase in stress and anxiety, the long-term effects of which we will not be able to appreciate or quantify for years to come.

Brands, and anyone associated with selling those brands, want to be involved with happiness, too, which makes sense. Coca-Cola alone has given us campaigns with taglines such as "Open happiness," "Happiness starts with a smile," and #choosehappiness (not to mention that the company pretty much single-handedly developed our modern imagery of the veritable king of consumer happiness, Santa Claus). And here's the thing—Coke makes me happy.* But if I can get that feeling from a Madison Avenue–marketed carbonated beverage, perhaps there is actually more to the happiness equation.

Prior to the ancient Greek philosophers, happiness, like most things in life, was seen as a benefaction granted by the gods. (The English word *happiness* comes from the Icelandic root *happ* or "luck," so at least etymologically, luck seems to have always played some role in our happiness.) It was the great iconoclast Socrates who became the first to suggest that happiness was a cognitive and meaning-making pursuit, something in a person's control, rather than simply a gift bestowed by the gods.

About fifty years after Socrates's death, two competing interpretations of Socratic happiness emerged: hedonism and eudaemonism. Aristippus developed the notion of hedonism, i.e., happiness found in the pursuit of pleasure. He was an original libertine who reveled in excess and disdained delayed gratification (Madison Avenue would have loved Aristippus!). Aristotle, on the other hand, found hedonism vulgar. As described in his series

---

* I know this is an emotive topic for some—Coke vs. Pepsi. Please understand that I'm from Atlanta, hence loving Coca-Cola comes with the territory. We loved Coke so much in my childhood home that when the company launched New Coke, my brother built a shrine to mourn the passing of the old formula. It was a mausoleum of sorts built with sugar cubes, teenage angst, and unbridled creativity. It was, in my humble opinion, a masterpiece. But I digress.

of writings titled *The Nicomachean Ethics*, Aristotle felt that the summum bonum—Cicero's ideal of the "highest good"—was to live a
life of virtue (*arete*), and in this journey toward the highest good,
one found eudaemonia, or the conditions for "living well."*

Between scientists, philosophers, and marketers all telling us how to be happy, it's easy to get confounded. How do we
achieve happiness? But perhaps that is the wrong question. What
if we're so fixated on happiness that we've failed to question
whether happiness is what we should be pursuing? Maybe other
emotional experiences are more beneficial and more achievable.
What if, after two millennia of debating the relative benefits of
varying types of happiness, we actually could be focusing on
another, more enduring, more impactful emotional state that
would bring us both happiness and more significant benefits? A
bit like on a game show—"But wait . . . there's more!"

Why not wonder? If we are to get to the heart of what most
happiness science is exploring, it's the answer to the question,
How do we achieve summum bonum? And if that is the question, then
wonder may actually be a better (and perhaps less fraught) path
to the "highest good" in life. Simply put, it feels like we are on a
racetrack and chasing the wrong rabbit.

Let's look at the self-transcendent final element of wonder,
awe, for example. When researchers study awe, they must be
confident they are actually studying its effects and not confusing them with other positive emotions like joy, humor, or happiness—which, in many pieces of research, leads to awe being
compared directly to happiness. Consistently, happiness, while
undoubtedly positive, does not create the quantum of beneficial outcomes that awe does. And further, the materialism of

---

* The Greek etymology of the word is Eu for "good" and *daimon* for "soul." This is
similar to the French *bonheur*, which comes from the Latin *bonum auguriim*, or "good
omen." The direct Greek translation would be something akin to *flourishing* and what
modern psychologists might today call *well-being*.

hedonic happiness is actually oppositional to awe. That makes sense, as hedonic happiness is a self-focused pursuit, whereas awe is a self-transcendent one.

When I spoke to psychologist and philosopher Kirk Schneider, he referred to happiness as "potential fool's gold." This may sound strange coming from a leading figure in the positive psychology movement, but Schneider believes the "compulsion to think positively" (i.e., toxic positivity) is equally as bad as the "compulsion to think negatively" and can actually block us from experiencing the "wonder-amazement of living." He maintains that embracing negative emotions adds to the richness of our human experience. "I would say it adds to the vitality, the intensity of living, at least for many people. A fuller sense of being alive means that one has access to one's fuller ranges of thoughts, feelings, sensations, imaginings."

Melanie Rudd, associate professor of marketing at the University of Houston and an expert in the science of making us happy, isn't even making happiness a goal for herself anymore. "Personally, I stopped with the whole 'I'm pursuing happiness' thing because it's not only impossible, but I don't think it's optimal." And Rudd is hardly somber. Judging from the short time we spent together, her personality is one I would describe as ebullient. But she says that tackling happiness can feel too big, and more than that, we're actually lousy at finding it. "It's tricky because we're all so bad at pursuing happiness. There's so much research that shows that we're horrible at predicting what will make us happy." This phenomenon of misjudging what will make us happy is called *affective forecasting*, and as humans, we "miswant" a lot of things that we have been conditioned to believe will make us happier than they actually do. Negative emotions are also one way to broaden our emotional vocabulary, which helps us call up a greater variety of coping skills.

In fact, people with higher emotional granularity, or *emodiversity*, use more positive coping mechanisms and recover more quickly from stress. Rudd agrees. "We shouldn't be so focused on happiness only because there are some other reasons why we might want to broaden our positive emotion portfolio. But I think the idea here is that the better the average person understands different positive emotions, what they do, and why they exist, it makes us better able to say, I don't just want to feel good, I want to feel wonder, or I want to feel pride, or I want to feel happiness," Rudd explains. "And I think what we should be pursuing is the right emotion for our goals."

More recently, a new path to "the good life" has emerged. Shigehiro Oishi, from the University of Virginia, has been developing a theory on "psychological richness," a type of summum bonum found in a life full of a "variety of interesting and perspective-changing experiences." Oishi had research assistants review and code obituaries for an entire year from a major US newspaper and found that there were three primary ways people were described as having lived a good life—it was either happy, meaningful, or filled with fascinating encounters and experiences; that is, psychologically rich. Researchers then explored, across several different countries, people's expressed desires for the future. While wanting a happy life trumped a psychologically rich one, when participants were asked to consider what they most regretted missing out on from the past, those regrets reflected elements of a psychologically rich life (like missing the chance to attend university) more so than a happy or meaningful one, supporting Melanie Rudd's take on people often "miswanting" what will make them happy.

What kinds of people typically pursue a "psychologically rich" life? Those high in openness, intellectually curious, with a flexible world view, who experience big emotions and like to make meaning out of them—wonderprone people. And, like wonder, these psychologically rich experiences can be light and uplifting, but they can also be dark or traumatic. Oishsi's research on the benefits of a psychologically rich life would also appear to be direct evidence of the benefits of a wonder-based life as well and moves the notion of summum bonum beyond that of just the hedonically happy or eudaemonically meaningful binary.

The world, the people in it, and our experiences are not binary. Two things can coexist in opposition to each other, and both can be true at the same time. Wonder embraces that beautiful, messy complexity of life in a way happiness doesn't. It allows for nuance and depth. It allows for the reality of suckitude. That uncomfortable balancing coexistence feels more true to me than a manufactured cajoling toward happiness.

Here's the thing, though. This isn't either-or. Wonder actually begets eudaemonic happiness. Open people are happier. Deeply curious people are happier. People higher in absorption are happier. And people who are awe-prone are happier. So seeking and finding the composite elements of wonder, as opposed to happiness, is a twofer. It's more attainable, and along the way, as we get the benefits of the entire wonder cycle, we have a good chance of being rewarded with happiness too. It's great to be happy, but it's even better to be in wonder.

What you can expect from this book

There are two ways we can study an idea. We can dissect it, pulling off its wings, pinning it to a board, and filleting it open. Or we can explore ideas more holistically and look for connecting points between them. One of the scientists I spoke to put it this way: "You're either a lumper or a splitter." Lumpers like to see elements that connect and group them, finding insight in not just the elements themselves but their additive relationship to one another—what philosopher Ludwig Wittgenstein described as finding the "family resemblances" of an idea. Splitters prefer to cleave elements off and examine them down to smaller and smaller minutiae, finding value in reductionism. Wonder, with its intertwined complexity, lends itself to lumping, and because I'm a fan of the Aristotelian philosophy that the total is greater than the sum of its parts, we're going to lump and explore wonder as a composite of related states, traits, and emotions.

If we're to think of wonder as f*cking magic, consider this your wonder spell book. Look to it for ideas, theories, stories, knowledge, wisdom, inspiration, and a reminder of what you may already know in your soul but need to see written in front of you. I am sorry to report that this book will not solve all your life's problems. It will not make you thinner or improve your eyesight. It will not make your partner less annoying, and it probably won't help you quit smoking (although it could, as you'll see in Chapter 16). But it may give you a new perspective on getting the most out of life, even in the face of some really lousy times. Well, in the face of life.

In Part 1, we'll find an introduction to wonder and all its traits, states, facets, and flavors. This is where we'll build our wonder vocabulary and define each of the interconnected elements of the wonder cycle. By the end of this section, we'll be able to identify the building blocks of the holistic wonder experience. Part 2 makes the case for wonder, leaving no stone of the human experience unturned: birth and death, learning and creativity, leading and moving people to action, health and well-being, and time and space. Here we explore wonder research and illustrate ways it can be applied to all the fundamental areas of our life. This is where we find the bulk of the evidence for wonder. We'll also gain practical knowledge on building a wonder practice, cultivating a wonder mindset, and identifying wonder-bringers in our day-to-day life. And in Part 3 we explore how to become a lifelong wonder practitioner and see how releasing ourselves to the transcendent magic of wonder can be the antidote for our move-fast-break-things world, setting us up for living a life steeped in wonder's mystery.

This is the sort of book that is chock-full of concepts, studies, and stories. To help summarize, there will be a short "Wonder Wrap-Up" at the end of every chapter, ensuring you're clear on the key concepts before moving on. The footnotes and endnotes also offer additional insights, resources, references, and trivia that will allow you to further your wonder exploration as you see fit. My hope is that this is a book you will return to and reference again and again, finding it resonates with you for different reasons over time.

Openness, curiosity, absorption, and awe each have their own stories to tell, but under this wonder umbrella, toggling between wonder as a noun and a verb, we start to see all the ways they link—overlapping, sometimes converging, occasionally leapfrogging, at times nesting one inside another. What also becomes clear as we learn more about wonder is the degree to which each element connects with the others and the additive nature of those connections. The wonder whole is greater than the sum of its parts.

When I was young, my mother had a small kaleidoscope that sat on the coffee table in our living room. It was a lovely handmade tchotchke she had probably received as a gift, picked up by a friend perhaps at a craft fair or quaint curio shop. It had a polished brass tube where the mirrors hid, and at the end sat a small disk-shaped container with multicolored shards of matte beach glass that tumbled gently around inside. It was pretty from the outside, but when you peered in the peephole—*wow!* Spectacular! A riot of color and gemlike twinkling. So brilliant and so *surprising*. And with the slightest twist of the disk, the scene changed again. It was different but just as breathtaking. That's what I imagine when I think of wonder and all its elements: a kaleidoscope of different layers, each lovely and worthy of attention when parsed, but when you look at them together through just the right lens—*whoa!* A magically unexpected experience!

A sunset can just be a sunset, or it can be the thing that connects you to the universal good in humanity. Who's to say what it will be on any given day? And why? Who is more likely to experience wonder? And why did we as humans even develop wonder in the first place? These are the questions we'll try to answer about this magical and sometimes elusive experience.

Understanding wonder is part science, part soul; part praxis and part luck; part précis and part good yarn. Samuel Taylor Coleridge said any good story requires a "suspension of disbelief," or even more lyrically, "poetic faith." A dose of poetic faith is what's needed to study wonder. So might I suggest during the course of our wonder exploration, we embrace poetic faith? Allow science to tell its story and let soul have its say, too. And just enjoy the f*cking magic.

WONDER WRAP-UP

- Wonder has five elements: *watch* (openness), *wander* (deep curiosity), *whittle* (absorption), *wow* and *whoa* (awe).

- Emotions are tough to study for several reasons, and wonder is no exception. They are often difficult to define, made more complex across cultures. It's challenging to separate them from one another and even more so to study them in a lab.

- There is a bit of a tug-of-war between the perceived certainty of hard (natural) sciences and the subjective nature of soft (social) sciences. Neuroscience is undoubtedly exciting but is still an incredibly nascent field. Both natural and social sciences are critical to understanding the human condition.

- Two dominant interpretations of happiness emerged from ancient Greek philosophy—*hedonic* and *eudaemonic*. Hedonic happiness focuses on maximizing pleasure, whereas eudaemonic happiness is a balanced, meaning-making path to happiness. Eudaemonic happiness is associated with wonder, while hedonic is contrary to it. A third path to *summum bonum* could be a "psychologically rich" life, whose characteristics are directly aligned with those of wonder.

- When we push all negative thoughts from our minds, we fall into the trap of toxic positivity, and in doing so, we lose the opportunity to make sense of those experiences. Wonder allows for positive and negative emotional tone, and because of that, wonder is both more beneficial and more achievable than happiness.

- What was a mystery today may be explained tomorrow. What is thought to be understood today may be disproved tomorrow. The process of exploration is valuable in and of itself. And wonder doesn't have to be understood to be experienced.

1

Watch

This is the story of a very unlikely friendship.

Born into a family of intellectual elites in the mid-nineteenth century, William James was the first person to teach a university psychology course in America, joking that the first psychology course he attended was the one he taught. Now considered the father of American psychology, James spent twelve years penning his twelve-hundred-page masterwork, *The Principles of Psychology*, and his writings are foundational to the field. Young William's life was a peripatetic one. His father believed he and his siblings (including authors Alice and Henry) would benefit from a global education, so he moved the family from the United States to Europe and back again several times, with James having lived in eighteen different homes (and even more if including hotels) before age sixteen. James begrudgingly attended Harvard University Medical School (he wanted to be a painter), but in the end, he discovered he was interested in the inner workings of the mind and soul, not the body. A contemporary of great thinkers like his godfather Ralph Waldo Emerson, Bertrand Russell, Mark Twain, Horatio Alger, Carl Jung, Sigmund Freud, and W. E. B. Du Bois, it was the latter, Du Bois, who introduced James to his young friend.

Helen Adams Keller was born a healthy baby girl in Tuscumbia, Alabama, on June 27, 1880. When Helen was about a year and a half, a fever, perhaps caused by rubella, left her blind and deaf, completely cut off from the world she had known. She would later describe that time in her life as being "at sea in a dense fog." For years following, she descended into a semi-feral state of headstrong chaos until a kindly Alexander Graham Bell took a shine to young Helen and arranged for a recent Perkins Institution for the Blind graduate, Anne Sullivan, to teach her. Sullivan transformed the child's life (Helen referred to the day she met Sullivan as "her soul's birthday"), and their relationship—and Helen's transformation—became lore.

And so it was in Boston, where James and his brilliant radical friend and classmate Du Bois, having taken a short journey from Cambridge to Roxbury, met the then eleven-year-old Keller at the Perkins Institution for the Blind. James brought her a gift that she was deeply moved by, and years later, she still recalled their first meeting vividly. "When I was a little girl he came to see Miss Sullivan and me at the Perkins Institution for the Blind in South Boston. He brought me a beautiful ostrich feather. 'I thought,' he said, 'you would like the feather, it is soft and light and caressing.' We talked about my sense perceptions and he wove a magic web into his discourse." This poignant and perceptive gift was the beginning of a friendship that would last for the best part of two decades until James's death in 1910.

W. E. B. Du Bois also maintained a friendship with Keller. Despite being deaf, Keller had a voice, and it was one she used in support of several issues of the day, including civil rights. "Perhaps because she was blind to color differences in this world, I became intensely interested in her, and all through my life I have followed her career." Du Bois, who went on to found the National Association for the Advancement of Colored People, nurtured Keller's activism, and he remarked on her maturation from child to racial equality advocate (and eventual cofounder of the American Civil Liberties Union), "So it was proven, as I knew it would be, that this woman who sits in darkness has a spiritual insight clearer than that of many wide-eyed people who stare uncomprehendingly at this prejudiced world."*

Throughout their friendship, James and Keller often spoke of the ideas of perception and consciousness. James felt strongly that many humans develop their external senses at the expense of their internal ones, and he was in awe of Keller's exceptional aptitude in deploying her interior senses. "You have escaped from your prison-house," he wrote in one of his many letters to Keller. "Most of us are still beating about in the dark round the walls of our prison, and we seldom find the secret door of exit." Du Bois, James, and Keller, each in their own way, were exploring the meaning of watching and openness. Of sight and vision. People can be invisible, and people can be seen—sometimes not for who they are but for who they are perceived to be. People can be sighted, wide-eyed, looking but not *seeing*. And we can be without the physical faculty of sight but, like Keller, blessed with insight. James described this sort of aspirational, open awareness as "the capacity of the soul to be grasped, to have its life-currents absorbed by what is given . . . the non-thinking level, the level of pure sensorial perception."

What say we open ourselves to the life-current of pure sensorial perception?

The first element: openness

Watching—openness to experience—is the first element of wonder. The watcher is open and present, always mentally seeking,

---

* Helen Keller was considered such a radical that the FBI kept a substantial file on her political activities.

searching, and seeing, examining the familiar with new eyes to find undiscovered details and delights. Openness to experience is a personality trait associated with a number of characteristics like cognitive flexibility, intellectual curiosity, unconventional thinking, and absorption, and researchers have consistently found people high in openness to be naturally energetic, inventive, and compassionate. And because of these characteristics, and the broader nature of the experiences open people typically seek out and encounter, people high in openness frequently live nonconforming, less traditional lives.

By the time we're about twenty years old, a lot of who we are is fairly fixed, as our elemental qualities as humans—our personality traits—have pretty much settled into place. How we react to or approach any given situation will be based on both our traits—our deeply ingrained personality features—and our states—our temporal and variable emotional reactions to a given situation. Attributes like our propensity for happiness, our political views, and the jobs we might like are all heavily influenced by our personality.

Analyzing personality traits en masse began in World War I when the United States military had soldiers fill out personality questionnaires to assess their preparedness for war. Since then, similar questionnaires have steadily grown in popularity, especially in the corporate sphere. Today, there is a proliferation of what are erroneously called "personality tests" on platforms like Facebook and Instagram, where you can find out who your life partner should be based on the length of your middle toe or what your perfect job is based on your Harry Potter house. (Before social networks, these "tests" were all the rage. Those of a certain age may remember the saucy questionnaires in the back of women's magazines that promised to help libertine ladies determine which sex position was right for their personality type.)

One would hope it goes without saying that such tests are "for recreational purposes only." Arguably, though, many people also consider the Myers-Briggs Type Indicator (MBTI) or the Enneagram valid personality tests.

While tools like the MBTI can be beneficial as a reference point for discussion and self-awareness, the reality is that for all the years the MBTI has been used, it is still viewed as scientifically dubious. Loosely based on the theories of Jungian psychology, the MBTI has been called "bogus," "corporate astrology," and "shockingly bad" by scientists, but despite this, it is still taken online 1.5 million times a year. There are, however, several validated personality inventories, the most commonly cited being the Five-Factor Model of Personality, or the "Big Five," which comprises the personality traits openness to experience, conscientiousness, extroversion, agreeableness, and neuroticism (also called OCEAN or CANOE).

Part of what makes the Big Five an improvement over other ways of analyzing personality is that it looks at traits across a continuum rather than in discrete and oppositional categories, meaning someone can be high, medium, or low on agreeableness, but not outright disagreeable (although your significant other might like to differ). This continuum model allows for more nuance than the MBTI, which forces respondents to identify with one quality or another when, in actuality, those who straddle two qualities may be a little of each depending on the day, mood, or context.

But the most fundamental difference in the Big Five, as opposed to these other tools, is that it is predictive. (And not predictive in a dystopian *Minority Report* sort of way, but simply consistently indicative of certain life outcomes.) Presumably, we want to use a personality inventory to support our understanding of ourselves and our decision-making. If a tool isn't predictive, the result is only a few steps removed from a fortune cookie. It can give us some food for thought, but we can't confidently apply the result to our lives. However, in an overwhelming number of studies, across cultures, demographics, and eras, the Big Five has been demonstrated to predict everything from life, job, and relationship satisfaction to work and school performance, physical health, longevity, and more. And this is consistent across all manner of variables, including intelligence and socioeconomic status.

Among the Big Five personality traits, the one linked to the most positive life outcomes is openness to experience. Open people are more likely to live more creative lives, have greater imagination, and be more innovative and intellectual, and they are highly perceptive and insightful. Another outcome this trait is predictive of? Wonder! People high in openness are more wonderprone.

These attributes might be the result of open people literally seeing the world differently. In 2016, a team of researchers from the University of Melbourne wanted to explore the connection between openness and a visual quirk known as binocular rivalry, a phenomenon that occurs when the left eye is shown one image and the right eye a different one. "Because the brain cannot extract a coherent picture from these incompatible percepts, the two images seem to flip back and forth in our mind's eye, each image rivaling the other for dominance," explains study author Luke Smillie. "But sometimes both images do break through into conscious perception as a scrambled mash-up." The study showed that open people could hold the mash-up image in their heads for longer. This "permeability of consciousness" appears to make open people more comfortable with complex emotional experiences.* "It is as though the gates of perception are agape,

---

* Those same participants also reported experiencing mixed emotions (like nervous excitement and awe) more frequently than their less open counterparts.

allowing more visual information to flow into consciousness for open people."

It's worth clarifying that when we talk of openness, it's not the interpersonal openness we might see in an outgoing extrovert. In fact, openness to experience doesn't necessarily correlate to extroversion, but rather is an experiential and intellectual receptivity to different, unfamiliar, and even uncomfortable things, experiences, and ideas. "People high in openness to experience enjoy aesthetic experiences, live more creative lives, and pursue and support the arts," says Paul Silvia, professor of psychology at the University of North Carolina, Greensboro. "People low in openness to experience, in contrast, are more conventional, practical, and down-to-earth." And it likely won't come as a surprise that being down-to-earth is not so conducive to wonder.

Nature versus nurture

Whenever the topic of personality traits comes up, the concept of nature versus nurture is soon to follow. An intriguing way to explore this connection is to study identical twins separated at birth. We've all seen the TV shows in which separated twins are reunited and they turn out to have strikingly similar jobs, haircuts, or taste in partners, and these similarities are typically the result of the genetic personality traits they share. Several studies looking at twins separated at birth have shown that personality traits are almost equally influenced by genetic heredity and one's environment, with the percentage influenced by the environment typically stable by adulthood. Whether we can change our personality is a hotly debated topic, but there is mounting evidence that our brain isn't entirely as immutable as some think and can shift when presented with a compelling enough reason. The question is, how compelling is compelling enough?

Psychologist Carol Dweck from Stanford University believes that while our personality is set by adulthood, there are "in-between" parts of our personality that are more malleable. Features like our overarching belief systems, self-belief, goal-setting behavior, and coping strategies are all changeable with self-awareness and practice, and these also significantly impact the way we view the world and the decisions we make. Dweck believes these adaptable features can underpin the ways we "grow and learn, sustain satisfying relationships, achieve well in school and careers, be caring toward others [and] recover from setbacks" potentially as much as our personality.

In one study of Dweck's, a group of junior high school students undertook an eight-week study skills course. Those in the control group were given no prompt, whereas those in the experimental group were told that intelligence isn't innate but instead is like a muscle that simply needs to be exercised. Those told that intelligence is mutable performed better. These "in-between" elements impact not only our intelligence, but our sense of self. If a person is congratulated for doing well because they are intelligent (i.e., a set trait), their self-esteem suffers, whereas if someone is lauded for their work (i.e., their effort, which is variable), they are more eager to learn and more resilient in setbacks.

This is just to say that we shouldn't feel constrained by our personality—we still have free will—but understanding our personality, and the tendencies and proclivities our personality engenders, helps us create strategies to harness or mitigate those tendencies. Don't worry if you believe you are on the lower end of the scale in some of these wonderprone attributes. First, no one is devoid of a particular element of the Big Five. We all have some openness, for example. Second, there is more evidence that over time we can shift the needle on these traits (somewhat), although doing so takes concerted effort or a life-changing experience. Last, we can always build other in-between skills around our personality to enhance, support, and counterbalance our existing traits, and we'll learn some of the ways to do just that throughout the book.

In defense of daydreaming

William James spoke of the "prison-house" of our mind, and for many, the prospect of being left alone with only our thoughts can feel like entering a prison. People don't want to be alone with their thoughts, but this is nothing new. Blaise Pascal, the seventeenth-century mathematician and philosopher, wrote, "the sole cause of man's unhappiness is that he does not know how to stay quietly in his room." Victor Frankl believed that "the existential vacuum manifests itself mainly in a state of boredom." In 1930, philosopher Bertrand Russell said, "We are less bored than our ancestors were, but we are more afraid of boredom." He believed that boredom had its benefits, and when we allow ourselves the comfort of "fruitful monotony," we are not so hungry for a quick fix of entertainment. Without a bit of boredom, Russell feared, our focus will "always be directed towards the next pleasure." For wonder seekers, an openness to our internal thoughts is just as valuable, if not more so, as our external ones.

What is new is the ease with which we can occupy our mind with external input. There are those of us who remember a card catalog, looking for a book using the Dewey Decimal System, perhaps pulling out microfiche of the Encyclopedia Britannica, and then photocopying pages to transcribe later. It took time. The amount of information we could gather was limited because our tools were not as efficient or effective. Today, we have just about the sum total of all human knowledge (as well as a surfeit of pet pics and political rants) in the palm of our hand, which means we never have to be bored again. And maybe that's not such a good thing.

It has gotten so inordinately easy to be entertained, it's understandable why we constantly crave the novelty of new information. Many theories on boredom revolve around our need for arousal and suggest that in the absence of enough stimuli, we will engage in anything that provides newness. Humans in a sensory-deprived environment will willingly listen to boring newscasts repetitively, just for exposure to novel stimuli. Rats will take a lesser-known route in a maze simply to do something different.

We have so much noise surrounding us these days that our "exciting stimuli equilibrium" has shifted significantly higher, meaning our boredom threshold has dropped even lower. Without boredom—without staring into space while we wait for our late-arriving dinner companion, without watching the clouds when we're stuck waiting for our big brother to finish his soccer match, without contemplating the ceiling at the doctor's office after having read all the out-of-date magazines (including the Highlights with the puzzles already solved)—how will we daydream?

Oft derided and the topic of many a teacher's report card comment (Monica likes to daydream. I do wonder what she is thinking about.), daydreaming, or mind-wandering, is generally seen as an undesirable activity, especially among school-age children from whom the education system demands unrelenting focus. And yet, on average, we daydream 47 percent of our waking hours. If our brain spends nearly half of our awake time doing it, there is probably a good reason why.

The term daydreaming was coined by Julien Varendonck in 1921 in his book The Psychology of Day-Dreams (with a foreword by Sigmund Freud, so sort of a big deal). While both Freud and

William James saw benefits to daydreaming, the past twenty years have yielded research that portrays daydreaming as "a cognitive control failure." One exception is the work of psychologist Jerome Singer, who spent most of his professional life researching daydreaming (he preferred the term to mind-wandering). Singer identified three types of daydreaming, and while two can have negative impacts, one is quite beneficial.

The first is guilty dysphoric or fear-of-the-future daydreaming, when we either think about the past, perseverating on a negative experience (like the time six years ago we joked how ancient someone's cat was, only for it to die the next day), or we catastrophize the future (like imagining your presentation will be so bad that someone will pull the fire alarm just to make it stop).* Then there is poor attentional control, in which a person struggles to focus on a particular thought or task, particularly troublesome for those with attention deficits. These two kinds of daydreaming don't have identifiable benefits. But the third type, positive constructive daydreaming (PCD), in which we cast our mind forward and imagine future possibilities in a creative, positive way, can be quite beneficial.

PCD is the bridge that links watching and wandering by connecting our internal observations with the forecasting required for future exploration. It's associated with openness to experience, curiosity, absorption, and an exploration of ideas, feelings, and sensations, all ingredients of wonder. Helpful for planning and creativity, PCD can also change the structure of our brain, thickening the cerebral cortex, or what's known as our brain's gray matter, the thinning of which is associated with the cognitive decline of aging.

The day I first spoke with cognitive scientist and humanistic psychologist Scott Barry Kaufman, he shared that he was

---

* True story. Not my finest moment.

feeling a bit down, which was unexpected news, as he greeted me with such a warm smile. His mentor and friend Jerome Singer had recently passed away, and he was tasked with writing Singer's obituary at the family's request. Kaufman, however, had a deep interest in daydreaming that had begun well before his tutelage with Singer. As a child, Kaufman had an uneasy relationship with schooling and experienced firsthand the derision cast at daydreamers. As a tyke, young Scott had a rough medical start. Before he'd reached the tender age of three, he'd already had twenty-one ear infections, which left him with an auditory processing disorder, and this hearing lag made him appear developmentally delayed. By the time he was given an IQ test for school placement, Scott couldn't hear the questions and performed poorly. This led to years in special education classes, being bullied, and being found either daydreaming or disruptive, until a thoughtful teacher questioned whether he really required the supports of special ed, and Kaufman's life was transformed. He went on to teach at Columbia, Yale, New York University, and the University of Pennsylvania, as well as to become a bestselling author and the host of the most downloaded psychology podcast in the world.

Kaufman is proof that daydreamers are not lazy failures. "We tend to make a false dichotomy between attention and daydreaming. We treat daydreaming as though it's bad and attention is always good. It's such a simplistic view. Daydreaming is not always a negative, you know. There's positive constructive daydreaming. We can intentionally focus so that our daydreams are productive. It's very good to run simulations in our head. It evolved for a reason, this capacity."

The part of our brain most often associated with daydreaming is called the *default mode network* (DMN). To make studying and understanding the brain more manageable, scientists break it down into regions called *networks*, each containing a few million neurons, having similarities at a cellular level, and sharing coordinated functions and activity patterns. Of the seven networks identified, two are particularly applicable to wonder—the default mode network and the *salience network*. (More about the salience network in Chapter 4.)

The DMN is a bit of a media darling in neuroscience. In recent research, it has been identified as playing a pivotal role in the neuroscience of not only daydreaming, but autism, ADHD, meditation, flow, awe, psychedelics, and Alzheimer's disease, to name a few, so it is not uncommon to see the DMN referenced in science reporting. The term *default mode* refers to the part of our brain associated with our resting state and is responsible for our ability to reflect on our own consciousness and internal narrative. The term *resting state* is really a misnomer, however—our brain is never really at rest; it simply shifts neural activity. The DMN is an anti-correlational system, active during contemplation like daydreaming and quiet when our working memory becomes engaged. Sometimes it is described as the "autopilot for the brain." The brain is always working in the background to help us make sense of our life, processing thoughts of our past and our imagined future.

The DMN is also something of a hub, with lots of connections running through it that impact a host of other activity patterns. But more interesting and somewhat mysterious, the DMN is responsible for much of our abstract conceptual thought—the introspective, self-referential kind that separates us from primates—and it recalls and constructs social scenarios to help us make meaning of our life. Given its association with openness, absorption, and awe, as well as memory, empathy, mirror neurons, and Theory of Mind (more about those last two in Chapter 11), this is a particularly intriguing network for wonder seekers.

The DMN can become disrupted during cognitive decline, such as dementia, and while this link isn't fully understood yet, we know that a well-functioning default mode network, in which we cast our mind's eye forward in time or reflect on our past experience, plays a pivotal role in our healthy mental functioning. It also appears to be more active in people who are high in openness to experience as well as frequent daydreamers, and we can strengthen the DMN through slow thought activities like meditation and daydreaming.

Philosophers have long stressed the importance of the type of inner reflection associated with PCD. In addition to Bertrand Russell's ode to boredom, most of the enlightenment philosophers like Diderot, Locke, and Kant believed it was inward reflection, not external drivers, that empowered humanity to direct their own lives and lead themselves. In his 1690 work, *An Essay Concerning Human Understanding*, John Locke coined the word *consciousness*, describing it as the "perception of what passes in a man's own mind." For Locke, consciousness was "inseparable from thinking" and represented an integral awareness of the working of our own mind. Open observation of our internal consciousness paves the way for curious exploration of our external world.

Franz Kafka once wrote, "You do not need to leave your room. Remain sitting at your table and listen. Do not even listen, simply wait, be quiet still and solitary. The world will freely offer itself to you to be unmasked, it has no choice, it will roll in ecstasy at your feet." A strangely sanguine quote for someone known to be a fairly dark fella, but toward the end of his life, Kafka was engrossed with the metaphysical "world within" and the power that resides in an open still awareness. Imagine young Helen Keller—cut off from so much, in a fog at sea—and yet she was still open, ready to absorb the life-currents in her sphere. And then this stranger hands her an ostrich feather. Picture her hands dancing across the spine of the feather, starting at the quill and moving up the rachis, gently grazing each slender barb, mapping the landscape of the object in her mind's eye. It would have felt so delicate. So light. I'm certain she would have let the feather caress her face, too. Did it tickle? Did she giggle with the sensation? Perhaps she felt the light eddies of air swirl about her as she fanned the diaphanous plume. She wouldn't have made a conscious decision about transitioning from openness to curiosity. It would just happen. As humans, when we are open to experiencing new things, our brain naturally wants that openness to blossom into exploration. Why? To know.

WONDER WRAP-UP

- Openness to experience—*watch*—the first element of wonder, is a stable, universal personality trait associated with intellectual curiosity, creativity, artistic expression, and cognitive flexibility, among other characteristics.

- The most frequently cited personality trait model is the Big Five, which includes conscientiousness, agreeableness, neuroticism, extroversion, and openness to experience. Using a validated personality test like the Big Five is better for understanding who we are than a tool like the MBTI.

- Our personality is the lens through which we see the world, and it can influence all manner of decisions we make and how wonderprone we are. About half of our personality is hereditary (nature) and about half is based on our environment up to adulthood (nurture).

- While most personality traits are stable and set by

adulthood, we can still build attitudes, beliefs, and strategies to enhance or mitigate our personality traits and make us more wonderprone.

- There are different types of daydreaming, and one of them, *positive constructive daydreaming* (PCD), is very beneficial for us. PCD is reflective and imaginative but not negatively ruminative. It links the internal exploration of openness with the external exploration of curiosity.

- The *default mode network* (DMN), the part of the brain associated with daydreaming, is a relevant area of the brain when understanding wonder, as it is responsible for our reflecting on our own consciousness and experience of being human. The DMN is made up of subregions associated with memory, Theory of Mind, and mirror neurons, all elements associated with how we perceive wonder. It also appears to play a role in several areas of neuroscientific study such as autism, ADHD, meditation, flow, awe, psychedelics, and Alzheimer's, to name a few.

2

Wander

My aunt Jacqui and uncle Selwyn have a marvelous little home. Unassumingly suburban from the outside, when you enter, you are transported. It is filled with the most gloriously curated collection of bits and bobs. From Chinese joss sticks to Victorian figurines; a scroll player piano to a polished brass ship's Chadburn; kinetic or fixed, Asian or African or American or British, antique or modern, expensive or simple, nothing was off-limits. As a child, I was allowed to hold, explore, touch, play with, and ask for the story of anything. This place was the physical manifestation of deep curiosity because everything had a story. And that story, warm and patient and detailed in the telling, could always connect to another item and another story. I was free to wander to my heart's content.

I always left there feeling like the world was a wonderland so much bigger than my small snapshot of it. I left inspired and enriched. I left hungry, but not for a quick fix. Hungry for all of it, for every nook and cranny of knowledge the cabinet of curiosities holds. That's wondrous curiosity, and you'll know it when you feel it, for it is visceral as much as it is intellectual. Humbling in the presence of so much that can never be understood despite a valiant desire to try.

The second element: curiosity

I loved the Curious George books as a child. What could be better than a cheeky monkey always getting into some kind of trouble because of his insatiable curiosity? This is how curiosity is often packaged—as a child's naughty pursuit, or, as seen in many a horror film, as the punch line of a cautionary tale.

Humans have a fraught history with curiosity. If we go back hundreds of years, the early Catholic Church was the primary benefactor of most higher education and scholarly inquiry; however, that beneficence came with a caveat—the discoveries could not undermine the Church's power. This ecclesiastic gatekeeping to knowledge led to a certain chilling of epistemic exploration in Europe, where curiosity was forced to hide in corners and merely expressing it in some contexts became an act of resistance and rebellion. But the Church was not alone in its disdain for the trait. Several centuries later, even Freud saw curiosity as a type of malady. He (unsurprisingly) thought it was brought on by sublimated sexual exploration, calling it *schaulust*, the "pleasure in looking."

This fraught history has some basis, as curiosity *can* sometimes drive us to experience unpleasant things. We have all had one of those cringe-it-was-so-terrible-but-I-couldn't-look-away moments, in which morbid curiosity overrides good sense. Researchers from the University of Chicago wanted to test the limits of that phenomenon. Participants were asked to choose a set of cards. One set had pictures of various rocks, while the other had a mixture of images—rocks and truly grotesque pictures of dog poop. Participants wouldn't know which image they were getting until they flipped the card over. Researchers found people *enjoyed* the thrill of flipping over the mixed cards in anticipation of the "eww!" elicited from getting a dog poop image. They were experiencing pleasure even as they were simultaneously repulsed. Why are we motivated to explore unpleasant things?

The evolution of human curiosity

The biology and neuroscience of curiosity are based on a dopamine and opiate response triggered by our brain's stimulation and reward cycle. This cycle serves a vital purpose. The dopamine release associated with the seeking phase of curiosity motivates exploration. At the same time, our hippocampus, the part of the brain responsible for embedding information into long-term learning, is activated, enhancing our incidental memory. If what we discover is interesting enough, that's followed by the natural opiate endorphins, which give us a pop of pleasure once we scratch that curiosity itch. That, in turn, releases more dopamine to motivate exploratory behavior again.

This cycle is crucial to keep us curious, but it also explains why we may be driven to explore unpleasant things, too. We show even greater curiosity when topics are negative or controversial, with people showing almost twice the engagement on social network posts that are negative. (If you've ever doom-scrolled well past your bedtime, that's the dopamine feedback loop keeping you hooked.) And trust me, internet and social media moguls know this research, too, which is why the internet, while an incredible curiosity tool, can also become our worst kind of rabbit hole filled with dopamine hits of conflict and negativity.

And yet curiosity is, as author Ian Leslie described it, "such a basic component of our nature that we are nearly oblivious to its pervasiveness in our lives." We spend countless hours seeking and consuming information, the majority found on the internet, which also happens to be a facilitator of much of our society and economy. Also known as *exploratory behavior*, curiosity plays a valuable role in our psyches. Cicero once described curiosity as an "innate love of learning and of knowledge . . . without the lure of any profit." William James called it "the impulse towards better cognition." Einstein so revered curiosity he called it "holy curiosity," continuing, "I have no special talents. I am only passionately curious."

Curiosity is a quality we share with other animals—we've all seen a pooch sniff tentatively at something tasty, curious to know if it's edible and how quickly their human might be distracted so they can steal it. And while some scientists believe we first evolved curiosity as a drive to satiate a knowledge gap, just like a dog is driven to satiate hunger or thirst, wonder-type curiosity is a purely human trait. Animals have what is known as an "exploration-exploitation trade-off." This means they spend about 20 percent of the time exploring for new opportunities and information, and the other 80 percent exploiting that knowledge. But curiosity must be more than just this trade-off; otherwise, why would organisms seek out new knowledge that is not associated with a direct need? Why would we explore just for the fun of it? This is because our instinctual exploratory drive runs deeper than simply satiating base animal needs. Rather, human curiosity is aligned with the very human need for sense-making.

This drive to gain knowledge for knowledge's sake is unique to humans and a differentiating feature of wonder-type curiosity versus the kibble-type curiosity a hound might have. Our human brains evolved to create everything from the Great Pyramids to the Mona Lisa to the smartphone, but this level of cognitive development is only made possible by curiosity for the enjoyment of it and not just to close a cognitive gap.

One of the areas of the brain associated with curiosity, the caudate nucleus, is also associated with romantic love. This coupling links primal pleasure with the pleasure of learning. Clearly, our brain wants more out of its curious pursuits than just a pure exploration-exploitation trade-off—it wants us to be head over heels for discovering more.

Types of curiosity

Curiosity is not a monolith, and like so many ubiquitous emotions that seem simple enough to define, there is still no single agreed-upon model. Several models are based on the concept of two (or more) dimensions of curiosity that illustrate the motivation or rationale for exploratory behavior. These models include dimensions like *sensational/theoretic, perceptual/epistemic, diversive/specific, interest/deprivation, exploration/absorption,* and *stretching/embracing.*

At the end of the nineteenth century, William James was the first to propose a two-dimensional model, the *sensational/theoretic* model. According to James, the first dimension, *sensational,* we share with animals and is like the curiosity of childhood that seeks to understand the animate or the concrete. The second dimension, *theoretic* curiosity, also called *intellectual* curiosity, is a purely human emotion engaged during times of "scientific curiosity or metaphysical wonder." James did not expand on this theory in great detail, and it wasn't explored in earnest until psychologist Daniel Berlyne picked up James's thinking in the mid-twentieth century, creating two similar dimensions, *perceptual* and *epistemic* curiosity. Berlyne believed perceptual curiosity, described as the drive to pursue novel stimuli, was an exploratory behavior we shared with animals, whereas epistemic curiosity, an internal drive for acquiring knowledge for enjoyment and reward, was unique to humans. Most recently, psychologist Todd Kashdan aggregated elements of previous curiosity research to develop his comprehensive Five-Dimensional Curiosity Scale. This five-factor model includes *joyous exploration, deprivation sensitivity, stress tolerance, social curiosity,* and thrill-seeking, and integrates Kashdan's belief that curiosity is piv-otal to personal growth.

While each of these models is different in its own way, a few conceptual threads are to be found. First, we see that the purpose of curiosity is to explore, seek novelty, and immer-sively learn. Second, we see a differentiation between the type of curiosity motivated by filling a directive or immediate need (information, safety, snacks)—what we'll call *surface* curiosity—and the curiosity driven by the epistemic *pleasure* of acquiring knowledge—what we'll refer to as *deep* curiosity.

Surface curiosity is associated with scattershot exploration, or Google searches to settle a bet. We use this category of curios-ity to seek novelty or keep boredom at bay. Surface curiosity tends to be driven by a need for filling in specific knowledge gaps or queries (*What is that sound? Has the milk gone off? Who shot JR?*). When I visualize this concept, I imagine a rock skipping on a pond—it covers a lot of ground but just barely skims along the surface.

Deep curiosity, on the other hand, is based not just on a need to acquire knowledge for a purpose, but on an interest in that knowledge, a love of exploration, and a comfort with, even an enjoyment of, complex, nuanced answers. (*Is there a god? Is there a pattern to prime numbers? What is the political position of antidises-tablishmentarianism?*) Its purpose is meaning-making, epistemic, and learning as pleasure.

It's a pity curiosity has been so misunderstood throughout history, as this second element of wonder has so much to offer. Cu-riosity improves our life skills, decreases bias, and increases well-being. Curious people are more empathetic, and, as with openness, they are also happier, less stressed, and more comfortable with am-biguity. In contrast, the absence of exploratory behavior is associ-ated with an increased risk of everything from self-harm and body dysmorphia to groupthink, prejudice, and low empathy.

The Single Right Answer

Two "in-between" aspects of our personality that significantly affect our curiosity style are our *need for cognition* (NFC) and *need for cognitive closure* (NFCC). Both of these play a prominent role in our motivation for seeking out information and how comfortable we are with ambiguity in the answers we find. The first trait, need for cognition, describes our tendency to seek and become immersed in cognitively challenging activity. A person high in NFC is naturally open, creative, mentally flexible, and deeply curious. They enjoy not only seeking out information but reflecting on it, mulling it over. In comparison, people low in NFC tend to use their preexisting worldview and take mental shortcuts to make sense of what they experience.

Our need for cognitive closure (NFCC) describes the degree to which we need order, predictability, a definite answer, or a sense of finality. A person high in NFCC is mentally rigid. They display a desire to reach a conclusion quickly and a discomfort with gray areas or nuance, especially once the "Single Right Answer" has been identified. While these two traits aren't on a continuum at opposite ends, people high in NFC tend to be low in NFCC and vice versa. Research shows that wonderprone people are high in NFC and low in NFCC and thus are not motivated by finding the Single Right Answer. They are comfortable to sit in the unknowing. This concept of mental rigidity and the Single Right Answer is a theme we'll see throughout the book and one that impacts everything from learning to leadership style and teamwork to religious tolerance.

In a series of letters to an aspiring poet, author and philosopher Rainer Maria Rilke encouraged his young recipient to embrace this state of unknowing. "Be patient towards all that is unsolved in your heart and try to love the *questions themselves* like locked rooms," he wrote. "*Live* the questions now. Perhaps you will then gradually, without noticing it, live along some distant day into the answer."

The gifts of wandering curiosity

On any given morning, in any given city, you might find David Pearl standing on a street corner leading a workshop on the art of wandering. The founder of social enterprise Street Wisdom, Pearl gets busy people to take three hours out of their day to "ask the street a question." On their seemingly aimless walk, participants are often surprised to find answers present themselves in almost magical, uncanny ways. A sort of synchronicity scavenger hunt, folks in this wandering experiment find they can connect the dots, foster a mindset in which mental tumblers fall into place, unlocking questions and unblocking answers that have nagged them for years. Some of the stories are astonishing.

One participant, Scott, asked the street whether he was wise to take the leap and start a business. He feared he wouldn't be able to find the right people or projects to make his dream come true. During his walk, Scott ran into three separate friends he hadn't seen for ages. Each friend gave him a different piece of valuable advice about his new venture, including contacts to the exact types of people and projects he was seeking. Each also gave him similar encouragement—go for it! He did, and he credits that Street Wisdom walk with cultivating the business he has today. "I arrived thirty minutes late for the debrief, full of euphoric energy," he recalled. "I summarize Street Wisdom as simple, soulful, and life-changing—I don't say that lightly as it completely transformed my life." Scott's open, present curiosity unblocked his fear-based mindset and allowed new thinking to emerge.

Another story is of a woman who asked the street what she should do with herself now that her fifth child had left the nest. On her walk, she inexplicably discovered a diary tucked behind a drainpipe. As she read the diary, she found herself connecting with the author, reminiscing about her own passion for writing when she was younger. Her Street Wisdom walk gave her the nudge to reconnect with her creative side and embrace her newfound time and space. From seeing their name in lights or running into old friends to sometimes quite literally tripping over an answer, the synchronicities Pearl's wanderers experience are really best described as small droplets of wonder, a bit of sea mist from the ocean of interconnectedness between our thoughts, the animate world, and each other.*

Pearl looks like a man who enjoys a good walk. Lanky and lean, his legs could easily traverse a city block in just a few strides. When he speaks, he has the calm erudite tone of a public radio announcer, and his background as a performer comes through. "I am a musician, and early in my life, when I was a kid, I was taken to the opera house. I'm eight years old, and, the long and short of it is, I was standing next to [Placido] Domingo. He was the lead, and I was a small soloist, but hearing him sing in a rehearsal near me, blew my mind. And it was a kind of confirmation of a suspicion that I'd had, but that the adults wouldn't fess up to, which was daily reality was a very dimmed-down version of what was possible." It was as if a switch had been flicked, or perhaps a curtain pulled back. Pearl's relationship with what was "real" had changed. "In nature programs, you see underwater documentaries

---

* The theory of synchronicities was introduced by psychologist Carl Jung as a metaphysical "meaningful coincidence" that is imbued with a certain magical numinous quality. While Jung saw synchronicities as possible evidence for the existence of a collective unconscious, there are also theories that they are a tool for our brain to bring forward ideas from our subconscious that help us pattern match and find solutions.

about fish. And at some point, a whole shoal of fish will turn at one time. That's what happened in my brain when I heard that sound. It whet my appetite for higher states of awareness."

Into adulthood, Pearl remained curious about the things we choose to question and those we don't, either out of familiarity or mores or haste. What drove him to start Street Wisdom was a desire to mine that curiosity for stories and meaning. Launched in 2013 in London, Street Wisdom is now a nonprofit open-source experience found in forty countries from Kenya to Croatia.

What becomes apparent when listening to Pearl or his fellow Street Wisdomers is that while wandering seems to be the whole point, walking is just the physical mechanism that motivates exploration. It allows people to be exposed to new and different stimuli, to become sponges of receptivity, forced out of rigid habit and into literal, metaphorical, and metaphysical discovery. When I asked Pearl how staying curious helps people find solutions, he became philosophical. "There's a kind of message in a bottle quality to [what we find]. It's like a future memory. And it's basically you winking back to yourself."

Wandering curiosity won't always bestow these sorts of epiphanic gifts, but when we are open and deeply curious, we create the environment for wonder. And then, when we find that one thing that truly ignites our mind, we become absorbed, falling down Alice's rabbit hole, not particularly caring if we find our way back out. In the next chapter, we'll learn that, just like for Alice, the rabbit hole of absorption is the gateway through the looking glass to a magical and transcendent world of wonder.

WONDER WRAP-UP

- Curiosity—wander—the second element of wonder, is both a trait and a state, meaning we have our natural disposition toward curiosity and situational curiosity prompted in the moment.

- Exploratory behavior developed in humans to gather specific information needed for survival, but it has further evolved into a mechanism for meaning-making.

- Curiosity is associated with many benefits, including better relationships and increased well-being, but despite these, it has not always been viewed as a positive attribute.

- Curiosity is driven by a dopamine response in our brain that motivates exploration. It also triggers our hippocampus, which enhances our incidental memory. Curiosity is a generally pleasant experience, but the lure of dopamine means we may engage in exploratory behavior even when it is unpleasant or not good for us (e.g., unhealthy internet usage).

- Two aspects of our personality play a significant role in our wonderproneness: *need for cognition* (NFC)—our tendency to enjoy intellectual pursuits—and *need for cognitive closure* (NFCC)—our desire for the Single Right Answer. People high in NFC and low in NFCC are more wonderprone.

- There are several different models of curiosity, but they share notable similarities that can be generally lumped into two categories: *surface* and *deep*. Surface curiosity is motivated to close a specific knowledge gap, whereas deep curiosity encompasses the enjoyment of learning for learning's sake. Both serve a purpose, but deep curiosity more directly contributes to wonder.

3

Whittle

When I was a child, I used to travel up to Appalachia to visit my best friend's extended family. These were country mountain folk, whose environs and pastimes were leagues away from those of my suburban life in Atlanta. It was full of the exotic for me. The smell of woodsmoke and pickling spices combined with the earthy loam of farm life, sharing the air with cricket song and buzzing midges. We would pop morning glories, suck honeysuckle, and eat home-baked sheet cake topped with canned fruit cocktail. On Sundays, we went to church, where music and the occasional speaking in tongues were their connection to the holy. Doors stayed open, screens closed against the bugs, and you could catch glimpses of their quotidian through the mesh. Every grown-up was warm and welcoming and wrapped little girls like me in love as if we were their own. It was idyllic.

One of the things I recall most vividly from my trips up north was an older local gentleman there who liked to whittle. A quiet, wizened soul, he would sit and carve little figurines and crosses with a penknife. My favorite of his whimsies was a ball in a cage. It seemed like a sort of magic trick. That from a solid piece of wood, he could set free that perfectly round ball, once fixed, now sitting loose such that it could roll and knock around inside a delicately carved cage. It took such focus, such skill.

When he whittled, curls of wood snowing from his hands, he was perfectly absorbed in the moment, content within a complete and comfortable abandon. So total was his absorption that I would almost fall into his rhythm myself, gently rocking with every light stroke of his arching knife.

The third element: absorption

We all know the feeling of being absorbed, be it lost in thought, transported by a good book, or wholly entranced by an activity. When I think of being absorbed, my whittler always springs to mind. A lovely metaphor of paring down his carving while paring down his attention as well. Absorption as a psychological concept was first defined in the 1970s by Auke Tellegen, a psychology professor from the University of Minnesota, as part of his exploration into why some people are more hypnotizable than others. Tellegen described absorption as "a full commitment of available perceptual, motoric, imaginative and ideational resources" in which we are open "to absorbing and self-altering experiences." In this absorbed state, the object of our attention becomes hyper-real, deserving of our total emotional and attentional energy, even if that object is fiction, like a film, or seemingly banal, like a penknife figurine.

Openness is a personality trait, and curiosity is both a trait and a state, but where does absorption sit? There is some debate about whether absorption is a trait and therefore dispositional, or a state triggered by an event and therefore experiential. But research suggests that it can be both. For example, explorers tested before and after a period of Antarctic isolation scored higher on the absorption scale, even post-isolation, than they had prior to their expedition. Cannabis users also reported greater absorption when simply reflecting on their experiences involving cannabis, even if they didn't show naturally high trait absorption. Those two pieces of evidence would suggest that absorption is a state we can dial up with practice.

Wanderers and watchers are great whittlers, too. People higher in absorption tend to be more open, more curious, and bigger daydreamers, and they have greater mental flexibility. Like other elements of wonder, absorption has a physiological impact as well—high absorption shows a relationship to lower blood pressure. The whittler represents all the ways we can narrow our field of distractions, pare away the extraneous, and enjoy a purity of focus that can, under the right conditions, lead us to a state of transcendence.

Flow

For many people, if they were to hear the story of my whittler, the word flow would spring to mind. Developed by psychologist Mihály Csíkszentmihályi and popularized in the 1990s, the concept of flow has become synonymous with "being in the zone," a state of complete focus that overtakes people when they are engaged in an activity at which they are adept. Csíkszentmihályi was originally a happiness researcher, an interest he developed after spending his childhood in Europe during and in the aftermath of World War II (a period that included a stay in an Italian prison camp as a child, all while mourning the loss of both of his older brothers). He couldn't help but observe that the adults in his orbit postwar, while resilient and resolute, never seemed to find the vibrancy and happiness they had enjoyed before. From that observation, Csíkszentmihályi became interested in deriving the ingredients of a life worth living.

He looked in several places—philosophy, art, literature—before stumbling upon a lecture, purportedly about flying saucers but actually about trauma-based hallucinatory projections, that turned his mind toward Carl Jung and the field of psychology for the answer to the happiness riddle. "I tried to understand: where—in everyday life, in our normal experience—do we feel really happy?" Csíkszentmihályi explained. "And to start those studies about forty years ago, I began to look at creative people—first artists and scientists, and so forth—trying to understand what made them feel that it was worth essentially spending their life doing things for which many of them didn't expect either fame or fortune, but which made their life meaningful and worth doing."

What Csíkszentmihályi found is that the artists were in a type of "optimal state" that he termed flow (named as such because when he asked people to explain the experience to him, they described that the work seemed to "flow from them"). Typified by a sense of effortless attention, flow is a state of peak performance in which all our abilities and attentional energies are engaged in a challenging (i.e., hard but not too hard) task, leading to deep, unyielding absorption. This absorption can be so deep that we lose time and ourselves in the work, treating primary needs like food and sleep as distractions to be ignored.

This element of "hard but not too hard" is crucial. Neither absorption nor flow can be achieved if the task at hand is too subjectively difficult. It must be aligned such that the task maintains a balance between too easy (boring and menial, so we bail) and too hard (outside of our skill set such that we become frustrated, so we bail). The flow sweet spot is where our abilities are stretched but not overly stressed. Csíkszentmihályi explained,

"Enjoyment appears at the boundary between boredom and anxiety, when the challenges are just balanced with the person's capacity to act."

The reason behind that enjoyment, and a central part of Csíkszentmihályi's flow thesis, is that focus *and* purpose allow people to be happy, as the intensity of flow fully occupies the mind, leaving no room for the noisiness of negative thoughts.* According to Csíkszentmihályi, when a person is in flow, "he doesn't have enough attention left over to monitor how his body feels, or his problems at home. He can't feel even that he's hungry or tired. His body disappears, his identity disappears from his consciousness, because he doesn't have enough attention. . . . Existence is temporarily suspended."

Like many artists, Lego brick artist and creator of the world-famous *The Art of the Brick* touring show Nathan Sawaya enters a flow state when he works, and he often describes this creative state as transcendent. "There's been moments where [my process of creation] is really a flow state. I'm in a groove, and I don't realize time is passing. I've been told that it looks like I'm in a trance."

Sawaya's journey as an artist is an unusual one. He started out as a successful corporate lawyer but secretly wanted to be a sculptor. For years he "buried that soulful resistance way down deep" until the day his passion excavated his dream, and Sawaya

---

* Csíkszentmihályi defined seven conditions that are present when we are in flow, and these are true across the globe, regardless of education, culture, or skills, from nuns and football players to mountain climbers and Lego brick artists. One of those is a sense of intrinsic motivation, or what Csíkszentmihályi called having an "autotelic personality" (the term coming from the Greek *auto*, meaning "self," and *telos*, meaning "goal"). Openness to experience, curiosity, and a willingness to learn are all characteristics of an autotelic personality, so it makes sense that flow would be connected to wonder, but the where and how are still a bit unclear.

left the legal world behind to become a Lego brick artist. His flow state stems from the comfort and expertise in working with his medium combined with the challenge of his complex creations. Sawaya has been playing with Legos his whole life. "Growing up, I had a 36-square-foot Lego city. And as a boy, I didn't have a lot of creative toys, but Lego bricks was one of those things that I had. This was in Oregon, in a town called Veneta. Population 2,500 on a good day. That was my respite." Now Sawaya creates sculptures with as many as eighty thousand pieces, which is sufficiently cognitively challenging to send him into a light transcendent flow state.

As with many topics in psychology, there is debate about how to categorize flow. Some scientists view it as a type of curiosity, seeing similarities between the two states, specifically in the motivation required to direct our attention so completely to a specific task. Others suggest that flow might be a type of self-transcendent experience (STE), an experience of expanded awareness that takes us out of ourselves and makes us feel more connected to others. Csíkszentmihályi's description of existence being "temporarily suspended" during flow certainly supports that latter theory.

Scott Barry Kaufman even finds flow a bit of an oddity. "I've been confused about flow myself and where that fits in when we talk about self-transcendence. . . . The flow research literature is very disorganized and often confusing because people use the term to mean different things at different times." Kaufman does believe that if sufficiently intense, flow could be potentially categorized as an STE, but it would be at the extreme end of the absorption spectrum. Perhaps think of flow as "turbocharged absorption" or "transcendence lite" or "a liminal amorphous gateway between curiosity and self-transcendence."

I guess "flow" has a better ring to it. Let's just stick with that.

Absorption as a gateway to self-transcendent experiences

"I realized I could no longer define the boundaries of where I began and where I ended. . . . Everything blended together as one. I felt that I was as big as the universe. I wasn't terrified. I wasn't feeling anything other than an awe for the fact that, 'Oh my gosh, I am alive!'" Those are the words of stroke survivor and neuroscientist Jill Bolte Taylor. In her popular book and stirring TED talk, both titled *My Stroke of Insight*, she movingly and matter-of-factly recounts her self-transcendent experience brought about by a stroke. As she describes it, her left brain shut down and her right brain was left without the filters it usually employed. The result was overwhelming. "Sound coming in through my ears was chaos. Light coming in was burning. . . . If you were talking to me, I wouldn't be able to pick your voice out from the background noise." But when she shut out the stimuli and released herself to the transcendence, she felt free. "I was experiencing bliss and euphoria. I was happy. I also lost all my emotional baggage," Taylor shared. "That was freeing. Imagine what it would be like to just be in the present moment. All I had was the wonder and the splendor and the magnificence of the present moment—and it's beautiful."

When we hear the term *self-transcendent*, we may conjure up images of a bearded guru sitting in the lotus position, but in the most basic sense, *to transcend* means "to rise above or exceed," so self-transcendence is just rising above our own self-focus. STEs can be achieved through all manner of experiences, from mindfulness to psychedelics to even a neurological condition like Taylor's. And they appear to sit on a spectrum of intensity, with flow at one end and the complete dissolution of the ego at the other (quite a range!). STEs were first explored in the psychological literature by William James and Sigmund Freud, each with differing opinions. In his *Varieties of Religious Experience*, James wrote that STEs, and mystical experiences, in particular, were positive and allowed us to view "the universe in its totality." Freud, on the other hand, felt these moments of "oceanic oneness" were "likely neurotic regressions to the womb and a symptom of psychopathology."

Research scientist David Yaden, a student and admirer of William James's work, has since picked up James's study into STEs with his own *Varieties* research. "Even before William James," Yaden explains, "the history has not treated self-transcending experiences very kindly." Yaden disagrees with Freud, arguing that STEs are certainly not indicative of mental illness, with Yaden's decision to enter this area of study actually prompted by his own self-transcendent experience, which sounds strikingly like Taylor's.

> This was during my college years . . . and I was sort of searching for myself in some way. I was trying to decide what to do with my life as a lot of people are during that time. . . . I was lying on my dorm room bed, and I start to feel this heat in my chest, which I initially think is heartburn or something very physical. But this heat slowly begins to spread over my entire body eventually, and at some point, in my mind, I hear the words, "This is love." And so at that point, I went entirely into my mind and sort of felt like I went out of my body in some way. It felt like I could just see 360 degrees around myself. And I was completely part of this intricate fabric that spread out in every direction. . . . And so immediately, I feel this sort of wave of love towards everyone around me, especially friends and family. Everything seemed new, life seemed fascinating. And future possibilities opened up in my mind. . . . It

*was just an incredibly profound and meaningful moment. But more
than anything, I was wondering what the hell just happened to me.*

Typified by moments of decreased attention to ourselves
(known as lower self-salience) and increased feelings of connectedness to others, STEs go by any number of descriptors, including sublime, numinous, transpersonal, religious, spiritual,
sacred, epiphanic, ecstatic, near death, mystical, or simply a time
of "regression in the service of the ego." The term psychologist
Abraham Maslow coined for a self-transcendent experience was
peak experience. Maslow was not religious and therefore wanted a
term that didn't conjure up the religiosity expressed in William
James's *Varieties,* but the characteristics were still those shared
across all STEs, including absorption, heightened aestheticism,
wonder, awe, and surrender.

These experiences are universal and incredibly common.
According to the Pew Research Center, 49 percent of people have
reported a religious or mystical experience that changed their
life, but Yaden thinks the number of people who have experienced some form of STE is much higher than research reflects.
He fears the language focusing on the intensity of an STE "leaves
a lot of people out." Instead, Yaden asks his students, "'Who here
has had an experience of a mind-blowing idea, sweeping natural
scenery, amazing art, or music?' and then usually, every hand in
the audience goes up."

The psychological theory of STEs is that those things we focus
on intently—be they ideas, objects, or activities—develop an "importance and intimacy" imbued with a particular mystical association, and that mystical intimacy facilitates these altered states
of consciousness. The focus achieved in absorption primes us
for wonder and acts as a portal to these sorts of self-transcendent

experiences.* And because people who are high in absorption are more likely to lose themselves in music, art, or literature, they naturally gravitate toward activities that are known wonderbringers. As we'll see later in the book, absorption is not only a gateway to altered states of consciousness like STEs; it also prompts stronger feelings of awe and enhances the benefits associated with several wonderbringers such as meditation and psychedelics.

In a study using the experiences of mountain climbers to explore the relationship between flow and STEs, researchers found that those who cited achieving an absorbed flow state while climbing were also more likely to report having had a transcendental, awe-like experience. Csíkszentmihályi observed, "The mystique of rock climbing is climbing; you get to the top of a rock glad it's over but really wish it would go on forever. The justification of climbing is climbing, like the justification of poetry is writing; you don't conquer anything except things in yourself." And perhaps that is another way to view transcendence, as the conquering of things in yourself.

Polar explorer and world-record mountaineer Alison Levine knows a thing or two about conquering things inside herself. Levine served as team captain of the first American Women's Everest Expedition and completed the Adventure Grand Slam, a feat that consists of climbing the highest peak on each continent and skiing to both the North and South Poles, an accomplishment she shares with only twenty other people in the world. Her adventures are even more impressive given she has had three heart surgeries and suffers from Raynaud's disease, putting her at greater

---

* While the first two elements of wonder—openness and curiosity—are fairly straightforward, absorption brings us to a bit of a fork in the road. STE researchers believe if we are in a very intense flow state, our focus might actually become so narrow that we miss the wow moment of the wonder cycle. But if flow were less intense, it could serve as a type of high-absorption state that leads us into awe.

risk for frostbite than typical climbers. (And if that didn't already make her cool enough, she has a beer named after her, too.)

While on the mountain, Levine's focus is completely absorbed with the climb. "You have to pay attention to every step. You can't just go on autopilot when you're in these extreme environments." While she doesn't always enter a full flow state on her climbs—they are frequently too technically challenging for that—her heightened absorption makes her more wonderprone. "I want to absorb everything along the way, because I think that's what helps me build curiosity about other mountains and reflect on the lessons I learned."

As she transitions out of her absorbed state, her transcendence begins to unfold. Levine's wonderbringer is not the climb itself, but rather reflecting on the small fraternity of men and women who have preceded her up some of the world's most challenging peaks. "Wonder for me is, I immediately start picturing the explorers of the past. Whether I'm on the side of a mountain or in the middle of Antarctica, and I start wondering, What was it like for these early Arctic and Antarctic explorers? What did it look like when they were here? What were they thinking when they were here? What were they dreaming about? What were they worried about?" Almost priming herself for wonder, Levine reflects on these questions before she heads up and upon her return, connecting her in a profound way to the climbers who came before her. Her absorbed state opens a gateway to awe, transcending herself and the bounds of time.

WONDER WRAP-UP

- Absorption—*whittle*—is the third element of wonder, posited to be both a state and a trait. It is described as becoming so engaged in a task that we commit our total attentional resources to it.

- People higher in absorption tend to be more open, curious, empathetic, imaginative, and flexible, and they naturally gravitate toward artistic activities that are known wonderbringers.

- Flow, a concept developed by Mihály Csíkszentmihályi, is a type of absorption characterized by deep, effortless attention. This feeling of "being in the groove" is achieved when we strike the right balance between our skills and the difficulty of an activity (i.e., hard but not too hard). Flow is difficult to categorize but is likely both a deep form of absorption and a light form of self-transcendent experience, and it is associated with many benefits, including improved well-being.

- A self-transcendent experience (STE), also known as a mystical, numinous, sublime, or peak experience, is a moment of expanded awareness that takes us out of ourselves and makes us feel more connected to others. STEs are universal, with at least a third of people, but likely substantially more, having experienced one.

- The focus achieved in absorption is a known portal to self-transcendent experiences like awe (the final element of wonder). Absorption positions us to be more wonderprone and enhances the effect of STEs.

4

Compression and Release

F
rank Lloyd Wright spent twenty-two years building
Taliesin West, his sprawling winter home just outside
Scottsdale, Arizona. Often considered his most personal
work of architecture, Taliesin West was initially conceived as a
camp for student architects (and as respite from brutal Michigan
winters) but eventually grew to a compound of almost six hundred acres that comprised home, office, and school for Wright
and his family.

The compound as it stands today is equal parts inspired,
threadbare, and odd. Grand crescendos of rooms open from
small, cramped doorways or halls that at certain points are so
narrow and low you feel you must dip your head ever so slightly
to avoid whacking it, not unlike the doorway in a small boat
or RV. This seems rather awkward for such an accomplished
architect until you realize, of course, it is intentional—a technique he referred to as "compression and release." A keen student of the psychology of space, Wright knew, without the need
for scientific validation or explanation, that the contrast of dark,
pent hallways, some "the width of a Pullman aisle," opening into

light-filled cantilevered spaces would elicit eye-blinking wonder in its viewers.

Also known as "tension and resolution" or "embrace and release," compression and release allowed Wright to express the impact and significance of contrast. It was a technique he used repeatedly, from his Oak Park, Illinois, Home and Studio to the Johnson Wax Headquarters, the Solomon R. Guggenheim Museum, and more. The technique was effective because it hinged on how our brain perceives stimuli. If you've ever closed your eyes when thinking about a tough problem, only to open them when the solution erupts from your consciousness, you understand the benefit of filtering the stimuli we take in to get a clearer picture. Lloyd N. Trefethen, professor of numerical analysis at Oxford University, coined a phrase: "shrink the diameter of intellectual space." Our brain regularly shrinks the intellectual diameter of stimuli so we can more effectively move through the world. And when it reduces what we notice, contrast like what Frank Lloyd Wright used in his designs becomes a mechanism for telling our brain, "This is worth noticing."

This chapter is about a moment—a single pivotal instant that serves as a catalyst. Just as Frank Lloyd Wright constructed a moment in which an observer would move from claustrophobic hallway to a wonder-inducing dining room, the moment I'm referring to serves as an inflection point between what we thought we would experience and what we are surprised to find instead. The term for this moment is an *expectation violation*, and it is the lighting of the touch paper that moves us from absorption to the final element of wonder, *awe*. From compression to release, a differential, or contrast, possesses within it a magical synergist that awakens our senses from the expected to the unexpected. And the magnitude of that moment defines the doorway of our perception and what we see on the other side.

What gets noticed and what gets filtered

Contrast is a dominant force in how we observe the world. In many ways, contrast, or change, is *all* that we see. For example, in our visual field, the ways we notice colors, light, and depth are all built around contrasts. The same goes for our mental field, which is driven by how we collect and process stimuli. Our brain picks up about eleven million bits of stimuli per second, but we can't possibly notice all the input we take in. To help us make sense of what would otherwise be a debilitating cacophony of information, it sorts these stimuli based on what appears to be the most urgent or relevant. This filtering could be based on ancient protective reactions (loud noise = danger) or on recent knowledge (jackhammer = annoying but not dangerous). It builds easy patterns, what are called *heuristics* or *schema*, for us to follow, and registers what is different enough for us to notice and what is similar enough that it can be ignored. This system of pattern matching and noticing incongruity is the basis of many of our mental processes.

A simple example is the feeling of your clothes as you wear them. You notice the feeling of the fabric against your skin as you initially put your clothes on—your brain registers a new sensation. But after a few seconds, you don't really perceive it any longer. Your brain has decided that that information is no longer relevant, and instead, the red signal at the crosswalk is more deserving of your cognitive focus.

The optical illusion known as the Troxler effect or Troxler's fading, discovered by Swiss physician Ignaz Paul Vital Troxler in 1804, demonstrates this phenomenon of contrast and relevance. There are many online examples you can try yourself, a common one involving staring at a dot set on a field of various muted colors. If you stare intently at only the dot, the colors in the background will begin to fade from the visual field fairly quickly. That is until you look away and back again, and then the colors reappear. This type of information filtering is called *habituation* and can be experienced with every type of sensory stimuli. To be efficient and reserve energy, after a while our brain ignores stimuli that are "static." We can become habituated to almost anything, and during habituation, our brain isn't just ignoring these stimuli; it is also adapting by creating new patterns of thinking based on the things it sees and the things it has trained itself to ignore.

Sea legs are a great illustration. If you've ever gone out on a boat, you may notice when you return to land, you can still feel the gentle swaying of the sea despite being on terra firma. Your brain adapted to what it needed to in order to keep you balanced while out on the water, responding to equilibrium shifts and triggering core muscles to keep you upright. All this activity, unnoticed by you as it happened, created a new model—a new heuristic—in your brain about balance. Once back on land, the brain still operates on that heuristic. It has adapted, and in an incredibly short period of time. And now, because of the contrast of being on shore, you notice the adaptation, and thus have to reshift your balance heuristic back to the one appropriate for being on land.

It's not just physical sensations that can be impacted by this contrast, but psychological ones as well. One of the reasons people root for the underdog is because of the burst of additional pleasure we feel when the underdog wins. That expectation violation of winning against the odds, as opposed to always rooting for the winning team and getting the expected outcome (i.e., habituation), lends added meaning to the moment.

Another mental process that filters our perception of the world is *latent inhibition*, also known as *learned irrelevance*. Latent inhibition is a phenomenon whereby we are less likely to notice new details of something familiar than with something we've never encountered before. This is an unconscious response that our brain might employ so we don't become distracted by multiple voices in a crowd, but we will notice if someone yells "Fire!" Newness gets noticed.

Let's use the example of a light switch. If you had never seen a light switch before, you might be amazed when you flicked this little protrusion of plastic and the lights came on. *How does it do that? Will it do it every time? Is there a lag? Do all light switches work the same way?* Imagine all the details you might examine when a light switch is new and the stimuli associated with it are novel. (I felt this way upon being introduced to an all-singing, all-dancing toilet on my first visit to Japan.) Over time, your brain becomes habituated to the idea of the light switch, so at some point, the details of it are no longer noticed, and all light switches fall into the same mental category, regardless of whether or not they have different features. In essence, the pattern of habituation to the details of a light switch becomes a type of learning.

People with low latent inhibition don't lose their fascination with the light switch. While they will learn its functionality, their brain's reduced filtering means more details continue to be noticed. As a result, such people can be more creative, as they may connect the dots in an unexpected way, and they also don't find unlearning old patterns as challenging. At the same time, that number of stimuli may be overwhelming, and for certain neurodivergent people, such as people with ADD/ADHD or people on the autism spectrum, the filter that attenuates information allows too much in, causing distraction and sensory overload. Extremely low latent inhibition, a state known as *cognitive disinhibition*, has even been connected to psychosis, and in some cases of schizophrenia, latent inhibition vanishes entirely, illuminating a potential connection between creativity and mental illness found in the stereotypical "mad genius."

We can decrease our sensitization to habituation by regularly introducing novelty into our lives, as well as integrating attention-training strategies such as meditation. While extremely low levels of latent inhibition are usually treated pharmacologically, we can train our brain to self-regulate our inhibitory control through various methods like cycling, singing in a choir, listening to books on tape, and, as with habituation, certain types of mindfulness practice.

Latent inhibition is closely associated with the psychological and neuroscientific theory of *salience*, yet another way our brain acknowledges and transmits information. The area of our brain that manages many of these filters—picking and choosing what is brought to consciousness based on the patterns it sees and the importance it assigns to various novel stimuli—is called the *salience network*. The salience network is anti-correlational to the default mode network (meaning when the DMN is activated the salience network is quieted, and vice versa).

Somewhat intuitively named, the salience network is the area of the brain that filters external stimuli and then labels and ranks those stimuli in order of salience, or relevance and relative importance. Central to our sense of motivation and action, the salience network determines what should draw our attention and then triggers our drive system. This is a pivotal brain area for wonder, as it is associated with features like heuristics and expectation violations, which impact stimulus-driven attention like curiosity.

Sometimes the brain notices things that seem more salient, but we assign an outweighed importance to them. For example, shark attacks are less likely to kill you than slipping in the shower, but we don't have TV channels dedicating a week of programming to deadly bathroom mishaps. The vivid, novel, and gruesome nature of a shark attack makes it more salient; that is, more noticed.

From an evolutionary point of view, pattern matching developed as a means of survival. When a community is at the mercy of the weather, crop growth, and animal migration, noticing key patterns is the difference between life and death. But we aren't the only creatures who process stimuli this way. Animals with far smaller brains than ours employ this technique, and with good reason, as it is an incredibly efficient way to use limited cognitive processing power. Reptiles are a great example of a species that has primarily functioned on an "if it's not changing, it's not worth noticing" model for millennia. (Jurassic Park dinosaurs, terrifying as they were, could still be outwitted by simply standing veeeeeeery still.) And consider some of the stimuli we simply can't perceive even if we want to. For instance, elephant trunks are so sensitive they can pick up vibrations from other elephants as far as ten miles away. Pit vipers can see infrared at night, a light spectrum completely invisible to the human eye. Bats (as well as toothed whales and some shrews) employ echolocation using high-frequency pulses undetectable by human ears. Although, if you're interested in communing with your local bat population, researchers like neuroscientist David Eagleman have learned how to "turn on" this capability in humans through neural implants.

Basically, "out there" (waves hands) is a lot less about what's "there" or "not there" or "real" or "not real" than what is "perceived in the moment" or "not perceived in the moment." It's all a matter of perception.

Unlocking the doors of perception

Let's imagine a scene. You are on the phone as you're racing out the door, frazzled and dreadfully late to a meeting. As you leave the house, you flick the light switch off, and nothing happens. The lights stay on. You would be annoyed, perhaps a bit surprised, but it would likely not create such a vast knowledge gap that you would feel the need to cancel your plans to figure out the reason behind it. There would undoubtedly be some cognitive dissonance, meaning your brain would expect one thing and experience something else, and because our brain doesn't usually like cognitive dissonance (especially in those of us with a high need for cognitive closure), we would scramble in our noggin for some reasonable explanation to fill in the gap. After a few seconds, you would likely be satisfied with the guess that the wiring is faulty or some such, and you would go on your way, making a mental note to call a repair person.

Now, imagine you flick the light switch, and the lights in a *different* room start turning on and off. This would be unusual based on what we know about how a light switch operates, and as a result, it would cause a decent-size expectation violation. There would be a knowledge gap, but your brain might still try to connect the dots between electricity, lights, on-and-off, and so on. Such an event would be unexpected and highly weird, but not life-changing. It may or may not, depending on how comfortable you were with that unanswered question, and how urgent your meeting was, make you stop and reroute the course of your day.

But what if every time you flicked the light switch on and off, your cat disappeared and reappeared? That would be freak-out inducing, going against not only what you know about light switches but also what you know about physics. And cats. Such a phenomenon would be a massive expectation violation and require an even larger knowledge gap to be closed, as the disappearing and reappearing cat would be impossible to ignore. Your pressing phone call and meeting would be forgotten as your brain rerouted more cognitive energy to make sense of this very big contrast between your heuristic (lights in our room turn on and off when we flick a switch) and what you are experiencing (Mr. Bigglesworth vanishes when you flick a switch). This is an extreme example (obviously) but demonstrates that what we experience is all contextual.

The concept of expectation violation is actually part and parcel of the way we *wander* and *whittle*, as this moment of discovering something unexpected inspires us to be curious and become absorbed in finding a subsequent explanation. But for the *wow* and *whoa* of awe, the expectation violation is of an even greater magnitude. Piercarlo Valdesolo, director of the Moral Emotions and Trust Lab at Claremont McKenna College, describes it this way: "You're in the presence of something novel, something that you can't immediately understand, or something that defies your everyday experience. An emotion like surprise can be merely that—something happens that's unexpected. . . . You wonder what is going on—you're curious." The difference with awe, Valdesolo explains, is the *whoa* moment that shifts our perspective. "Awe, I think, involves an extra ingredient; not only does something happen that violates your expectations— not only is there a gap in your knowledge that's made salient— but the expectation-violating event challenges the schemas, the knowledge structures that you have, to such an extent that . . . you cannot assimilate this information into those structures." So the lights staying on is surprising and makes you curious. The cat disappearing is awe-inducing and would be big enough to profoundly shift your view of the world.

Einstein described an expectation violation as the moment "an experience comes into conflict with a world of concepts already sufficiently fixed within us." He related a wonder-filled moment as a child when an expectation violation regarding a heretofore "unconscious world of concepts" changed his perspective indelibly. "A wonder of this kind I experienced as a child of four or five years when my father showed me a compass. That this needle behaved in such a determined way did not at all fit in the kind of occurrences that could find a place in the unconscious world of concepts (efficacy produced by direct 'touch'). I can still remember—or at least believe I can remember—that this experience made a deep and lasting impression upon me. Something deeply hidden had to be behind things." Einstein's description poignantly touches on each element of wonder—the observation and curiosity of the compass, the absorption in the needle, his youthful schema suddenly disrupted by a bigger world of knowledge than the one he had previously known, and the magical moment of awe-filled awareness that changed him.

Now imagine on your way out the door, you were so distracted with your call and the day's upcoming meetings that you didn't notice anything. The light switch is bedeviled, Mr. Bigglesworth vanishes beyond the veil, and you simply missed the whole freaking thing because your brain was completely focused elsewhere. We'll cover more in Part 3, but when we fail to be present in the moment, we close ourselves off from opportunities to become curious and absorbed and hence may miss glimpses of wonder. Sometimes the expectation violation isn't so much an indication of the size of the cognitive gap as it is of the attention paid to the gap in the first place.

In future chapters, we will see that the way our brain filters, sorts, and analyzes information greatly impacts what we remember and the depth of meaning we assign to any experience. Lights in the other room going on and off might mean a prank. Cat vanishing might mean a brush with the mystical. Beau Lotto and his consulting team, known as the "Lab of Misfits," focus much of their research on this idea of perception, the meaning we assign experiences, and the context in which we have them. "If everything in perception is grounded in meaning, even seeing red is seeing 'a meaning,' as in seeing 'the behavioral significance of something,'" Lotto explains. "What you're doing is seeing the relationships between things, not the thing. The brain is only looking at relationships, not absolutes. So red is actually a direction. It's a relationship."

This idea that perception is relationship-based makes me think of a beautiful bottle of raki I purchased on vacation in Turkey. I had taken a shine to the anisette-flavored aperitif during my visit and was excited to bring a bit of my vacation back home with me. But—and we have all had this experience—it just didn't taste the same back in my living room. Out of the context of my Turkish holiday experience, absent the sand and sun and seafood, my perception had shifted. Nothing had presumably happened to the bottle of liquor, and my taste buds and olfactory senses were still operating in the same fashion, but the context was different, thus my perception had changed. This line of thinking, if you allow it, can throw up all sorts of fascinating philosophical, almost ontological questions. *What is color? Would colors exist if humans didn't exist? Does anything exist if we don't experience it? What else exists that we simply are unable (or unwilling) to perceive? If a tree falls in the forest and no one is there to hear it, did it make a sound?* (You get the picture.)

Seventeenth-century French philosopher René Descartes explored this concept in his book *Passions of the Soul*. Through a compilation of a series of letters between himself and Princess Elisabeth of Bohemia on the nature of human emotions (what he called "passions"), Descartes noted the link between novelty, curiosity, and perception. He introduced, in many ways, the idea that not only is the very nature of perception a cognitive experience, but that wonder is an epistemic one; that is, focused on meaning-making and knowledge-gathering. "When our first encounter with some object takes us by surprise, and we judge it to be new, or very different from what we have previously experienced or from *what we expected it to be* [my emphasis], this causes us to wonder at it and be astonished. And because this can happen before we have any knowledge of whether the thing is beneficial to us or not, it seems to me that wonderment is the first passion of all. And it has no contrary, because, if the object that presents itself has nothing in itself to surprise us, we are not moved by it in any way and we consider it without any passion."

These examples illustrate a fundamental piece of the wonder puzzle: all perception exists within a context. And when a pattern we expect to complete is interrupted, when our expectation of what we think should happen next is violated, our brain pays attention, encodes memories, and kicks into wonder overdrive. We are now ready to transition from our moment of absorbed compression into the expansive release of awe.

WONDER WRAP-UP

- A moment known as an *expectation violation* sits between the wonder elements of absorption and awe. When what we expect to experience and what we actually experience are vastly different, it acts as a catalyst for transitioning from absorption to awe. This phenomenon occurs because the brain notices and responds to contrasts.

- To be as efficient as possible, our brain filters and pattern matches stimuli to determine what is salient, relevant, and worth noticing. These filters and patterns form the building blocks of our knowledge structures known as

schema or *heuristics*. When we experience something worth
remembering, our schema will change to take on that new
information.

- The *salience network*, an area of the brain that is anti-
  correlational to the default mode network (DMN),
  is responsible for filtering external stimuli and then
  labeling and ranking that data in order of relevance
  and importance. This is one of the key networks when
  studying wonder, as it is linked to how we experience an
  expectation violation.

- *Latent inhibition*, also known as learned irrelevance, is a
  phenomenon whereby we are less likely to notice new
  details of something familiar than something novel. If our
  latent inhibition is too high, we may miss opportunities
  for wonder.

- Latent inhibition is a form of *habituation*. Habituation is a
  way our brain adapts to persistent stimuli that it deems
  non-salient. As happens with sea legs, we can become
  habituated to stimuli and build new schema very quickly.

- Slow thought activities that focus on practicing presence,
  like meditation, help us self-regulate our inhibitory
  control, as do other cognitive training exercises like
  martial arts or singing in a choir.

- All perception is contextual, and that context determines
  how we perceive wonder—its magnitude and its meaning.

5

Wow and Whoa

In July 1969, 600 million people watched the moon landing on television. That moment remains one of the largest shared human experiences ever. After that "giant leap for mankind," the world was never quite the same again. This global transformation had already begun six months prior when, on Christmas Eve of 1968, *Apollo 8* astronaut William Anders snapped a photo called *Earthrise*—a poignant image of Earth as a small, fragile marble suspended in inky dark. Borders erased, nations and nationalities almost nonsensical constructs, this image confronted our most deeply held beliefs about humankind's place in the universe and set in motion a defining moment of the twentieth century. Nineteen sixty-eight marked a period of massive turbulence worldwide—scenes of the Vietnam War beamed into homes, the May '68 student riots in Paris, the assassination of Martin Luther King Jr., followed by Robert Kennedy only two months later. Humanity was having a violent reckoning with itself. The *Earthrise* photo and seeing the whole Earth for the first time in human history jolted people out of their individual egoic concerns, turning their eyes heavenward. *Earthrise* (and a subsequent photo titled *Blue Marble*) has since become the most widely disseminated image in human history, changing our relationship with this shared common home.*

Our journey into space changed humanity's relationship with itself, but we Earthlings weren't the only ones affected. When the astronauts returned from space, they were fundamentally changed people. Shuttle astronaut Kathryn D. Sullivan said, "No amount of prior study or training can fully prepare anybody for the awe and wonder this inspires." International Space Station resident Ron Garan remarked, "it was as if time stood still." When *Apollo* 9 lunar module pilot Russell "Rusty" Schweickart saw Earth from space, he said, "From the moon, the Earth is so small and so fragile and such a precious little spot in that universe that you can block it out with your thumb. Then you realize that on that spot, that little blue and white thing, is everything that means anything to you—all of history and music and poetry and art and death and birth and love, tears, joy, games, all of it right there on that little spot that you can cover with your thumb. And you realize from that perspective that you've changed forever, that there is something new there, that the relationship is no longer what it was."

What Schweickart was eloquently describing was the "Overview Effect" and the metamorphic power of wonder. A term coined in 1987 by space writer Frank White, the Overview Effect describes the unexpected, powerful, and profound shift in perspective astronauts experience when they view Earth from space. White described those fundamental, enduring shifts as "truly transformative experiences involving senses of wonder and awe, unity with nature, transcendence, and universal brotherhood."

How big a shift? When *Apollo* 14 astronaut Edgar Mitchell returned from space in 1971, he said he'd developed "an instant

---

* It also coincided with, and some would argue triggered, what is today's modern sustainability movement.

global consciousness," continuing, "From out there on the moon, international politics look so petty. You want to grab a politician by the scruff of the neck and drag him a quarter of a million miles out and say, 'Look at that, you son of a bitch.'" Upon his return, Mitchell felt compelled to start the Institute for Noetic Sciences. (Noetic sciences comprise a scientific wildland that includes a huge range of exploration from meditation to altered states of consciousness all the way to full parapsychology, such as telekinesis.) "When I went to the moon I was a pragmatic test pilot," Mitchell said. "But when I saw the planet Earth floating in the vastness of space the presence of divinity became almost palpable and I knew that life in the universe was not just an accident." Quite a leap from "pragmatic test pilot," but wonder can do that to you.

Apollo 15 astronaut Jim Irwin had an epiphany while in space, saying, "I felt the power of God as I'd never felt it before." Despite having left the church at age ten, Irwin became a born-again Christian upon his return and spent the rest of his life as a preacher. Russell Schweickart became a devotee of Transcendental Meditation and committed his life to volunteerism. All of these personal and career metamorphoses were undeniably the result of having experienced the *wow* and *whoa* of wonder's final element, *awe*.

Reviewing the astronaut interviews, one is struck by how they describe not just a feeling of breathtaking beauty or terrifying void, or even how the experience changed their individual lives, but how it changed the way they see themselves in relation to the rest of the world. Canadian astronaut Chris Hadfield, who spent a record-breaking 166 days in space, shared this sentiment by saying, "It was when I took a picture, actually, of Karachi, Pakistan, and I read what I wrote about it the next day, which was: 'There are 6 million of us living in Pakistan.' Six million of 'us'? When is that no longer 'them'? How did that part of the world, which I've never even been to, now, suddenly, because of the cumulative effect of where I am, start to feel like us? I think that's when the world became one place for me."

Fascinated by the consistency of the narratives from returning astronauts, our STE researcher David Yaden decided to team up with pioneering radiologist Andy Newberg to study the Overview Effect and better understand these astronauts' transformations. Newberg was one of the first scientists to put meditators and "veteran contemplatives" into an fMRI scanner to see what was happening in their brains when they entered what Yaden calls "deep states of unity." Yaden and Newberg found that the Overview Effect had all the characteristics of an altered state of consciousness, and, more specifically, the self-transcendent state of awe.

The final element: awe

While philosophers, artists, writers, and religious scholars have explored awe for millennia, the science of awe is less than twenty years old. Academic interest was ignited in the topic in 2003 when psychologists Dacher Keltner and Jonathan Haidt published their paper "Approaching Awe, a Moral, Spiritual, and Aesthetic Emotion" and shared the first real conceptual framework of an idea as old as humanity. They described awe as the feeling we experience in the presence of something so vast—physically or cognitively—that it challenges the way we see the world (wow!), and thus our perspective is forever changed (whoa ...).

Even just meeting Dacher Keltner over a video call, I got the impression that this is a man who has cultivated a strong wonder practice. No sense of rush or pressure. He'll just amble with the complete confidence that wonder is there, and he's the man to find it. Keltner's manner is mellow and generous, and his easy demeanor quickly gives way to exuberance as he talks excitedly about all the various discoveries that have been made about awe. "The deep reason [I began studying awe] is, I was raised by kind of countercultural types who were really interested in art and literature and politics, and when I got into the field of emotion around 1990, our understanding of all the kinds of the prosocial positive emotions was impoverished. So, we just didn't have a literature on compassion, and we didn't have a literature on awe. Here I was out at musical concerts and out in nature and seeing Nelson Mandela come out of prison, and I was just like, 'What is this emotion?'"

Keltner shared a sentiment echoed by many scientists—that prior to the 1990s, the psychology profession was predominantly focused on viewing people through a deficits-based lens. The *Diagnostic and Statistical Manual of Mental Disorders*, known as the DSM, is the bible of mental pathology; that is, what's "broken" with humans.* From anxiety and ADHD to trichotillomania and voyeurism, it is a compendium of every "validated mental disorder," and the conditions contained therein were the primary focus of psychology researchers for more than one hundred years until psychologist Martin Seligman, in his role as president of the American Psychological Association, started the positive psychology movement in 1998. Keltner, like Seligman and many other entrants into the psychology profession at the turn of the millennium, said he was drawn to explore not the negative aspects of the human condition but rather "what really matters in people's lives." Keltner channeled this passion into the Greater Good Science Center (GGSC), whose tagline is "Science-based insights for a meaningful life." Begun in 2001, the GGSC has served as a research center and training repository whose basic, if not gargantuan, mission is to help people improve their

---

* To be clear, I am not suggesting people are broken, rather that the DSM's deficits-based approach makes some people feel that way.

emotional and social well-being and live more meaningful lives. "There's a sense in psychological science and evolutionary theory and emotion science that it's all about fight-or-flight. And here's America—things are broken—so we focus on what we want to fix, right?" Keltner explains. "But awe is just the opposite. Our imagination has evolved our capacity for wonder, our hunger for art and music and transcendent meaning. So, [choosing to study awe] was a perfect confluence of a lot of different forces."

The stages of awe

Keltner and Haidt's conceptual assumptions about awe have largely been proven true in subsequent research, including their proposed components of awe. First is the trigger—the expectation violation—an eliciting event that challenges our previous heuristic in a particularly novel and profound way. This could be as simple as Frank Lloyd Wright's compression and release or as earth-shattering as losing your cat from a possessed light switch. This novel jolt to our schema makes us pay attention (remember—we only notice the contrast), and in that moment of recognition, our mind opens up to receive as many stimuli as possible.

The next stages are awe's two *cognitive appraisals* (i.e., how we emotionally interpret a situation): *vastness* and *accommodation*. Vastness is the *wow* moment, when something so moving has grabbed us and made us feel like a small piece of a much bigger world. And accommodation is the *whoa* moment, when our brain tries to make sense of that *wow* experience, and our view of the world is different because of it.

Awe can be found in countless places—nature, art, music, architecture, religion, rousing speeches, and even one another—and in each of these places, we may encounter an awe elicitor. These elicitors can be perceptual (like the strings in Edward

Elgar's orchestral masterwork "Nimrod") or conceptual (like trying to understand the theory of a folded universe). Within these
categories, awe can be further classified through the subcategories
of natural, cognitive, and social awe. And these can be further
identified through their "flavors" (beauty, virtue, exceptional ability, threat, and the supernatural), which is the term used to describe the different tones of awe experiences.

Awe is very individual. And as such, the same experience
will mean different things to different people. Let's take a view
of the Grand Canyon, which is no doubt awe-inspiring. If you
have ever stood on the canyon's rim, the void of the chasm
seems to almost suck the air out of your lungs like a vacuum.
For one person, this experience might be a perceptual natural
awe elicitor, as they are moved by the physical vista. For another,
perhaps struck by the canyon's geologic history, it could be a
conceptual cognitive elicitor. For some, the sheer beauty of the
view could be the quality that challenges their schema. For others, the immense abyss could create a sense of threat that shocks
the system. And with awe, it could even be all of these. This
makes for an incredibly multilayered emotion with any number
of ways to experience it.

After we have this vast, novel experience, our brain sets to
work trying to understand what it has just perceived. Now our
schemas kick in. Schemas are little building blocks of knowledge that we keep and recall when needed.* These blocks are

---

* It's easy to understand the model when you think of children and the way they
build knowledge. Imagine a child who knows what an apple is but has never seen
a pomegranate. She spies the pomegranate in the fruit bowl and her brain fetches
her existing apple schema: red, round, smooth, lives in the fruit bowl. This process
of calling up and applying an existing schema is *assimilation*. Once she learns that
the pomegranate is not the same as an apple, but is a different fruit, she will use the
process of *accommodation* to change her existing schema. This is a simple schema and
is easier to change because she's just a child. Schemas become much more complex
and thus harder to change when we are adults.

built up over our lifetime, so as children, we have fewer, smaller blocks that are easy to change, and as we get older and accumulate more knowledge, these blocks are more numerous, complex, and fixed. If the new stimuli create only a small cognition gap, our brain may just dismiss the experience. It will find a schema to match, ignore any discrepancies, and shift focus to other stimuli. But if the experience creates a larger gap, resulting in a significant cognitive challenge, then our schema will change to wrap itself around this new information. This is called *accommodation*. Whether that change is enduring or temporary depends on many factors, but research would say it's primarily a combination of our personality traits (the filters) and the intensity of the experience (the size of the cognition gap).

Like William James and Abraham Maslow, Keltner and Haidt initially regarded awe as an experience that had to be big, "fleeting and rare," such as summiting a mountain peak or seeing your child take their first steps. However, research has since shown even modest, simple, day-to-day experiences, such as a sunrise or a favorite song, can elicit awe. We'll learn more in Part 2 about how to find wonder in our day-to-day lives, but the discovery of quotidian awe has opened up the possibility of cultivating wonderproneness (and the meaningful outcomes it generates) regularly—not just on rare occasions.

The history of awe

As an English word, *awe* has quite a mythical creation story. From the Old Norse *agi* and the Danish *ave*, the word first appeared in Middle English in the thirteenth century. An evocative theme in Norse mythology, awe was most keenly seen through the mythical powers of Ægishjálmr (the Helm of Awe), which, according to the linguist Stephen Flowers, "was originally a kind of sphere of magical power to strike fear into the enemy . . . associated with the power of serpents to paralyze their prey before striking." The paralyzing power of serpents is a fine description of the terror, curiosity, reverence, and even desire—desire to control such a power—of awe. According to the *Poetic Edda*, a written collection of spoken-word Norse poetry, the Helm of Awe subsequently manifested itself into a sort of tattooed protection amulet worn by Viking warriors. The symbol was a collection of small trident runic shapes not dissimilar to the shape of a snowflake. This image was beaten into a soft metal such as copper or lead, dipped into stain, and pressed to the warrior's forehead directly between the brows, likely resembling a bindi. This has left some historians to posit that it was also meant to connect the wearer with the power of the third eye. This symbol carried with it the fierce power of awe, stunning foes and leading warriors safely into battle.

The Norse interpretation of awe was often one of fear, with the Helm of Awe sometimes translated as the Helm of Terror. This fungibility of awe and terror was not uncommon when describing the relationship between humans and their deities, with many descriptions of ancient mystical awe having a tinge of the terrible and supernatural to them. In the *Bhagavat Gita*, sixteen hundred years earlier, the word *bhītāḥ* appears, similarly often translated as "fear" but also as being "enraptured" by a "terrible and wonderful form."

In the biblical story of Paul's conversion, Saul, as he was then known, a pharisee and persecutor of Christians, encountered Jesus on the road to Damascus. "A light from heaven flashed around him," and he "fell to the ground." After three days of blindness, "something like scales fell from Saul's eyes, and he could see again." From this epiphanic experience, Saul converted and was transformed from a pharisee to a loyal Christian apostle. The *Bhagavat Gita* also tells its own dramatic conversion story of the warrior prince Arunja by Krishna. Krishna tries to persuade Arunja to lead his men into heroic battle, and certain death, on behalf of the forces of good. Despite Krishna's entreaties, Arunja is unmoved. Then, when Krishna gifts Arunja with spiritual vision, Arunja witnesses a revelation reminiscent of something out of 1960s psychedelia or a lively Hieronymus Bosch painting. He is blinded by the light of a thousand suns, dazzled by a million deities, and then enveloped by a kaleidoscope of swirling shapes and colors, including images of all living creatures, the entire cosmos, infinite faces, and various bodily incarnations of gods, jewels, serpents, sages, and Brahma seated on a lotus. The vision culminates with Krishna consuming all that has ever existed and destroying it in his mouth (whew!). Understandably, Arunja's reaction was . . . mixed. He felt both "ecstatic . . . joy, yet fear and trembling perturbed [his] mind."

As well as the realm of religious scholars, philosophers have also pondered awe. Thirteenth-century philosopher Thomas Aquinas believed that the very nature of philosophy and any meaningful creation of humankind such as poetry, art, and music finds its birth in awe. "Philosophy arises from awe," he said in his work Metaphysics. "A philosopher is bound in his way to be a lover of myths and poetic fables. Poets and philosophers are alike in being big with wonder." And, of course, writers, artists, and musicians revel in wonder and its composite element awe. Around the same time that the Vikings were adorning themselves with the Ægishjálmr, on the other side of the world, Sufi poet Rumi was conjuring a less fearful incarnation of awe. "Awe is the salve that will heal our eyes." And, in perhaps one of the most astute interpretations of awe, he wrote,

> You must have shadow and light source both.
> Listen and lay your head under the tree of awe.

Awe as shelter, as nurturer, as balm. Awe as smiter, as paralyzer, as destroyer. Either manifestation—tender or terrible—has power. But Rumi's insight of "shadow and light" touches on one of the fascinating aspects of awe: its duality.

Shadow and light, day and night, sun and moon, yin and yang—humans use duality as a way to link and make sense of seemingly opposing forces in the world. Some of those opposing forces are emotions, too, such as joy and grief, hope and despair, enthusiasm and malaise. Emotions, at their heart, are ways for humans to categorize and communicate their own experiences, and we naturally categorize them as positive or negative. Psychologists call this assignment of an emotion to a positive or negative pole its *valence*. So, happiness is "positively valenced," and anger is "negatively valenced." And while some emotions ride the valence fence, most can be put toward the end of one pole or the other. What makes awe quite unusual is that it can be either positively or negatively valenced, and sometimes even both at the same time, as in the story of Arunja. The word itself is something of a shape-shifter, too. The emotional tone of the word *awe* has morphed through the years, losing some of the terror that the etymology reflects and, at least in the Western world, migrated to a more positively valenced emotion.

Why should we care about awe?

I reverentially refer to Keltner as the "Awe Father," not just because he's the researcher who penned the seminal paper on awe, setting in motion a robust and growing body of awe research, but because he has spawned so many awe researchers from his own tutelage. It's hard to find someone working on the topic whose academic genealogy doesn't somehow trace back to him at the top of the awe family tree, including several leading contemporary awe researchers like Lani Shiota, Jennifer Stellar, and Paul Piff.

Michelle "Lani" Shiota, associate professor of social psychology and founder of the Shiota Psychophysiology Laboratory for Affective Testing, or SPLAT lab, a positive emotions lab out of Arizona State University, was one of Dacher Keltner's first PhD students researching the science of awe. Shiota reminds me of a bad-ass Marvel heroine—professor by day, superhero by night. She has an air about her that is both otherworldly and powerful. (Women with giant brains can have that mystique, and I am here for it.) Shiota is, by a fair margin, the most cautious of the researchers I spoke with, proudly proclaiming herself a "stickler." She is very precise with her explanations of the science and not shy in sharing those areas where she sees some over-enthusiasm. "I am absolutely not someone who reaches way beyond the science."

A trained ballet dancer before becoming a psychologist, Shiota began studying awe because she, like Keltner, had experienced it herself but saw a dearth of academic literature about it. "I come from this background of immersion in the theater and in dance and in music, where awe was part of why you live; that awe is kind of the point of being here. It was so central to my experience of the world." Keltner cautioned her, however, that studying awe on its own could be perceived as too fringe and that it would be more prudent to explore it in the context of other prosocial emotions (i.e., helping emotions). "People will think you're a flake, basically," Shiota explains. "So, if you're going to study it, let's talk about this broader category of potentially specific positive emotions, which was very, very new at the time."

Shiota was the first to take Keltner and Haidt's conceptual ideas and attempt to study experimentally elicited awe. To test for the emotion, she and her research team needed something easily accessible on the Berkeley campus that would reliably inspire awe. They landed on, of all things, the skeleton of a T. *rex* as the eliciting object. Osborn, the *Tyrannosaurus rex* in question, is a mammoth twelve feet tall, twenty-five feet long, 90 percent complete skeleton cast, weighing in at five tons (so named after Henry Fairfield Osborn, a paleontologist and president of the American Museum of Natural History who was the first to describe the *Tyrannosaurus rex* in 1905). Osborn is a striking beast, but researchers wanted to know if he was truly *awe-inspiring*. For the experiment, half the participants were brought to view the *Tyrannosaurus rex* skeleton, while the other half were brought to view an empty hallway. They asked participants in each group to share words they would use to describe the environment they had observed and to describe themselves.

The researchers were able to determine that those seeing the T. *rex* had experienced awe, whereas those in the empty hall had not, and further, that it was possible to differentiate awe experimentally from other positive emotions like joy and pride. Through this experiment, Shiota and her colleagues also established several principal characteristics of the awe state. They found those who had experienced awe had measurable changes to their self-concept—the image one has of oneself in relation to others—deemphasizing their sense of the individual and increasing their sense of connectedness to the whole. Based on these two characteristics, the researchers also determined that awe is an epistemic self-transcendent emotion elicited by information-rich stimulus, experienced when "one is presented with an opportunity to build informational resources, rather than material or social ones." Last, awe-prone individuals are more adept at and open to revising their mental schemas. In other words, wonderprone people are more willing to change their mind.

As we'll see throughout this book, it's not always easy to elicit a strong enough awe response to study it. To tackle this, Beau

Lotto and his Lab of Misfits had the clever idea of studying the audience of a Cirque du Soleil show. Part circus (hence the name), part extreme modern acrobatics, and part dream state, performers in Cirque du Soleil can bend, hoist, perch, writhe, entwine, pirouette, flip, balance, twirl, suspend, and generally contort their bodies in the most unbelievable, entrancingly beautiful, and yet logic- and sense- and gravity-defying ways. Lotto felt certain it would be a wonderbringer for most attendees. "We went to Las Vegas, and we recorded the brain activity of people while they watched over ten performances of O, which is an iconic Cirque performance. And we also measured the behavior before the performance, as well as a different group after the performance." The Lab of Misfits recorded attendees' brain activity using EEG imaging technology and was able to track the brain as it experienced awe in real time. Lotto claims they've identified the brain activity of someone experiencing awe to such a precise degree that they can train an artificial neural network to predict with 83 percent precision whether someone is in an awe state or not.

Lotto and his team found several intriguing results from this experiment, but the one they thought most striking was the way people viewed themselves after an awe experience. "Something that was really quite profound is that when we asked people, 'Are you someone who has a propensity to experience awe?' they were more likely to give a positive response *after* the performance than they were [before]. They literally redefined themselves and their history."

The evolutionary heritage of awe

One of the questions that naturally emerge when discussing emotions is "why?" *Why do we have a particular response? For what purpose did humans develop this way of reacting to the world?* Pinning down evolutionary psychology to a single historical theory can sometimes lead to some dodgy science since so much of it is hypothetical, and human behavior develops for more than just a single reason. Lani Shiota finds many in evolutionary psychology too keen to pinpoint the singular cause and effect of our adaptive functions. "I think that one thing that tends to happen with evolutionary biology, as well as evolutionary psychology, is this claim that if there is this widespread innate trait, and it has a function, it evolved for a reason. They have the same conversations about why humans walk upright, and there's at least five different arguments. But that's not how evolution works. It's not like a reality TV show where there was some design challenge, and then God was like, 'Okay, whoever comes up with the best design wins.'" Shiota prefers exploring our more holistic evolutionary heritage. "It's more like somebody's genes mutated, and they walked a little more upright. And if it was overall good, it was more likely to be preserved in the system, but that good can have come from many different sources. So, there isn't necessarily a singular adaptive function, but once you identify that it might be part of our evolutionary heritage, you start asking, 'What are those functions?'"

So, what is the evolutionary heritage of awe? Some scientists believe it might have been a way of communicating leadership to groups, with the most impressive person inspiring awe and, therefore, fealty. Some believe it was a mechanism for quickly taking in large amounts of information, such as when standing at the top of a hill and looking out at an endless vista. What seems to be consistent across the various rationales for the emotion of awe is that it is epistemic (i.e., meaning-making and knowledge-building).

Another area of study for many of Keltner's students was looking at the cultural variations of awe, and the findings are illuminating, if perhaps somewhat intuitive. We know from past research that emotions can have different nuances across cultures, with individualistic cultures like that of the United States differing from collectivist cultures like those in Asia or Latin America. Individualists tend to feel socially disengaging emotions like anger or pride more strongly than engaging emotions like friendliness or compassion, whereas collectivist cultures are the reverse. Americans also tend to value high-arousal states—we are an enthusiastic people—because these states support individual achievement. In contrast, collectivist cultures prefer calmer, low-arousal states that support harmony of the whole and allow for greater attention to be given to the emotional states of others.

In a study of twenty-six countries across six continents, these differences held true for awe as well. Individualistic cultures, in particular that of Americans, associate awe with a positive experience more frequently and are more likely to enjoy an increase in their self-esteem from the experience. In comparison, collectivists are more likely to ascribe an awe experience to a supernatural phenomenon, thus imbuing their experience with a tinge of fear and helplessness. Interestingly, David Yaden found this same variation among Western and Asian space travelers and their reaction to the Overview Effect.

Some of this may come down to the language differences in the word itself. For example, the Spanish term for awe, *asombro*, has a connotation of an emotion tinged with fear, and the Chinese term for awe, 敬畏, is a combination of the characters for "respect" and "fear." Jennifer Stellar, another of Keltner's advisees, has also seen this cultural variation. "We've done one cross-cultural study that suggests that fear is actually a larger component in a culture like China's that doesn't have these strong norms toward idealization of positive effect. Rather, they are very comfortable with contradictory states. So, it might be totally fine to feel positive awe mixed with fear because they haven't had the Western historical traditions of romanticism and transcendentalism." In fact, these days, between 70 and 80 percent of all awe experiences are reported as positive, but collectivist cultures still hold a greater degree of reverence and fear about awe.

Stellar, a psychologist and director of the Health, Emotions, & Altruism Lab at the University of Toronto, has also found that a culture's association with an emotion is not fixed over time. There has been a progressive shift through the years to a more positive and less "fear and trembling" view of the awe experience globally. "What I think we've seen over the past hundred years, but I would say even longer, is this transition to a more positive experience of awe as a culture, and again, modern culture prioritizes positive aspects. So I'm not surprised that we've almost washed out the negative parts, but I'm not sure that's a good thing. If you look at the definition of awe cognitions, like perceiving something as vast and having a challenge to your worldview, those are not inherently positive. They are, if anything, maybe a little scary."

But despite the variations, there are enough commonalities through culture and time to support that awe is a universal and innate trait. Beyond the heaps of literature and philosophy that describe awe as elemental to the human experience, the research into vocalizations and facial expressions of awe also illustrates this. For instance, researchers have identified the "awe face." First, there is the sharp intake of breath, raised eyebrows, and widened eyes (wow!), and then there is the exhale with an open, drop-jawed mouth (whoa . . .). (Strikingly similar to the description in the Nāṭyaśāstra from the Introduction.) In one Chinese translation of awe—惊叹 (to marvel or exclaim)—definitions of the two characters also reflect the physical commonalties of an awe experience. The first character, 惊, means "to startle," and the second, 叹, means "to sigh."

From a replica of a T. rex skeleton and the Cirque du Soleil to impressive architecture and TV shows like the BBC's Planet Earth, any number of elicitors have been used to study awe experimentally. More recently, virtual reality and psychedelics have been added to the mix of tools. All these experiments have firmly established three consistent characteristics of awe. First, awe is its own discrete emotion, separate from other positive emotions like happiness and pride. Second, awe makes us feel like a smaller component of a bigger system, also known as small-self, lowering our ego but not our self-esteem. And third, because of this small-self, awe makes us more prosocial, meaning it makes us want to be better to each other.

In the transcendence of awe we discover some of wonder's greatest magic, and many of the benefits of wonder illustrated in Part 2 result from awe as the culmination of the wonder cycle. But even if we don't achieve an awe experience every time we seek it, engaging in the other elements of wonder is still an incredibly worthwhile and beneficial endeavor. And when we strive to be more wonderprone, it means we are creating a personally optimal environment for our mind, body, and soul to be more open, curious, absorbed, and in awe. With every attempt to practice openness, curiosity, or absorption, we are kick-starting an additive, upwardly cyclical process in which we build greater capacity for all the elements of wonder and become more primed for the potential of awe.

WONDER WRAP-UP

- Awe is the last element of wonder and in many ways represents its ultimate manifestation as the pinnacle of the wonder cycle. Awe is a universal state and trait whose evolutionary heritage was likely associated with determining hierarchy, gathering information for survival, and building community.

- Awe is typified by two states—*vastness* and *accommodation*, or *wow* and *whoa*. Vastness is when something, be it an incredible vista, complex idea, or moving oratory, strikes us in a way that makes us feel small and connected to the broader ecosystem of humanity. As our mind wraps itself around this new, moving experience and accommodates it, our schema changes, as does our view of the world.

- Because of this *small-self*, awe makes us more prosocial, meaning we want to be better to each other through emotions like compassion, empathy, and generosity.

- An example of the power of awe is a phenomenon called the Overview Effect, a profound psychological shift that occurs after astronauts see Earth from space. But while this is an example of an intense form of the emotion, awe can also be found in simple ways, like at a museum or on a walk in nature.

- People who are open, deeply curious, and prone to absorption are more likely to experience awe, and awe, in turn, enhances these wonder elements. A wonder virtuous circle.

- Awe is an unusual emotion because it is *dually valenced*, meaning it can be positive or negative, and sometimes both simultaneously. It is now generally perceived as a positive experience, but the meaning has shifted over the years, as etymologically, it is typically tinged with fear.

Part Two

Wonder as a
Practice

6

Wonder Mindset

A llow me a bit of nostalgia, if you will. When I think of developing a wonder mindset, I imagine one of those Magic Eye posters from the 1990s. For those among the uninitiated, these wildly popular posters were pieces of digitally generated "art" (a term used very loosely here), something of an optical illusion but one that relied on a perceptual shift. A very complex and colorful variety of what's called a *random dot autostereogram*, the images on these posters looked like a staticky pattern of fractals or colored shapes. But you weren't trying to see that patterned image—you were trying to see *another* image hidden within the piece, something usually cheesy like a breaching dolphin or roaring lion. To view this magic image, one would stare at the poster (some folks longer than others), slack-jawed, head tilted, maybe squinting, until . . . *whoa!* The brain would sort through the noise of the patterns, until the hidden image would suddenly seem to jump out in 3D. *How had they missed it?* The more experience a person had looking at various Magic Eye posters, the more proficient they became. It was fun and a bit addictive, and for some, apparently, even a transcendent experience. This recollection reminds me that wonder is always there. Sometimes, we just need to train our mind to see it.

We don't need to passively wait to experience wonder. We can cultivate a mindset attuned to wonder instead. "This is the problem. People think that wonder is an experience of the world. It's actually a way of looking," explains Beau Lotto. "Ask, 'What is the lens that you look through?' And we say that's a daily practice. It doesn't just happen. You have to work at it. Every day you have hundreds of opportunities to practice creating that lens." This is the essence of a wonder mindset—taking every opportunity to practice creating that lens.

So why were the Magic Eye posters just a bit of weird fractal wallpaper for some but transcendent for others? And what does this have to do with a wonder mindset? First, wonder is very individual and subjective. Every person needs to discover what brings them wonder and understand how their mindset influences that. Second, the filters we employ, the lenses we use, and the perspective we bring will affect our perception of our experience. Too many shortcuts? We might miss some opportunity for wonder. Too rigid? We may explain away wonder rather than dwell in the wow. And finally, because it is our perception that determines the consequences of any experience, our mindset matters. Why does one person get chills when listening to certain music and another doesn't? Same music, but different perceptions, so different consequences. While an external event (an aria, the Grand Canyon, a religious ritual) might be the springboard, it is our own mind that actually embodies wonder. A wonder mindset is less about the synergist and more about our way of seeing. The wonder catalyst knocks on the door. A wonder mindset gives us the keys to open it.

So, what kind of mindset makes someone wonderprone? People who are wonderprone are present, open, mentally nimble, and curious about new ideas, people, and things in a deep and exploratory way. They enjoy the process of becoming intellectually engaged and absorbed in meaning-making pursuits. They are deeply moved by music and can get lost in vivid thought. They find satisfaction in chewing on abstruse ideas and are comfortable with the unknown and unknowing. They walk toward questions rather than away. And they seek and embrace opportunities for transcendence, growing in their desire to contribute and connect with others.

When looking at how to cultivate a wonder mindset, it's valuable to understand our "dispositional wonder"—the type of wonderproneness we bring to the party based on our heritable personality traits. Are you high in openness? Are you naturally curious? Do you feel comfortable with the ineffable? Having a wonder mindset isn't necessarily about changing who you are, so much as enhancing through a wonder practice those traits that contribute to wonderproneness and counterbalancing those that don't. These established trait baselines are what are known as personality trait "thresholds." By first understanding our pre-existing trait thresholds, we can then employ additional techniques that enhance or mitigate our ability to become more wonderprone.

As a guide throughout this chapter, I'll share a sampling of questions researchers use to test for the elements of wonder. It's striking how much overlap there is in the questions for openness, curiosity, absorption, and awe, revealing the sinews of connectivity within the wonder cycle. I'll also share a few tasters of some practical ways to strengthen our wonder mindset (and you'll see more as well throughout this and the next section, in particular in Chapter 15, "Slow Thought"). The goal is to build a strong mental picture of a wonderprone person, so we can create our own wonder practice to become one.

Watch—openness to experience

Do you:

- have an active imagination and enjoy using it while you daydream?

- love philosophical discussions or a good debate?

- feel chills when you listen to music or get teary during commercials?

- enjoy experiencing new cultures or viewing different kinds of art?

Watching, our first element in the wonder cycle, is about seeing the world through a lens of openness, observation, willingness, and the faith that there will be something worth seeing. Scott Barry Kaufman describes openness as "the drive for cognitive exploration of inner experience." It makes sense that our foundation for wonder would begin with inner exploration, to prepare ourselves for outer exploration. In his research, Kaufman has found openness to be associated with "creativity, authenticity, IQ, willingness to entertain a variety of perspectives, personal growth, enjoyment of imagination and mind-wandering, tendency to seek out and enjoy cognitive stimulation, curiosity, high tolerance for ambiguity, low need for closure, breadth, and depth of emotional experience, appreciation of beauty, aesthetic chills and awe." (Wow!) Almost all of these characteristics are associated with the wonder cycle in different ways.

Research has consistently shown that the more open we are to the world, the more wonderprone we are, simply because our "wonder threshold" is lower. In his studies, Paul Silvia found, "If we view traits as 'thresholds' for behaviors and experiences, then we can view openness to experience as, in part, a lower threshold for experiencing states like awe and wonder." But openness also predicts a greater motivation to seek out environments where we are more likely to experience wonder. As Jennifer Stellar explains, "If I'm somebody who's particularly open, I'm going to go travel, I'm going to go to concerts and art museums and go have these experiences that if I'm less open, I just wouldn't be able to have." Stellar points out that while openness isn't a prerequisite, it sets the stage for us to be exposed to more frequent wonder experiences. "I'm not saying it's the only way to have them . . . but I do think on average, the more open you are, the more likely you will be to just put yourself in a situation where you feel this emotion." But Stellar is keen to share that openness in this context isn't just about being more open to experience; it is about being open to the world, to ideas, and other people. "My impression is there might be something deeper about being open to the world, like being open to being challenged, being more humble, and less defensive and threat prone. Openness primes you to be in the right place at the right time, and maybe even be in the right mindset to take in these experiences." If we aren't watching, if our field of vision is too narrow, we'll be blind to the opportunities for wonder around us.

Becoming a watcher: strength training for openness

It can be challenging to shift the needle on the personality trait of openness to experience for us fully grown folk, as it's a very stable trait across our lifetime. One way, though, was discovered quite by accident during a cognitive training pilot program aimed at staving off cognitive decline in older adults. Based on a protocol researchers developed called ACTIVE (Advanced Cognitive Training for Independent and Vital Elderly), the program involved cerebral games like Sudoku, crosswords, puzzles, and pattern matching.

Participants were given progressively more challenging exercises during the sixteen-week at-home program, with researchers adjusting the activities to keep participants sufficiently engaged in the learning process. The program was structured around two elements. The first was using inductive learning (also called discovery learning), which increases fluid cognition. The second was helping participants strike the right balance of difficulty in their activities so they could achieve the sweet spot of flow.

"We wanted participants to feel challenged but not overwhelmed," said University of Illinois psychology professor Elizabeth Stine-Morrow, who led the research. And while the training did improve cognitive functioning, an additional side effect was that it made participants more open to experience—the first time a nonpharmacological intervention changed a personality trait assumed to be fixed by adulthood. "While we didn't explicitly test this, we suspect that the training program—adapted in difficulty in sync with skill development—was important in leading to increased openness." As Stine-Morrow explained, "Growing confidence in their reasoning abilities possibly enabled greater enjoyment of intellectually challenging and creative endeavors." And these changes were observed in adults as old as ninety-four, presumably a person whose personality traits were very well established. Cognition and openness have always been linked, so, understandably, there could be a correlation between improved cognition and increased openness, but this is a surprising shift, especially in such a short time frame, on a trait known to be so stable.

While these changes were moderate and enduring, I want to stress that entirely changing your personality is not necessarily a worthwhile nor realistic goal. What we can do, however, is incrementally increase the choices we make toward more open behaviors and use the wonder cycle to reinforce those behaviors into longer-term shifts. For example, try a new walk to work instead of the usual route, or get a membership to a museum and visit some exhibitions you would normally pass over. While this is about novelty, it's also about changing the context, so we notice more of what we are seeing. In time, as we experience more new ideas, in new contexts, we should experience more wonder, which in turn will maximize our existing openness threshold, creating another wonder virtuous circle. So equally beneficial to doing exercises like those from the ACTIVE study is simply developing an awareness and recognition of our individual openness threshold and working to take full advantage of that.

Wander—curiosity

Do you:

- like to study new subjects or discover different cultures?

- feel at your best encountering the unpredictability of day-to-day life?

- thrive when doing something challenging or complicated?

- struggle when life has too much structure or a set routine?

Wander, our second element in the wonder cycle, is about eagerly engaging with the world, being comfortable with the twists and turns life brings, and always exploring, searching, seeking, scouting, tinkering, hunting, questioning, challenging, probing, discovering, discerning, and noodling. Our goal is to put ourselves forward so our mind can be challenged.

Curiosity is both a state and a trait, so knowing what we do about changing traits, our efforts are best spent improving our curiosity state through a change in attitude or environment. As the saying goes, neurons that fire together wire together, meaning the more our brain engages in a specific activity, the more likely we will create a cognitive track that further precipitates that activity in the future. So perhaps boosting our state of curiosity will ultimately help boost our trait curiosity over time.

David Eagleman is a bit of an outlier when it comes to his take on changing personality traits. Unlike many of his contemporaries, he believes it may take less effort than we think to change who we are because, in fact, we are always changing. "Every moment of your life, your brain is rewiring. You've got 86 billion neurons and a fraction of a quadrillion connections between them. These vast seas of connections are constantly changing their strength, and they're unconnecting and reconnecting elsewhere. It's why you are a slightly different person than you were a week ago or a year ago." (I find that notion oddly comforting.)

We tend to become less deeply curious as we age because we perceive there is less to be curious about, so while this may require some extra effort, understanding how to bolster trait curiosity is a valuable lifelong skill. As David Yaden explains, "There are fewer things that can't readily fit into the existing schemas we have for how we interpret our surroundings. As we age, it becomes more and more important to actively seek out wonder because it's not simply delivered to us."

Seek novelty

We have looked at the role of novelty a few times already, as it is so strongly associated with the elements of wonder. Two European neurobiologists, Nico Bunzeck and Emrah Düzel, are responsible for much of what we know about novelty. Bunzeck and Düzel were able to locate what they believe is the primary part of the brain that responds to novel stimuli, an area of the midbrain called the *substantia nigra/ventral tegmental area* or SN/VTA. This "novelty center" is closely linked to both the hippocampus and the amygdala.

We've covered how the hippocampus is responsible for creating memories so we can call them up later and how the amygdala, responsible for our fight-or-flight emotive response, also plays a role in reinforcing memories.

Bunzeck and Düzel surmised this SN/VTA connection through what is called an "oddball experiment." They first showed test subjects a series of familiar pictures (faces, places, etc.), and then they inserted some "oddball" pictures of new and unexpected images. They found the SN/VTA was activated by the oddball pictures and the memory recall of these images was stronger than it was with the familiar images, regardless of how vivid or emotionally charged those familiar images were. But this activation only occurred when the images were *completely* new—when participants viewed the oddball pictures for a second time, there was no response, indicating that the novelty had already worn off. "When we see something new, we see it has a potential for rewarding us in some way. This potential that lies in new things motivates us to explore our environment for rewards." But as Düzel explains, this reward is short-lived. "The brain learns that the stimulus, once familiar, has no reward associated with it, and so it loses its potential. For this reason, only completely new objects activate the midbrain area and increase our levels of dopamine."*

So, there we have it. To increase our motivation toward curiosity, we need to seek out novelty. And, of course, because wonder is a meaning-making emotion, it's best if the pursuit is an epistemic one, too. As we'll see, many of the wonderbringers in the next few chapters offer novelty paired with some sort

---

* Our brains pay attention to new things and reward that attention with dopamine, but increasingly, research shows that dopamine alone isn't the reward. Rather, it motivates us to search out more novelty for more reward. (Novelty is one of the reasons we find it so hard to stop multitasking—switching from task to task feels good.) That's why novelty is so effective in learning—curiosity thrives on incongruity, and we notice and are motivated by newness.

of epistemic or intellectual component. It's a potent combo. So, take different routes, go to different places. Shake up your noggin a bit. Merely changing the lighting or temperature in a space can make it feel novel or new. Even wearing your watch on a different wrist can get you out of a mental rut. Most critically, begin to train yourself to see with fresh eyes.

Try to answer Rainer Maria Rilke's entreaty "to be always beginning." Think of the wide eyes of a newborn as they see everything literally for the first time. Embrace the Zen precept of shoshin, which is translated as "the beginner's mind." Be open, drop your preconceptions, and seek new possibilities. As Zen master Shunryu Suzuki observed, "In the beginner's mind there are many possibilities, but in the expert's there are few." Stop trying to be an expert at life. Revel in the wonder of a beginner.

Slow down

We know that being hungry for knowledge (high need for cognition) and comfortable with ambiguity (low need for cognitive closure) are two qualities that make us more wonderprone. While stable traits like openness are largely based on a mix of heredity and longitudinal life experiences up to adulthood, our need for cognitive closure is a lot less rigid—only slightly influenced by our predisposition and much more so based on situational elements like our environment and mindset. These traits can, however, become calcified with age. So how do we create a mindset comfortable with discomfort? We need to slow down.

When we're stressed or rushed, we lean heavily on our cognitive shortcuts and seek quick answers that are not mentally taxing. The same thing happens when we feel threatened. In essence, we raise our need for cognitive closure threshold. And this makes sense—when our brain is frazzled, we don't have time for open curiosity. We want to avoid ambiguity and find fast, simple answers. To feel comfortable leaning into ambiguity, we need to reduce our stress levels and hurriedness. Chapter 15 looks at other ways to integrate slow thought into our wonder practice as well, like meditation and journaling. We should also look to limit fast media consumption, like social networks and constant "breaking news," that tend to over-index urgency for viewership.

Whittle—absorption

Do you:

- listen to music so deeply that you almost feel like you are floating on the notes? Or perhaps see patterns and colors as you listen?

- have such an intensely vivid memory that when you think of the past, it's almost as if you're back there again?

- read a book or watch a movie and lose yourself, feeling like you're one of the characters?

- ever sense someone is near you without actually seeing or hearing them?

Whittle, or absorption, the third element, is the gateway to self-transcendent experiences. Think of absorption as the runway before taking flight. Someone high in absorption has big feelings. They are easily moved by a beautiful sunset or an evocative piece of music. They are creative and can craft entire worlds with fantastically striking mental imagery. With just the smallest of cues—a smell or a color—memories will come flooding back, and their recollection of the moment will be crystal clear. At their core, whittlers are *present*. They can't get caught up and become totally absorbed in an experience if they are distracted. Absorption, like curiosity, is both a state and a personality trait, so to strengthen this element, we want to make the most of our natural tendencies while crafting opportunities for more in-the-moment absorption.

Short-circuit rumination with presence practice

Not surprisingly, the primary thing that gets in the way of us being absorbed is distractions. Those distractions can be external, like a child tugging on our sleeve or our email notifications dinging, or internal, like rumination or stress. External distractions are a way of life, and although we can certainly learn to manage our response to them more effectively, to best position ourselves for wonder we need to first tackle the internal distractions. Perhaps it seems counterintuitive—be present so you can lose yourself—but how can we transcend ourselves if we are self-consciously buried so very far inside our head?

Rumination often runs amok when we are too engrossed in ourselves. In the same way that self-transcendence and prosocial behaviors are associated with all sorts of positive outcomes, self-absorption and rumination are associated with poor ones. Excessive self-focus resides in the same family of "self-conscious emotions" as shame and guilt and contributes to several adverse outcomes like depression, anxiety, OCD, and addiction. We want to avoid that spiraling, persistent negative narrative everyone has to some degree or another.

There is an expression that sounds like something Yoda might say: "Train, don't try." Learning presence takes practice. In Chapter 15, we'll cover several ways that help bolster attentional discipline and quiet rumination, and make us more wonderprone, like meditation, gratitude, prayer, and journaling. And in another virtuous circle, low self-focus makes us more likely to experience a self-transcendent experience, and self-transcendent experiences reduce self-focus.

Sit with boredom, and then banish it the right way

We have no reason to be bored. We know so little of the world, so little of ourselves, that the very notion of boredom seems almost irrational. And yet, many of us find ourselves frequently twiddling our thumbs (an outdated expression to be sure, as we don't twiddle our thumbs anymore—we employ them quite deftly to click and scroll). And while boredom can be beneficial in that it encourages us to seek and fulfill new goals, it can also be the product of a brain habituated to too many dopamine hits from novelty-seeking. You might be saying, "But, Monica, I thought novelty was good." It is, but we want the right kind of novelty.

Think about it—what do most of us do when we're bored? We pick up our phones. I'm not saying that tech is bad, but being distracted by the internet's endless capacity for entertainment can impact our ability to become absorbed. So what's the solution? Put down the freaking phone. Allow yourself to be bored. Feel that uncomfortable itch crawl up your back, and then rather than jumping on some device, sit with it. Observe it. See how long you can keep yourself from responding to it. And then, when you can sit no longer, find another outlet for that boredom, like going for a walk, writing in a journal, or picking up a good book.

Stepping away from our phone also helps us align our need for cognition and need for cognitive closure with wonder, as our internet echo chambers make us more susceptible to self-reinforcing ideologies, lowering our NFC and increasing our NFCC; that is, making us less wonderprone. "When you have closure, you don't look for information anymore, you close your mind to any other information and are not interested, as you think you know," explains Arie Kruglanski, social psychologist and director of the Motivated Cognition Lab at the University of Maryland. "So people who have a high need for closure are not open to persuasion or new information; they know what they know, and they have their truth." The key is to move from boredom to something mentally challenging instead of something pacifying so that a bit of challenge and interest is given a chance to develop into healthy absorption.

Wow and whoa—awe

Do you:

- love beauty and seem to find it everywhere?

- feel wonder almost every day?

- enjoy connecting the dots and spying patterns in your environment?

- seek out experiences that challenge your perspective and how you see the world?

Our final elements of wonder are wow and whoa—the breathtaking, mind-blowing, transcendent experience of awe. Awe-prone people are open, curious, creative, and tolerant. They take pleasure in cognitive tasks and are well suited for a complex and enigmatic world. Always hungry for new experiences, people higher in dispositional awe like to think big ideas and feel big emotions. They naturally put themselves in physical places and mental spaces where they are more likely to experience wonder.

Awe is both a state and a trait, so we'll be looking at how to make the most out of awe-inspiring experiences and, in particular, finding those in the quotidian. And, of course, improving the other elements of the wonder cycle will also contribute to becoming more awe-prone. There are so many wonderbringers, but we don't always see them. Too busy, too cranky, too tired to experience the wonder around us, we miss countless opportunities. But if we prep ourselves for a wonder experience, we are far more likely to recognize it.

Priming

While being naturally more open primes us to be in the right place at the right time to experience wonder, we can create our own primes to become more wonderprone, too. Priming is an explicit, subtle, or subconscious cue that prepares our brain to influence future memories, emotions, or behaviors. A simple example would be product placement in a film. You may not notice the brand consciously, but in the future, you might associate it with the pleasant feelings you had while watching the movie—you've been primed to think positively about the product. Mentalists use priming tricks, such as wearing a yellow shirt to prime you to "randomly" say the word *banana*. A rather famous *nudging prime* is used in the men's bathroom at Amsterdam's Schiphol Airport, where men kept missing the urinal and leaving a mess for sanitation staff. The airport etched images of small flies into the urinals that, without explicitly saying anything, encouraged men to aim in the right place, thus making less mess.* Advertisers, app developers, politicians, and government officials all use primes to drive specific behaviors. And primes work because, similarly to how it treats other biases and heuristics, our brain logs the information and makes it easier to process and pattern match in the future. This encoding, or *behavioral pump*, prepares

---

* Nudge theory uses subtle techniques to influence choice architecture without actually restricting choice. The idea is that we often don't respond when a direct request is made of us, like a sign saying, "Be careful and don't have an accident," but we will pay attention to a sign saying, "x days since our last accident." A nudging prime is some cue in the environment that unconsciously drives decisions. The head of the Schiphol program is quoted as saying, "When a man sees a fly, he wants to hit it." That's the nudge.

our brain to notice and create associations with certain stimuli more efficiently.

People who write down their goals are more likely to achieve them partly because they are priming themselves to reach those goals, and we can create personal conscious primes, such as daily manifestations, intentions, or motivational phrases. So if your goal is to cultivate a wonder mindset, priming is an excellent tool to include in your wonder practice. Why does goal priming work? If the outcome of the goal is rewarding, then our brain commits more cognitive energy toward achieving it. The prime reroutes our thinking to a new path, eventually creating a new behavioral track. How might we prime ourselves to be more observant of wonder in our day?

William Blake once wrote, "The tree which moves some to tears of joy is in the eyes of others only a green thing which stands in the way. As a man is, so he sees." Wonder is in the eye of the beholder. Catalysts for wonder exist everywhere in the world around us, whether we are moved by them or not. A wonder mindset means making wonder an attitude, not just a specific experience. It attunes us to the certain knowledge that wonder exists and prepares us to see and receive it. As we are, so we see. See wonder.

WONDER WRAP-UP

- While our propensity for many of the elements of wonder has a hereditary component, it is also influenced by our attitude and environment. Learning and practicing the skills that support a wonder mindset positions us for wonder.

- Open people have an active imagination and enjoy new experiences. As a personality trait, openness can be challenging to increase, but certain cognitive exercises that induce flow can help.

- Deeply curious people like to challenge themselves intellectually and thrive on unpredictability. We can increase our state of curiosity in a few ways. Curiosity thrives on novelty, so seeking newness helps jump-start exploratory behavior. When we are too busy, we may lean too heavily on our mental shortcuts and rush through exploration. Slowing down allows us to notice wonderbringing details.

- People prone to absorption have vivid recollections of the past and love to lose themselves in a film or book. Absorption is derailed when we ruminate. By cultivating a presence practice, we short-circuit rumination and can become absorbed.

- Boredom is a natural state, but in our tech-enabled world, we too often banish boredom by staring at a device. This impacts our need for cognition, need for cognitive closure, and curiosity. Try something mentally challenging rather than pacifying.

- Awe-prone people see beauty and magic everywhere. One way to increase our likelihood of experiencing awe is to prime ourselves for it. A prime is a conscious cue (like writing down goals) or a subconscious one (like product placement in a film) that influences our future perception. By telling ourselves we will find ways to experience awe, we are more likely to do so.

7

Identifying a Wonderbringer

In the days before TripAdvisor, TripTiks, and Michelin Guides, there was a travel guide of antiquity known as the Wonders of the World. As the Greek empire grew in the fourth century BC, so did the appetite of its citizenry to travel to newly accessible exotic locales. Conceived as a celebration of Greek culture, the initial list of the Seven Wonders of the World included totemic sites like the Colossus of Rhodes and the Hanging Gardens of Babylon. Tragically, by the fifteenth century, all but one of the original seven wonders, the Great Pyramid of Giza, had been destroyed. Yet, this list remains enduring, even after the structures themselves have turned to dust.

Why? What is it in the hearts of humans that makes us want to seek out these places that take our breath away? Many of these wonder sites, including the modern-day Wonders of the World (like the Taj Mahal and Machu Picchu), have some religious or spiritual context, with a palpable weightiness, an intrigue, that simultaneously baffles and bewitches, all characteristics of wonderbringers that are incredibly consistent across cultures. As Lani Shiota, who has extensively researched the universality of awe, explains, "We've proposed that awe is part of human nature, that it's an evolved capacity that all humans have, and there's pretty decent evidence that all humans can feel this. When you look at the anthropological record, we clearly build things and make things and idealize places that evoke this state. When you think about sacred places around, they tend to be awe-invoking places."

Though wonder is individual, there are commonalities in wonderbringers derived from thousands of years of humans engaging with our external world. So, what are those features that make something a wonderbringer? How do we know we're in the presence of wonder? What is the magic, the aura, the frisson that these items or places or experiences seem to inspire? And how will we know it when we see it?

While wonderbringers are highly subjective, some themes are built into our innate sense of what evokes wonder, and these make up the anatomy of a wonderbringer. For example, most cultures prefer natural settings to built environments. Within natural settings, people are more moved by scenery that has some degree of mystery or inspires exploration, like a meandering path or hidden spot. Impressively large environments like skies showcasing dramatic weather systems, panoramic vistas, mountain ranges, and ocean views are also universally enjoyed, as are repeating patterns like symmetries, waves, spirals, tessellations, and fractals (the gentle undulating ripples we see in the sand and mirrored in the clouds is one example, and the spinning cluster of a galaxy similar to the swirled pattern of a Romanesco is another).

Physicist Richard Taylor from the University of Oregon wanted to understand our attraction to fractals. What he found was that our eyes actually examine our environment using a fractal pattern, so rather than finding these patterns chaotic, we find them soothing. "Your visual system is in some way hardwired to understand fractals," said Taylor. "The stress-reduction is triggered by a physiological resonance that occurs when the fractal structure of the eye matches that of the fractal image being viewed."

In the same way the Greeks created a guide to their wonders, this chapter will hopefully help us find our wonders. There are commonalities in the attributes of wonderbringers as well as the emotions and physiological responses they evoke. Understanding some of these common features can give us a bit of a lexicon of wonder to identify it, seek it, discuss it, and share it. And the better we are at recognizing these elements, the more adept we will become at bringing wonder into our lives. Again, this isn't about capturing the lightning bug in a jar to study it, so much as having a basic treasure map with "x marks the spot" so we can find those gems again.

Aesthetics and the sublime

The prevalent features we have found appealing for millennia, like a broad vista or a calming forest, have also shaped the way we create and experience art, design, music, and beauty in general. The field of philosophy that emerged to explore these ideas is known as *aesthetics*, derived from the Greek word *aisthetikos*, meaning "pertaining to sense perception." While the early Greek philosophers were interested in the role of beauty as part of the human experience, a group of eighteenth-century philosophers including Alexander Baumgarten, Immanuel Kant, Edmund Burke, Arthur Schopenhauer, and G. W. F. Hegel began exploring an emerging subset of aesthetic philosophy that they dubbed "the sublime."* And as aesthetics became interwoven with the notion of the sublime, wonder began to feature heavily in

---

* I.e., Baumgarten's "the science of how things are cognized by means of the senses."

philosophical writings. These writings on aesthetics, and more specifically the sublime, help illuminate the consistent features of wonderbringers and our reactions to them.

Kant described the sublime as something difficult to "get our head around," ascribing it to experiences that are vast, overwhelming, and, in some cases, potentially terrifying, like being in the presence of an imposing structure or fierce storm. These experiences are either "mathematical" (vast in physical size) or "dynamical" (emotionally or cognitively overwhelming), but Kant notes that while the sublime has a tinge of fear, it is generally a positive experience. He attributed this dichotomy to the "rapid alternation" between feeling overwhelmed and understanding that the state of overwhelm is actually manageable, mirroring the vastness and accommodation of Keltner and Haidt's awe theory. Kant wrote in his *Critique of Pure Reason*, "The sublime is limitless, so that the mind in the presence of the sublime, attempting to imagine what it cannot, has pain in the failure but pleasure in contemplating the immensity of the attempt." *Pleasure in contemplating the immensity of the attempt . . .* love that!*

According to David Yaden, the features of the sublime align almost directly with those of awe. They are mixed emotional states, with the same concepts of vastness and accommodation, both lead to an increase in connectedness and a decrease of ego, and they have similar temporal qualities. Another feature Yaden found comparable across both concepts was the physiological

---

* Some philosophers have embraced the concept of *aura* to describe aesthetic wonder, defining it as a quality that resides within a sublime object, and the aura generates a sort of disturbance in the air we feel from art that moves us. Apropos to describe aesthetic emotion in that way, as the word *aura* comes from the Latin to mean "breath" or "breeze." Architectural historian Russell Quacchia called the feeling of experiencing an aura "the wonder experience." (Quacchia, Russell. 2016. "The Aesthetic Experiences of Aura, Awe, and Wonder: Reflections on Their Nature and Relationships." Contemporary Aesthetics [Journal Archive] 14 [1]: 10.)

response. When we're experiencing both awe and the sublime, we'll gasp, our eyes will widen, our pupils dilate, and our jaw will likely drop. Our chest may swell with a sense of warmth as if our heart is full (what we might call "heartwarming"). We could get goose bumps, and tears may spring to our eyes. Experimental psychology researcher William Braud called these tears of "wonder-joy," describing them as the "bodily indications of the functioning of the eye of the soul, of the spirit, of the heart—direct responses to the true, the good, the beautiful, the sacred." These types of goose bumps, known as *aesthetic chills*, are incredibly common, accounting for as much as one-third of the goose bumps we experience. Initially called thrills to distinguish them from chills of cold, this physical manifestation is a helpful indicator in identifying our wonderbringers.

Goose bumps and aesthetic chills

When you have goose bumps, can someone else feel them? That was the question the team at Sensoree asked and, in their own way, answered. Sensoree, a wearable technology design lab, linked up with scientists from the University of Twente in the Netherlands to see how they could make that goose-bumpy feeling more contagious, believing that the more people shared their wonder experiences, the more meaningful those experiences would become. From this collaboration, AWElectric was born. Described as "bioresponsive animatronic fashion," AWElectric is wearable technology that "exhibits *extimacy*—externalized intimacy." Using a series of sensors, one wearer seeks experiences that give them goose bumps, be it music, a gentle touch, or a poignant film. When the sensors pick up the user's heart rate, breathing, and skin conductivity that signal the user is experiencing awe, their partner's AWElectric suit responds. Using pneumatic fabric and frequency sounds meant to induce goose bumps, the second wearer can share the moment virtually with their mate.*

If donning a goose-bump-inducing suit is a bridge too far, Matthew Sachs, a Columbia University researcher, believes that we can use music to share goose bumps, and he has created a formula to predict goose-bump-inducing music: $Pgoosebumps = CF (Sc + Id + Ap)$. Measuring various characteristics from social context, like a singing crowd, to song qualities, like lyrics, pitch, and harmonics, Sachs can predict the likelihood of music giving us that tingling feeling. The most goose-bump-inducing musical genre, according to Sachs? Rock 'n' roll.

Goose bumps, or piloerection, is a vestigial attribute from our ape ancestors. First, it was a mechanism to get warmed up after a chill. The hair standing up would capture air underneath and create a layer of warmth against the skin. Second, emotional goose bumps were a response to facing something unexpected or threatening, resulting in the ape's hair standing on end to make it appear larger and more intimidating. This attribute evolved and now exists in humans as an unconscious response, and in some people it lies completely dormant—as many as 55 percent of healthy people don't experience goose bumps at all, but those who do appear to enjoy greater well-being.

Aesthetic chills, or psychogenic shivers, are a type of *somatic marker*, a bit of ancient emotional DNA. The somatic marker hypothesis suggests that emotions have a sort of fingerprint handed down through time, and these inherited emotions use bodily signals to communicate information to us. Some believe the insula plays a role in the biological markers that trigger these neurochemical physiological responses, and we interpret

---

* Other "emotional prosthesis" researchers have found these sorts of technologies to be highly effective in producing chills of significant intensity to also trigger the associated emotional effects of goose bumps, such as empathy.

those bodily signals, our "gut feeling," to help us make decisions. Think of the queasiness you experience when you look over the side of a tall building, or the hair that stands up on the back of your neck when you're aware of someone following you. Those physiological messages are telling you the situation is dangerous, and that information guides your decision-making. These physiological responses illustrate how emotions like wonder are not purely psychological experiences; they are physical, too.

Mitchell Colver is a goose bump expert out of Utah State University, and he says wonder goose bumps likely result from a lag between the two parts of our brain. "You can divide the human brain in two. We have an emotional brain and a cognitive brain. And our emotional brain—which is responsible for our response to threats—responds quicker to external stimuli than our cognitive brain. The response shifts from fear to pleasure, and the brain releases dopamine as a reward for correctly assessing the lack of an actual threat. That dopamine causes a wave of good feelings, and you recognize the stimuli as enjoyable again." In other words, if we experience something inexplicably moving, this elicits an initial brief fear response in the emotional brain, resulting in goose bumps while our cognitive brain catches up.

People higher in openness tend to be more goose-bump-prone, with one study across fifty-one cultures showing chills as one of the most consistent cross-cultural markers of openness. Mitchell Colver wanted to explore this finding further and discovered this correlation held only for a subset of openness—openness to *ideas* (just as Jennifer Stellar theorized in Chapter 6). People high in openness to experience self-reported more goose bumps, but when participants were hooked up to skin sensors, researchers found that people open to experience were overreporting their chills. In actuality, people who were open to ideas were getting them more often. And this openness to ideas reflects a type of emotional openness associated with imagination, deep curiosity, and absorption.

It is fascinating to see the translations of aesthetic chills that researchers used when testing this cultural hypothesis globally. Each culture has a unique way of describing this physical manifestation of wonder. In Tigrigna, it is to have "a strong feeling invade me." In Marathi, to "experience a stimulating impulse within me." In Swedish, to "get shivers of delight." In Korean, to "be moved tremendously." In Malay, to "feel the feeling of enchantment." In Indonesian, to "feel the steam of happiness."

Our mind and the "hard" questions

My husband sold Uri Geller some office furniture years ago. From this fairly banal connection, the two struck up a sort of friendship, and so it was on the basis of this friendship that my husband, stepson, and I went to visit Uri at his home in the Berkshire village of Sonning on a slightly gray, very English, early spring day. For those born after 1980, Uri Geller may be an unknown character, but most know of him as a wildly popular illusionist and mentalist from the '70s and '80s. He is a big personality, as well as a bit boastful, and on occasion, to put it delicately, his mouth wrote checks about his abilities that his rear couldn't always cover. That being said, he was nonetheless a beloved and frequent guest on talk shows like The Tonight Show, The Merv Griffin Show, and others. His biggest claim to fame is bending spoons.

Uri is, to put it mildly, frenetic. Bouncing from one story to another, one artifact to another, he was charming and gracious. Ever the showman, he showed us his Cadillac covered in spoons bent by the good and the great, from Salvador Dalí and Albert

Einstein to Bridget Bardot and Elvis Presley. He pontificated on everything from sports to politics to alien visitations to problems he had with his neighbors (he was attempting to "donate" a sculpture of a colossal bent spoon to his local park and had been met with, shall we say, some resistance). He made predictions, telling us that our impending marriage would be a solid one (a prediction he got right) and that England would win the World Cup that year (one he got wrong), but, of course, we were there for the spoon bending.

I was, honestly, a skeptic, so we had brought our own very distinctive and very strong spoons to hedge against any funny business. (In fact, the entire day prior I had spent trying with the utmost strength to bend our spoons, just to ensure they were of suitable mettle.) First, he bent a few of his own spoons. Then he had my stepson, Jude, just five at the time, hold a spoon and bend it himself, with only a little help from Uri, who touched the top of Jude's hand ever so lightly. We were all delighted, most especially Jude. But of course, it was Uri's spoons from his own cutlery drawer he was bending, so I was certain it was some kind of, albeit marvelous, magic trick. (I also had to giggle thinking about his preparation for our inevitable spoon-bending request: "Honey, we have guests coming over. Can you grab some more bendy spoons from the cellar?")

Then came our spoons' turn. The effect was no different. Each time Uri held one of our spoons, they—and I have no other word to describe it—melted in front of our eyes. After he handed them back (and signed them, of course), I studied them. Other than being a bit warm where they had bent, I could not see or feel anything that would indicate how he had done it. I tried to bend the spoon back to its original shape, but it was impossible. They were solid when I handed them to Uri and solid when he handed them back. It was inexplicable. It was also super cool.

When I tell people this story, they naturally say I was duped. It was a magic trick, sleight of hand. And for all those James Randi wannabes (Geller's archnemesis), I fully accept it may have been. Or maybe Uri has preternaturally strong thumbs. Or maybe he has learned some way to channel his psi. Or maybe he is an alien. Or maybe all of the above. But even without explanation, I felt wonder. Just like without explanation, I felt a sense of wonder when visiting Frank Lloyd Wright's Taliesin. Or how a child feels wonder at the "gotcha nose" game. Explanations are great but not necessary. You wouldn't say to a child, "Grow up. Of course I didn't take your nose." (Well, you could, but then you'd be a jerk.) But we are still so young in our understanding of ourselves as humans. Why can't we keep that open, childlike curiosity of the unknown while also finding joy in the new knowns?

So, would I like to know how Uri did it? Sure. Do I feel compelled to explain it away within my heuristics of known phenomena? Not particularly. I can hold that moment in wonder and be equally fascinated, whether I have an explanation or not. And more important, just because there is no current explanation doesn't obviate its existence, meaning, or worth.

William James called this glimpse into the unknown the "filmiest of screens," which to me conjures up the images of old-school illusionists, or perhaps even the Wizard of Oz. James was one of the early scientists who openly explored different theories of consciousness, a topic that has become somewhat verboten for scientists today. James embraced mystery. He saw the difference between our standard operating procedure consciousness and a superpowered type of consciousness, the kind triggered by wonder. "Our normal waking consciousness, rational consciousness as we call it, is but one special type of consciousness, whilst all about it, parted from it by the filmiest of screens, there lie potential forms of consciousness entirely different. We may go through life without suspecting their existence; but apply the requisite stimulus, and at a touch they are there in all their completeness."

So, what is consciousness, and what does it have to do with our study of wonder? "Philosophers do this annoying thing of saying it depends what you mean." David Chalmers likes to discuss what he calls the "easy problems" and the "hard problems." Chalmers, a philosopher and cognitive scientist exploring the essence of consciousness, is the type of guy who could give you a frighteningly plausible answer to the question Are we living in the Matrix? Or Can robots feel sad?

For Chalmers, the easy problems are questions like Why do we experience emotions? These are frequently explicable by current scientific systems, or at least broadly testable. The hard problems are questions like How does matter give rise to consciousness? Though questions like this can't be answered in any current scientific paradigm, they still exist and, for now, are left to the philosophers. "There was no consciousness at the start of the universe. There may be none at the end. But this thing happened at some point in the history of the universe—consciousness developed," shares Chalmers. "Without consciousness, there'd be no meaning, no true value, no good versus bad, and so on. So with the advent of consciousness, suddenly, the universe went from meaningless to somehow meaningful. Why did this happen?" (That question alone should have your noggin in full wonder state!) "I think life has meaning for us because we are conscious. So without consciousness, no meaning. What's meaningful in life is basically what we find meaningful."

So we close here with a small keepsake for you to tuck away in your mind and carry for the rest of the book and beyond. Wonder is as much a feature of our brain as our mind. It is as much an experience of our body as of our consciousness. It is a subject of both science and soul. And only within this duality can we fully understand and harness its meaning and impact in our lives.

WONDER WRAP-UP

- There are many commonalities in what inspires wonder in humans, such as dramatic vistas and repeating patterns.

- The field of philosophy that examines beauty is called aesthetics. First explored by the Greeks, the aesthetic concept of the sublime was developed by a group of eighteenth-century thinkers. Kant, Burke, and Schopenhauer all describe the sublime as similar to awe: vast, moving, and perhaps a bit frightening.

- When someone encounters an aesthetic wonderbringer, they often experience aesthetic chills, or goose bumps. This is a common and universal indicator of a wonderbringer.

- People higher in openness to ideas are more prone to aesthetic chills, and these chills are one of the strongest cross-cultural markers for openness.

- Exploring wonder requires a combination of easy questions and hard questions. Easy questions are those that are generally answered by current science or at least testable. The hard questions are those best fielded by philosophers, theologians, and artists, as they can't really be answered by science.

8

Wonderbringers

I t's difficult to say which was her first love, nature or writing. Conservationist and author Rachel Carson would probably say nature, as it is something that is most easily felt: "It is not half so important to know as to feel." Carson's observations of the natural world are foundational to modern environmentalism, and her essays and books on the topic ignited the passions of an inchoate sustainability movement. Still, one finds a depth of emotion in her reflections on wonder that stretches beyond mere activism. Carson was entranced by the wonder of her rural surroundings on the Allegheny River from her earliest childhood memories. "I can remember no time," she wrote, "when I wasn't interested in the out-of-doors and the whole world of nature." Carson was still a child, though, when she recognized writing as her other great love. She is best known for Silent Spring, the book that lit the touchpaper for the modern ecology movement and the ongoing fight against pesticides (Carson's obituary in The New York Times described the impact of Silent Spring as clobbering the "affluent chemical industry and the general public with the devastating effect of a Biblical plague of locusts").*

---

* Carson is generally credited with providing the impetus for the institution of the EPA and the subsequent banning of DDT.

But her most poignant work is undeniably her essay *The Sense of Wonder*, published posthumously, after she died of cancer at age fifty-six.

Carson recognized wonder as a mighty instrument for social change. She shared in her 1963 acceptance speech for the National Book Award, "The more clearly we can focus our attention on the wonders and realities of the Universe about us, the less taste we shall have for the destruction of our race. Wonder and humility are wholesome emotions, and they do not exist side by side with a lust for destruction." She also recognized wonder as a meaning-making emotion, writing in *The Sense of Wonder*, "Drink in the beauty and wonder at the meaning of what you see." But really, Carson's *Wonder* was written almost as a letter of encouragement to all parents cum love letter to the earth itself—paying homage not only to the rustic and rambling Maine coast but to the wonder-filled relationship between her and her grandnephew, four-year-old Roger, whom she adopted when Carson's niece Marjorie suddenly passed away, leaving him an orphan.

Carson and her grandnephew's relationship was riven with deeply challenging moments, and yet their shared sense of wonder provided respite and resilience. Together, she, Roger, and the great outdoors forged a beautiful relationship among the neon lichens and dew-drenched nettles. "A child's world is fresh and new and beautiful, full of wonder and excitement," wrote Carson. "It is our misfortune that for most of us that clear-eyed vision, that true instinct for what is beautiful and awe-inspiring, is dimmed and even lost before we reach adulthood."

Though Carson and Roger had only a decade of wondrous exploration together before Carson died in 1964, her writing showed that she was more than an ecologist extolling the virtues of sustainable living or even a philosopher sharing the phenomenology of wonder with others. She was perhaps most preciously a mother sharing her love of nature's wonders with her adopted son. A beautiful, interwoven story of love, friendship, teaching, and the sublimity of nature—all wonderbringers.

Wonderbringers of the mind and heart

I am a nerd. I don't see this term as a pejorative—I love nerds. I come from nerdy stock. We were not a sporting breed. Other than a bit of running and some racquetball in the eighties, it was nerdy pursuits for us. A typical evening in my childhood involved Dad quizzing me from the *Word Power* book before dinner, followed by tea and Lemon Thins in front of PBS (*Rumpole of the Bailey* and *Hercule Poirot* were favorites). Perhaps a rousing game of Trivial Pursuit where Mom would hem and haw about how hard the question was and then answer it perfectly, to the eye rolls and groans of her competitors. When we traveled, my brother and I would be assigned a city to research, and we'd be the tour guides. (This practice bestowed upon us the titles Nervil the Navigator and Nerva the Navigatrix, names conjured from the quirky mind of my father.) Life was filled with choir practice and High-Q competitions, theater rehearsals, and extra courses in the summers. You get the picture. Nerd central.

So, while I appreciate and can be wowed by nature's majesty, it's the brainy wonderbringers that do it more for me. Subjects like art and music, poetry and literature, physics and philosophy, neuroscience and astronomy. And even when I experience a naturally evoked wonderbringer, it's more often some intellectual attribute—the meteorology of the weather or the geology of a landscape—that gives me pause. If we are to examine wonderbringers holistically, it could be argued that there is almost always some cognitive element at play with wonderbringers, as they are actively molding our mental schemas.

As you'll see in this section, there is a socially derived facet to wonder, too, even when it might appear at times to be purely intellectual or solitary. Some researchers describe it as a "quintessentially collective emotion," and given that wonder's evolutionary heritage stems from how we create community, thrive together, and share knowledge, this notion makes sense. While wonder can be experienced alone, the act of experiencing it or sharing stories of it with other people expands the impact— wonder shared is wonder multiplied. Wonder struggles to flourish if we don't engage with others.

In fairness, however, these differentiations between wonderbringers, be they of the heart or the mind, nature or art, are really just a means of categorization to help us understand what tickles our wonder fancy. While wonderbringers have a depth and richness that defy being put in a box, giving language to our sources of wonder fosters an emotionally nourishing life and more meaningful relationships. In this chapter I've shared some universal wonderbringers that resonate with me, but a complete list of potential wonderbringers would be endless, because we contain multitudes. The question to answer is, What are yours?

Art

Rain. Swelter. Snow. Hail. In any condition, six days a week, you are likely to find Kanami Kusajima in New York City's Washington Square Park, dancing. Atop a large piece of poster paper measuring about six feet square, with splashes of pigment reminiscent of a Jackson Pollock, Kusajima dances, her only partner black sumi ink and white paper. She is a classically trained dancer, but during COVID lockdowns, she became despondent at the inability to share her art with an audience. After an initial collaboration with another local artist, Kusajima decided to strike out on her own, and now she is known as Let Hair Down.

The name refers to her long sable mane, which acts as austere costume, prop, and curtain. Swinging or whipped by the weather. Sometimes draped around her shoulder. But most often hanging, her face obscured for the entirety of the composition. And with her baggy gray T-shirt and black jersey pants, one leg cut off at the knee, she becomes Everyman captured in timeless monochrome. Without race or gender. An androgynous proxy for embodied emotion. A human body in mesmerizing motion.

When she dances, her movements are trancelike, seemingly absent of any awareness of her bustling, frenetic environment. She shares the park with young men hawking cannabis and a drummer bashing away at the skins, and yet they seem only stage furniture to her principal role, as she draws those around her into her world. When a few members of her audience emerge from their own wonder state and begin to clap, her head pops up, the hair falls from her face, and a bright smile emerges. Kusajima gives a small namaste bow, and then, like the stage lights dimming, her hair drops, and she reenters her wonderland.

"The pandemic made me realize how important it is not to forget human connections, emotions, and feelings, while the system of the world now often forces us to forget all of those," Kusajima shares. "I have been dancing every day to not forget the warmth of humans." When I ask where she goes in her head when she dances, she says that while she does enter a transcendent state, her primary focus is to maintain a sense of open awareness so that she can connect with her audience. "Sometimes I feel like I enter a spiritual space. It feels like being aware of everything. In this state, I feel all of my cells in my body activated, and my consciousness catches everything happening around me."

Kusajima is clear that while she is not concerned with the message observers take from her performance, the interplay between herself, her audience, and the broader world is an indispensable aspect of her creative process. "I like observing and interacting with nature, humans, and events happening around me with curiosity. I find a lot of wonder from that experience. That experience resonates in me, and I believe those experiences somehow affect my body and dance movement unconsciously." Kusajima admits that dancing in the same place every day could become boring, but she credits her wonder practice with keeping her artistic expression fresh and meaningful. "With an open, curious mind, you can discover new things limitlessly."

Art is a window into the history of human emotion. We are inspired to make it, and then we cherish it, protect it. George Bernard Shaw said, "without art, the crudeness of reality would make the world unbearable." Leo Tolstoy called art a "means of union among men" and "indispensable for the life . . . of humanity." René Magritte believed art "evokes the mystery without which the world would not exist." Prisoners in concentration camps risked their lives to make furtive sketches or sing forbidden songs. The Mona Lisa was moved five times to be kept hidden from Nazi hands. Refugees carry with them a book of poetry and nothing more. Holocaust survivor and founding member of the London Chamber Orchestra Anita Lasker-Wallfisch was held in Auschwitz and Bergen-Belsen as a young woman. She credits playing the cello in the camps with saving her life, remarking, "Hitler destroyed endless things, but music . . . you can't destroy it."

While the subject matter or the technical prowess with which a piece of artwork was rendered may move us, something visceral occurs when viewing art. Otherwise, why would we be so enthralled by the graffitied remains at Pompeii or the animals painted in vermilion on the cave walls at Lascaux? Those aren't technically inspiring. We're moved, instead, because of some connection to the artists themselves, a transference of their energy to the viewer. We become a character in their ancient story. Modern painter Mark Rothko, who took his own life after battling with depression, observed, "The people who weep before my pictures are having the same religious experience I had when I painted them." Aesthetic emotional contagions evoke empathy. And, using the example of Rothko, or perhaps a more well-known artist like Vincent van Gogh, knowing their tragic backstory adds to the emotion we feel while viewing their art.

Empathy researcher Jamil Zaki describes art as "empathy boot camp." Bill English, artistic director for San Francisco Playhouse, calls their space an "empathy gym." Art arouses openness and curiosity, even if it may not evoke awe all the time. Some researchers believe the act of viewing art qua art—meaning viewing the Mona Lisa as a piece of art in the Louvre as opposed to seeing a print of the Mona Lisa on a sweatshirt—activates a specific type of schema in our mind, making us more open and curious as we experience the work through our "art schema" rather than within our "day-to-day schema."

If we're looking for an accessible wonderbringer, art is an enriching way to evoke the benefits of wonder in our home or office. While art as a wonderbringer is subjective, some design attributes consistently evoke wonder, like those that are rich, ephemeral, rare, grand, or evocative of a higher power. We also connect to patterns that we find in artwork, even if we don't pick up on those patterns consciously. Fractal researcher Richard Taylor actually chose to study fractals after becoming entranced by Jackson Pollock's work as a child. Taylor examined different fractal patterns found in nature and compared them to Pollock's work using computers. He found that Pollock's pieces are far from random; rather, they follow fractal patterns similar to those of trees and snowflakes.

And to be clear, art in this context isn't just something visual hanging on the walls. It imbues all parts of our life, from fashion and decor to design and architecture (and I would happily argue even food).* Art is poetry and spoken word, theater and music. It is film and photography and dance. It is a perfect pillow of agnolotti on a pool of tomato cream. Borrowing Tolstoy's definition, art is anything that communicates emotion.

Architecture

Buildings are ubiquitous, and while they primarily serve to fulfill some of our basic human needs, they are also incredibly accessible wonderbringers. Just as there are certain qualities of wonderbringing art, certain architectural features tend to evoke wonder, too. In her research at Princeton University, artist and filmmaker Wendi Yan identified four primary attributes of awe-inspiring architectural design: infinity (e.g., magnitude, repetition, and totality), silence, the illusion of threat (what she calls "safe threat"), and nature. A study out of Canada examining different qualities of the built environment found three primary wonderbringing attributes: immensity, adornment, and sanctity. The consistency of these characteristics sheds light on why impressive structures, ornate churches, and somber monuments inspire such strong wonder responses.

Admittedly, not all built environments are wonderbringers, but museums are particularly adept at delivering wonder-inducing design. They do this through features like the immensity of an entrance hall or by employing Wright's technique of compression and release through physical space or lighting. The United States Holocaust Memorial Museum in Washington, DC, where dark galleries telling dark stories are punctuated by the solace

---

* When I discussed this idea with a friend at lunch she remarked, "Sharing a meal with the people I love is like prayer to me."

of halls flooded with light, is an excellent example of this technique. And researchers from Belgium theorized that these structures don't just serve to evoke awe but also facilitate openness, community building, and social cohesion.

Museums are wonder labs. When people enter a museum, be it art, science, or history, they are open and curious, "with expectations to see wondrous things that they cannot see in their everyday lives," things that wow us. Good museums tell a story, and we feel a greater depth of emotion when we have the story behind the pieces we're seeing. And as we learn even little nuggets of information, that priming dose of knowledge spurs our curiosity. We become absorbed, and then we are poised for the wow and whoa of awe.

A massive opportunity for wonder-based design exists in our office buildings as well. Biophilic design, which applies the thinking of E. O. Wilson to interior design by integrating elements like plants, organic lines, water features, and natural light, colors, and materials, is growing in popularity, and these are top design features consistently desired by office dwellers. (More about biophilia in Chapter 12.) Despite the desire, according to one study, 47 percent of office workers still lack access to natural light, and 58 percent lack plants in their work space. The benefits of biophilic office design are the same found in the "green advantage" studies you'll see in Chapter 10, such as attention restoration and stress reduction. In addition to those benefits, access to natural light increases morale and reduces eyestrain, headaches, and fatigue, and plants can improve poor indoor air quality, which is responsible for the illness of an estimated 64 million employees a year. People are willing to pay more for houses or hotel rooms with biophilic features, and they are more desirous of working in environments with biophilic design. Given Americans spend 90 percent of their time indoors, biophilic design offers a practical and effective remediation for a nature-deprived populace, and a way to bring wonder into the work-built environment.

Music

Growing up in the South, there was no escaping the outsized role music had in connecting the community. In religious worship, it was used to knit together a congregation, the call-and-response choral tradition serving as a musical conversation to express emotion and consolidate shared beliefs. That tradition fed the songs of the civil rights movement, in which music catalyzed a unified identity. The Pentecostal Church is just one example of a denomination that uses music to facilitate religious transcendence, with researchers showing it as the single most consequential elicitor of religious wonder within that community. Of course, this is not unique to the southern United States—the African Igbo use the same word to mean "religion" and "music," as an example. Singing is known to trigger certain wonder-related physiological responses and when performed in a group, involves the wonder-enhancing elements of fellowship and moving in sync, as well.

Music, and its role in our lives, is universal. Researchers in the Department of Human Evolutionary Biology at Harvard University analyzed ethnographic data from 315 societies globally and found that the attraction to, connection with, and usage of music is something we share as a human race. From lullabies to love songs, dances to dirges, music is a part of our shared human experience and a primary form of expression and social bonding. It also serves as a universal source of aesthetic wonder—as we explored earlier, one indication that music is a wonderbringer is that it's such a common cause of aesthetic chills.

Early research into aesthetic chills found that goose bumps were usually felt at transitional points of a musical composition, such as shifts in texture, dynamic, key, or modulation. These transitions, like a harmonic key change or a dramatic crescendo, appear to act as an aural expectation violation, evoking wonder. Aesthetic chills are associated with higher connectivity between both the DMN and the salience network, and it is likely that the interplay between the two networks, in response to an expectation violation (in this case in the form of musical shifts), is what triggers the goose bumps.

Scientists from the University of Oxford gathered excerpts of varying types of music and analyzed their wonderbringing characteristics. Their hypothesis is that the score's perceptual qualities of size and amplitude inspire wonder via a sort of musical smallself. Not surprisingly, just as high openness to experience and low need for cognitive closure predicts wonderproneness in general, people higher in openness and lower in need for cognitive closure are more likely to feel wonder and get chills from music. But our preferences in musical genre matter, too, as we are most likely to find wonder in the type of music we like.*

Chills aren't the only connection between music and the DMN. Research from 2021 showed that while the executive control network, the brain area responsible for problem-solving, was activated while performing rehearsed or memorized musical pieces, it was the DMN (the same area associated with daydreaming) that became active when jazz musicians improvised. The theory is that during these periods of free creativity, musicians enter a type of flow state in which the filters employed by the active brain drop, and the DMN becomes active, allowing for greater freedom of expression.

---

* Researchers found that music with "a large sonic envelope, use of crescendo, and major shifts in energy and volume" was most likely to move people. For vocal music, narrative storytelling added to the wonder, and owing to the dually valenced nature of wonder, both happy and sad music are known to provoke the emotion.

The salience network, one of the DMN's anti-correlational networks, also has linkages to music beyond aesthetic chills. It's a well-known phenomenon that playing familiar music to Alzheimer's sufferers appears to open a window of lucidity, even at the latest stages of the disease. Researchers at the University of Utah found that it was the salience network that becomes active during these moments, calling it "an island of remembrance" that is spared the ravages of Alzheimer's.

Within the salience network is the insula, a slightly mysterious part of the brain that is still not fully understood. Tucked away in an area called the lateral sulcus, the insula's hidden location meant it went unnoticed for a long time, and due to the imprecise nature of neuroimaging, there is still debate about what role it plays. Various theories suggest it could involve not only the enjoyment of music but also anything from love, craving, pain, addiction, and our concept of self-awareness, to even the taste of wine.

Love

The phrase coup de foudre is such a marvelous double entendre in French. Directly translated, it means "strike of lightning," but colloquially, it means "love at first sight." What astute observers of love the French are. Love at first sight does feel like a lightning strike, and sometimes wonder does, too. Some human experiences are of such immense profundity that they knock us back and defy explanation.

Wonder is a natural fit for love, right? I am a child of the seventies, so my tender young heart was bathed in the sweet, smooth sounds of 1980s R&B love songs. Billy Ocean, Luther Vandross, Teddy Pendergrass, Lionel Richie, and, of course, Stevie Wonder all crooned lyrically about the wonder of love. Victor Hugo described it in Les Misérables when he wrote, "Love is the sublime crucible in which is consummated the fusion of man and woman. . . . When two mouths, made sacred by love, draw near to each other to create, it is impossible, that above that ineffable kiss there should not be a thrill in the immense mystery of the stars." Sublime, ineffable, and a thrill in the immense mystery of the stars? That's the wonder of love! And even further back in history, *The Love Song for Shu-Sin*, the oldest known love poem, dating back to circa 2000 BC, contains these verses: "Bridegroom, dear to my heart, Goodly is your beauty, honeysweet. Lion, dear to my heart, goodly is your beauty, honeysweet. You have captivated me, let me stand tremblingly before you." Trembling in the presence of beauty—love is indeed a wonderbringer.

Like so many profound emotions, words seem to do poor justice to the experience of love, but you usually know it when you feel it. (*Merriam-Webster* has twelve different ways to define love, thirteen if we include the tennis term.) As our life span and brain size increased throughout history, humans developed myriad types of love. Bonding between parent and child, connection to a survival group, and most recently (evolutionarily) pair-bonding all developed as mechanisms for ensuring stable communities. Empathy is very likely an evolutionary precursor to love, and it now serves as the primary nourishment in all our relationships, as well as being an outcome of a wonder practice.

The chemicals associated with love, dopamine and oxytocin, are also found in the elements of wonder. Dopamine drives us to seek the pleasure and avoid the pain of love experiences, just as it provides the lure of pleasure from curiosity. Dopamine also impacts the hypothalamus, which drives many primal urges such as hunger and thirst—interestingly, words often associated with lust, the very definition of hedonic love. Oxytocin is a bonding chemical, and some researchers believe it could prove to be a pivotal link to some of our evolutionary and biological drivers toward curiosity and awe. For now, it is only conjecture, but what we do know is that many occasions of oxytocin release are also associated with wonder experiences, including orgasm, breastfeeding, dancing, meditation, prayer, being in the presence of charismatic or spiritual leaders, and shared fellowship.

Sex

If the French have good expressions for love, they have a great one for orgasm—*le petit mort*, or "the little death." For some, sex, or more specifically, orgasm, precipitates an altered state of consciousness, a moment of ego death. One such type of orgasm, known as "expanded sexual response" (ESR), is defined in the scientific literature as "being able to attain long-lasting and/or prolonged and/or multiple and/or sustained orgasms and/or status orgasms that lasted longer and more intense than the classical orgasm patterns defined in the literature." (I imagine it feels better than it sounds.) While both men and women can experience an ESR, it is more common in women, as is experiencing an altered state of consciousness from one. One Swiss researcher described an ESR as "experiencing a sense of unity with everything and a sense of the Divine." This researcher also noted that such intense sexual experiences were not uncommon in his studies and even suggested the response is similar to that of someone under the influence of N-Dimethyltryptamine (DMT), a potent hallucinogenic drug. "We call it the DMT-effect. . . . Women feel they are receiving messages. They see things, visions. Or they dissolve."

The idea of the female orgasm being a portal to a transcendent state is an ancient concept, and one quite freely explored in eastern Taoist and Tantric traditions (the *Kama Sutra* being a well-known example). This is less so in other cultures where sexuality, and in particular female sexuality, was repressed, cast as evil, and tolerated only as a means of procreation, not pleasure. In 2011, sex researchers Mike Lousada and Elena Angel, while exploring the methods and benefits of Tantric sex, developed a three-tier model of human orgasm: intrapersonal, interpersonal, and transpersonal, the latter being described as an "experience that transcends the personal or egoic level of awareness" or what has also been referred to as a "soul orgasm." While sex is not always a social endeavor—people can obviously reach orgasm alone—transcending, peak experience, wonderbringing sex is usually reported as sex with another person.

Sex therapist Emily Jamea wanted to determine what type of sex was most likely to lead to a peak experience. (Don't get too excited—it's not that kind of book!) Through her research, she identified four qualities of an optimal sexual experience: sensuality, curiosity, imagination, and relationship attachment. Upon examination, these qualities share many of the same attributes as the elements of the wonder cycle. As an example, Jamea's quality of sensuality relies on wonder's first element of mindful openness; her sexual curiosity is deep and empathetic like wonder's second element; the imagination facet is fueled by the sort of daydreaming and vivid mental imagery associated with people high in absorption; and, as during an awe state, wonder's final element, participants shared that during an optimal sexual experience they felt "as if the rest of the world disappears" or "time seems to stand still." Given that people who are more wonderprone have a higher appetite for sensation-seeking, Jamea's model suggests that sensual, creative, and imaginative sex within an attached loving relationship can indeed be a wonderbringer.

Parea

The Greeks have a much-honored concept of friendship called *parea*. Directly translated, the word means "company" or "companionship." More broadly, however, it means a group of friends who regularly gather together to enjoy one another's company, share life experiences, explore philosophies, and generally put the world to rights. Your parea is your group of ride-or-die, family-you-choose people you can just "be" with. The Greeks saw this kind of connection as not just enjoyable but an indispensable shared human bond that was fundamental to well-being. As it does for many types of ancient wisdom, modern science backs this up. Friendships improve our physical and mental health, and some research shows they contribute to as much as a 50 percent increase in longevity, equal in impact to stopping smoking or taking up exercise.

These types of deep friendship groups are usually formed by the time we close out our twenties. As we age, however, this dynamic shifts. We tend to seek out fewer new friendships, and most of us find we have more "friends" on social media, but perhaps fewer friends IRL. This is partly due to the exploratory nature of our twenties that transitions into our nesting thirties. Also, as our life evolves, it becomes harder to meet the conditions of friendship. The ability to confide in each other or the freedom to pop by and hang out is not as easy as it once was. We live in a mobile society, and often that runs counter to the proximity and frequency needed to build deep friendships. Not to mention that our curiosity, which helps us make friends, decreases as we age. This is why our college years, time spent in the armed forces, or other formative experiences in our lives as young adults are so conducive to making lifelong friends.

Wonder fosters the bonds of a parea. Entering a new friendship with openness and a flexible mindset nurtures the early days of a relationship, even in new adult friendships, which can be harder to forge. Wonder helps us drop some of our walls and develop empathic curiosity about others, strengthening the interconnectedness between us. Sharing wonderbringers, like relaying to a friend the details of an incredible hike or moving play, is another powerful way to deepen a relationship. When we experience something exciting or interesting and share it with our friends, the experience takes on new, enhanced meaning. In fact, the recollection becomes more potent in our mind's eye and ignites our curiosity, encouraging us to seek out more new experiences and people. Climber Alison Levine described it as "when you see other people and where their curiosity can take them, that spurs curiosity in another."

Friendship itself may also inspire wonder, especially if we see our friends perform deeply compassionate or impressive acts. More often, however, a parea acts as an amplifier and multiplier of wonder. We know that people who regularly experience wonder are more generous with their time, more likely to offer a helping hand, more compassionate, and more empathetic. They also deprioritize their needs for the needs of the group. Those are unquestionably great qualities in a friend, and wonder serves to cultivate them all.

Fellowship

Political rallies, religious rituals, music concerts, sporting events, theater, and dance all enhance and are enhanced by wonder. Wonder creates a deeper level of affinity and communal engagement when we gather.* It strengthens social relationships and consolidates collective identity into one cohesive unit. And that

---

* Paul Silvia describes this as a sense of "heightened connectedness," which makes group members feel "less isolated, less singular, and more related to something bigger, sometimes to the point that they feel engulfed or consumed."

shared identity drives us to make sacrifices for one another, such as being more helpful or generous. This wonder-driven connectivity of groups can enmesh families, communities, and nations even more deeply than pride. And as we make sacrifices for each other, when we see ourselves as just one star within a swirling galaxy, we realize that the world doesn't revolve around us. It broadens our perspective and increases our openness to people and experiences outside our immediate sphere. This broadened perspective, in turn, makes our problems feel smaller, too.

The *vagus nerve*, a cranial nerve that connects the brain to the rest of the body, also viewed as the seat of awe and other wonderbringing emotions like gratitude, plays a prominent role in linking the psychological and physiological. Dacher Keltner described it as one of the great "mind-body nexuses," with his research finding those with healthier vagal tone are less focused on themselves and show "an increased propensity for transformative experiences of the sacred." Stephen Porges, neuroscientist and developer of the "polyvagal theory," considers the vagus nerve the root of "social engagement behaviors," "self-intimacy," and love, as it connects to the oxytocin system, and vagal tone appears to be associated with oxytocin release. Porges also sees the role the vagus nerve plays in the wonder of fellowship and religion. "The Sufis use dance, the Buddhists chant, and the Muslims and Jews use posture and vocal prayers. These are all vagal triggers that promote self-intimacy, but they are framed in contexts that promote social engagement; it's not only bodies moving, it's bodies moving in a social context. This socially engaged movement helps stimulate both parts of the vagal system, evoking a deep state of connection of the kind that fosters not just awe but also empathy and love."

The longest of all the cranial nerves (*vagus* is Latin for "wandering"), the vagus nerve runs all the way from the brain stem to the colon. It connects the insula to the rest of the body and is part of the unconscious parasympathetic system responsible for the "rest-and-digest" response, which balances the fight-or-flight response by controlling things like our heart rate, gut, and immune and vascular systems. When we are stressed and it is overwhelmed, the vagus nerve precipitates a visceral response that shuts down our higher-order thinking and puts us into a primal fight-or-flight mode. When we are calm and have good vagal tone, meaning our vagus nerve is healthy, our heart rate decreases, our breathing is slow and deep, and we can be more relaxed, open, and creative.

Having good vagal tone is connected to general well-being, and in fact, an implanted vagal nerve stimulator, which serves to activate healthier vagal tone, is approved by the FDA as a treatment for both depression and epilepsy. The vagus nerve appears to link our emotions, perceptions, and physical bodies somehow, and also aligns with the somatic marker hypothesis (the innate association between our emotions and physical feelings, a.k.a. our "gut feeling"). And many believe this linkage could have broader implications for how we develop social connections, as the vagus nerve is also activated during prosocial emotions like nostalgia and prosocial activities like shared fellowship.

Social wonderbringers like fellowship are the ways we connect and commune. Fellowship doesn't have to be structured or extroverted or a symbiotic sorority of people who know the secret handshake. It can be amorphous and introverted, ad hoc, a ragtag group of randomers who find themselves thrown together for a common purpose—purpose being the operative word. Fellowship can stem from the family we're born with or the family we choose, through our church, mosque, or temple. It can be found in a garage band or by volunteering for a beach cleanup; with a group of friends who visit museums or go quarry jumping. Perhaps it's travel or teaching or learning. The question to ask when seeking the wonder of fellowship is, *What creates a sense of meaningful connectedness for me?*

Virtual wonder

In 2018, a group of scientists from Canada launched an experiment called the AWE (Awe-inspiring Wellness Environment) project. They created an immersive virtual reality (VR) space designed to mimic the same *wow* and *whoa* as the Overview Effect. The goal was to "evoke a sense of awe and wonder" and prompt "wellbeing benefits and an increased sense of interconnectedness" for participants. To project a sense of welcoming mystery, participants were first greeted and brought to a small booth decorated in fairy lights. Next, participants entered the booth, encountering a dark, private space complete with a comfy chair, blanket, and a set of virtual reality goggles. Then, they settled in to watch a series of moving and dramatic scenic journeys of a forest, lake, or outer space, each designed to induce a sense of wonder. The most common reactions, other than frequently uttering the word *wow*, were combinations of wonder, curiosity, fear, and connection.

The researchers shared what they thought made for a successful VR wonder experience. The first criterion was a sense of ritual at the beginning, to set an appropriate mental context, which they felt was achieved by the fairy lights and enclosed tent space. Next, providing each participant with a private area allowed the experience to unfold with an open mind and absent any judgment. Last, the researchers found that having a safe, cozy environment helped assuage any fear or uneasiness that might emerge during the intensity of the VR "trip." As you'll see in Chapter 16, these elements of ritual, set, and setting are components of a successful psychedelic trip, too. If you can't get your hands on a VR set, fear not. Even watching video footage of awe-inspiring places has been shown to elicit wonder. Watching them using the guide of ritual, privacy, safety, and comfort will enhance the experience further.

It bears saying again—wonder is subjective. And the research shows that we will experience more wonder if our wonder-bringer is something we connect with. So, while we share similarities as humans, remember that someone else's wonderbringers don't have to be ours. The beauty of wonder is that much of the magic comes through discovering those things that bring us wonder and then sharing that magic with others. Whether it's gardening, gratitude, meditation, reading, writing, interpretive dance, drum circles, skydiving, surfing, magic tricks, science fairs, poetry jams, flower arranging, wood carving, bedazzling, or underwater basket weaving, wonder is about what moves you. Find that captivating, emotionally daunting, enchanting, perspective-inducing, ineffable experience that makes you feel like a small piece in a grand cosmic puzzle, and whatever that is, do more of it.

WONDER WRAP-UP

- Identifying and giving emotionally granular language to our wonderbringers helps us learn and share more about them. Just as there are common features of wonderbringers, there are universally common characteristics of wonderbringing art, architecture, design, and music.

- Wonder does not fit precisely into categorization, but many wonderbringers have a large brainy component like those found in art, science, and philosophy. So it might not be just the visual element of an incredible lightning storm that is a wonderbringer, but the meteorology behind the storm that gets the cognitive wonder juices flowing.

- Wonder thrives in social environments. Wonder in groups builds stronger relationships and communal engagement. Wonder shared is wonder multiplied.

- The vagus nerve, a cranial nerve that connects the brain to the rest of the body, is the longest nerve in the body, and is associated with wonderbringers like fellowship, as well as prosocial emotions like awe and gratitude.

- Virtual reality can inspire wonder by mimicking wonderbringing environments, like the profound vastness of the Overview Effect. This is enhanced by creating a ritualized process and a secure, comfortable setting.

9

Time

It was more than 150 years ago when French historian Alexis de Tocqueville remarked that Americans are "always in a hurry."* Not much has changed. The United States remains one of the few countries that don't legally mandate paid vacation, and the average vacation time taken by American workers is about half that of their European counterparts, most of whom have five weeks of mandated holiday time (that they unfailingly take). In the US, many of the days offered by companies are being left on the table, with more than half of Americans not taking their full allotted time away, in part because for many, the aphorism "time is money" rings true. The phrase, attributed to Benjamin Franklin, equates time to cash and creates a scarcity mindset regarding time, even though factors like labor laws and technology have resulted in people having more free time than

---

* De Tocqueville went on to say, "In America the freest and most enlightened men placed in the happiest circumstances that the world affords, it seemed to me as if a cloud habitually hung upon their brow, and I thought them serious and almost sad, even in their pleasures. The chief reason for this contrast is that [they] are forever brooding over the advantages they do not possess. It is strange to see with what feverish ardor the Americans pursue their own welfare and to watch the vague dread that constantly torments them lest they should not have chosen the shortest path which may lead to it." This has not changed, and it is oppositional to living a life of wonder.

they did a hundred years ago. In fact, the more our collective affluence has grown, so has our obsession with time. Our expenditure of time must be "worth it," and for a growing population of money-rich, time-poor people, time feels like the more precious resource. For those who feel a sense of time paucity, time is a scarce resource, whether the "facts" of time availability show that to be true or not.

To test this phenomenon, scientists asked participants to listen to one of the most delicately stunning operatic performances, the aural gossamer that is the "Flower Duet" from the opera *Lakmé*. Half the participants were asked to calculate their hourly wage before listening, while the others simply listened. Those who did the wage calculation were more anxious and enjoyed the music less—until that group was paid for their time participating in the experiment. At that point, their anxiety decreased, and their levels of enjoyment improved. The reality is, we have wired ourselves to have some sort of Pavlovian response to grinding. Wonder doesn't flourish in grind culture. It doesn't thrive in a rushed environment.

But what if wonder could make us feel like we had *more* time?

Time is a funny thing. When we talk about our "sense of time," we aren't talking about perceiving time through any of our senses per se. We don't smell, taste, feel, hear, or see time. But as William James noted in *The Principles of Psychology*, time is a matter of perception, and because everyone perceives things differently, time is not nearly as fixed as we might think. Fifteen hundred years before William James, theologian and philosopher Saint Augustine recognized time as a function of memory and measurement, meaning we measure our concept of time against our memories of what occurred prior. In essence, time is contextual and relative. Einstein proved Saint Augustine right—time is relative according to physics, too. (Although Einstein was reflecting not on physics but rather on psychological temporality when he mused, "Sitting with a pretty girl for an hour seems but a minute; sitting on a hot stove for a minute seems an hour.") Time is perception, and our perception can be altered.

When time is elastic

When David Eagleman was eight years old, he was a curious sort, as are many boys his age. Growing up in Albuquerque just outside the Sandia Mountains offered him and his older brother ample opportunity for suburban exploration. This was the '70s, a time when parents didn't hover quite so much, when kids were left to wander their neighborhoods, staying out until the streetlights flickered on, beckoning them home.

Despite David's father admonishing the boys not to play on a nearby building site, the two couldn't resist. While David was walking along the roof of a home under construction, he stepped down onto what he thought was solid material but found out the hard way that it was just tar paper. Down he went, spiraling to the floor. Luckily, he didn't end up with any serious, lingering injuries, although he did badly damage his nose—and ego. (His father jokes, "He made a one-point landing." His face.) What did stay with him from that experience was a fascination with time, as his recollection of that incident, as for many people who have a terrifying experience, gave him the impression that time had slowed down.

As he fell through the roof, David can recall the glinting nails on the house floor, the feeling of turning in midair. He even had time to reflect. "I was thinking about *Alice in Wonderland*, how this must be what it was like for her when she fell down the rabbit hole." Once he recovered sufficiently to think straight, David tried to make sense of the fall. If he'd had to guess how long it had taken him to drop through the tar paper to the floor, he would have reckoned four to five seconds. But later, he calculated how long it takes an average person to fall twelve feet and found it was just under a second—.86 to be precise. Why such a large discrepancy? Why does time seem to slow down in moments of acute crisis?* And why do we remember the details so sharply? Those questions were in part what drove Eagleman to become a scientist.

Scientists aren't usually considered very rock 'n' roll. Between Einstein and Dr. Bunsen Honeydew, perhaps our mental image of a scientist (mad or otherwise) is somewhat fixed to the nebbish and nerdy. But David Eagleman defies the stereotypes. (I won't say he is cooler than you, but he is definitely cooler than me.) Named one of Houston's best-dressed men with a self-proclaimed fashion style of "rock star," Eagleman is obviously a different species of scientist. A neuroscientist, bestselling author (both fiction and nonfiction), technologist, entrepreneur, host of the PBS show *The Brain*, and science adviser for the HBO series *Westworld*, Eagleman has academic qualifications from Rice and Baylor and currently teaches neuroscience at Stanford University. His latest entrepreneurial effort, Neosensory, uses sensory substitution to aid people with everything from tinnitus to blind navigation. While he is now looking at brain plasticity from a hardware intervention point of view, his early work focused on time perception, inspired by his tumble.

The flip-book of our mind

Ten miles north of downtown Dallas sits the picked-over remains of an abandoned amusement park. Found along the access road to I-635, between Big City Crushed Concrete and Liquid

---

* A phenomenon known as *tachypsychia*.

Environmental Solutions in an industrial area, Zero Gravity, once marketed as "the world's only thrill amusement park," now looks forlornly like something out of a dystopian film or dust bowl literary tale. The rides, including experiences simulating flying, free fall, and high acceleration, with names like Sky-coaster and Texas Blastoff, were auctioned off in 2021 in a sort of "everything must go" fire sale after the landlord sold the land and evicted the tenants. With the shuttering of Zero Gravity, the last remaining SCAD—"Suspended Catch Air Device"—in the United States closed.

When the amusement park was thriving, however, it was a mecca for people from all over the world looking to test their bravery and intestinal fortitude. One particular ride, called Nothin' but Net, flung willing participants sixteen stories down and into a waiting net . . . for fun. Clearly, Nothin' but Net was meant to scare the bejeezus out of its riders, and this is precisely what David Eagleman was looking for. He had a theory. He thought that time seems to slow down amid a crisis because our brain processes information more quickly during life-and-death experiences. To explore his theory, he needed two things: a life-and-death experience and a way to test processing speed. To simulate the feeling of a life-and-death experience, he initially tried roller coasters but, while he said the participants had loads of fun, the coasters were not scary enough. That's what led him to the SCAD, which he determined was sufficiently panic-inducing. To measure processing speed, he used a small perceptual chronometer that the victims, I mean *participants*, wore on their wrist as they were hurtling down one hundred feet.

The chronometer was set to rapidly flash random numbers—too rapidly for the brain to recognize typically. Eagleman theorized that if the brain was processing information more quickly, then the people falling would be able to see and identify the flashing numbers (assuming they kept their eyes open, which at least one participant was unable to do). Eagleman was surprised to find he was wrong—no one could read the flashing numbers. But strangely, all the participants estimated their drop as taking much longer than the actual fall did, mimicking Eagleman's childhood recollection from the building site. But if the reason wasn't that our brain processes information more quickly in life-and-death situations, what explains the perceptual memory shift?

Eagleman concluded that it isn't that our brain speeds up—it's that our brain embeds more detail in a shorter span of time, giving the illusion of time slowing down. The theory (supported by several other subsequent experiments) is that the amygdala, the driver of our fight-or-flight response, is triggered during the "OMG" moment, and this encodes richer emotional memories. "The key thing is it's not intuitive when people first think about this," Eagleman explains. "It's just that you actually write down very little in your memory. I mean, if you think about what you did last Thursday, you probably don't remember more than thirty seconds of footage at most." When we pay more attention, we encode more memories.

Once, in a fit of entrepreneurial zeal, my mom purchased a crate of Pelé flip-books—hundreds and hundreds of small hand-held books containing full-color cascading images of the 1960s Brazilian soccer phenom Pelé performing one of his famous overhead bicycle kicks. I'm not sure what untapped futebol flip-book market she was hoping to corner, but suffice it to say, I think she missed the peak, and so we had a lot of those books hanging about in my home as a child. While a real Pelé kick took about one second, the fastest I could get the thing moving was about ten seconds because the flip-book effect was executed over so many images.

Think of our memory as a flip-book. When our memory works in "regular" gear, we might embed ten memories per hour. I mean, really, how much do you remember at any given time? I have to give a good noodle to even recall what I had for lunch most days. And this is for a reason. We only have so much cranial real estate allocated for memory, and our brain is keen to hold on to only what we absolutely need to recall. This feature of memory is one of the reasons eyewitness testimony is so faulty (and only one reason . . . there are many more). Unless we are given a compelling reason to remember something, we won't.

On the other hand, something scary, something life-threatening, sends a message to our brain to pay close attention. So instead of logging ten memories an hour, when our amygdala is triggered, we might log ten per *second*. Our brain isn't processing more quickly—we're encoding more detail. When we go to the flipbook of our mind to recall a scary or intense experience, there are many more images embedded than usual, and we feel all those memories must be associated with a more extended amount of time.

If a life-and-death experience makes us feel like time is standing still, what about a wonder-inducing one? Absorption can have a temporal quality about it. Especially in a flow state, people report feeling as if they lose a sense of time. And research consistently shows that spiritually transcending or moving experiences make people feel like "everything was in slow motion," a phenomenon that isn't fully understood yet. Eagleman's research points to the amygdala, but awe experiences created in labs and measured on fMRI don't usually show a strong amygdala reaction. Nonetheless, the same type of time perspective shift is reported.

Lani Shiota thinks this probably comes down to the hippocampus, which she explains is adjacent to and intermeshed with the amygdala. As a result, during specific brain processes, it becomes quite difficult to parse these two areas for analysis. She explains, "The primary thing in humans that the hippocampus does . . . is facilitate the encoding of vivid episodic memory. The kind of memories that you can call up and re-experience in a rich sensory way." And as Shiota suggests, scientists have recently discovered "time cells" in the hippocampus that they believe play a role in episodic memory. You'll recall that the hippocampus was also the structure at play in encoding memories during a state of curiosity. So what appears to occur during both terrifying and transcendent moments is an interplay between the amygdala and the hippocampus that embeds richer memories, and more of them.

Eagleman also notes that it's not just awe moments that we recall more vividly. When we are curious, we also encode more vivid memories into long-term memory, in part because of the way our brain responds to information we find interesting. "When you ask a question in the context of your curiosity, then you've got these neurotransmitter systems [that kick in], mostly acetylcholine [also known as the "memory molecule"], but others as well. And you're really making plastic changes, as opposed to when you're just being told information."

Awe stretches time

Two hundred fifty miles down I-45 from Zero Gravity, in Houston, we find Melanie Rudd, our happiness researcher, who also tries to understand how people spend their money and their time, with the end goal of improving their well-being. While the relationship between marketing and wonder may not be apparent, Rudd recognized that people's perception of time paucity or abundance could influence consumer decisions. "If you don't feel you have time, you're less likely to do things that require an expenditure of time, whether that be volunteering, and whether that be going out and seeking any other kind of leisure experience. It's almost like this horrible, vicious cycle."

Rudd wanted to understand what emotions made us feel less time-poor, and her research uncovered a primary benefit of wonder for time-stressed people—*awe stretches time*. In one of Rudd's studies, participants were shown different videos designed to evoke either awe or happiness, and then they were asked to take a survey that contained questions about time perception. (The goal of testing awe against happiness was to ensure it was not just "feeling good" that made this difference in time perception, but rather "feeling awe" that did it.) Rudd's hypothesis was correct. Participants who watched the awe videos felt they had more time compared with those who watched the happiness videos.

Just as Eagleman found with life-threatening experiences, awe experiences force us to become absorbed and focused on the present moment. Like our flip-book of memories, we string together a greater number of memories when experiencing awe, which not only makes our recollections richer but also makes us feel that we have more time. "The more you encode along with an experience, the more rich that experience feels, and then the more expansive it feels," Rudd explains. That expansiveness, in turn, can make us more willing to spend our time on other people or ourselves, acts that modern life can make a struggle.

Not only is the notion of extreme time scarcity unhealthy, it's often inaccurate. Even when we are experiencing leisure, as during the "Flower Duet" operatic score experiment mentioned earlier, we can still feel anxious and time-pressured. Rudd shares an example of this dynamic that she found particularly illustrative. "We did some data collection here in Houston at a kite festival. Families show up, and they fly kites in this big field on a big hill. It was a beautiful day, and we went around and asked people, 'How busy do you feel right now?' And they were like at a six or seven. At a kite festival!" Rudd believes it's not so much our modern life as our modern perception of time that's one of the most significant barriers to mitigating our sense of time pressure. "Our perception of time is off-balance. And we are becoming trained to feel busy all the time, at least especially in our culture.

"Up until this point, technology has been used against the average worker in terms of increasing our time stress. We have more technology and can do things faster and easier, and yet we feel we are still working just as much, if not more." Rudd says this time pressure can impact sleep patterns, fuel depression, and manifest physical health symptoms like headaches and high blood pressure. "People tend to view time as a lot more scarce than it really even is, so our perception is out of whack. We need some recalibration." Rudd hopes her research into wonder's time-effects can help tip the scales to a more realistic appraisal of our time so that we become less stressed, healthier, and more generous. "I think anything that expands our perception of time is a good tool that we can use to help at least fight back against that tendency for us to constantly feel like we have no time."

So, if people were to feel as though they had more time, would they also be more generous with how they spent that time? And would that generosity extend to other things, such as money? To find out, in a subsequent study, Rudd had participants write narratives about a moment they felt happy or a moment they felt awe. Rudd once again found that awe decreased impatience and increased perceived time availability, and people who experienced awe were more willing to use that "extra time" volunteering. She went on to show that awe both improved life satisfaction and influenced the types of consumer decisions people made. Specifically, people were both more generous with their time and less materialistic—preferring experiences to stuff. This phenomenon is particularly interesting as experiences rather than stuff create longer-term eudaemonic happiness and well-being benefits as well.*

"A small dose of awe even gave participants a momentary boost in life satisfaction," shares Rudd. "These results also have implications for how people spend their time and underscore the importance and promise of cultivating awe in everyday life." These sorts of utilitarian benefits illustrate that small moments of wonder can provide enduring, useful shifts in perception, behavior, and physical and mental health.

There has also been extensive research in tourism marketing that shows people are more inclined toward wonder-inducing leisure activities. For instance, research indicates that awe contributes to a greater sense of heritage. After a wonder-filled visit, people tend to develop what's called "place attachment," meaning if they experience a wonder-inducing event at a particular place, they will return there in search of the same experience again. Combine these findings with those that show awe encourages environmentally responsible behavior in several ways (such as reduced littering), along with an increased tendency toward volunteerism due to wonder's time effects, and we can see how wonder provides a potential mechanism for greater conservatism, restoration, and stewardship of wonder-inducing destinations. This kind of insight could also support more sustainable tourism and reduce the exotification of wonder-driven leisure. Local communities could leverage heritage and place attachment, helping tourists find wonder-inducing venues closer to home,

---

* Further research out of Belgium, Canada, and China replicated Rudd's findings vis-à-vis time perception and volunteerism, finding that awe as an emotion inspired not just donations of time, but money as well.

making wonder-based travel not only more sustainable but infinitely more accessible as well.

Rudd takes satisfaction in the practical ways this research can be applied to everything from encouraging volunteerism to lessening road rage, and as we'll see in the next two chapters, it can also be applied at school and work. "I'm not going to change the world or anything, but I think that it's great to be able to work on something that people find helpful and beneficial. And I think awe really is a very useful tool." Rudd also hopes that her research will help people better identify different positive emotions, particularly awe, so they can connect to them more regularly and move from the vicious cycle of time paucity to a virtuous one of wonder. "It seems to have so many effects and downstream consequences of things that are on people's top checklists for a better world—helping others, not feeling so time-stressed, helping the environment, being more open and curious. I want people to say, 'Oh, this is great. I want more of this. How do I get more of this?' Once they understand the importance of it, they're really motivated to pursue it."

WONDER WRAP-UP

- We have been conditioned to see busyness as a laudable state, so we often perceive we are more time-poor than we actually are. But when we are too busy—or perceive we are—we miss opportunities for wonder.

- Our perception of time is contextual. Under different conditions, we can experience time as running at different speeds. (We see this in an expression like "Time flies when you're having fun.") Part of this has to do with how our brain encodes memories.

- When we experience something deeply meaningful, scary, or wonder-inducing, we encode more detailed memories about the experience; thus, the recollection of the time feels longer.

- Because of this dynamic, we can use wonder, and specifically absorption and awe, to stretch our sense of time and reduce our sense of time paucity.

- This benefit of wonder has many potential practical applications at school and work, such as improving well-being and decreasing stress. These findings can also be extended to marketing initiatives in experiential purchasing, wonder-based leisure activities, sustainable tourism, and volunteerism.

10

Learning

Kruti Parekh came into the world swaddled in wonder. For parents Jaishri and Subhash, it was more than just the parental wonder of the birth of their first child. Parekh was India's first test-tube baby. In her stage show *Illusions of Mind*, Parekh, now a mentalist and magician, performs sleight of hand, reads people's minds, makes elephants disappear, and, yes, even bends a fork (a treat she shared with me when I mentioned how enchanted I was by Uri's talent). Besides performing magic, Kruti has a PhD in applying magical techniques to teaching and learning, and she uses this in her work for kids with disabilities and their teachers. "I like to joke that magic is my birthright," she says, laughing, "because I'm born by the magic of science."

Magic means making the impossible possible, she explains. "I use magic as a language to create wonder." Working with researchers from the University of St. Gallen, Parekh is studying how the wonder of magic can ignite interest and recall in subjects like math and science in children with disabilities. She found that using magic tricks as a teaching medium with these children enhanced their foundational knowledge in areas like colors, numbers, and depth perception. More important, Parekh says she has seen children find a joy in learning that they didn't have before.

Parekh also uses magic as a way to help teachers better understand their students' unique needs, explaining, "Magic is where logic fails." Using the temporary suspension of logic that occurs when witnessing something magical, Parekh helps teachers view their students' experiences through a new lens. "[Teachers] don't know how it feels to lose an ability. So I said, you know what, I'm going to take away your ability to comprehend. I do a trick where I show them a word, and they are not able to read what the word is, but the rest of the audience is able to read it. Now they know how it feels to be on the other side. It helps them connect with these kids."

Because wonder is an epistemic emotional experience based on meaning-making, it makes intuitive sense it's linked with learning. Education researchers Cathie Pearce and Maggie MacLure describe wonder as "a liminal experience—a sort of shimmering apprehension on the threshold between knowing and unknowing, in which aesthetic, cognitive, and spiritual experiences are simultaneously mobilized." Descartes called wonder "a sudden surprise of the soul." He also saw it as a learning tool. "We can say of wonder that its particular utility is to enable us to learn and retain in our memory things of which we were formerly unaware. . . . And so we see that those without any natural inclination to this passion are ordinarily very ignorant." Other philosophers agreed—Socrates opined that "wisdom begins in wonder," and Saint Thomas Aquinas viewed wonder as a "desire to learn."

We find another wonder virtuous circle in learning and education—learning is facilitated by and facilitates wonder. It's easy to see how the building blocks of wonder—openness, deep curiosity, absorption, expectation violation, the closing of a cognitive gap, making room for new information resulting in a new perspective—follow the best kind of learning journey, and, hence, why research supports wonder as a teaching and learning technique.

Deep learning, and are we losing it?

At the core of the learning process are two fundamental approaches: deep learning, which, like deep curiosity, lends itself to wonder, and surface learning, which does not. Deep learning encourages learners to actively and critically engage with the content, motivated by an intrinsic desire to know more. Deep learners relish exploring the meaning of a topic area and creating new cognitive structures based on the connections between different topics, allowing the gained knowledge to be applied to other areas of learning. Knowledge gained by deep learning is more often embedded into long-term memory and has enduring applicability for learners. This approach to learning is most often observed in those with high openness, high-trait deep curiosity, high need for cognition, and low need for cognitive closure (mirroring the states and traits of wonderprone people). And this learning approach is additive, as previous positive learning experiences also contribute to deep learning.

In contrast, surface learning is a superficial approach to learning that skims the surface of a content area, gathering facts with the primary focus being the eventual regurgitation of those facts for assessment. Surface learning doesn't illuminate connective patterns, and it lacks engagement in the learning process; rather, facts are accepted uncritically and are stored as unconnected items. What's more, surface learning is perceived as a task to be completed and is rooted in extrinsic motivation. This sort of learning is associated with the short-term recall of content but doesn't show particularly enduring results. It tends to be found in those with low trait curiosity, low need for cognition, and high need for cognitive closure, but it can also be indicative of learners with anxiety or previously poor learning experiences. Last, surface learners struggle with ambiguity—if they are assessed on the Single Right Answer, they will seek to learn only the Single Right Answer.

All experience is contextual, and learning is no different—some teaching styles facilitate deep learning while others facilitate surface learning. When education is focused on assessments and tests, is rushed, or doesn't encourage interaction, or when a teacher is negative toward or disinterested in the content, a student may revert to surface learning, regardless of their natural learning approach. On the flip side, when a teacher is engaged and engaging, connects the content to real-life examples, allows for a more holistic means of assessment, and encourages questions (and mistakes), deep learning can be fostered. Teachers who are keen watchers and wanderers inspire keen watchers and wanderers.

If we were to define wonder-based learning, it would be learning that promotes openness and intrinsically motivated curiosity, leverages the power of an expectation violation, and inspires a sense of awe in students. And investing in wonder-based learning is well worth the effort, as the benefits are manifold. For instance, people higher in trait openness are more inclined toward deep learning (openness being the only Big Five trait associated with deep learning) and creativity. Openness is also associated with higher verbal cognitive performance and abstract thinking, so fostering openness in early education significantly impacts learning outcomes as a child grows.

It's been said that curiosity is the wick in the candle of learning, and if so, deep curiosity burns longer and brighter. As revered educator John Dewey said of learning, "The most vital and significant factor . . . is, without doubt, curiosity. . . . Eagerness for experience, for new and varied contacts, is found where wonder is found." Dewey believed that if the powers of curiosity "are not used and cultivated at the right moment, they tend to be transitory, to die out, or to wane in intensity [and become] easily dulled and blunted." But then the reverse must also be true—curiosity must be able to be honed on an exploratory whetstone. This is how the education system and parenting styles can mold children's curious tendencies from a very early age.

Curiosity supports learning and improves critical thinking. Allowing students to work with rather than against their natural curiosity also means working with and not against the neuroscience of learning. When someone's curiosity leads them to an answer, what they learn is encoded more deeply and thus retained longer, even more so when the curiosity is intrinsically motivated. Edward Deci, a psychology and social sciences professor at the University of Rochester, published a set of revolutionary findings that showed not only that intrinsically motivated curiosity results in better long-term recall, but extrinsically motivated curiosity (driven by external rewards like money or grades) actually kills intrinsic curiosity. As David Eagleman explained in the previous chapter, asking questions in the context of our curiosity makes plastic changes within our brain. "I use the analogy, your teacher says, 'Okay, here's ten important dates in Mongolian history,' but you just don't care. And so it's just really hard to remember. But if it's something that you really care about, it makes all the difference."

So what happens if you have to learn about Mongolian history, and it's just not your jam? Find anything to be deeply curious about and explore that at the same time as the boring topic, and your recall of even the humdrum bits will be improved. Cognitive neuroscientists out of the University of California, Davis, found that intrinsic curiosity doesn't make us more adept just at learning things we are interested in but also in learning the stuff we find boring. "Curiosity may put the brain in a state that allows it to learn and retain any kind of information," says Matthias Gruber, lead author of the study. It's "like a vortex that sucks in what you are motivated to learn, and also everything around it."

Awe also appears to make students more engaged learners. Melanie Rudd, the researcher who discovered awe slows down time, wanted to see how awe might positively impact learning and our desire to engage in types of learning-based experiences called "experiential creation." She and her research partner, Kathleen Vohs, ran an experiment just before Valentine's Day in which they showed participants videos of either awe-inducing, happiness-inducing, or neutral imagery. Afterward, they offered participants a choice between a voucher for a box of chocolates or a recipe to make chocolates for gifting (i.e., experiential creation). Those who viewed the awe-inducing videos were more likely to choose the experiential creation, or the "engaged learning" option. Subsequent studies further supported those findings. The researchers explained that awe gives you "openness to learning and curiosity. . . . You have a desire to create, because that's a natural way that we learn. Putting our hands on things is a very primitive way that we learn as we start doing. We just do and make." Another virtuous wonder circle. Openness and curiosity make us more awe-prone, and awe makes us more open and curious for learning.

While Rudd says there is a lot of research about awe prompting prosocial emotions like empathy, she'd love to see more of a focus on the relationship between awe and learning. "It certainly could have an impact for learning environments. I'm particularly interested in how it would be applicable to getting people in an open mindset for discussions and dialogue, which is something we need more of."

Before shifting gears, I think it's worth noting that while wonder and awe boost deep learning, monotony negatively impacts both curiosity and absorption, and therefore all learning. This effect happens because awe's impact on learning is initiated by the contrast, and excitement, of an expectation violation. An expectation violation enhances incidental memories and triggers the hippocampus associated with long-term memory and learning. Monotony, however, shrinks the hippocampus. For this reason, curiosity coupled with an expectation violation leading to a *wow* and *whoa* moment—like a magic trick or cool chemistry experiment—is a powerful strategy to motivate and reinforce learning. This intriguing contrast is at the heart of a magician's artistry and why Kruti Parekh's approach is effective.

Deep play, and are we losing it?

Play is one of the most ancient and primal ways of learning. Before any sort of pedagogy, play served as a way to learn our most basic living skills. The power of play as an effective learning strategy is easily recognized when watching babies, little wonder machines that they are, learn about the new world they inhabit. Babies have so few schemas, so few building blocks, that their brains are constantly observing, exploring, and accommodating new information. And this development of new schemas is almost always done in the context of playful activity.

One foundational theory on the evolutionary purpose of positive emotions like happiness and wonder is the *broaden-and-build* theory. Broaden-and-build says that positive emotions allow us to feel secure enough to broaden our horizons and look for new opportunities, either on the savanna or on the cul-de-sac, to encourage us to do things that might otherwise seem a bit unpleasant. In turn, that allows us to build the relationships, skills, and elemental components of a more fruitful existence. The scientist who developed the broaden-and-build model, Barbara Fredrickson, was particularly intrigued by the joy children experience in play, and, in turn, how many intellectual, social, and communication skills stem from play.

Play is where self-directed, deep learning begins to take root. Poet, academic, and naturalist Diane Ackerman's description of deep play reflects the wonder of learning through a flow type of transcendence. "Deep play is a fascinating hallmark of being human; it reveals our need to seek a special brand of transcendence. In deep play, one's sense of time no longer originates within oneself. When it happens, we experience a sense of revelation and gratitude. . . . It's so familiar to us, so deeply ingrained in the matrix of our childhood, that we take it for granted." In this quote, she describes the openness and curiosity of play, as well as the absorption and potential for the transcendence of revelatory awe. "Wonder is the heaviest element in the periodic table of the heart. Even a tiny piece of it can stop time."

While play may look simple, children demonstrate some of their most advanced verbal skills while engaged in free, unstructured play. Research also shows that almost 50 percent of free play time is spent utilizing the basics of mathematical learning, and children who engage in guided play, such as playing a game like Chutes and Ladders, show increased numeracy in areas like counting, numerical magnitude, and estimation. "We may think of play as optional, a casual activity. But play is fundamental to evolution," shares Ackerman. "Without play, humans and many other animals would perish." Play creates its own motivation through enjoyment and bonding and is about trying new approaches without judgment of failure. Play is steeped in the wonder of open exploration, curiosity, and awe.

According to anthropologists, observation, play, and exploration were the primary teaching methods for children in ancient hunter-gatherer cultures. Exploratory play allowed children to acquire the essential knowledge of flora and fauna required for life within their community. Creativity, initiative, trial and error, and freewheeling curiosity were tools enough for learning. This behavior was not just allowed but encouraged and trusted until children were in their late teens. (No helicopter parents here.)

Once humans became agrarian, everything shifted. Land meant a need for labor. A need for labor meant a need for larger family units. Larger family units meant more time caring for the family and less time for play. Property ownership drove hierarchical structures of servitude, and obedience overtook independence as foremost to survival. From the start of feudalism in the ninth century to the end of industrialism in the nineteenth, children generally spent their days working. As the need for child labor declined, it was replaced with the belief that children should learn. But for what purpose? Some saw the role of schooling as primarily religious education. Others saw it as a tool of control and subjugation. And indeed, some saw it as a means to support and protect children, but still within a curriculum consisting predominantly of morals and memorization. In short, self-directed exploration and play were out, and inculcation and regurgitation were in. But though play was quite literally beaten out of children ("spare the rod, spoil the child"), our basic evolutionary desire to play as a means of learning persisted.

Experiential learning

Education today is (mostly) more humane, but play is still overwhelmingly seen as ancillary, and structured curricula set against standardized benchmarks are the norm. There are,

however, outliers, including well-known alternative schooling philosophies such as Waldorf and Montessori and a rapidly
growing number of independent, nontraditional schools, including micro-schools, learner-led schools, and project-based
learning. There's Blue School in New York, started by the members of the Blue Man Group and their families, which even has
a "Wonder Room" complete with a black light for relaxing "glow
time." Another is the Innovative Schools Cooperative, a network
of independent schools across the US that focuses on experiential learning.

One such wonder-filled, play-embracing environment is
Beau Lotto's i, scientist, a science-education program run in part-
nership with the UK's London Science Museum. As Lotto explains, "It's so different from other science-education programs,
where the aim is to learn facts." Lotto is clear about what catalyzes
this different approach. "The first stage of that process is wonder.
We're effectively turning the school into a science lab. And we're
saying that science—in fact, anything that is creative—is play
with intention. And play begins with wonder." Lotto echoes David Eagleman's opinion that interest is a critical factor in learning. "If [children] don't care, they're not going to ask a question.
And so what we're doing is, we're actually turning school into a
lab itself. So they aren't learning about science; they're *becoming*
scientists." Lotto describes i, scientist as a place where children
are taught to be open to new experiences, move toward uncertainty, and celebrate curiosity.

This type of wonder-based, early education significantly impacts young kids' learning outcomes, mainly due to its focus on
curiosity. In a longitudinal study that tracked children from age
three to age eleven, those kids who were highly curious three-
year-olds were more intelligent and higher-performing eleven-
year-olds. The curious kids had better verbal skills and scored

twelve points higher on intelligence tests than their less inquisitive classmates. In another study, children with "gifted curiosity" also outperformed peers in a number of academic outcomes. What this indicates is that deep curiosity is a mechanism of high performance in and of itself and could be just as contributory to future performance as cognitive giftedness; that is, high IQ.

Science learning, in particular, lends itself to a wonder-based approach because of the abundance of opportunities for novelty, which embeds learning and impacts memory.* Even just changing a learning environment can boost a student's memory and learning. Novelty researchers found that mixing novel information with information that was only slightly familiar increased the retention not just of the new information but also of the slightly familiar information. It appears that novelty contributes to greater plasticity in the hippocampus (the part of the brain responsible for storing memories for long-term recall). After the exercise, participants had a 19 percent higher recall of the slightly familiar information when it was mixed in with the novel bits. (Real-life application? Studying for an exam works best if you sprinkle in some entirely new elements with the vaguely familiar stuff you're trying to learn; even better if the novel stuff is something unrelated—similar to the Mongolian history example earlier, we want to create a curiosity vortex.)

But are kids learning in these different educational models?

---

* Some curiosity researchers even view awe as an intense form of curiosity. The appraisals found in awe—vastness and accommodation—are a less intense version of a set of factors that promote curiosity—novelty and comprehensibility. They see curiosity and awe on a continuum where the novelty is increasingly more difficult to comprehend. (Think of the light switch from Chapter 4—turning the lights off in the other room is curious. Making your cat disappear is awe inspiring.) (Campos, Belinda, Michelle N. Shiota, Dacher Keltner, Gian C. Gonzaga, and Jennifer L. Goetz. 2013. "What Is Shared, What Is Different? Core Relational Themes and Expressive Displays of Eight Positive Emotions." Cognition & Emotion 27 [1]: 37–52.)

Some of them must be, as one i, scientist cohort of eight-to-ten-year-olds from Beau Lotto's Blackawton Primary School became the youngest scientists in history to publish their research in a peer-reviewed journal. Despite lacking references ("The kids weren't really inspired by that") and having hand-drawn illustrations, their research on bee behavior was found by reviewers to be sound science with well-documented methods and novel findings.

These experiential learning environments and others like them follow the basic tenets of largely self-directed, autonomous, playful, and wonder-filled exploration. And despite some criticism of perhaps being too esoteric, these schools, by and large, have the same or better academic outcomes as more rigid environments but with much higher degrees of reported well-being and creativity.

Unlearning

Jim Garrison is an educator with a lifetime of social and political activism roles, including cofounder and president of the Gorbachev Foundation, chairman and president of the State of the World Forum, and, most recently, president of Ubiquity University. A child of Christian missionaries in China and Taiwan, Garrison grew up surrounded by competing ideologies. "The most important experience of my whole life happened when I was five years old. I was playing, and I entered a Buddhist temple. And there, sitting on the floor, was a monk in his saffron robes facing the Buddha. And he was absolutely quiet. He mirrored the Buddha." Garrison can recall the moment in vivid detail. "I peeked around to see what he looked like, and he was perfectly still. And then a fly landed and crawled across his forehead. He didn't move. Then the fly flew away, and I just started to gaze at the stillness of this man. Then the fly came back and started to crawl across his lips. He didn't move a muscle. And in that instant, everything I thought I knew disappeared." Garrison is clear that this moment of wonder in that temple laid the foundation for his entire philosophy of life.

Over time, he found the fixed religious worldview he had been brought up in "was debilitating to the spirit of inquiry, rather than fostering it." He discerned early in life that for those with a rigid worldview, curiosity is apostasy. "Curiosity is dangerous. Curiosity leads to heresy. And, as I can tell you from personal experience, that heresy has a high price." Garrison rejected the formalized religion that shaped such a central role in his family's life, and what grew in that void was a love of curiosity and a disdain for ideology. For a man who eschews ideologies, his academic background was spent studying them, receiving his MA in the history of religion from Harvard and a PhD in philosophical theology from the University of Cambridge. Now Garrison wants to impart that holy curiosity to his students in his role leading Ubiquity University. "I believe that modern contemporary education is at the root of our contemporary crisis. We have designed an educational system not around questions but around facts you need to know and tests which ascertain how well you memorize them. So curiosity, subjectivity, personal growth is irrelevant to whether you get a 98 percent or 99 percent."

When education systems seek to obviate wonder and ambiguity in exchange for standardization and rigidity, this impacts our ability not only to learn but to unlearn as well. Researchers predict that a child today will have eighteen jobs in six careers throughout their lifetime, so the ability to learn and unlearn rapidly is critical. What do I mean by unlearning? Our brain has only so much changeable cognitive terrain, and new skills can't always just be layered on top of the old.

Alvaro Pascual-Leone is professor of neurology and director of the Berenson-Allen Center for Noninvasive Brain Stimulation at Beth Israel Deaconess Medical Center and Harvard Medical School and is widely accepted as the person who coined the term *neuroplasticity*. He explains the way we learn—and potentially unlearn—using the metaphor of a ski slope. The topography of the slope—the contour of the hill, the trees, and rocks—is what our genes contribute to our brain, whether it be our personality or sexual orientation or perhaps our propensity for certain mental health conditions. But when we ski down the slope the first time, although it's shaped by the topography, we can choose which route to take. That part is in our control. "But," Pascual-Leone says, "what will definitely happen the second time you take the slope down is that you will more likely than not find yourself somewhere or another that is related to the path you took the first time. It won't be exactly that path, but it will be closer to that one than any other." Over time, as we take the same route repeatedly, it becomes harder and harder to take a new one, and those routes become ruts that become habits, both good and bad. "At the end, you will have some paths that have been used a lot, some that have been used very little . . . and it is very difficult now to get out of those tracks. And those tracks are not genetically determined anymore." So we are locked into neural pathways by our genetics (the topography) and our habits (the tracks), and while it's *possible* to change our route, it's difficult to do because our brain likes a fast shortcut, and those ruts are fast. Wonder is a way to clear the piste and lay new tracks.

Our slope is completely clear when we are young—fresh, pristine powder waiting to be carved. But as we get older, those tracks become deeper and deeper. As author Virginia Woolf wrote, "As one gets older one has a greater power through reason to provide an explanation," so over time, "this explanation blunts the sledgehammer force of the blow." Woolf imagined our heuristics as almost defenses to change. When a significant change happens to a child, they have fewer "heuristic defenses," and thus, their schema is easily altered. But as adults, we have built up sufficient explanations, sufficient heuristic defenses, to "blunt the blow." This means that while adults may not be as knocked off-balance by changes in their life as a child could be, they are also less adept at unlearning than children are.

As it turns out, one of the keys to unlearning is latent inhibition, the phenomenon of learned irrelevance that we looked at in Chapter 4. "Learning what to ignore is critical for effective psychological functioning—it would be simply overwhelming to process the full stream of information available to our senses as we make our way through the world. So we cull through this information for relevant details, screening out everything else. The problem is, the screened-out information might be useful later, but by then, we are slow to realize its significance, to unlearn its irrelevance," shares Luke Smillie, our openness researcher from Chapter 1. "For the average person, this preexposure stifles subsequent learning—the critical stimulus has been rendered 'irrelevant' and fails to penetrate awareness. Not so, however, for those high in openness, who are less susceptible to latent inhibition."

Psychologist Kurt Lewin, an early-twentieth-century pioneer in change management theory, developed a vivid illustration of unlearning. He saw change as requiring us to "thaw, reframe, refreeze." While there are some valid critiques of this idea, primarily that change is never really "set" but rather a constant, Lewin's description conjures a really useful visual of just how difficult unlearning can be. Think of it this way—I loved ice pops as a kid. We would make them in ice cube trays with plastic wrap and toothpicks until my folks really splurged and upgraded to those chichi ice-pop molds with the fancy save-your-fingers-from-drips handles. I could never wait long enough, though. They always looked frozen on the outside, but inside? Still liquid. *Sigh.*

The disappointment of having to stick those ice pops back in the freezer and waaaaaaaaaaait. It was so painful. Now imagine you've been behaving in a certain way for years, maybe decades. Consider how much time and energy it would take to melt twenty years of behavior, reframe it, and then refreeze it until it is solid again. That's unlearning. Futurist and philosopher Alvin Toffler explained, "The illiterate of the 21st century will not be those who cannot read and write, but those who cannot learn, unlearn, and relearn." Wonder-based education that focuses on the process of inquiry rather than on the answer itself produces a more nimble learner, making us more proficient at not just learning but unlearning, too.

Modern education, polarization, and the Single Right Answer

Garrison, like many others, views modern education as not just lacking play but lacking cooperation. He believes the school environment promotes a competitive and ultimately harmful culture where the mental health of children is not considered. "These kids come into a system starting in kindergarten where they know they have to perform, and they've got to eliminate curiosity because that's the point of the game." Garrison fears that this decrease in curiosity and empathy in schools may make students more prone to bias and poor mental health.

As one might expect, the emotional health of students has an impact on academic outcomes, but the extent to which it impacts those outcomes is appreciable. For example, one in eight children in the US has an anxiety disorder, and those with clinical anxiety are 1.4 times more likely to drop out of high school. Anxious children also perform worse on both comprehension and standard-ized intelligence tests. But even without clinically significant levels of anxiety, the executive functioning of students who experience test anxiety can be impaired enough to hamper learning. When anxiety increases and the fight-or-flight response is triggered, exec-utive functioning, which manages attention regulation, focus, and absorption, as well as mental flexibility, diminishes, and a student's ability to retain or recall information plummets.

"Right now, our educational system, particularly business school, is not only antisocial, it's psychotic," exhorts Garrison. "Our business schools are training generations of psychopaths without conscience, without compassion, or empathy. Ruthless, tough competitors, where you win at all costs, and the guy with the most toys wins. And it's in complete violation of evolution. The more they're learning about evolution, the more they're finding out it's motivated and sustained by cooperation, not through com-petition." Garrison recognizes the power of wonder to foster more cooperative cultures in schools. He believes "wonder is inherently a social enterprise," continuing, "Awe and wonder, from an exis-tential point of view, are not only social phenomena but I think they're linked to the willingness to imagine something different."

Garrison maintains learning is best as a cooperative rather than a competitive process, and he sees wonder as a mechanism for cooperative connection.* It would seem that as children, we

---

* This idea is exemplified by a popular team-building exercise titled "The Marshmallow Challenge." The challenge is to build the tallest tower possible with a fixed amount of dried spaghetti, tape, and string, that is capable of supporting one large, fluffy marshmallow at the top. While the Marshmallow Challenge has been performed with many different types of groups, from small children and university students to great scions of politics and industry, one cohort consistently performs the best—kindergartners. And one cohort consistently performs the worst—MBA students. Why? As Tom Wujac explains, because none of the kids are "trying to be CEO of Spaghetti, Inc." MBA students tend to be competitive among themselves and obsessive planners, while small children are highly cooperative and engage in a constant, playful, iterative wonder cycle. With kindergarteners, all ideas are good

are initially encouraged to embrace this highly open, curious approach but are dissuaded from it over time. And that reality is at our peril, as an absence of exploratory behavior can have long-term negative impacts. Psychologist and personality theorist Silvan Tomkins described a lack of curiosity as so detrimental to learning it's akin to the "destruction of brain tissue," explaining, "there is no human competence which can be achieved in the absence of a sustaining interest." Cultivating curiosity from an early age matters because that is when the natural brain plasticity of a child is at its highest. As we've explored, while about half of our personality attributes are hereditary, the other half are environmental, so our schools and learning institutions can have a fundamental impact on not just *what* we learn but the *way* we learn over the course of our lifetime.

Our peak awe periods in life are between six and twenty years of age—also the time of maximum plasticity—and then again after age sixty-five when mortality looms. Given this timing, Dacher Keltner views wonder-based schooling as a tremendous opportunity for positively impacting not just a child's learning but their emotional capacity throughout their life. "There's probably a pedagogical philosophy that's going to come out of wonder science. Just asking questions. Getting people to think big and then small. I think that [wonder] has this opportunity, much like gratitude in schools, to reorient our young people to [questions like], 'How do you listen to music? How do you look at a painting? How do you think scientifically?' "

Using Ubiquity University as a model, Garrison hopes to design a wonder-based education system that encourages cognitive

---

ideas (openness). Every solution is worth collaboratively exploring (curiosity). The individual ego is lost in the pursuit of a solution (absorption). Every failed attempt results in learning (expectation violation). The solution changes their schema (awe). (Wujec, Tom. 2010. "Build a Tower, Build a Team." TED2010. 6:35. https://www.ted.com/talks/tom_wujec_build_a_tower_build_a_team.)

flexibility and fosters the growth of children's better nature. "If you've got a billion people, how do you design a learning system that makes people prosocial? How do I come into a relationship with you as a stranger and be instinctively curious about who you are, rather than afraid of who you are?" This is the question we should be asking not just for the betterment of the world, but for the betterment of students' academic outcomes as well. Evidence shows learners who link their learning to a prosocial or self-transcendent purpose, like helping people or making a difference, perform better. This is also a necessary question to answer if we're going to tackle the polarization of the current educational model. In the book *Wonder-Full Education*, Laura Piersol wrote, "In my view, students in our current education system are taught to be more like dogmatic puppies than humble wonderers. . . . What happens to wonder in a world that appears to be filled with solvable problems? It vanishes; it is swept under our neat and tidy paths of learning."

Garrison believes this questioning philosophy should be foundational to how we approach life; otherwise, we risk becoming calcified in our thinking and conforming to the Single Right Answer. "Instilling, through a pedagogy and an ethos, the importance of questions is the key to curiosity and wonder, and even imagination. Because if you think you know, then curiosity or wonder or imagination becomes irrelevant. Because you already know." In other words, if children learn there is only the Single Right Answer to every question, they may naturally develop into entrenched thinkers in the future.

"The most worrying part about the lack of wonder in the classroom is that we don't just ignore its potential, we often actively discourage it," Piersol explains. "Instead of guiding students to dismantle existing assumptions and gain the courage to consider 'strange' new ideas, we lead them to concrete answers and present most subjects as static entities in which there is little left that is unknown." And that entrenched thinking impacts our political, social, and economic behavior. Psychologist Kirk Schneider agrees. "It's a profound tragedy what our culture, and many cultures, do to dampen that primal sense of humility and wonder about life, discovery, and amazement. We've got all these rules and regulations that bombard kids so quickly with the fixation on a single point of view to the utter exclusion of competing points of view." Of course, people predisposed to discomfort with ambiguity will still likely gravitate toward more concrete answers. Nonetheless, wonder-based education could help *all* children approach uncertainty with more openness, curiosity, adaptability, and nuance, potentially resulting in a more tolerant society.

Garrison believes his Ubiquity University is one such wonder-based learning environment that pushes back against the norm. The school claims its nontraditional teaching style can be traced back to Plato's Academy, "the mystery schools of antiquity," and "the shamanic traditions of indigenous peoples." While the school is accredited, the coursework is not what one would expect at a traditional university. For example, students at Ubiquity University get credit for working at a coffee plantation in Nicaragua or teaching themselves wood-turning. "That's just human life experience born out of a person's curiosity and passion for learning," explains Garrison. "We believe that should be counted for credit."

Garrison shares the university's mission so casually that one could almost miss the manifest enormity of it. "If we can catalyze transformational experiences with young people at a mass level, I'm a happy camper." What's more, he sees wonder as not just a critical component to learning but as a guiding principle for his life and work. "I made a vow to myself as a young man that whatever I was going to do would be out of acts of imagination. So my life has been one act of imagination after another.

Because I've tried since that experience of awe with the monk when I was five years old to always ask myself, 'Where's the wonder here?'"

Nontraditional learners

There are nontraditional schools, and then there are nontraditional learners. One of the biggest challenges facing schools today is how to meet the educational needs of children who are what author Deborah Reber calls "differently wired"—children with neurodifferences such as ADD, ADHD, autism, learning disabilities, or giftedness. As Reber explains, "Differently wired children frequently struggle in conventional learning environments, and yet they represent more than 20 percent of students." But even with one in five children falling into this category, Reber feels there is an education gap. "There are many aspects of traditional educational models that are simply not designed to support students who learn and think differently," Reber explains. And this failure to provide these students with appropriate learning environments can have lifelong impacts. "Many differently wired children struggle to succeed in school, internalize the message that they are 'broken' or stupid, and fail to launch, and often carry with them residual pain and trauma well into adulthood."

It's incredible the lengths society will go to in order to fit children into the current structure of school. In America, two-thirds of children with an ADD/ADHD diagnosis are on stimulant medication. And while these drugs offer substantial, meaningful benefits for many students with ADD/ADHD, there are also times they are used simply to manage behavior that doesn't work well in traditional classrooms. The message is clear. Children should sit, pay attention, and work quietly, and if they can't, we can "fix" that. Reber's goal in writing her book

Differently Wired was to help parents "shift away from a deficits-based parenting style (i.e., one rooted in 'fixing' their children) to parenting in a way that focuses on the individual child and their unique strengths." Reber has seen firsthand the failures of traditional education. She comes to this work from personal experience, as her own child is differently wired, both being gifted and having ADHD. "The majority of systems, traditional timelines, educational models, and communities don't actually respect or support the lived experience of kids like mine."

While ADHD has often been woefully oversimplified as a lack of discipline or a malady that affects kids who can't sit still, it is much more complex than that. As we learned earlier, curiosity is fueled by the neurotransmitter dopamine, a "feel good" chemical messenger that communicates between neurons and is tied to our brain's reward or motivational system. But dopamine also plays an essential role in attention and absorption. For many years researchers believed people with ADD/ADHD had lower dopamine levels than neurotypical people. The prevailing thinking today is that people with ADD/ADHD have enough dopamine, but their dopamine receptors work too efficiently, meaning the dopamine gets gobbled up too quickly. So people with attention deficits will continually seek out the curiosity dopamine hit, but the chemical doesn't stick around long enough to get them absorbed in the topic at hand. Most currently prescribed medications for ADHD act as a stimulant to block dopamine uptake, so the dopamine is removed more slowly. Absent such medication, either a tremendous amount of mental effort or something fascinating is required to give the person with an attention deficit the boost needed to transition from curiosity to absorption.

That's where wonder comes in. Certain wonder interventions appear to benefit students with ADHD, as well as autistic and other neurodivergent students who are poorly served by conventional classroom settings. In fact, wonder-based therapies have already been shown to ameliorate symptoms of ADHD, particularly aiding in the element of absorption. For instance, environmental psychologists Rachel Kaplan and Stephen Kaplan's Attention Restoration Theory (ART) finds that children suffering from attention fatigue can get relief from that mental effort by simply staring at a natural or green environment (more about that in Chapters 12 and 13). Another piece of research, out of the University of Illinois Urbana-Champaign, studied children who lived in identical apartment blocks and found those with an enriched green space view, as opposed to a barren landscape, performed better on impulse control tests. These results are bolstered by further research showing unmedicated children with ADHD who took "greener" walks had better performance on attention tests.

It's worth noting the "green advantage" in those experiments. Artificially built outdoor environments such as paved playgrounds didn't yield the same results, so this isn't simply a matter of children "burning off energy." Rather, there is something specific about green, natural environments that is beneficial to these children, even when tested across geographic, economic, and racial demographics.

Last, we can't explore the connection between wonder, neurodivergence, and learning without including daydreaming. Unfortunately, just like fidgeting, daydreaming is strongly discouraged in most traditional learning environments, even though we know daydreaming has a multitude of benefits, including making children more reflective, developing their sense of compassion, and supporting moral decision-making. Most schools dwell so much on an assumption of high attentional demand that they've failed to balance the potential benefit of "constructive internal reflection." When we consider that daydreaming, or "spacing out," is a hallmark of ADHD for both boys and girls, one has to question how many children are being labeled as "underachievers" or "troublemakers" when it's the educational approach that is failing them, not the other way around. Reber calls for paradigm-shifting approaches. "Encouraging differently wired children to dwell in their many strengths and follow their interests and passions is the key to their unlocking their potential and growing up to be self-actualized adults," Reber explains. "Many neurologically divergent students languish in traditional schools only to thrive when their parents opt to pull them out and homeschool or unschool them (usually after a period of 'detoxing' from negative school experiences), encouraging their children to take the lead in their pursuits, and using their interests as a launching pad for deep exploration, skill-building, and growth."

Rabbi and educator Harold Kushner echoes Reber's thoughts on encouraging children to take the lead in their own education. "I would tell the teachers in our religious school, 'I don't want to hear that on the day of the first serious snowfall of winter, you called the children back from the window to return to page forty-three in the textbook. A young child's gasp of delight at the beauty of the snow will be as authentic a prayer, and as religiously grounded a response to the wonder and beauty of God's world, as anything in your lesson plan for that afternoon.'" The message Dacher Keltner wants students to hear is a bit more blunt. "Stop fucking worrying about the exam, open your mind, and get out and wonder about things."

In the same way that wonder changes the lens through which we see the world, wonder-based learning requires seeing things differently. Although teaching approaches are slowly shifting, conventional educational models still focus too heavily on standardized benchmarks, failing to leverage a time of maximum malleability in a child's mind. Educators have a unique opportunity to not just teach subject matter but to contribute to the way these children will think, interact, and solve problems as adults. As Kruti Parekh is fond of saying, "Magic yesterday is science today. And today's magic will be science tomorrow." A wonder-based education that allows for deep learning, play, and a healthy dose of magic is more likely to mold open, inquisitive, broad-minded adults, and open, inquisitive, broad-minded adults are more likely to make great parents, bosses, and leaders.

WONDER WRAP-UP

- Like deep and surface curiosity, there is deep and surface learning. Deep learning is characterized by active engagement and an intrinsic desire to know more. Deep learners are flexible, appreciate nuance, and retain what they learn for longer. Surface learning is learning for the purposes of assessment. These learners dislike ambiguity and seek the Single Right Answer, resulting in a rigid mindset and short-term recall.

- Play is fundamental to learning, and wonder-based learning is steeped in deep play. Deep play engages each element of the wonder cycle and is characterized by open exploration, deep curiosity, flow-type absorption, and moments of revelatory awe. Deep play also encourages cooperative behaviors.

- Curious kids are better learners, and novelty spurs curiosity and helps us embed information. Wonder-based education seeks opportunities for novelty and aha moments, not rote memorization.

- Many school environments neglect play, or even open exploration, as a learning technique, which leads to decreased empathy and increased polarization. Wonder-based pedagogy is cooperative, not competitive, encouraging greater tolerance and cognitive flexibility.

- Learning is contextual. Certain learners perform better in certain environments, and nontraditional learners need nontraditional solutions. Wonder-based learning appears to be particularly beneficial to some nontraditional learners.

11

Wonder at Work

The Oude Kerk in Amsterdam is a towering structure that sits a bit out of place in De Wallen, the city's labyrinthine red light district. Begun as a humble wooden chapel in 1213 and consecrated as a stone church about one hundred years later, the Oude Kerk is Amsterdam's oldest building and now serves as a contemporary art and culture center when not undergoing its long-term restoration. The granite structure has survived fifteen generations of wars, fires, looting, and mob vandalism, and while it has had several renovations, it looks pretty much the same today as it did when Rembrandt had all four of his children baptized there. It is an imposing structure—36,000 square feet, four pipe organs, with a soaring steeple made of Estonian wood, the biggest of its kind in Europe. Simply put, it is awe-inspiring.

Scientists from the Netherlands used the Oude Kerk as the backdrop for studying the psychological phenomenon known as *small-self*. Prior to the study, small-self had typically been conceptualized as a psychological smallness, as in a decrease in ego and self-salience. But these researchers wanted to understand the effects of awe on our *physical* body perception. Recalling Keltner and Haidt's two elements of an awe experience—vastness and accommodation—they set out to understand how and why a sense of vastness might shift our mental schemas in this way. To study this, the researchers had church visitors fill out surveys before and after they went inside, asking them to estimate their body size compared to the large entry door of the church. They found that visitors who reported higher levels of awe after the visit perceived themselves as physically smaller. The researchers also found two additional pieces of wonder data—those higher in trait absorption were more likely to have an awe experience, and older participants were less likely to experience awe.

This small-self phenomenon is one of the primary ways wonder evokes humility, empathy, and many other prosocial emotions. Small-self precipitates a decrease in self-interest and shifts attention and behavior away from our own needs and onto the needs of others. It allows us to atomize our difficulties into more metabolizable units and grants us the room to consider what those around us may be thinking and feeling, and respond compassionately—obviously a great attribute to have in a manager or team member.

Leading with wonder

Overwhelmingly, people want to work for humble, empathetic leaders and be a part of open, trusting, supportive teams. We have all heard the expression that people don't leave their jobs, they leave their bosses, and with good reason. Leaders have an outsized impact on employee satisfaction, and managers set the tone of an organizational culture. In one 2018 study, of those employees who had bosses they thought were great, 94 percent of respondents said they had passion and energy for their job, as opposed to only 59 percent of those with reportedly bad bosses. Managers have a direct impact on engagement. Besides empathy, what makes a good boss? Humility, honesty, patience, authenticity, selflessness, and openness to new ideas—all characteristics that are enhanced by wonder.

Organizational culture is tricky. It's not as easy as a leader proclaiming, "This is our culture," and then the organization magically operates that way (although many seem to think this is the case). Instead, it is the reverse—the behaviors come first, and those behaviors need to be forged by conscious efforts. Think of culture as the wake we leave behind a series of behaviors. If those actions are inconsistent or diffuse, then the wake is weak, and other turbulence can break through the ripple effect you're trying to create. But if the actions are aligned and authentic, the wake is quite formidable, and it takes a lot of effort to disrupt it. (And this remains the truth whether those actions are positive or toxic, which is why it is so difficult to change an entrenched corporate culture.)

What sorts of behaviors contribute to a great culture? It depends on the aspirations of each organization, but cemented into the behavioral foundations of a wonder-based workplace culture we'll usually find characteristics like empathy, humility, ethics, altruism, trust, creativity, flexibility, openness, curiosity, emotional intelligence, and cohesive, inclusive teamwork. Each of the composite elements of wonder—openness, curiosity, absorption, and awe—contributes to these prosocial leadership qualities, and wonder in the workplace can germinate this kind of culture. (I know I'd want to work at a place like that!)

Empathy

Consistently a feature of good leadership, personal relationships, high-performing teams, and healthy organizational cultures, empathy is vital to employees. So much so, in one 2021 study, 75 percent of employees said they would take a lower salary to work for a more empathetic company. That number increases to 83 percent when asking Gen Z employees (those born after 1996). Empathy has a bottom-line benefit, too. Another study found the top ten most "empathetic companies" showed twice the growth in value as that of the bottom ten and generated 50 percent more earnings. So what makes a company empathetic? An empathetic company is one that does business with compassion. It listens, supports work-life balance, invests in people, is ethical, trusted, and trusting. And it's easy to imagine one reason why empathetic companies perform better—because that's where good people want to work.

Empathy likely evolved as a mechanism to keep groups supportive of one another for improved survival, and it is made possible in part because of a social-cognitive skill called the Theory of Mind (ToM). A notion developed by Immanuel Kant, ToM is the ability of individuals to recognize that other people have thoughts, emotions, and beliefs separate from their own. This recognition allows us to interpret and infer the mental states and behaviors of others around us through our social interactions, and we then use those inferences to determine whether we feel motivated to engage in prosocial emotions like empathy or compassion.

Over the past decade, there has been significant interest in the discovery of a subset of neurons called mirror neurons. As the name suggests, these neurons appear to mirror the actions and emotional state of people we observe, and researchers believe they play a sizable role in empathy. What's fascinating is that when eighteen-month-old children watched a human show them how to use a toy, they learned the action, but when they watched a machine engage in the same action, they didn't learn how to use the toy. What made this discovery so groundbreaking was that mirror neurons appear to play a role in several neurocognitive functions like speech and language, imitation and knowledge-sharing, empathy, social cognition, and the Theory of Mind, as well as having tremendous implications for the way we learn from and interact with one another.

Yet, despite what we know about the benefits of more empathetic workplaces and a more compassionate society at large, according to philosopher and author Roman Krznaric, "We are facing a chronic and growing empathy deficit." Krznaric claims that empathy levels have dropped almost 50 percent since the 1970s. In a 2010 analysis of nearly fourteen thousand college students, Krznaric was able to track empathy over the prior three decades, and the research showed a steady decline in both "empathic concern" and "perspective-taking." Krznaric believes this drop in empathy is likely due to a society replete with virtual activities that don't allow for the kind of community socialization that builds empathy skills. He also pinpoints the rise of narcissism, which has been increasing over the past several decades.* "Digital culture has created an epidemic of narcissism and exacerbated political polarization that divides rather than unites people."

But there is hope. Contrary to the thinking that humanity comprises selfish jerks, research is building that, actually, humans are what Krznaric calls "homo empathicus, wired for empathy, social cooperation, and mutual aid." Stanford researcher Jamil Zaki echoes Krznaric's findings, sharing that while he

---

* In a 2006 study, 81 percent of eighteen-to-twenty-five-year-olds reported that getting rich was one of their generation's top goals, and 61 percent listed it as their number one goal. (In 2006, this study segment would have represented people born between 1980 and 1996, who would now be age twenty-five to forty-one.) Jamil Zaki's more recent research from 2020 aligns with these findings. Empathy researcher Sara Konrath attributes this to the increasing pressure on those generations. "Rising inequality makes it very hard for average people to have a sustainable lifestyle economically and so on. All of these different pressures on young people, I think crowd out their focus on their own self-care and care for others."

believes there is currently a pronounced trend away from empathetic concern toward a culture of blame, dehumanization, and polarization, we also share an innate drive toward empathy that can be strengthened. "Empathy is like a skill. It's like a muscle," he explains. "We can practice it like any other skill and get better at connecting with people."

Krznaric sees the wonder element of curiosity as a way to build that empathy muscle. "Curiosity expands our empathy when we talk to people outside our usual social circle, encountering lives and world views very different from our own. And it is a useful cure for the chronic loneliness afflicting around one in three Americans." (I'm not sure if it was Walt Whitman or Ted Lasso who said, "Be curious, not judgmental," but they were both spot-on.) But reaping the empathy-building benefits of wonder requires more than just surface curiosity. We need to be deeply curious about others. "Cultivating curiosity requires more than having a brief chat about the weather," explains Krznaric. "Highly empathic people (HEPs) have an insatiable curiosity about strangers. They will talk to the person sitting next to them on the bus, having retained that natural inquisitiveness we all had as children, but which society is so good at beating out of us." Hence, another wonder virtuous circle: curiosity breeds empathy, which breeds curiosity.

Researchers have also consistently found that absorption is associated with empathy. If someone pays close attention to what another person is saying and feeling, that absorption translates to greater compassion. And this empathetic behavior is further reinforced by a greater tendency toward unconscious mimicry or imitation in interpersonal interactions, too, like using the same body language or tone of voice as another person. Mimicry puts people at ease and builds rapport. (It also plays a role in charisma, which we'll look at in Chapter 14.)

One study following people who play fantasy role-play games like Dungeons and Dragons found they have higher dispositional empathy. A possible theory behind both the mimicry and role-playing correlations is that people high in absorption are particularly deft perspective-takers. The skills and capacity required to take on the persona of a fantasy character translate to the skills and capacity to take on other people's perspectives in real life. In essence, the definitions of interpersonal absorption—to lose one's self in the story of another—and empathy are functionally similar, and the ability to step in and out of different worlds (fictional or otherwise) is transferable. This sort of perspective-taking is a primary feature of emotional intelligence as well, and yet another reason wonder is vital to leadership and teamwork.

Humility

It's understandable why humility is so desired in the workplace. Humility is the personality dimension most highly correlated with moral character at work and indicates a motivation toward better organizational citizenship. Humble people have a secure, balanced sense of self, so they appreciate and recognize the contributions of others, and they are also more open, particularly in the face of negative feedback. In a 2015 study, Amy Ou from the University of Singapore found that humble CEOs lead stronger management teams who are, in turn, more effective at collaboration, information sharing, decision-making, and crafting a shared vision. In another study, she found CEO humility to be associated with empowering leadership behaviors and, further, that this empowerment prompted greater integration between top and middle management, contributing to increased engagement, commitment, and job performance.

Positive emotion researcher Jennifer Stellar found a close link between wonder and humility in her research. In one study, she had participants self-report their own perceived level of humility and then asked their friends how humble they perceived the participants to be. The research subjects who reported feeling awe more regularly, be it small doses of quotidian awe or more intense experiences of awe, perceived themselves as more humble, *as did their friends*. According to Stellar, "Emotions not only function to influence behavior but also change the self-concept and broader patterns of thought about one's relationship to others and the outside world."

Wonder offers us the gift of perspective. As Stellar explains, "Awe shifts self-perception [and helps us] fully appreciate the value of others and see themselves more accurately, evoking humility." A bit like the Overview Effect, when we view our world of work from a wonder vantage point, the borders become erased, hierarchies are less focal, feedback becomes easier, and we can see, and appreciate, individuals for who they are.

Altruism and ethics

A research colleague of Stellar's, Paul Piff, found the same small-self prosocial effects in his experiments, this time using as the awe elicitor a grove of towering Tasmanian eucalyptus trees on the Berkeley campus. This is not just any old campus copse, but at two hundred feet tall, it's the tallest stand of hardwood trees in North America. Piff split participants into two groups, asking one group to look up at the trees and the other group to look up at a building of approximately the same height. At the end of one minute, the experimenter approached the participants with questionnaires and "accidentally" dropped a box of pens to observe the participants' reaction. Using the number of pens the participants picked up as a measure of helping behavior, the study showed that those who had spent their minute looking at the grove of trees were more helpful. After the accident, participants then completed a questionnaire, and the tree-viewing group also showed an increase in ethical decision-making and a reduction in feelings of entitlement.

Piff conducted several subsequent experiments, including one in which participants watched videos, some of them awe-inspiring, and then played a game where each point gained could be exchanged for a ticket to a $100 raffle—serious money for a college student—or gifted to another research participant. Those students who watched the awe-inspiring videos gave more points away and kept fewer for themselves. Piff found this same relationship between awe and altruism in each of his studies, indicating awe serves a prosocial function.* These kinds of altruistic behaviors are also associated with honesty, and according to a 2014 Pew Research study, 84 percent of employees listed honesty as the most desirable quality in a leader, calling it "absolutely essential."

The fact that results were seen in such a short time—participants in Piff's Tasmanian eucalyptus experience spent only sixty seconds viewing the trees—lends credence to the theory that quotidian awe can make a difference in our attitude and behavior and that the other elements of wonder contribute to a healthier organizational culture. Imagine what a sixty-second wonder break or a five-minute wonder writing exercise could do for our workplaces.

Authenticity

We've all heard corporate culture gurus tell us that we need to "bring our whole selves to work," and many diversity, equity, and

---

* In a further study in which people were asked to write a five-sentence narrative recalling an awe-inspiring time, they subsequently behaved more altruistically in hypothetical scenarios like returning a lost wallet. What's more, these results held for negative awe and non-nature-based awe, and against a number of other prosocial emotions like happiness and pride.

inclusion efforts focus on cultures in which employees are free to be their authentic selves. But there is a continued gap between leaders who believe they support an authentic culture and their employees' perception. This lack of cultural coherence significantly impacts our work life. Research out of Utrecht University found that those who felt they could be authentic at work had higher job satisfaction, engagement, motivation, and performance. In another study from 2019, people who felt they could be themselves in the workplace reported stronger work relationships and improved well-being. And entrepreneurs who were their authentic selves in a pitch rather than trying to cater to the crowd made better first impressions, according to a later Harvard study.

Wonder helps people be more authentic. An extensive multinational study by a group of researchers out of China found that awe makes us more desirous of pursuing our authentic selves. The theory is that self-transcendence contributes to higher degrees of authentic prosociality, meaning people do nice things for others because it aligns with their inner beliefs instead of doing them for show, which creates a self-reinforcing drive toward authenticity. Another recent study found that both openness and curiosity contributed to people enjoying more meaningful, authentic lives. Curiosity also supports authentic leadership. Curious leaders are more open, ask questions that show genuine interest, actively listen, and are more willing to reframe their opinions, all desirable qualities in a leader.

Wonder in teams

Teams at work, as in life, help share the load, make us happier, help us learn and develop skills, increase our productivity, and reduce our stress levels. Team members can show us our blind spots, and with the support of a team, we are more willing to take risks—and have those risks pay off in innovative solutions. Working in teams where respect, honesty, and openness were encouraged, team members were 80 percent more likely to experience higher well-being. What are some ways to build teams like this? Focus on open behaviors like transparency, collaboration, and change-readiness, encourage honest feedback from everyone (regardless of where they sit in the org chart), and make diversity and inclusion a cornerstone.

Stitching inclusive teams together

As humans, we have evolved to naturally cooperate within tribes—empathy likely developed in part as a way to bond us to our compatriots. But at the same time, we have also evolved to reject those outside of our group. This ingrained behavioral phenomenon of pattern matching to find friend or foe is known as ingrouping or outgrouping and developed in humans as a means of survival, identity, and community. We naturally ingroup and outgroup at work, too, and that ingroup bonding can create solid, effective teams. It can also inhibit us from developing the best teams, as the best teams are almost always diverse teams, and outgrouping bias runs counter to diversity.

Time researcher David Eagleman wanted to understand how entrenched our tendency toward ingrouping and outgrouping was. He ran an experiment in which participants were placed into an fMRI scanner and shown images on a screen above them. First, they watched a hand being stabbed with a needle, and as the scientists expected, the observer's pain center in their brain was activated as though they themselves had been stabbed. Next, the researchers showed the same images but with superimposed labels, including "Jewish," "Christian," "Muslim," and "atheist." While the researchers expected to see a difference in the brain scans, they were shocked at how marked the change was. When people saw the hand of their ingroup being impaled (e.g., a Christian viewing a hand labeled "Christian"), their pain centers were activated. But when they saw the hands of an outgroup being stabbed (e.g., a Christian viewing a hand labeled "atheist"), there was almost no response. This reaction was so pronounced that researchers could estimate an outgroup response almost 75 percent of the time just based on the pain center reactivity.* "The lesson it paints for me is just how hardwired we are to make groups," Eagleman shared. Usually a proponent of brain malleability, even he was shocked at how ingrained this ingrouping behavior was.

But while this instinctive drive to quickly discern who is "on our side" has served a purpose evolutionarily, in creating teams, diversity is almost always better. Diversity in teams makes us more open, creative, and higher performing, and inclusion in teams increases psychological safety and innovation. In study after study, not only are diverse teams better, they are better than teams of "the best." Meaning that even homogenous teams of superqualified and skilled people still don't do as well as teams with mixed skill levels and experience. In just one example of many, diverse teams of stock pickers were 58 percent more likely to pick better stocks, and they made fewer mistakes. So this innate heuristic to exclude those whom we don't recognize can sometimes conspire against us in our effort to create top-notch teams. The goal in crafting high-performing teams is to find ways to recognize ingrouping bias and leverage this tribe philosophy to our benefit.

The good news is, we can train ourselves out of outgrouping. As Eagleman explains, "We are predisposed to just go for the simplest answer fast because that's really efficient to do that. But you can

---

* And as Eagleman observed, this phenomenon held true for the atheists, too, who presumably ascribe no meaning to religious labels, so this is not an experiment about religion; rather it's about any number of labels we use to include and exclude people.

train a person to be more thoughtful and less habitual." Eagleman ran another experiment to test this idea. First, he assigned people to teams, and as expected, the same ingrouping and outgrouping effects were observed. Then, he told participants that the teams had created alliances with each other. With just that additional information, the previous outgrouping effects disappeared, and new ingrouping was formed in the alliance teams. In a subsequent study, researchers found similar results. Simply priming participants that their assigned group would be expected to cooperate with other groups in the future decreased ingrouping bias again.

Eagleman was surprised and heartened by how easily empathy could be generated for people previously identified as outsiders—just a single sentence instruction. "In most things, I'm maybe more cynical and say it's not that simple, but in terms of [ingrouping], it's pretty straightforward," shares Eagleman. "One of the most important lessons for me that came out of that work was just the fast flexibility of groups." In a rapidly changing business landscape, the flexibility of team creation should be considered a core competency. "It means that nothing about us is permanent. But it means that we as a society have to work on ways to make sure we're doing this right. And make sure that groups can be cross-stitched in some way."

Wonder is one of the threads that can stitch teams together. For example, people who embody the wonder trait of curiosity tend to be more engaged, infuse more excitement into meeting new people, and are more likely to seek and build on what they learn about a person. One study had strangers ask each other personal questions and found that those who showed genuine curiosity about their interlocutor were rated friendlier (and more attractive). Research also indicates highly curious people appear to be less affected by social rejection, making them less hesitant to socially engage.

Awe also encourages inclusivity. In a study using mock student trials, those who were induced to be happy recalled negative stereotypical information about the case file and meted out harsher sentences, whereas those in the awe condition were less reliant on their previous stereotypes when making a judgment. And awe makes us feel a stronger connection to social groups, too, as do other self-transcendent experiences. Researchers of aboriginal tribal behavior noted that shared STEs formed a core feature of their cohesive tribal culture. And similar to the findings of Paul Piff in his eucalyptus grove study, more intense STEs like deep absorption, awe, and peak experiences can contribute to prosocial behavior that lasts for several months.

"What if we could use awe, not to get rid of conflict—conflict is essential, conflict is how your brain expands, it's how your brain learns—but rather, to enter conflict in a different way?" asks neuroscientist Beau Lotto. "And what if awe could enable us to enter it in at least two different ways? One, to give us the humility and courage to not know. . . . To enter conflict with a question instead of an answer. . . . And the second is, in entering conflict that way, to seek to understand rather than convince. Because everyone makes sense to themselves, right? And to understand another person is to understand the biases and assumptions that give rise to their behavior."

Flexibility and openness to change

Unexpected change is frequently unwelcome change, and when confronted with it, most of us will do whatever we can to exert control in other areas of our life, just to feel we have a grip.* It is

---

* If you think people like change, try telling one of those "pineapple on pizza" people that their tastes are an abomination to the entire citizenry of Napoli, and you'll see what I mean. Seriously. What is up with this? Warm pineapple and marinara?! What's next? Pineapple in pasta? Pineapple lasagna? It's a slippery slope, people.

far easier to deal with change if we hold our view of the world a bit more loosely. Think of it as mental inertia. A mind with fixed ideas stays fixed. A mind with fluid ideas stays fluid.

"Especially in modern times, people are not willing to change and keep their minds open," explains Melanie Rudd. "And the idea of changing and evolving how we think about things—it's terrifying." Rudd believes awe can help us manage change and keep an open mind. "Something about awe specifically seems to make [change] less scary. There's something about it. It's simultaneously threatening your current cognition and your schema, and yet because of the positivity of the emotion and all the other things surrounding it, you don't feel so scared about it. And you actually are more open to changing. That's such a rare thing."

We covered the concept of need for cognitive closure (NFCC) and the ways it might impact our cognitive flexibility in Chapter 2. But NFCC can influence leadership styles and how people operate in teams, too. According to Professor Arne Roets from Ghent University, people high in NFCC "tend to prefer an autocratic leadership and hierarchical group decision structure, while derogating group members with deviant opinions." In a nutshell, if someone has a high need for cognitive closure, they're the type of person who likes everyone to know "their place." This need is also associated with greater prejudice, as people high in NFCC tend to fall back on their preexisting stereotypes rather than build new schemas.

"Basically," writes Roets, "anything that seems to provide quick and definite closure can be appealing to people high in [NFCC]; most commonly these are things they know and are familiar with (traditions, the majority perspective) or things that are very clear (e.g., what authorities state, but sometimes also extremist views, for these are usually very unambiguous)." But, like Eagleman, Roets believes these behaviors can be changed, and wonder can facilitate that.

Wonder lowers our NFCC, and people low in NFCC appear to be particularly "susceptible to the positive effects of inter-group contact," so once the outsider becomes the insider, their attitudes can shift. They are also more open and tolerant and eschew rigid hierarchies. That attitudinal flexibility translates to cognitive flexibility, too. Cognitive flexibility (i.e., low NFCC) in teams is associated with greater creativity, increased knowledge-sharing, better performance under pressure, and a higher tolerance for change. (Openness and curiosity both predict creativity as well.) And this cognitive flexibility brought on by wonder plays a significant role in how people handle change and risk, too. Through his research of Cirque du Soleil attendees described in Chapter 5, Beau Lotto found people increased their tolerance to risk after watching the awe-inspiring show. "Not only did they want to take more risk, but they were also better able at taking it. People were in less need of cognitive closure, better able to sit with uncertainty."

Another benefit of wonder is what's known as the *paradox mindset*, or the extent to which people embrace the tensions of competing ideas. People low in NFCC are better able to leverage this paradoxical tension as an opportunity for innovation and growth as opposed to analysis paralysis. And divergent thinking activity increases when people are primed with these sorts of paradoxical statements.* Nobel Laureates, authors of great literature, and other prodigious thinkers are known to be energized by considering seemingly oppositional concepts. Embracing paradoxical thinking increases organizational dexterity and makes for more nuanced and cognitively flexible thinkers and learners.

While people are the biggest component of wonder at work, certainly the work environment has an impact as well. In Chapter

---

* Those who were primed with the paradoxical statements performed 14 percent better than the control group.

8 we briefly explored how wonder can be found in art and architecture, and office buildings are no exception—or at least they needn't be. (Imagine the implications of Paul Piff's eucalyptus grove experiment if applied to commercial architectural design.) We also saw in the previous chapter how we can leverage the "green advantage" for better school performance, and that is true in our workplaces, too. And in the next few chapters we'll learn more about the power of wonder in nature and how biophilic design can create wonder-filled work spaces that are healthier and support resiliency.

I appreciate that going to your boss and saying, "I want more wonder at work" might get you a bit of side-eye, but the truth is, work isn't working for so many people, so what have we got to lose? Imagine trainings on openness, curiosity, absorption, and awe, on wonder-based leadership, on how to take wonder breaks, on how to meet our teammates with wonder. Wonder at work is achievable, and given the unrestrained influence large corporations have in shaping global policy, culture, and social mores, better work makes for a better world. Who wouldn't want a world shaped by wonder-based work cultures built on empathy, humility, trust, and inclusivity? I know I would.

WONDER WRAP-UP

- Wonder has many applications for the workplace. Empathy, humility, authenticity, creativity, inclusivity, flexibility, ethics, trust, emotional intelligence, and innovation are just some of the characteristics one might find in a wonder-based organization.

- Many of the positive characteristics of a wonder-based organizational culture stem from the prosocial outcomes of a small-self. When we put the needs of our team ahead of our own, we become better leaders and colleagues.

- Empathy, humility, and honesty are all qualities we regularly seek in leaders, but we have pervasive empathy and trust problems in the workplace.

- Via the mechanism of self-transcendence, awe makes us more desirous of pursuing our authentic selves. Authenticity increases job satisfaction, engagement, and performance.

- We are hardwired to create tribes for security and acceptance, but this ingrouping and outgrouping can cause us to reject people based on biases. Wonder decreases bias and allows us to broaden our ingroup.

- Wonderprone people are more cognitively flexible. This flexibility is associated with tolerance, creativity, innovation, and better management of risk and pressure.

12

Health

The rustling of leaves, soft and fluttering in spring, wet turning to brittle as autumn shifts to winter. The uniquely sylvan smell of petrichor and bark and a musty stratum of windfall decay. The wind whispering gossip to the trees, each branch passing it on. Stippled sunlight winking through the canopy. Muffled crunches underfoot. Quiet but certainly not silent. At least not after attuning your hearing to the wild. Companionless, and yet you can't resist the urge to peek over your shoulder, as it feels, somehow, like you are not alone. Like you are being called. Five senses, and an inkling of a sixth, all roused and at attention. Your entire body a hound's twitching nose, eagerly tasting the air.

We have all felt the magic of the forest. Transcendentalist philosopher and essayist Ralph Waldo Emerson had a deep connection to the woods, and when he writes of his time there, his words are suffused with wonder. "In the woods, we return to reason and faith. There I feel that nothing can befall me in life . . . which nature cannot repair. Standing on the bare ground—my head bathed by the blithe air and uplifted into infinite space—all mean egotism vanishes. I become a transparent eyeball; I am nothing; I see all; the currents of the Universal Being circulate through me; I am part or particle of God." The dual nature of reason and faith.

The quiet open awareness. The dissolution of the self. The oneness with all universal energy. Emerson spent more than three years honing and crafting his forty-one-page thesis *Nature*, inspired by his walks in Walden Woods surrounding his home in Concord, Massachusetts. (He would later share those woods with his friend Henry David Thoreau, who went on to pen *Walden*.) Published in 1836, *Nature* has become known as the first meaningful work of philosophy authored by an American. Emerson didn't just see God in the woods—he saw healing, too.

From Emerson to Aristotle, Shinto to the Transcendentalists, we've witnessed great thinkers and great philosophies that honor the healing power of nature. Even the Father of Medicine, Hippocrates, believed "Nature itself is the best physician." For most of human existence, medical science as we currently know it didn't exist (it hasn't even been two hundred years since the invention of anesthesia; less than one hundred for penicillin), yet nature-based medicinal practices date back to the Neanderthals. Ayurvedic medicine and traditional Chinese medicine have been practiced for thousands of years, and because of the continued prominence of nature-based medicine in some African and Asian countries, natural therapies remain the primary health care for almost 80 percent of the world's population. But the West, too, had a great appreciation for nature-based medicinal practices well into the mid-1900s.

Before it was relegated to "alternative medicine," natural medicine was incredibly popular, especially during the Industrial Revolution. A prime example is the use of sanatoriums, which grew by more than 15,000 percent between 1900 and 1925, peaking at more than 600,000 beds in the United States alone. Seen as an escape from the pollution, noise, and chaos of overcrowded cities and a rapidly expanding urban landscape that encroached on wild and rural land, sanatoriums were located in high-altitude places like the Adirondacks and the Swiss Alps, and dry locales like Arizona and California. Tuberculosis was also epidemic, accounting for a staggering one-third of all deaths at the time, and besides antibiotics, the fresh air and sun of sanatoriums were some of only a few remedies available to patients.

Doctors prescribed treatment at these bucolic health resorts for everything from rheumatism to depression. But as the medical breakthroughs of the mid-twentieth century emerged, the attitude toward natural medicine shifted. More attention and resources focused on results that could be reproduced in a lab, so sanatoriums were soon shuttered, replaced by modern medical facilities. There is no question that some early medical treatments were dubious at best and diabolical at worst (no one is suggesting a return to bloodletting). Still, nature-based therapies are making a comeback, this time supported by a great deal of rigorous science, and some of that science points to the beneficial role of wonder.

While there is increasing attention being paid to the impact of nature on the human condition—and the results are undeniable—the reason why we experience these benefits is still being debated. Many focus on the biological and chemical features of nature, whereas the feelings we experience in the great outdoors, the emotional features, are unquestionably contributory to the benefits as well. When we explore forest medicine, the "green advantage," and other nature-based health approaches through an emotional lens, rather than a purely physiological one, we can see the ways wonder plays a key role in why the human psyche finds time in nature so healing.

Forest medicine

In 1988, Qing Li was a young medical student in Tokyo. As a child, Qing had lived in a small village in Datong, Shanxi

Province, China, nestled in a forest of poplar and apricot trees. After moving to Japan for school, he found himself burnt out. Needing respite, he took up an invitation from friends to spend the Japanese spring celebration of Golden Week on the small island of Yakushima, known for its pristine forests housing native *Yakusugi* (ancient Japanese cedars) more than two thousand years old. After camping in the woods for a week, Qing emerged revitalized—and intrigued. He wanted to understand what curative properties of the forest may have contributed to his renewed vigor. He has since dedicated his life to understanding what healing these ancient forests have to offer us.

"Some people study forests. Some people study medicine. I study forest medicine to find out all the ways walking in the forest can improve our wellbeing." Qing posited, if we feel less stressed after a trip to the forest, might this also have a physiological impact? To date, Qing has run at least twenty studies to answer just that question. "It is well known that the immune system, including natural killer (NK) cells, plays an important role in defense against bacteria, viruses, and tumors," Qing explains. "It is also well known that stress inhibits immune function." Among his team's observations was an increase in the activity of intracellular anticancer proteins and antiviral cells, changes that remained significant for an entire week after the visit. Qing concluded that four to six hours in the forest could boost the immune system for a week, and a weekend in the woods can benefit immune function for a month.

Qing's research has identified certain atmospheric benefits in the forest, like terpenes (compounds responsible for the smells, flavors, and color of any given plant) and the dappled sunlight through the leaves (the Japanese have a word for that—komorebi). But the research also indicates more than a physical interaction is at play. Some emotion is triggered by the natural environment that also contributes to these benefits. "[Forest bathing] is like a bridge," Qing muses. "By opening our senses, it bridges the gap between us and the natural world." When asked about any kind of spiritual or metaphysical connection one might find in the forest, he says there is no doubt that he becomes filled with an emotional awareness that the Japanese call *yuugen.* "I don't have the data. I just have a feeling." The word doesn't quite have a direct translation, but it's something like "subtle grace" or "mysterious profundity." To hear the description—being moved by an ineffable sense of oneness with the universe—it sounds an awful lot like wonder to me.

Six years prior to Qing's trip to Yakushima, the Japanese government had already founded the Japanese Society of Forest Medicine (JSFM) and introduced the concept of *shinrin-yoku,* or "forest bathing," to encourage city dwellers to take leave of their small, crowded homes and immerse themselves in some of the three thousand miles of pristine woodland that blankets almost 70 percent of Japan. They hoped this antidote to the tech boom of the eighties would also inspire a renewed sense of environmentalism and stewardship of these native woodlands.

Around the same time the Japanese government began studying the healing effects of nature, seven thousand miles away, American evolutionary biologist E. O. Wilson devised a theory similar to Qing's. As Wilson hypothesized in his book *Biophilia,* humans have a biological imperative to nurture and be nurtured by nature. Our ancient brain still seeks the natural cues of our savanna-dwelling past—open spaces meant safety from predators; water, trees, and flowers were signs of refuge and food sources. Many of these features, like "safe threat," water, and hidden areas of refuge, are those same features in art and architecture that are known to inspire wonder. Wilson suggested that humans evolved to "affiliate with other organisms," and because Mother Earth represents the birth of our very existence, we will always yearn to be connected to her. Wilson called that ancient yearning *biophilia*, from the Greek *bios*, meaning "life," and *philios*, meaning "love."

That same year, 1984, Roger Ulrich of the Centre for Health-care Architecture proved Wilson's thesis when he became the first to demonstrate the health outcomes of nature in a formal-ized medical research experiment. Ulrich and his team reviewed the medical records of patients recovering from gallbladder surgery, and they found that patients whose rooms had windows overlooking trees healed, on average, one day faster, had fewer surgical complications, and needed significantly less pain medi-cation than patients whose view consisted of a brown brick wall. Like Qing, Ulrich had firsthand experience with the healing characteristics of nature. As a teenager, he suffered from kid-ney disease and spent much of his youth bedridden, either in "gloomy, sometimes brutal, healthcare buildings" or in his home, where he contemplated a lone pine tree. In an interview decades later, he said, "I think seeing that tree helped my emotional state." Ulrich's life-saving tree is not unusual. As we'll see in the next chapter, when we are deprived of our human connection to nature, not only is our physical health impacted, but our won-derproness atrophies too.*

Another one of JSFM's researchers, Yoshifumi Miyazaki of Chiba University, found that those who took forest walks had lower cortisol levels than those who took the same-paced fifteen-minute walk in a city setting. Natural environments appear to make our brain happy by activating the insula and the anterior

---

* In another study, in Uppsala, Sweden, patients in the ICU were randomly assigned one of six images—two abstract paintings, a white panel, a blank wall, or simulated views of a dark forest or a tree-lined stream. Ulrich found that those looking at the tree-lined stream had better health outcomes (less anxiety and less pain medication) than those with the other interventions.

cingulate cortex, two areas linked to well-being, emotional stability, and reduced blood flow to the part of our brain typically associated with ruminating on negative thoughts. As we'll see in Chapter 16, one of wonder's greatest benefits is also its ability to short-circuit negative rumination. Miyazaki believes our response to nature is woven into our very essence. "Genes cannot change over just a few hundred years," he suggests. In his book *Shinrin Yoku: The Japanese Art of Forest Bathing*, Miyazaki explains that since the dawn of man, we have lived in nature and that not only have our genes evolved based on our responses to it, but our genetic makeup isn't equipped to manage a world so devoid of it. "In 1800, only 3 percent of the world's population lived in urban areas," he explains. That number now is closer to 55 percent and is expected to be 68 percent by 2050. "We live in our modern society with bodies that are still adapted to the natural environment."

Kaplan's Attention Restoration Theory (ART), which suggests that we have finite attentional resources and our capacity to direct attention can be renewed by contact with nature, builds on the work of William James, who observed that certain features in natural environments ("strange things, moving things, wild animals, bright things . . .") are "effortlessly engaging." These features only require *involuntary* attention, while environments that aren't effortlessly engaging require *voluntary* mental energy, or what Kaplan called *directed attention*. The challenge is that endless directed attention wears us out, which is exactly what we see in the more than half the world's population who are urban dwellers. The psychological stressors of urban lifestyles impose high demands on attentional capacities, and according to ART, this cognitive overload results in attention fatigue. The fix is to take time out from our attention-hungry modern life by exposing ourselves to less demanding natural environments that allow us to rebuild our cognitive and attentional resources.

While Ulrich's research focused on the benefits of the visual component of nature, the benefits of nature are omnisensory, and Qing is quick to note that forest bathing is more than just taking a walk in the woods—it must engage all the senses. Just the scent of nature is beneficial. Qing found that even in very low doses, the protective chemicals secreted by trees, known as *phytoncides*, increase the immune function of natural killer cells, which are known as anticancer proteins. And the terpenes found in these phytoncides, specifically those in the Japanese cypress, have been linked with improved immune functioning, reduced anxiety, and a higher pain threshold. In future studies, Qing wants to see what effect forest bathing may have on Alzheimer's patients. He hopes to show that the olfactory response triggered by the phytoncide in the forest will have a beneficial effect on memory.

Wonder heals—in nature or otherwise

Jennifer Stellar always knew she wanted to study positive emotions. "I think I always was interested in the positive side of psychology. I thought, if I'm going to devote my life and research to something, I'm actually genuinely more interested in understanding what's good about people than how we're flawed and, you know, hostile and racist." While she recognizes the importance of studying those more negative aspects of human nature, she wanted her copious amounts of time spent on a PhD to be something she enjoyed. "I always was just fascinated by the idea that we're supposed to be these selfish creatures, yet we aren't. We have these cooperative tendencies—we have empathy, we have compassion; all that really binds us together."

When her PhD adviser, Dacher Keltner, suggested she look at awe as one of those prosocial emotions, Stellar wasn't convinced. "It wasn't like a love at first sight," she says, laughing at the recollection. "It was more like, *What is this emotion? Why should I care about it?*" As Stellar began to stick her toe into the world of wonder, she was surprised at how prolific philosophers, writers, and religious scholars have been on the topic, and yet there remained a lacuna of scientific study. "The more I read about it, the more I found that there's so much going on, and there's so little we know." She appreciated the topic's potential and wanted to rectify this research gap. "It's so rich. It's a complex, complicated emotion to work with. We know less than we should, I think."

In simplest terms, negative emotions make us sick, not just mentally but also physically. Fear, sadness, shame, anxiety, and stress all prompt an unhealthy biological response, and one way those negative emotions make us sick is by stimulating inflammation. In the case of physical injury or infection, the immune system releases small proteins called *proinflammatory cytokines* to trigger a robust immune response in the form of inflammation. These proinflammatory cytokines are then balanced with anti-inflammatory cytokines to keep the response proportional and in check, and this interplay over time results in healing. But if our inflammatory response occurs absent injury or illness, it can actually give rise to health issues, including cardiovascular disease, diabetes, depression, rheumatoid arthritis, asthma, and Alzheimer's.

Although a considerable amount of research had previously explored the relationship between negative emotions and proinflammatory cytokines, Stellar wanted to find out if *positive* emotions might also have an impact. As anticipated, she found positive affect did indeed impact the proinflammatory cytokines, and awe was the strongest predictor of lower cytokines out of all the positive emotions tested.* The researchers don't know why awe is such a strong predictor of lower inflammation,

---

* This was true for both dispositional and experiential awe.

but they suggest that proinflammatory cytokines tend to en-courage withdrawing socially, perhaps as an adaptive response for solitary healing. Stellar explains that as awe is associated "with curiosity and a desire to explore," wonder's combination of openness, curiosity, and awe drives social connection and explo-ration that counteracts this isolation impulse, in turn spurring a healthier balance of cytokine expression.

While there is a great deal of evidence illustrating psyche-delics arouse a hypercharged awe experience, what Stellar found in her study is that it's actually the little wonder experiences that really matter. Stellar shares that the participants in her cytokine study weren't asked to think about "those ephemeral, very fleet-ing, heavy experiences" but relatively small wonder moments in their day. "So if anything, I feel like from my experience, where we have people do daily diaries every night of awe experiences, we're typically working in that more quotidian experience of awe." Stellar cautions (as do many other researchers) against extra-polating too much from her findings, but the results are promis-ing, and many of her colleagues, like Dacher Keltner, agree that an additive "dose effect" of quotidian awe can have considerable and consequential effects over time. As Keltner explains, "Those less intense experiences are probably activating pretty similar parts of the brain [as self-transcendent awe experiences]. Awe reduces cortisol, elevates vagal tone, and reduces inflammation, so for the next week or two, your body's in a different state. And you're talking to your romantic partner differently. And you're handling your disease differently."

Wonder walks

We've covered at length the impact of time spent in nature, but wonder walks are really as much about the effectiveness of setting an intention for wonder as about the wonder benefits of nature. Psychologists from the University of California, Berkeley, wanted to see if awe might be a catalyst for getting seniors (adults age sixty to ninety years old) to be more mobile, a goal that would benefit their mental and physical health. The researchers split participants into two groups. They were each instructed to take a fifteen-minute walk every day for eight weeks and then asked to complete narrative surveys about their walk and their emotional state throughout the rest of the day. One group was sent on a "regular walk," meaning they had no priming instructions before they set off. The other group went on a "wonder walk," meaning participants were "taught how to orient their walks to experience awe by tapping into their sense of wonder and walking in new locales." Researchers counted on the wonderbringing supports of priming and novelty to make the wonder walks more beneficial.

The results confirmed their hypothesis—the wonder walkers "shifted their attention to the details of the world around them and encouraged wonder." In contrast, the control group walkers got caught up ruminating about mundane tasks like packing for an upcoming trip. Researchers also discovered an additive, dose-like relationship between the wonder walks and prosocial emotions like compassion, finding that these emotions incrementally increased with each walk. Another way they knew the wonder walkers had a better time? Bigger smiles! Researchers had the participants take selfies before and after each walk, and wonder walkers consistently had bigger smiles than the regular walkers.

If ever there was a group of folks who knew about a wonder walk, it would have to be the transcendentalists, followers of the early nineteenth-century religious and philosophical movement focused on idealism, unity, the innate goodness of humanity, and the wonder of nature. They believed that the divine was found in everyday activities, and their raison d'être was to commune with nature via a good meander. Ralph Waldo Emerson, a leading voice in transcendentalism, eloquently described the frisson he felt from just a simple walk home one evening, observing, "Crossing a bare common in snow puddles, at twilight, under a clouded sky, without having in my thoughts any occurrence of special good fortune, I have enjoyed a perfect exhilaration. I am glad to the brink of fear." "Glad to the brink of fear" is the perfect distillation of the sublimity of a good wonder walk.

So what makes an ideal wonder walk? Go big. Look for high vistas or sweeping panoramas. If we can't go big, go small. Stay curious about all those little things we might breeze by on a usual walk, taking no detail for granted. Try an entirely different route to set ourselves up for novelty and an expectation violation. We want to attempt to counter habituation by challenging our heuristics. And, of course, prime ourselves that this will be a walk full of wonder, so we are open to finding those wow and whoa moments. To open her eyes to "unnoticed beauty," Rachel Carson used to ask herself the questions, "What if I had never seen this before? What if I knew I would never see it again?"

The majority of wonder experiences are positive. People find being open, curious, absorbed, and in awe to be generally enjoyable, so it's not surprising that wonder experiences can have positive health benefits. But sometimes, curiosity and awe can be brought about from crisis or tragedy. Part of what makes wonder so special is that even when its genesis is a negative experience, it appears that we can still often gain positive outcomes like stress reduction, compassion, and resilience. This is where wonder becomes more than just an emotion that has certain benefits; it becomes a way of life.

WONDER WRAP-UP

- Nature heals mentally and physically, and the evidence is mounting that it's not just the physical environment but the feeling of wonder it evokes that bestows the benefits.

- Time spent in nature, or even just viewing or smelling nature, lowers pain, speeds healing, lessens anxiety, and generally makes us healthier physically and psychologically. There are several different philosophies that have formed to explore this phenomenon, including forest medicine, biophilia, and Attention Restoration Theory. While some of these benefits are attributed to the biological and chemical features of nature, the emotional features of nature have strong linkages to wonder.

- In nature or otherwise, wonder also reduces cortisol, elevates vagal tone, and lowers proinflammatory cytokines, proteins associated with several inflammatory diseases such as heart disease and rheumatoid arthritis. These do not need to be big wow moments but can be small doses found in the quotidian.

- Wonder walks are an excellent way to practice priming ourselves for wonder. Studies show that people who took a wonder walk (i.e., primed for wonder) felt better and had bigger smiles than those who had regular walks. When planning an ideal wonder walk, look for new routes or novel elements. Also, notice big vistas or small details.

Part Three

Living in Wonder

13

Resilience

Union Correctional Institution (UCI), where most of Florida's 330-plus male death row inmates are held, sits just off State Road 16 on the outskirts of the town of Raiford, population 224. About 135 miles east of Tallahassee, it's all gangly pines punctuated like patchwork by overgrown fields and the occasional cow pasture. It's not interesting enough to be bleak. It just is. Like many prisons, UCI is not a particularly easy place to get to. Land and labor are cheaper in the sticks. But although the town is picayune, the Raiford prison complex is home to more than five thousand incarcerated souls across several facilities. Initially established in 1913 as a prison farm for inmates too infirm to be leased to private businesses as unpaid penal labor, it slowly metastasized into the meandering prison compound it is today.

I remember my first visit there. I was working as an investigator for a division of the Florida State Department of Justice that seeks to defend and exonerate people on death row via post-conviction relief, or what are known as collateral appeals.* Our team of attorneys and investigators helped these defendants

---

* After guilt and innocence has been established and direct appeals have been exhausted, collateral appeals are used to request that the court examine specific parts of the trial or sentencing, usually applying to a failure in the procedural elements of the case or trial.

either prove their innocence or build a case for a reduced sentence. This work had me visiting a fair number of prisons, prisoners, and their families all over the country, and it was the reason I found myself at UCI on that claggy spring day. The sound of a prison door closing behind you has a sort of sepulchral finality to it—one I never really got used to—and despite knowing I would get to leave later, it sent a chill up my spine that even the oppressive north Florida heat couldn't thaw.

The walk from receiving to the death row visitor rooms was a narrow, caged pathway, fenced in on both sides and along the top. A few inmates were on the other side of the fence tending to the grounds, but their blue shirts indicated they were general population, not the death row guys. The death row inmates are not allowed work detail. They are only let out of their cells for yard time (twice weekly), showers (five minutes, three times a week), and visits (mostly legal with the rare social visitor).

These men lived in a wonder vacuum. An almost total loss of autonomy. Social death as friends and family moved on. What is known as the "perfect boring situation" phenomenon—the triple insult of the monotony of the same environment, with the same people, doing the same activities every day. Their sense of openness bricked up, entombed like a living corpse. This soulless existence takes an incalculable toll on the human psyche. Studies show that people subjected to even a few days of solitary confinement exhibit a shift in their EEG activity to an "abnormal pattern characteristic of stupor and delirium."* And Florida's death row isn't even the most restrictive. Prisoners can still communicate with other inmates through the bars, and most have a view of

---

* This includes patients in intensive care units, those with injuries that make them bedridden or immobilized, and patients who lose sensory capabilities. This is also seen in isolated, confined, or extreme (ICE) environments like those experienced during space travel or on submarine missions.

some natural light. Many death row inmates in other states see no sunlight or sky, their only view a small window that, when not filled with the face of the guard doing welfare checks, looks out to a narrow interior hallway. Most have no physical contact, with the exception of guards attaching their shackles, for the entirety of their incarceration, some stretching into decades. They represent a growing number of people within the US, now at almost 5.3 million, who have limited access to the natural world. Be it in hospitals, nursing homes, or prisons, these people are denied the physical and emotional benefits of being in nature. If we include those in inner cities who are nature deprived, that number skyrockets to 100 million—28 million of them children.

What stuck with me about that first visit to UCI—most of them, really—were the conversations my clients and I had after the talk of their case was finished. Starved of stimuli, void of novelty, with nothing to explore, these guys were happy to talk about most things, but what so many of them wanted to chat about, at least with me, was the weather. The tone of the sky during a summer rainstorm. The kinds of trees I saw on the drive. One loved to reminisce about the winters in his native New York. (*Snow up to my neck! Have you ever seen snow like that?*) I recall one investigator who would sneak in the rare fall leaf or a surreptitious pressed wildflower. These precious artifacts of a world of wonder long left behind became treasured contraband. It has taken me years to wrap my head around that level of deprivation and the resilience it took to withstand it.

In 2012, a group of prisoners from Pelican Bay, California, sued over their treatment while held in Pelican Bay's Secure Housing Unit, or SHU (another name for solitary confinement). A psychologist testifying about the conditions said the environment perpetuated "chronic and overwhelming feelings of sadness, hopelessness, and depression," which caused inmates to "lose their grasp on their sanity." This psychologist noted that the prisoners' "capacity to function as remotely effective, feeling, social beings atrophies." Inmate Kevin McCarthy said of his time in Pelican Bay, "Solitary confinement is like being stranded at sea. Your whole existence revolves around the hope of being rescued. You have no sense of direction and no idea whether the end is in sight. As time passes, though, your hope weakens, and you start to think you will drown." Another inmate lamented, "I haven't seen the moon since 1998."

To support people like McCarthy, ecologist and academic Tierney Thys and her colleagues are testing an experimental sanctuary space called the Blue Room, where incarcerated people are able to connect with a simulacrum of nature. For one hour, five times a week, inmates at Snake River Correctional Institution in Ontario, Oregon, are taken to a room where they can choose to watch nothing or one of thirty-eight projected videos of nature scenes. The most popular videos are those devoid of people, with wide-open spaces like mountains and beaches, showing blue skies and sunlight, accompanied by nature sounds—"Places to daydream about" was how one participant described them. Inmates shared that their improved mood lasted for hours and, for some, even days, after the intervention. Thys explains that "even just digital depictions of gorgeous nature scenes displayed on the concrete walls of their confines had lasting effects on the mental status of the inmates." Thys believes the Blue Room experiment demonstrates that separate from the health benefits of being in nature, the wonder of nature can support resilience in even the most extreme of environments.

Nearly one-half of inmates reported feeling calmer and less irritable after watching the nature videos, but beyond improved mood, which we covered in the previous chapter, Thys observed a more profound response. One inmate described the experience as helping him "think clearer to know there is so much more beauty in this world then [sic] this prison." They could zoom out of their confinement and recall the vastness and variety of the world again. The men were more resilient, better able to withstand and recover from the intense stressors of prison life. Just reflecting on the Blue Room imagery later helped them manage their emotions more successfully, saying that the videos made their time inside more bearable.*

I recall one client of mine at UCI, a man I was pretty sure hadn't done the crime he was accused of. He'd been on death row already for almost twenty years, and there were times when he mused if it would be easier for him to just "volunteer" (a request made by some death row inmates to end their appeals and request an execution date). But more often than not, he was in incongruously good spirits and happy to have the visit, even if no progress had been made on his case. I would ask him what he did to pass his time (most guys didn't have access to TVs then). He read what he could get his hands on, and then he spent the rest of the time in his head. He said he imagined himself like a bird flying over the places he could remember from before his time inside. He described it almost like astral projection. A sort of transcendence. The reverie was so vividly constructed that he could just about convince himself he was actually there observing it, perhaps not corporally but metaphysically.

It wasn't nature, or even freedom that his avian self represented, so much as the expansive richness of his figmental flight. His world had shrunk to a six-by-nine cell, but his soul

---

* Despite initial resistance to the Blue Room experiment from the guards, including comments about the prisoners not being deserving of such "coddling," staff surveyed agreed that the inmates were calmer after viewing the videos, with the effects lasting for hours. Most striking was the reduction in violent behavior. Blue Room inmates had 26 percent fewer disciplinary reports and fewer incidents of cell extraction (forced removal of an inmate from their cell), which is a traumatic process for both inmate and guard.

needed space. It needed detail. It needed something to explore. It wasn't just the natural world that he was deprived of, but the vastness and variety requisite for wonder that so many of us take for granted. So he conjured these experiences, confessing to me that some days, the wonder of those trips was all that kept him from utter hopelessness and despair.

Lost at sea

Steve will never know for sure what his boat hit that night. He suspects a whale was what sunk *Napoleon Solo*, his twenty-one-foot sailing vessel, in the middle of the South China Sea. What he does know is that he had only a few minutes to abandon ship and take as much as he could get his hands on to help him survive what came next. Though Steven Callahan was a keen solo sailor and no stranger to the unyielding loneliness and impassive brutishness of the sea, he was not prepared for the severity of his plight—what became seventy-six days adrift at sea.

The tale seems like something out of old seafaring lore. Days stretching one into another without water and food. Moments of sheer terror and crisis when he was sure to perish. Yet somehow, Callahan managed to keep a sense of calm about him. Amid the chaos of uncertainty and powerlessness, he never became blind to the world of "natural wonders" he was flung into. He remained wonder-struck by his surroundings, and this became his life buoy. The notes Callahan kept in his log didn't refer just to survival logistics and tidal patterns but also to "acrobatic dorados," "ballets of fluffy white clouds," "whirling, flaming sunsets," and the "glistening galaxies flung out into deep black night." The dichotomy was undeniable, described by Callahan as "a view of heaven from a seat in hell." But it was more than just beauty that gave him the will to survive. Rather, he said that it was a "heartfelt realization of one's insignificance" that yielded "a calming sense of being completely connected to the greater whole." It wasn't the majesty that moved him so much as the meaning. His sense of wonder allowed him to pull back his hesitating foot from the precipice of panic and focus on staying alive.

John Leach is a senior research fellow in survival psychology from the University of Portsmouth, and he interviewed Callahan after the seafarer was rescued. Much of Leach's work focuses on those first few minutes or days following a crisis catalyst, studying how extreme crises or time in isolated, confined, or extreme (ICE) environments impact decision-making and survival. Leach's findings are applied to improve emergency response and training in practical ways such as abandon-ship routines. As he describes it, "It's the training that provides the means to survival, but it's the psychology that provides the *meaning* to survival." Leach has interviewed survivors of plane crashes and prison camps, shipwrecks and kidnappings. On the day I spoke with him, he had just interviewed a man captured in the Caucasus by guerrillas and kept chained in a hole for several months before being rescued.

Every story has a consistent trajectory, Leach shared, and survival tends to hinge on one decisive element. "When people start to lose meaning in life, and it doesn't have to be even in an extreme environment, their life sort of disappears quite quickly," he explained. "I get quite a lot of correspondence from oncologists. One of their concerns is that when they've got to give a diagnosis to a patient and say, 'Look, you've got cancer, you've got this terminal illness,' that it doesn't trigger this sudden loss of meaning in their lives. Because if the patient is triggered, they perish quite quickly."

Philosopher and Holocaust survivor Victor Frankl said that self-transcendence and meaning were his salvation during his time spent in a Nazi concentration camp, writing after that "striving to find meaning in one's life is the primary motivational force in man." But Leach is quick to point out that "meaning" doesn't have to be of the Frankl existential sort. It can be much more prosaic. "The disproportionately high number of survivors tend to be those in the medical profession. And, of course, this makes sense. Because if you're in a survival situation—POW camp, or a life-raft, or a shipwreck or something like that—whether you're a doctor, whether you're a nurse, whether you're a paramedic, you have that purpose given to you. Other people don't tend to have that sort of purpose. And they need to find it." Leach explains that pursuing purposeful goals and succeeding at them is a crucial component of resilience. This kind of purposeful goal-setting hinges on staying open and curious, as exploratory behavior feeds the day-to-day drive required to set and achieve goals. Additionally, engaging in intrinsically motivating pursuits helps us manage emotional trauma and maintain lucidity in decision-making.

One of the most extreme ICE environments would unquestionably be space, and NASA has been studying how to mitigate the effects of that extreme environment on astronauts. As the urban legend goes, on December 28, 1973, astronauts from the *Skylab* 4 mission went on strike for about ninety minutes because their work schedule was so packed that their stress levels had become untenable. What did they want? One hour every day to look out the window back at Earth in order to meet "their needs to reflect, to observe, to find their place amid these baffling, fascinating, unprecedented experiences." There are various versions of this story that refute the degree to which the astronauts actually "downed tools." Still, what is agreed about that mission is that the crew was overworked, they complained, and a healthy dose of Overview Effect–induced awe by way of window-viewing time was one of the compromises.

Future missions recognized this need for a dose of wonder

and began providing astronauts with cameras as well. Initially available exclusively for research purposes, cameras can now be used by astronauts during their personal time. They've proven to be an effective means of stress management during long space flights, not to mention resulting in almost 200,000 awe-inspiring pictures of Earth from space.

These are extreme examples, but for our castaway Steve Callahan, "there is no distinct dividing line between 'normal' life and survival. It's largely a matter of amplitude and ultimate risk. Downs are incredibly deep, but ups are awesomely high." Callahan shared with me that in the midst of this harrowing cycle of ups and downs, holding the world in wonder provided him with a sense of enduring resilience. He writes at length in his best-selling book, *Adrift*, about how his ceaseless curiosity, deep transcendent absorption, and resulting awe granted him the alacrity to survive. "The entire focus of 'successful' survivors is to transcend the immediate threat. One only triumphs when fully present." And that sense of wonder in a time of crisis can be so mighty and moving, Callahan explained, that sometimes crisis survivors wish they could return to the time when their life had such sparkling clarity and meaning. "Virtually every survivor to whom I have spoken finds things of sublime value in their experiences that we actually miss, from personal knowledge to the spiritual."

As a result of these transcendent experiences at sea, Callahan's religious views have changed, too. Today, he defines his faith as "scientific mysticism," sharing, "I, and many others, found the divine in many ways. As they say, there are no atheists in foxholes. I think that is an oversimplification, but you get the point. Every experience can be a gift."

Though we've been looking in this chapter at wonder as it relates to extreme crises and environments, the majority of reported awe experiences are positive, with researchers estimating only 20 to 30 percent of reported awe events to involve some sort of threat. But even within those threat-based awe experiences, 69 percent of this group experienced events that contained what researchers called "silver linings." Threat-based awe often triggers a reduced sense of personal control, whereas the silver lining effect may contribute a modicum of personal control, which grants greater resilience.

For instance, researchers studying the impacts of COVID-19 found that while the pandemic elicited feelings of threat-based awe, there were silver linings seen in the collective response of health care workers and the community as a whole. The feelings of awe prompted by the vastness and need for accommodation of the public health emergency provoked a sense of small-self that led to people adopting what's known as *problem-focused coping*. Problem-focused coping strategies involve people taking direct action to manage stressful events, demonstrated in this case by an increase in handwashing and mask-wearing. Researchers posited that this action was driven by awe's social bonding and collectivist nature. Like Callahan's gift of experience, these "silver lining" acts of altruism, self-sacrifice, and resilience amid tragedy, despite stemming from negative experiences, still offer some potential for post-traumatic growth.

Post-traumatic stress disorder and post-traumatic growth

Craig Anderson, a postdoctoral researcher and fellow at the University of California, Berkeley, who was part of Jennifer Stellar's team, wanted to further develop Stellar's proinflammatory cytokines research. Specifically, he wanted to understand the impact of wonder on post-traumatic stress disorder (PTSD). Rather than do the research in a lab, he teamed up with the Sierra Club and took his research to the field—or to the rapids, to be precise. For his study, Anderson invited seventy-two military veterans and fifty-two inner-city youth on a series of white-water rafting trips along the South Fork of California's American River and Utah's Green River to study the participants' reactions to the awe-inspiring experience.

First associated with the "shell-shock" of veterans returning from combat, as many as 35 percent of US veterans have PTSD, compared to about 7 percent of the average American population. But it can occur from experiencing any number of traumatic life events and can be triggered by a seemingly banal experience—a smell, a sound—leading to severe nightmares, flashbacks, anxiety, and panic attacks. Chronically difficult to treat, it can be a lifelong, sometimes debilitating condition, with some vets from the Vietnam War still reporting PTSD symptoms as many as fifty years later.

Anderson wanted to study if awe, beyond other positive emotions, would improve well-being, reduce stress, or decrease PTSD symptoms. More important, he hoped to illustrate that the wonder effects of nature contribute to well-being outcomes such as resilience and that these effects can be found not only in extreme environments like white-water rafting, but in day-to-day life, too. To measure the effects of the experience, researchers tested participants' stress hormone levels before and after, as well as had them complete well-being surveys and keep journals about their experiences. They also affixed GoPro cameras to the front of the rafts to capture the participants' facial expressions throughout the excursion.

Participants experienced, among other benefits, a 21 percent drop in overall stress levels and a 29 percent reduction in PTSD symptoms as a result of their white-water raft experience. Those resiliency effects lasted for a week and, even more surprising, every participant on the boat experienced these benefits. "We found that people who shared the same raft expressed similar emotions and hormone profiles," Anderson explained, and he believes this means that wonder is contagious. The team also found "it was curiosity that most strongly aroused [the participants'] desire to step outside their comfort zone and learn more about the world around them, especially for those accustomed to acting tough around their peers." Anderson went on to explain that for the group of inner-city kids in particular, "If you're in a rough neighborhood, it doesn't pay to be open. You have to keep up a facade because if someone challenges you, you have to fight them. Otherwise, you're a pushover." From hardened vets to at-risk children, the rafting experience brought them out of their self-imposed shells and made them more open, curious, and awe-filled—more wonderprone.

To compare "riding the rapids" wonder to day-to-day wonder, Anderson and his team also had a separate group of participants complete journals and take daily and longitudinal surveys about their quotidian awe experiences. Surprisingly, the day-to-day participants reported the same benefits as the rafters. The more nature they experienced, the more wonder. The more wonder, the better their emotional regulation on the day and over time. "It's the active ingredient that explains why being in nature is good for us," shared Anderson.

As I consider PTSD, an incredibly complex condition that exhibits itself both physically and mentally, it almost feels like a type of *awe-interrupted in extremis*. Sufferers experience the intensity of a vast moment, but rather than achieving accommodation, the experience tips into terror, and the terrifying memories are encoded in a way that becomes triggering in the future. When I run this idea past Lani Shiota, she agrees. "Your instinct is actually dead-on." Although PTSD "cranks up your physical arousal in the exact opposite way of what awe does," the amygdala and the hippocampus are deeply interconnected. The mental triggers in someone with PTSD cascade to physical triggers like an increase in the stress hormone cortisol; the increase in cortisol signals the inflammatory system, releasing proinflammatory cytokines. "So, PTSD, if you think about it, is an overload response. Awe is helping you put that aside, and [it] creates this brief moment of malleability in our understanding of the world." That malleability allows the person with PTSD to carve out new neural pathways that, rather than resulting in panic, lead to a more resilient emotional state where they can process the emotions.

Not every trauma results in PTSD. Some people transition from a traumatic crisis into a period of post-traumatic growth, a phenomenon in which the trauma serves to prompt healing, connectedness, and emotional strength. But why do some people develop PTSD after a traumatic event, whereas others experience post-traumatic growth? The answer may lie in the hippocampus. As you recall, the hippocampus plays a significant role in memory collection and recollection. In studies of twins in which one twin experienced trauma resulting in PTSD and the other did not, brain scans showed a smaller hippocampus in both people. While it was previously thought that PTSD might shrink the hippocampus, researchers from California now believe it might be the smaller hippocampus pre-trauma that makes individuals more susceptible to PTSD. Ongoing research now appears to point to a sizable hippocampal role in emotional resilience, meaning resilience is likely significantly predisposed by genetics and heredity.

Curiosity as a route to resilience

Captain Alia Bojilova was an army psychologist and UN military observer working for the New Zealand Defense Force's Special Air Services and Counter-Terrorist Tactics Group, based in the Golan Heights, Syria. While serving in the area in 2013, she and two colleagues were taken hostage at gunpoint by thirty-eight members of the Syrian Free Army. "We were taken into the hot zone where we knew our fate was very much sealed. Or they ensured that we felt that way about it." Bojilova managed to use her psychology background to talk her way into a release. After first determining that she wasn't being taken to trade for some specific resource like weapons or another prisoner, she began asking questions. Lots of them.

Rather than seeing their captors as monsters with only negative intent, Bojilova tried to understand what might drive such a dangerous and monumental decision like taking a team of UN representatives captive. "Chopping our heads off didn't appear the smartest way of achieving a positive intent so we needed to find a way to understand what it is that they were wanting." Bojilova tried to get to know them as people—their fears, their hopes, their desires. "Along the way, what we realized is that little cracks were beginning to present on the wall that was keeping us between where we were and our safety. And it dawns on me that if you stare at a surface long enough, you begin to notice these cracks." Bojilova believed that if she kept observing and stayed curious, she could keep fear at bay, and a solution would present itself. The turning point for their captivity was when a lead captor asked for a translation dictionary and pointed to the word humility. It became clear to them that Bojilova's curiosity wasn't self-focused, but rather empathetic, and that humility moved her captors. Bojilova's genuine curiosity in her captors'

plight revealed footholds of humanity the captives could leverage for their release. Bojilova believes that in "finding a way to
have a conversation with your adversary and maintain that unbridled curiosity," she was able to create a meaningful, and life-
saving, connection.

"I might stand there in front of something that seems seemingly insurmountable and overwhelming. But if I look at it from
a different perspective and from a different angle, perhaps I can
find an opportunity in this. So this is the moment in which my
study of resilience became very focused on the connection between resilience and curiosity." Bojilova is now a world-renowned
expert in resilience and studies curiosity as a vehicle for resilience-
building. She believes that with curiosity, we "begin to ask more
questions, wonder more, create more space . . . to create the conditions within which we can nurture mutual reliance with others
through intimacy and lower degrees of self-interest."

Echoing Anderson's rafting findings, researcher Todd Kashdan believes curiosity could be a pivotal contributor to resilience
and post-traumatic growth. "Not everyone is prepared to benefit from opportunities for personal growth, but for the majority who are, curiosity is proposed to be a primary facilitator,"
explains Kashdan. He theorizes that curiosity promotes growth
and resilience by helping us process the triggering stimuli of
traumatic events more effectively. "Facilitating curiosity can
build the self-regulatory resources to withstand the avoidance
and disengagement that tends to occur following episodes of extreme anxiety and depression [and might serve as] a backdoor
route to approaching, processing, and making meaning of difficult emotional material."

Leach has also observed the importance of cognitive flexibility in resilience. "People don't make decisions under immediate
threat. Because, as the prefrontal cortex is a late development in

our evolution, it's very slow. . . . And because of that, the prefrontal cortex is effectively taken off-line. It's starved of resources,
which means that the sort of things that go into cognitive flexibility, which is prefrontal cortex function, are not there during
that moment. It comes back later when your immediate brain
starts to come back into action. But it can take time." Tapping
into cognitive flexibility is not easy under intense stress, but
keeping an open, curious mindset helps us find equilibrium.

Curiosity promotes resilience, but what of the other elements of wonder? Research shows that people who are higher
in openness enjoy better stress regulation and recovery, and
Scott Barry Kaufman, who also studies post-traumatic growth,
suspects "that an 'awe junkie' would be quicker to reframe a bad
situation in a way that gives them a sense of wonder and motivation to transcend the situation." Whereas horror makes us recoil,
the wonder cycle makes us willing and able to step forward.

From openness to awe, every stage of wonder supports a more
resilient psyche. For Steven Callahan, even terrible wonder
brought about meaningful growth, humbling in its profundity.
"There is a magnificent intensity in life that comes when we are
not in control but are only reacting, living, surviving. . . . For
me, to go to sea is to get a glimpse of the face of God. At sea I am
reminded of my insignificance—of all men's insignificance. It
is a wonderful feeling to be so humbled." Callahan will declare
his time lost at sea as horrific, but he cannot deny the wonder of
the experience and the way wonder kept him emotionally afloat
and granted him the resilience to survive. "The heartfelt realization of one's insignificance yields a calming sense of being
completely connected to the greater whole. As a tiny part of the
world and humanity, I now feel more at peace and much larger
than I ever felt as a man alone."

WONDER WRAP-UP

- More than just a simple ameliorator, every element of the wonder cycle, from openness to awe, supports a more resilient psyche in even some of the most extreme and terrible situations. This attribute of wonder means we can reap some benefits even in challenging times.

- From prison to space, wonder even promotes emotional regulation in what are known as isolated, confined, or extreme (ICE) environments.

- An absence of wonder, which can occur from a dearth of any of the wonder cycle elements, creates emotional and physical distress. Other than the lack of stimuli and human connection, one of the causes of this distress is a loss of meaning-making, as humans need meaning to metabolize our experiences and find life-sustaining purpose.

- Post-traumatic stress disorder (PTSD) is an often debilitating condition brought about by trauma. Wonder decreased the symptoms of PTSD by almost 30 percent in one groundbreaking study.

- Not everyone experiences PTSD after trauma. Some people experience post-traumatic growth (PTG), the positive processing of trauma characterized by increased emotional strength and resilience. The mental malleability triggered by wonder allows for the redevelopment of less reactive emotional schema.

14

Religion

I am what is referred to (with kind jest) as a second-generation recovering Catholic. My parents were raised by old-school nuns in Catholic schools and have the corn kernel–dented knees to prove it. On the one hand, they rejected Catholicism for its dogma, often cruel discipline, and tragic failures to its most vulnerable. On the other, they recognized and honored the importance of ritual, deep gratitude, and reflection, something the Catholic Church offers. So, in the end, my mom decided to seek out ritual and reverence in another denomination and left Catholicism for a more ecumenical congregation. My dad, however, lives in New Orleans, a community long girded by the conventions of Catholicism, and he finds comfort and value in the communion of that fellowship. He is comfortable taking what resonates with him and leaving the rest. Both paths work for their spiritual stewardship, so good for them.

As a child, I was expected to go to church every Sunday. When I was old enough to drive, my mother told me I didn't need to attend church with her anymore, but I had to go somewhere to shift my focus off being a stroppy teenager and instead practice reverence once a week. That meant I hopped around quite a bit, sampling what different friends had on offer—Jewish synagogues,

AME churches, Hindu temples. And after that experience, my approach to organized religion is now summed up best by the aphorism "religion is a multicolored lantern through which shines one light." (Perhaps the late Archbishop Desmond Tutu said it better when he remarked, "God is not a Christian. God accepts as pleasing those who live by the best lights available to them that they can discern.") So, like 27 percent (and growing) of the world's population, I consider myself spiritual but not religious. And while research has shown those with a belief in God experience wonder more frequently than the average person, the data also suggest that religion is not a requisite mechanism.

In a 2014 Pew Research Center study looking at the connection between religion and wonder, almost half of Americans surveyed reported feeling a deep sense of wonder about the universe once a week or more, and almost three-quarters of those who were wonderprone also had a greater sense of spiritual peace and well-being. Both prayer and meditation increased their sense of wonder, but it was those religious adherents who took their scripture less literally who were more wonderprone. This finding mirrors Jim Garrison's experience—rigid ideologies do not make room for wonder. Ritual, gratitude, and reverence are good habits to practice, however one may come to them—*practice* being the operative word. These habits nurture wonder and sit at the heart of the symbiosis between wonder and religion, but what denomination these wonder-seekers follow is inconsequential. Wonder responds to the light, not the color it shines through.

The structure of religious and social movements

It would be impossible to explore every religion's relationship to wonder, but we can gain insight by looking at the similar wonder-filled patterns shared by all faiths. While some may bristle at the idea of a universal structure to religion, it's important to note this isn't suggesting a "universal religion" in which all distinctive features of a singular faith are lost. On the contrary, it is only by finding the common threads within and throughout different religions that we can effectively identify, express, and highlight the distinctive characteristics of each singular faith.

The first of these universalities is that religion creates a framework for meaning-making. It provides a shared compass of beliefs through which to chart the human experience. Abraham Joshua Heschel, a Jewish theologian and philosopher, said of religious wonder, "[It] is more than an emotion; it is a way of understanding." Religion creates a salient frame for the wonder experience to find its home, an idea first put forward by William James in his book *The Varieties of Religious Experience*. What James meant is that religion can exist without wonder, and in fact religion as dogma or as a system of strictures is not aligned with wonder. And wonder can exist outside a religious context, as the secular world does not deny or eschew wonder. But the "religious experience" is a place where wonder and religion coalesce. So when a religious person has a wonder experience, that wonder experience will often find its meaning and context—its salience—within the framework of their religious practice.

As cultural anthropologist R. R. Marett observed, "Religion is the domain par excellence that offers standardized procedures to generate in religious practitioners—over and over again—a sense of wonder." Ritual, music, mystery, narrative storytelling, nostalgia, incense, prayer, chanting, candlelight all intermingle to conjure the magic of wonder.

A Christmas tradition in my home when I was very young was to attend midnight mass. To keep us kids happy, squirm-free, and awake until the end of mass we would be bribed—um,

I mean incentivized—by being allowed to open one gift early, but truth be told, I enjoyed the pomp and ceremony. Midnight mass always meant a trip to the big church, the Basilica of the Sacred Heart of Jesus, in downtown Atlanta. A very different experience from our humble little rural congregation, where Father Flaherty was often spotted in a flannel shirt and overalls when not donning his clerical collar. Sacred Heart is a strikingly imposing structure built in the late 1800s whose rust-hued stone seemed to almost glow, even at night, like a red sky at sunset. Inside, creams, yellows, and gold leaf reflected the light of candles and hanging lanterns. And despite the darkness outside, the stained-glass windows lining the walls still threw shards of color into the space, illuminated by the streetlights lining Peachtree Street. Those nights were nothing short of mystical. The heady combination of the swinging censers, the sounds of the choir drifting down from their hidden perch behind us in the nave. The huge, vaulted ceilings bouncing bombastic organ music through the space. The priest in vestments of sparkling gold thread telling the story of an arduous journey, a magical star, and a baby sent to save us. This could apply to so many holy days of any religion. It is by design, regardless of the specific doctrine. These "standardized procedures" are intended to consistently and reliably evoke wonder-filled transcendence in the observer. Social movements do the same with marches, chants, and vigils.

At their core, all movements, secular or religious, follow a similar framework: *ideal, need, deliverer.* The *ideal* serves as both the source of meaning and the wonder-filled goal of the follower. The *need* is a flaw or problem that separates the follower from the ideal. While this flaw or problem can be seen as a negative defect, it can also become a sinew of camaraderie between followers, which fuels the ideal. The *deliverer* possesses the rarefied power to fulfill the need and deliver the follower from their flawed state toward union and resolution with the ideal. Religious or not, people higher in cognitive flexibility and openness are more likely to experience an event of wonder. But when there is a preexisting belief in the awe of God, the wonder event will find a home in the salience framework of religion, thus reinforcing the religious context, beliefs, and their connectedness to the faith community. This same ideal, need, deliverer model can also be applied to many social movements.

The second common thread shared by all religions is that the origin story is frequently tinged with loss, fear, or mystery, elements that commonly overlap with wonder and awe experiences. Consider the fear and mystery in Arunja's story with Krishna. Or Jesus rising from the dead to save mankind, proving his identity to his friends by letting them stick their fingers in his wounds. There is the Taoist origin story, in which the Earth was a giant cosmic egg from which the god P'an Ku grew. After 18,000 years, P'an Ku died, collapsing and shattering to pieces. His blood formed the rivers, his flesh the earth, his breath the winds; his eyes became the sun and the moon, and his teeth the rocks; last, the insects living on his body became the human race. Zeus instructed his son Prometheus to create man, but when Prometheus gave humans the gift of fire, intended only for the gods, he was tortured for all of eternity. These are not particularly cheery tales, but rather much darker, mysterious beginnings. While social movements are not usually quite so gruesome, they are still often inspired by some sense of loss, such as the Triangle Shirtwaist Factory fire in 1911, one of the deadliest industrial accidents in US history and the catalyst for the occupational safety movement in America.

Indeed, most philosophers examining wonder over the centuries have ascribed some aspect of mystery to the wonder taxonomy. For instance, Rabbi Heschel said that religious awe "is the sense of wonder and humility inspired by the sublime or felt in the presence of mystery." In his seminal study of religion, *The Idea of the Holy*, Rudolf Otto introduced the concept of the numinous, which he defined as the *mysterium tremendum*—the *mysterium* being the ambiguity and transcendence of the experience; the *tremendum* evoking the fear, trepidation, gravitas, and awe of religious wonder.

Another universality within religions is the way in which they can have an enduring and positive impact on their practitioners. For example, feeling a sense of wonder about God is associated with greater long-term life satisfaction. And research shows that people who've experienced spiritual transformation—even if they frequently experience negative emotions like sadness, worry, or guilt—reported long-term positive shifts in their outlook and sense of purpose. It's worth noting that average "churchgoing" in and of itself won't lead to the same type of enduring effects that people who've had a numinous experience may enjoy. Those benefits, and many associated "godly" prosocial behaviors, quickly ebb in the once-weekly churchgoer who does not engage in religious activities throughout the rest of the week. (For example, the average churchgoer was found to be more charitable than non-churchgoers on Sunday, but not on weekdays. They also watched less porn—but again, only on Sundays.)

The way in which religions leverage and enhance social cohesion is yet another universal element. Common religious practices include group prayer, live musical performances, and movement-focused worship, like the followers of faiths like Sufism, whose devotees known as the whirling dervishes chant, twirl, and dance in unison to commune with God. Ritual, call-and-response, and song all serve to synchronize, unite, and power a following. Wonder's origins as a collective engagement mechanism are supported by research that shows highly religious people, after watching awe-eliciting videos, felt an increase in their sense of oneness with others.

Finally, all religions and social movements leverage charisma, be it of the idea itself or the orator of the idea, as a means of authority and as the fuel for change. The deliverer is the holder of the charisma, and the followers are the receivers, with this symbiosis constituting a primary condition of socially derived wonder.

Social movements act as a type of what sociologist Robert Bellah called our civil religion. Civil religions don't require deities (although they may include them), but they do take steps to inspire widespread passion and commitment to the same belief system. Bellah saw civil religions—anything from cults to jingoism ("Americanism" being Bellah's example) to even sports teams—as also fitting into the tripartite structure of ideal, need, deliverer. When Bellah published this theory in the late 1960s, churchgoing, which had been relatively stable throughout the early and mid-1900s (hovering at around 70 percent), was just beginning its decades-long decline. Some believe the Apollo missions of the 1960s might have contributed to that decline. Seeing Earth from space led to a more personal sense of reverence, gratitude, and perspective, making the church and formalized religion less relatable.*

The dark side of wonder

His followers wouldn't have heard the gunshots from the airstrip, so they couldn't yet know that the deaths of five people, one of them a congressman, would change their fates that afternoon. But they could tell that Jim was different at the compound.

---

* Environmentalism could be viewed as a type of civil religion inspired in part by the moon landing.

Edgier. More intense than usual. So, when he announced over the loudspeaker that it was time for their "White Night"—aka their revolutionary deaths—everyone knew this wasn't a test like last time. Today was to be their last day on earth.

The children drank first. The sickly sweet, powdered fruit drink masked the bitterness of the cyanide enough, so they swallowed. The sedatives mixed in for good measure ensured they would go peacefully—Jim was clever that way, to have the little ones go first. The parents would be hungry for the heavenly release awaiting them once their babies were gone. Many prayed. Some cried. None really resisted, only a handful hid, and in the end, in less than an hour, Jim Jones led 909 people to their deaths. It was the largest loss of American civilian life by a deliberate act until the terrorist attacks of September 11th. All in service of his command. What cruel mesmer overtook those victims? Why did they drink the Kool-Aid? Why does anyone ever?

How can an emotion like wonder, which increases our epistemological humility, increases prosocial emotions, and lowers our tendency toward dogmatism, play a role in perpetuating a cult? One reason is that the cognitive flexibility leveraged and enhanced by wonder fosters ambivalence to previously held beliefs. This ambivalence creates fertile ground for new ideas to flourish, even if those new ideas are not always great ones. Combine that with the fuel of charisma and the increased social cohesion wonder builds, and it's easy to see how wonder can create a movement, even if it moves people toward a negative ideal. Lani Shiota explains this dynamic, sharing, "If what awe does is create a moment of malleability, that malleability is not going to go in any particular direction. Cult leaders use awe to reshape minds routinely. It's all about what you present afterward."

Wonder has the power to influence, shift perspectives, and drive change, and while this power can have positive consequences, there exists the potential for it to be leveraged in negative ways. Jonestown is a painful example of how the charisma of wonder can be wielded as a weapon.*

Charisma as a vehicle for wonder

Charisma was initially a religious, or at least a supernatural, concept—the term originated in Greece, meaning "gift of grace." Historically, it was seen as just that. Great philosophers, teachers, and prophets had charisma, granted by the Almighty, and it was the direct and active connection between God and human that bestowed a charisma compelling to followers. Rooted in what Aristotle called the *ethos, pathos,* and *logos* (values, passion, and arguments) of a charismatic leader, this phenomenon was labeled "divine magnetism" by twentieth-century British evangelical author Arthur Wallis. Charisma was used in this magnetic sense in the first century by the apostle Paul, who said charisma was a supernatural "gift" spiritually bestowed by God as a means of building the Christian faith. Though Paul's view of the religious charismatic was discouraged by later church authorities and was eventually sidelined for a more subdued and less fervent type of worship, the Pauline interpretation did not die out. In fact, the Pentecostal movement, which was established in the United States in 1906, represented the culmination

---

* While many will argue Jonestown was murder and not suicide—undoubtedly easy to do when more than three hundred of the victims were children—one cannot deny the autonomy of those who willingly followed Jones's instruction to die. Cults are obviously more complex than a group of people blindly following charismatic leaders. They involve various levels of dehumanization, isolation, and often abuse. The term *brainwashing,* however, is generally rejected by cult experts, as they feel it does not adequately represent the self-determination of many cult members. Author Haruki Murakami described cult members as having "deposited all their precious personal holdings of selfhood" in the "spiritual bank" of the leader. (Murakami, Haruki, Alfred Birnbaum, and Philip Gabriel. 2013. *Underground: The Tokyo Gas Attack and the Japanese Psyche.* London: Vintage.)

of several evangelical movements spawned during the nine-teenth century, and it reignited belief in the individual Christian charismatic, divinely bestowed with the powers of healing and prophecy, brought forth through religious ecstasy. The 1960s saw a further revival in the charismatic renewal movement, sparked in part by evangelicals like Billy Graham and his crusades, align-ing with the emergence of true charismatic leaders like Martin Luther King Jr. and "false prophets" like Jim Jones.

It was also around this time that the work of sociologist Max Weber became popularized in leadership vernacular. In his fifteen-hundred-page tome, *Wirtschaft und Gesellschaft*, published posthumously in 1922 and translated into the English *Economy and Society* in 1968, Weber pulled a relatively obscure religious idea into the contemporary political and management lexicon. His book introduced a modern secular charisma, defined as a form of societal authority and control, and since then, it has taken on far greater scope and meaning. He described charisma as a divine gift "of the body and spirit not accessible to every-body," and charismatic leaders as being "endowed with super-natural, superhuman, or at least specifically exceptional powers or qualities." By Weber's assessment, charismatic leaders emerge during times of crisis, when the need for change is greatest, and they assume and maintain this power by offering "a big prom-ise." But given that they seemingly possess otherworldly powers bestowed on them by supernatural forces, if the leader can't de-liver on that promise, their charisma burnish fades, and with it, their hold on power.

Yale sociology professor Iván Szelényi emphasizes the dy-namic of reciprocity as central to the charismatic's influence. "[Weber] said the person is *considered* to be extraordinary and treated as endowed with superhuman or exemplary features. So— and what I think is extremely important to see—Weber does not tell us that this individual is *actually* extraordinary, that it is *actually* superhuman. In a way, it is in the eye of the beholder. It is among the followers who attribute these qualities to somebody."

The charismatic leader's authority depends on what Weber called *Vergemeinschaftung,* or "the making of a community of believers." This is why we see charismatic leaders in many authoritarian regimes go to extreme lengths to pursue "the big promise" (or "the big fallacy") just to keep their community of believers believing, often at the expense of the life and liberty of those who oppose them. "The big promise" also helps us understand the authoritarian leader's need to appear superhuman— like recovering miraculously from a deadly disease, exhibiting feats of strength, or using endless superlatives when describing themselves —when, to non-followers, those displays seem preening and hollow. "In a way, charismatic leaders are being made by the followers," explains Professor Szelényi. "To persuade you that you have to have a different kind of value system."*

When we revisit the elements of wonder, we can see how they align with charisma, religion, and social movements. There is an openness to new ideas, a curiosity for learning, and a dissolution of the ego, in which the individual feels small in the presence of the charismatic experience. That diminution of the self drives greater interpersonal connectivity, and in turn, communal sharing enhances the intensity of the experience. Followers then undergo a shift in their value system schema and freely donate money and time toward the fulfillment of an ideal. Both religious and social movements facilitate meaning-making, and

---

* From an evolutionary point of view, we can see the basis for the development of charismatic wonder and why it is an effective tool for moving people today. Emotions in words facilitate idea transfer. Charisma acts as a cue for humans to quickly identify the strong leader, and the resulting wonder spurs collectivist cohesion in pursuit of a shared goal. This shared "symbol of moral unity" creates a collective energy that can be a powerful change catalyst.

many followers report a sense of "being moved" or even transcendence when in the presence of a charismatic.

Today, rather than charisma being built by revelation and miracles, it's often endowed by virtue of media attention and scarcely more. Our need for cognitive closure is at play here, as it impacts the way we seek information and how tightly we hold on to that information when we find it. "Radicalisation occurs when this need for certainty is met by a narrative that provides certainty and is supported and validated by the network, which then creates a social movement," explains NFCC expert Arie Kruglanski. "If it is just an individual then he or she can change, but once it is part of a social movement then the individual becomes part of that larger shared reality, and it turns into a culture that gets validated and supported."

Once that occurs, any manner of conspiracy theories and "fake news" can be fed into a movement, and critical thinking is hindered, so it's all the more imperative not to conflate wonder-inducing self-transcendent charisma with celebrity or "influencer" status. They are not the same. Philosopher and theologian Philip Quinn wrote, "One is struck with awe in an encounter with what one takes to be a transcendent source of salvation or liberation, and one subsequently works to develop character traits, qualities of will and heart, that will attach one to what one believes to be a transcendent source of salvation or liberation." I do hope we aren't looking to influencers or reality stars to be our transcendent source of liberation, because, sister, it ain't there.

The uneasy alliance between science and religion

Today there seems to be a tug-of-war between science and religion as ideologies. Historically, however, religious and scientific leaders as individuals have seen the two as comfortable bedfellows, with wonder an evocative thread linking them. Immediately following the moon landing, astronaut Buzz Aldrin, an elder at Webster Presbyterian Church in Houston, asked for a moment of silence to take the Holy Communion he'd brought with him to space. "In the radio blackout, I opened the little plastic packages which contained the bread and the wine. I poured the wine into the chalice our church had given me. In the one-sixth gravity of the moon, the wine slowly curled and gracefully came up the side of the cup. Then I read the Scripture." Aldrin saw this moment of shared wonder as the ideal messenger to the world that science and religion can and should coexist. "Eagle's metal body creaked. I ate the tiny Host and swallowed the wine. I gave thanks for the intelligence and spirit that had brought two young pilots to the Sea of Tranquility. It was interesting for me to think: the very first liquid ever poured on the moon, and the very first food eaten there, were the communion elements."

Legendary theoretical physicist Albert Einstein, a devout follower of both God and wonder, said that his sense of God *was* his sense of wonder about the universe. "The most beautiful emotion we can experience is the mysterious. It is the fundamental emotion that stands at the cradle of all true art and science. He to whom this emotion is a stranger, who can no longer wonder and stand rapt in awe, is as good as dead, a snuffed-out candle." As he explained, wonder and religiosity intersect in the profound mystery of the unknown. "To sense that behind anything that can be experienced, there is something that our minds cannot grasp, whose beauty and sublimity reaches us only indirectly; this is religiousness. In this sense, and in this sense only, I am a devoutly religious man."

Einstein didn't mean to suggest that his wonder at the universe replaced God. On the contrary, like Galileo, Newton, and

Darwin, Einstein saw science as the ultimate manifestation of God's handiwork. Even Charles Darwin was deeply religious, despite his theory of evolution being seen by some as inconsistent with Christian teaching. In *The Voyage of the Beagle*, he wrote, "No one can stand in these solitudes unmoved and not feel that there is more in man than the mere breath of his body." Astrophysicist Carl Sagan echoed Darwin's sentiment, saying, "the notion that science and spirituality are somehow mutually exclusive does a disservice to both."*

Just as many scientists embrace religion, many religious leaders also embrace science. His Holiness the Dalai Lama, a man who has devoted his life to the leadership of the Buddhist faith since the age of fifteen, remains a fervent follower of science. "I have often said that if science proves facts that conflict with Buddhist understanding, Buddhism must change accordingly. We should always adopt a view that accords with the facts. If upon investigation we find that there is reason and proof for a point, then we should accept it." His perception of the world is enriched by an intermingling of faith, science, and mystery.

While I was writing this chapter, a friend reminded me of this quote by French philosopher Blaise Pascal: "There is a God-shaped

---

* There are few modern pieces of literature that better describe this tug-of-war than Sagan's book and the subsequent film *Contact*, a story of an agnostic scientist named Ellie, whose beliefs are challenged by a trip through a wormhole and a pastor she befriends. Ellie explains her belief that wonder is the common theme between science and religion, but that science is a more effective deliverer of that message. "Look, we all have a thirst for wonder. It's a deeply human quality. Science and religion are both bound up with it. What I'm saying is, you don't have to make stories up, you don't have to exaggerate. There's wonder and awe enough in the real world. Nature's a lot better at inventing wonders than we are." But during a transcendent moment, Ellie is awestruck by the ineffability of the experience and begins her journey of appreciating faith's role in the world, exclaiming, "No words to describe it. Poetry! They should have sent a poet." (Zemeckis, Robert, director. 1997. *Contact*. Warner Bros, 2 hrs., 30 mins.)

vacuum in the heart of every person, and it can never be filled by any created thing." The decline of formal religion has left many with a God-shaped hole in their lives. The universality of wonder means it can either become a secular instrument to fill that God-shaped hole or knit itself into and around a person's established religious practice, thereby enriching it.

WONDER WRAP-UP

- Religion is replete with wonder, as is potentially any movement that shares a widespread passion and commitment to a shared belief system (sometimes referred to as a civil religion).

- There is no particular religion that is more wonderprone than another. (Wonder responds to the light, not the color.) Rather, spiritual people in general are more wonderprone, but only if they are not too literal in their ideology, as mental rigidity in the form of NFCC is oppositional to wonder. Remember—rigid ideologies do not make room for wonder.

- Religious wonder's transformative power can also be used for negative purposes, such as in cults or jingoism.

- Charisma was a concept developed by the Greeks. A known wonderbringer, charisma was the direct and active connection between God and humans that bestowed the recipient with magnetism. The concept was made religious by Saint Paul and later the Pentecostal movement, then secularized by Max Weber.

- Charismatics gain their power from their followers, and in turn, followers gain their sense of belonging and purpose from their charismatic leader. This reciprocity is a key characteristic of charismatic wonder.

- As a wonderbringer, charisma provokes a transcendent sense of small-self, which builds a stronger shared identity and collective engagement.

- Religious and social movements share a similar construction across several features. They follow a *deliver, need, ideal* model that provides a sense of purpose, impetus, and drive to the community and its mission. They have compelling origin stories that engage followers through wondrous mystery. They also have the power to create enduring positive impact, and use charisma to fuel a shared cohesive community.

- Science and religion have not always coexisted comfortably. Although wonder is a scientific concept, it can also be woven into religion or remain secular.

15

Slow Thought

When journalist Carlo Petrini gathered his friends in a wine cellar in central Rome, he certainly didn't think he would become the figurehead of a movement spanning 122 countries. Protesting the arrival of a McDonald's in Rome's Piazza di Spagna, Petrini felt compelled to push back against the appearance of fast food in the heart of the revered gastronomic capital. McDonald's was emblematic of what he saw as the chief ill in the world: people are too fast. He tackled fast food as a symbol of a world that sees "slow" as an epithet, but his crusade grew so much larger than that. In the Slow Food Manifesto, he wrote, "We are enslaved by speed, and have all succumbed to the same insidious virus: Fast Life." Slow cities, slow parenting, and even slow sex—all sought to emulate this new slow philosophy.

Kirk Schneider applies this philosophy to our psyches in what he calls the "slow simmer." "The slow simmer approach to living requires cultivation over a lifetime throughout one's everyday experience. And to achieve that takes a great deal of practice." Schneider believes it is worth the effort, however. "I believe, at least for many people, that slow simmer can be, in the long run, more gratifying than something quick. I think we need to be careful, especially in our contemporary world where there is so much emphasis on speed and instant results." Speed kills. It kills empathy. It kills patience. And it kills wonder. Slow thought not only builds a wonder practice but embeds it in our life.

Meditation

Since 2015, the meditation industry has grown 306 percent, with a current market in excess of $2 billion. More than five thousand meditation smartphone applications are available, with some like Headspace and Calm generating as much as $200 million annually, and the app market alone is expected to exceed $4 billion by 2027. That doesn't even include the plethora of meditation studios, retreats, online courses, and books. Most of the Western world's understanding of meditation comes from a man named Jon Kabat-Zinn. In the mid-seventies, Kabat-Zinn, a recent PhD recipient in molecular biology from MIT, was interested in meditation and embarked on a two-week retreat in Vipassana meditation. *Vipassana*, a Pali word that roughly translates to "insight" or "clear-seeing," is a Buddhist spiritual meditation tradition that spans twenty-five hundred years. It had a resurgence in the US in the 1970s that included Kabat-Zinn and other leaders in the modern mindfulness movement, such as Tara Brach and Jack Kornfield. The approach focuses on breathing and body scans, where the meditator methodically pauses to observe, accept, but not react to bodily sensations.

During his two-week retreat, Kabat-Zinn sat completely still for hours on end in a cold, damp off-season summer camp. He later said he had never experienced such pain in his life, and yet through the practice of body scanning (observe, accept, but not react), he felt the pain "dissolve into pure sensation." This

experience inspired Kabat-Zinn to explore the idea of meditation for chronic pain management, and Mindfulness-Based
Stress Reduction (MBSR), a type of mindfulness-based intervention often combined with psychotherapy, was born. MBSR
is now taught worldwide in schools, workplaces, and prisons,
and while this is what most of us think of when we think of
meditation, there are a multitude of varieties of meditation, with
a variety of outcomes.

Which style is best for wonder?

Broadly speaking, meditation is a byzantine topic to research.
First, there are more than one hundred different meditation
traditions across many cultures, each engaging the brain in different ways and offering different benefits. Second, there are
massive discrepancies in the rigor, length, and frequency of
meditation training of research subjects, not to mention their
preexisting disposition before meditating. So, it's practically
impossible to compare someone who has been meditating on a
mountaintop for the past fifty years with someone who's been
going on weekend retreats for twenty years with someone who
has done twenty minutes of Transcendental Meditation twice
a day for the past ten years. Meanwhile, because of its ubiquity,
most of the research is focused only on MBSR. By researchers'
own admission, the meditation studies in the 1970s and 1980s
were not gold-standard, and the onslaught of new research into
various traditions and benefits has generated what psychologist and author Daniel Goleman calls a "tsunami of meditation
research [that] creates a foggy picture with a confusing welter
of results."

To make sense of this muddle, researchers have categorized
four primary styles of meditation. There is *focused attention meditation*, in which the meditator focuses on one particular element

like the breath, a sound, or a flame to narrow and sustain focus. *Open monitoring meditation* is a nonjudgmental observation, not dwelling, ruminating, or responding to a thought. (A combination of focused attention and open monitoring meditation is what most people would be familiar with from MBSR or apps like Headspace.) There is *loving-kindness meditation*, in which the meditator focuses on compassion and love toward other individuals and oneself. Last, there is the style of Transcendental Meditation (TM) called *mantra recitation*, in which the meditator focuses on the repetition—either out loud or in their head—of a word, phrase, or sound. These categorizations, however, are really just general typologies of approaches and don't highlight the importance of dose effects (i.e., duration and frequency), nor do they consider intensity, both of which are elements that influence the degree to which meditation impacts our body, brain, and mind.

The categorization put forward by Daniel Goleman and Richard Davidson in their book *The Science of Meditation* does include these elements of training, frequency, and intensity. They explain the concept of deep practice versus wide practice and further break that down into levels of proficiency and outcomes. In this categorization, we can start to see how one level flows into the other as a meditator's practice evolves with more time, commitment, and rigor. It also helps us appreciate that meditation research focusing only on specific modalities but not considering other factors like duration and depth can muddy the waters.

So how do we know which style is most beneficial to making us wonderprone? According to Goleman, Davidson, and some common sense, "The rule of thumb—that what gets practiced gets improved." They explain that while different people may respond better to different meditation styles (e.g., someone with anxiety and someone who wants pain management

LEVELS OF MEDITATION PRACTICE

Level 4: Apps or short "breathing at your desk" exercises—wide: These are watered down but also highly accessible. They focus on training attentional skills such as concentration and presence.

Level 3.2: MBSR, TM—wide—beginner: These are very user-friendly but require some training and regular practice. For beginners, these focus on training attentional skills such as concentration and presence. At this level, we can see some mild, short-term benefits. Long-term practitioners can observe significant and enduring trait changes.

Level 3.1: MBSR, TM, loving-kindness, Vipassana—wide—long-term: These are very user-friendly but require some training and regular practice. For long-term meditators, this involves moving from the attentional stage to a constructive one, where the meditator cultivates qualities like compassion and loving-kindness. Long-term meditators can observe significant and enduring trait changes.*

Level 2: Yogi, monk—deep—long-term: This is a more Westernized yogi that also entails years of constant, intense study but made more manageable for Western culture, removing some of the elements that are not well aligned to modern Western living. Lifetime hours in excess of 10,000. This is the level where deconstruction occurs, meaning cognitive barriers vanish, fundamental and enduring changes are observed physiologically and psychologically, and transcendence and altered forms of consciousness are possible.

Level 1: Yogi, monk—deep—long-term: This is full-on "yogi on a mountaintop living in a cave" level that entails years of constant, intense study within a totally immersive lifestyle of contemplation. Lifetime hours in excess of 20,000, ranging as high as 60,000 or more. This is the level where deconstruction occurs, where fundamental and enduring changes are observed physiologically and psychologically, and where transcendence and altered forms of consciousness are possible. (Only at this level do we find an equivalent effect to psychedelics.)

Based on categorization by Daniel Goleman and Richard Davidson
in their book *The Science of Meditation.*

---

* Goleman and Davidson don't break down level 3 like this, but given the differential between beginner and long-term meditator in results, this seems a bit clearer.

could potentially benefit from separate traditions), there are significant similarities in all meditation styles. "On a practical level, all forms of meditation share a common core of mind training—e.g., learning to let go of the myriad distractions that flow through the mind, and to focus on one object of attention or stance of awareness." This is why meditation as a means of attention training so effectively supports the wonder cycle and absorption in particular.

Even achieving mastery isn't a clear-cut route, as it's not as simple as "practicing ten thousand hours." It's not only the number of hours; it's the intensity, tutelage, and social bonds formed with teachers and other meditators that promotes mastery, and the benefits that mastery brings. So, years of solo TM practice, even in your feng-shui-ed converted guest room, is not as efficacious as the practice of someone who has performed fewer hours but in the context of more intense periods of retreats and professional coaching. As we'll see, this idea of context and support mirrors psychedelics, with the best results being seen not from people tripping on their own but from those with a qualified guide and aftercare.

Meditation as compared to psychedelics

Researchers see a prominent similarity when comparing the brain scans of people under the influence of psychedelics with those of highly trained meditation masters. (We'll learn more about that in the next chapter.) Cognitive neuroscientist Frederick Barrett made this observation in 2015, saying the brain imaging of the two were "quite similar, if not indistinguishable from" each other. Both psychedelics and meditation quiet the default mode network and increase brain entropy (i.e., a state of more complex and unexpected connections within the brain). While psychedelics are a faster route to these cognitive changes, a master yogi's way of processing and interpreting the stimulus of the world absent egoic reactivity is profoundly different from that of other people and is not comparable to the therapeutic effects of a single trip.

Meditation was never intended to benefit mental and physical health but rather to precipitate enduring trait-level changes that result in a kinder, more insightful level of being. It is, however, a happy outcome that health benefits can be achieved from meditation, and in some cases at the beginner level (although some of these changes may take time to appear). The field of science exploring different meditation traditions, known as contemplative science, is developing by leaps and bounds with advances in neuroscience. Contemplative science has found benefits at just about every level of meditation. While these are unlikely to be tantamount to those of an STE like a significant awe experience, they can support the building blocks of wonder, chiefly openness, presence, and attention, as well as align with some of the outcomes of wonder like empathy and compassion.

Attentional control

The human brain, as we have learned, is constantly filtering. It's managing our external stimuli and experiences, the internal dialogue and narrative that run in the background, and the biases and heuristics that try to help us behave efficiently (many of these running from the DMN). The brain's filters often compete with our presence, absorption, and attention in the process. Meditation helps minimize the effect of these filters while also lowering the volume from our chattering, self-centered ego. People who practice mindfulness meditation (MBSR or MBCT) are less distractible and have lower "attention interference." In fact, just eight minutes of focused breathing has been shown to decrease mind-wandering, while three ten-minute sessions of concentrated breathing markedly improved focus. After eight weeks of MBSR training, meditators showed even better focus and attentional control, and long-term Vipassana training enhanced their presence even further.

So why is attentional control so pertinent to wonder? One of the challenges of staying wonderprone is habituation and what's known as *repetition suppression*. Since novelty is a primary component of expectation violation, when something becomes too familiar, our brain downgrades the salience of those features it deems repetitive. This suppression hinders our presence and can impact our opportunities for observing wonder. But it's possible to defend against repetition suppression. For instance, master yogis showed almost no habituation in a test using noise distraction, paying as much attention to the first "click" as the twentieth. This is unusual—a "typical," non-meditating brain would start to block out that noise. It seems that by lowering our dependency on heuristic shortcuts, we're not only more present, but our reactivity to stimulus is reduced, helping us see more clearly and respond in a more deliberate, conscious way. In essence, mindfulness allows us to choose whether we want to be on autopilot or not. Again, as in most of these studies, the amount of time each meditator trained directly correlated to the amount of attentional control they exhibited.

There's notable evidence illustrating how MBSR, MBCT, focused attention meditation, and visualization can increase openness to experience while decreasing neuroticism (both Big Five personality traits), generally viewed as prerequisites to self-transcendence and foundational to wonder. For most people, shifts like these require regular practice to "top up" the response. However, for master yogis, it appears these changes occur at a trait level, meaning the yogis' brains have adapted such that they are in a constant state of open awareness and compassion.

Meditative practices can also lead to physiological changes in the brain over time, chiefly, a thickening of the cortical area of the brain that is associated with attention. Researchers have also found that deep breathing from meditation (and yoga), sometimes called *Ujjayi* or "oceanic breath," stimulates vagal activity, contributing to many meditation benefits, including lower blood pressure and heart rate. Meditation also lowers the stress hormone cortisol and proinflammatory cytokines (as with Jennifer Stellar's awe research). In fact, proinflammatory cytokines of MBSR meditators dropped after only three days of meditation practice, and experienced meditators who'd logged nine thousand hours or more not only had decreased signs of inflammation, but their levels of cortisol were 13 percent lower than those of the control group.

There is more research to be done, but it's clear that the level of meditation to reach a self-transcendent experience requires a tremendous amount of practice. The more intense the experience, the bigger and more enduring the benefit, and in meditation, that enduring benefit comes from intense training and time. This doesn't mean that a typical meditation practice of twenty minutes a day can't contribute to your wonder mindset. Moderate meditation using highly accessible meditation styles can make you more open, present, aware, and absorbed in the moment. The *wow* and *whoa* of self-transcendence might be harder to come by, but *watch*, *wander*, and *whittle* are all supported through contemplative practice, and those are elemental to a wonder mindset.

Gratitude

One way to slow down and cultivate a wonder practice is by stopping to consider the gifts we regularly receive in our life. In the same way that it's nice to thank someone who has given us a new teapot or a pair of slippers, it behooves us to consider the source of more meaningful gifts, like good health or a warm home, and give thanks for them as well. If comparison is the thief of joy, it is also the thief of gratitude. When we compare what we have to that of others, we often compare up and thus feel a sense of regret at what we don't have, and as those comparisons compound throughout our adult life, so do regret and resentment. If, however, we look at life through a wonder lens, like the open, curious eyes of a child, we can see the gifts we have with greater clarity. "We find gratitude journaling works so well with children because they have this innate sense of wonder. They don't have the layers added on with obstacles that come later in life," explains Robert Emmons, gratitude expert and author of the book Thanks! How the New Science of Gratitude Can Make You Happier. "There's a very intimate connection between a sense of wonder and a sense of gratitude."

Gratitude is associated with all manner of benefits, from fewer negative emotions and more positive ones to better coping strategies and an improved sense of well-being. It strengthens our interpersonal relationships, makes us better leaders, and imparts an increased meaning to our lives. Research has shown that engaging in just one act of gratitude each day for a week can lead to an increased feeling of well-being for up to six months after. (It even makes us healthier, sleep better, and want to exercise more!) Easy, accessible, and free, gratitude can be integrated into prayer or meditation and supported through gratitude communities online, all effective ways to embed gratitude in our day-to-day lives. Often described as a self-transcendent emotion (like compassion and awe), gratitude is a wonderbringer in and of itself. Therefore, as is the case with other self-transcendent emotions, people higher in openness and curiosity are naturally more likely to engage in a regular gratitude practice, too.

Because gratitude is attitudinal, we can consciously choose to invest in and improve this skill that not only has benefits in its own right but contributes to a wonder mindset. Gratitude puts the focus outside of ourselves, short-circuiting rumination and self-focus, prompting a type of psychic small-self. Once again, when we see our own smallness, we can better appreciate the magnitude of our own good fortune.

Gratitude is also another way we can use wonder at work. When we are grateful, we have a lower sense of entitlement, making us less selfish or greedy. It also lowers our tendency toward hostility or aggression by as much as 30 percent. Group-based gratitude can help form stronger teams, as it increases positive ingrouping behaviors like reciprocity and decreases negative outgrouping behaviors like prejudice. Emmons calls gratitude "the ultimate performance-enhancing substance," explaining that gratitude promotes the wonder elements of openness, cognitive flexibility, and deep curiosity, as well as innovation and creative thinking.

Reflecting on our life with thankful reverence acts as a cognitive reappraisal. A moment to pause, slow down, and consider the magic, mystery, and majesty of where we are at that very moment. There are many ways to practice gratitude, such as journaling and writing gratitude lists or even simply checking in a few times a day to ask ourselves what we're grateful for. But for gratitude to be a wonderbringer, we need to dig deep and find meaning in our thanks. This isn't just, "I'm grateful they had Chunky Monkey ice cream at the corner store" (although on some days, this can be very meaningful). We want to use gratitude to connect ourselves to others through empathetic consideration.

Prayer is also a type of gratitude or meditation practice, particularly meditative prayer, which centers on an intimate spiritual union with the divine. From a wonder and well-being point of view, meditative prayer is the most beneficial, as it activates the same areas of the brain as meditation and shares many of the same positive effects. In prayer, we find many other elements we know lead to greater wonder, including ritual, fellowship, empathy, and small-self.*

Narrative journaling

Stories are at the heart of how humans create meaning. They are how we construct context in our external world and process experiences in our inner world. Who of us isn't familiar with the childhood bedtime ritual of story time and the inevitable entreaty of "read me another one." Stories increase empathy and self-awareness, and researchers from the University of Southern California have discovered that the impact of stories on our psyches is universal. When participants from all over the world read the same story translated into their native language, they registered the same empathetic emotions, with neuroscientists finding that the DMN was activated in each reader. They concluded that all humans connect to, process, and make meaning about stories the same way, which is notable for wonder-seekers, as stories engage the entire wonder cycle, from openness to awe. The DMN may in fact be the link between slow thought and creativity, although awe researcher Lani Shiota cautions against putting too fine a point on some of these neuroscientific associations. "We're still sort of trying to guess or reverse engineer what it all means."

Science has illustrated that our empathy increases when we read stories in books. But interestingly, when we read and

---

* This is primarily through a sense of selflessness (very small-self), with that small-self being enhanced by the typical supplicant prayer posture of genuflection, bowing, or kneeling.

write stories, even about ourselves, not only does our empathy increase, but we become more wonderprone. The simple act of journaling can be reflective to recall and re-evoke a wonder experience, or it can be future-focused and used as a priming technique, writing about the wonder we anticipate experiencing. Critical to the success of journaling as a wonderbringer is the narrative feature. Sometimes journals can become a bit of a laundry list of our grievances or a regurgitation of our daily agenda, but we're looking to tell a story about ourselves.

One writing prompt researchers give their subjects is to think about a time they've experienced wonder and write at least five sentences to describe it. They use this narrative technique to help participants recall awe moments, extend these moments' longevity, and extract more profound meaning. The journaling process advances our awareness about what contributes to our individual wonder mindset, helping us identify our wonderbringers as well as the barriers we encounter that may hinder our wonder cycle.

Nostalgia

While there isn't a lot of direct research about the relationship between wonder and nostalgia, there are notable family resemblances that suggest a connection worth considering. Nostalgia, a sentimental longing for the past, is an often overlooked prosocial emotion. Though on the surface it could be perceived as negative because it is "self-focused," nostalgia is actually a dually valanced emotion, like curiosity and awe, that can serve as a very constructive coping mechanism, bringing positive affect to difficult times while also making us more open. Nostalgia has been shown to generate aesthetic chills, support meaning-making, ameliorate death anxiety, and make us more grateful. So we can begin to see how nostalgia, when deployed in the right way, can be a wonderbringer.

Many of our nostalgic ponderings are tinged with a sense of the bittersweet. Also known as *existential longing*, bittersweetness is that pleasant sense of melancholy that accompanies our reflections and mental meanderings. It's the part of us that likes listening to a sad song or reading an old love letter, and according to scientist and author Susan Cain, who wrote extensively on the subject, existential longing is quite beneficial, including by increasing our sense of meaning and gratitude. Cain joined up with Scott Barry Kaufman and David Yaden to develop a bittersweet measurement survey and found direct links between existential longing and wonder. "People who score high on the quiz, meaning that they tend to experience bittersweet states of mind, are also more inclined to states that predispose them to creativity, awe, wonder, spirituality, and transcendence," Cain explains. "These are some of the most sublime aspects of being human, and they happen to be connected to our appreciation of how fragile life can be, and the impermanence of life."

Nostalgia and other mixed or dually valanced emotions, like existential longing, curiosity, awe, and wonder, all contribute to greater resiliency, stemming potentially from the role of the vagus nerve in calming stress-reactive systems. Embracing both positive and negative emotions at the same time, also called *co-activation*, is a powerful coping mechanism. In essence, by holding both positive and negative thoughts in our mind at the same time, we are better able to metabolize traumatic experiences and make meaning of them. In one study of bereaved spouses, those widows and widowers who recalled both positive and negative elements of their deceased spouse were better able to manage their grief.

Nostalgia is also an excellent tool for wonder at work, and it's frequently utilized during icebreaker exercises or as a way to get to know teammates better. Simple questions can conjure nostalgia, such as, How did you celebrate your favorite holiday as a child? or What do you miss about your first job? The key is to construct a prompt that elicits a story of reverie and reflection, not just a one-line answer. Mixed emotions like nostalgia and wonder also support divergent or paradoxical thinking, which contributes to innovation, and mixed emotions appear to increase task accuracy as well. Given nostalgia's benefit to openness and general positive mood, embracing this emotion is a good thing to do regardless. And as with daydreaming and journaling, we want to steer clear of rumination and reflect from a position of gratitude or positive nostalgic contemplation.

Sleep

As a child, I had a nickname—one of many—granted to me by my father: "Nostrils Up." This was because whenever he looked into the backseat of the car, I was asleep, head cast back with my nose pointing heavenward, mouth agape like a bullfrog. When I was younger, I could sleep anywhere. Any surface. Any floor. Any chair. Any moving vehicle. Roller coasters and rock concerts. Playgrounds and practice fields. In my twenties, it was the naps. On cool hammocks and in warm nooks. On buses and subways. In the executive toilet at my day job because I had gotten in late from my night job. My delicious naps. Unfortunately, sleep is a more elusive companion these days. If you've ever suffered from chronic insomnia, you can understand why sleep deprivation is a form of torture. And, in fact, lack of sleep is a barrier to experiencing wonder, too.

Azizi Seixas is a biomedical researcher and assistant professor in the departments of population health and psychiatry at New York University Langone. Growing up in one of Jamaica's most deprived neighborhoods while attending one of the most affluent high schools on an academic scholarship, Seixas learned firsthand about social inequities. When he pursued a medical degree at Holy Cross College in western Massachusetts, he realized those same inequities existed in the United States. "I think I was the only person of color to graduate premed. Definitely, the only Black person to graduate premed. But I still ended up not going to medical school because I couldn't afford it." That unfortunate turn offered him the opportunity to do what he now sees as his vocation—studying the barriers to healthy sleep among racial and ethnic minorities and finding novel solutions to dismantle those barriers.

In the current grind culture, sleep deprivation is ignored and even lauded, which is unfortunate because, according to Seixas, lack of sleep is oppositional to being wonderprone. "Sleep helps from a mechanical standpoint, particularly through the lymphatic system, which is the transportation system during the night that clears the brain. . . . The brain is clearer, cleaner, and much more optimized." But, Seixas asserts, when our prefrontal cortex is operating under stress due to poor sleep, we are more likely to engage in hedonic decision-making and less likely to be open or curious, or engage in prosocial activities that contribute to wonder. And as we covered in some earlier chapters, when we are stressed, we lean on our shortcuts and heuristics. This means we are also less likely to experience mixed emotions like wonder. The thinking is that our emotions sit on a continuum from simple to complex. When we are stressed, we default to the simple emotions, and so rather than feel wonder, we may just feel a single-valanced emotion like happy or sad, instead of embracing the multidimensionality of wonder.

Dayna Johnson is an assistant professor of epidemiology at Emory University. Early in her academic career, Johnson was interested in the disparity of health outcomes for different populations and started looking at areas like diet, exercise, and stress.

The moment her focus shifted was when she learned that sleep is a risk factor for cardiovascular disease. Johnson grew up in Detroit and saw firsthand the impact shift work had on the sleep patterns of her Motor City community, most of whom were employed in the automotive industry. "I thought about shift workers and how common [sleep deprivation] is. My mother worked for an automobile company, and she doesn't sleep much. The idea of that as a risk factor for cardiovascular disease scared me in a way. I thought about my family."

The more Johnson learned, the more she came to appreciate just how foundational sleep is to every facet of our existence, including the presence and attentional control that support wonder. "Sleep is important because it truly controls your life. And it also determines your trajectory of health." Johnson notes that the onus of solving sleep deprivation should not be borne solely by the individual. There are structural barriers to sleep, and thus not everyone's route to wonder is as unencumbered as others. (For example, it's hard to prioritize presence and relaxation when you struggle with childcare or work two jobs.) "Sleep should be a right. But it's really something that's a privilege. Everyone doesn't have this same opportunity for many reasons, some of which are the direct result of structural problems."

While Johnson has yet to research if lack of sleep will make us less likely to engage in wonder-inducing behaviors, she is clear that sleep deprivation will make attention-training practices like meditation very difficult. She is also involved in some research that shows wonderbringers like meditation, journaling, and gratitude can support sleep. For example, people who keep a gratitude journal get about thirty minutes more sleep a night and wake up feeling more well rested. Sleep is likely another virtuous wonder circle—if we engage in a wonder practice, we get better sleep, which in turn supports engaging in our wonder practice.

Patience is considered a virtue in almost every major religion—Carlo Petrini even worked with the Pope to spread the word of a slower life—so there is an ancient recognition regarding the power of slow thought. Many of the wonder practice ideas we've explored in this chapter, like gratitude, narrative journaling, and nostalgia, are really about attention training. Once we become more adept at that training, our self-focus will minimize, and rumination will begin to drop off naturally. (Just being more patient increases empathy, decreases depression, and is associated with increased self-transcendence.) These slow thought skills are foundational for a life lived in wonder, priming us to see all the wonderbringers that exist around us, waiting to be revealed.

WONDER WRAP-UP

- Wonder is nurtured in a slow environment. There are several ways to achieve slow thought, like meditation, gratitude, and narrative journaling. These are more difficult to achieve without sufficient sleep.

- There are more than one hundred different types of meditation, one reason why studying it is so challenging. Different styles can offer different benefits, of which there are many, but the "best" meditation is the one we regularly do. This is because a consistent theme runs through all meditation traditions—building attentional control. Attentional control is the foundation of slow thought and a wonder practice.

- Master yogis have similar brain patterns to those of people undergoing a psychedelic trip, but achieving mastery is incredibly rigorous. While psychedelics may be a faster route to cognitive changes, it is important to remember that the speed train isn't the only ride in town.

- Gratitude and wonder are linked. Gratitude is both a wonderbringer and a way to build a wonder practice, especially when we use it to connect ourselves empathetically to others. Gratitude also contributes to a wonder-based work culture, as it makes us less aggressive and combats outgrouping bias.

- Narrative journaling harnesses the power of stories, and nostalgia imbues these stories with added emotion. When we recall wonder moments, journaling extends these moments in our mind, and we can extract more meaning from them. It also aids in our understanding of our individual wonderbringers and the barriers to wonder that we might encounter.

- Nostalgia, like other wonderbringers such as fellowship, is associated with the vagus nerve. When nostalgia is imbued with existential longing, it makes us more wonderprone.

- Sleep is foundational to every aspect of our life, including wonder. Lack of sleep kills attentional control, whereas good sleep improves it and allows us to engage in a wonder practice. Not everyone has the same access to sleep, and with sleep inequity comes wonder inequity.

16

Psychedelics

W hen is it going to come back? Where is it going to come back? What's going to happen to me? How's my family going to be able to deal with it?" Those were the questions fifty-five-year-old Pam Sakuda desperately asked herself when she learned her cancer had metastasized. Her diagnosis and prognosis were grim: stage four colon cancer with fourteen months, max, to live. She remembered thinking, "This is terminal. . . . This is basically what is going to kill you." Sakuda was devastated by the diagnosis, and as her days crept up to, and then past, the fourteen-month mark, she felt trapped in the most terrible kind of limbo. Waiting. Waiting. Waiting. In a purgatory, incapable of finding any hope or happiness. It wasn't just the existential fear of her own death, which she found paralyzing, but seeing the pain her illness was causing her devoted husband of twenty-four years as well. "There was the guilt of being the source of that pain, as well as all of my own fear. And it becomes almost overwhelming, where it infringes upon the time that you're enjoying. So crippled by this fear."

Despite beating the odds, Sakuda remained bereft. It became impossible for her to make plans for even the simplest activities for fear she would not be alive when the date rolled around. As the scope of her life shrunk to doctors' appointments and her regular grueling runs, Sakuda's anxiety grew. The pair of them, she and her husband, became locked in a morbid stasis. Her doctors tried psychotherapy and antidepressants, but the usually buoyant Sakuda showed no improvement. Feeling left with no other options, she volunteered for an experimental depression treatment trial at the University of California, Los Angeles. Two years after her initial diagnosis, Sakuda did something she could never have imagined prior—in a small hospital room, accompanied by trained therapists, she took a pill of psilocybin, the psychedelic compound found in "magic mushrooms." In that sterile space, decorated with some flowing fabrics and a few blankets and pillows to make it feel less so, Sakuda put on an eye mask and headphones, and slowly lay back on the bed, gripping some photos of loved ones. The soundtrack of her journey was an instrumental accompaniment specially designed to help her disconnect from her corporeal being and focus her mind inward.

What followed for the next seven hours was not what Sakuda would necessarily describe as pleasant—at several points during the trip, she found herself crying—but it was transformative. "I felt this lump of emotions kind of rolling up and firming up, almost like an entity. And I started to cry a little, and just to start to *feel* it all." The results were almost immediate. When her husband was invited into the treatment room after her trip, he said she was glowing. "There's my Pammy," he recalled, amazed. "She's just beaming with light, and I haven't seen that joyousness for so long. She was just totally alive; she was totally happy."

Sakuda was grateful for the insight and liberation the treatment unlocked in her. "I don't think the drug is the cause of these things. I think it's a catalyst that allows you to release your own thoughts and feelings from someplace that you wound them very tightly. And so, it allows you to open your own mind and your consciousness and release other feelings, explore other ways you might feel." Although Sakuda succumbed to her illness two years later, her single psilocybin trip allowed her and her husband to enjoy the time she had left. "There was a tremendous feeling of relief. And of happiness. And of hope."

Sakuda's results are not unique. In one randomized, double-blind, placebo-controlled study by Johns Hopkins, about 80 percent of patients suffering from depression due to terminal cancer found their mental health markedly improved, and more than 60 percent showed total remission of depressive symptoms after only a single guided psychedelic experience. Researchers are still debating precisely why psychedelics have this impact. Most believe it isn't the result of changed brain chemistry as one might find with the SSRIs in antidepressants or lithium in antipsychotics. Instead, the drug manifests a life-changing *experience* that grants participants a newly found mental flexibility to see life through an entirely different lens. After treatment, participants often report feeling a sense of small-self and a deep connectedness to others. This shift has led researchers to believe that it is wonder—the psychedelics acting as the fast track to an extreme expectation violation and *whoa* awe moment—transforming the participants' outlook, rather than any specific psychedelic pharmacology. And for many people, it takes only one session, and they are changed for life.

History of modern psychedelics

April 19 is known by many in the psychedelic world as Bicycle Day. It was this day in 1943 that Swiss chemist Albert Hofmann had his first trip on LSD, setting in motion what would eventually become a very fraught relationship between researchers and governmental controllers of a fascinating and potent drug. Hofmann first synthesized lysergic acid diethylamide five years earlier while working for Sandoz Pharmaceuticals, studying a rye fungus called ergot. He was looking for a stimulant to treat headaches and respiratory ailments, but when he tested it on animals, it didn't give him the result he was looking for, so he set it aside. Five years later, Hofmann felt compelled to look at the compound again, this time accidentally ingesting a minuscule amount. The reaction was mild, but he thought there might be some potential in the discovery. So, on a slightly gray Monday morning, a spring drizzle in the air, Hofmann decided to give himself what he thought would be a small dose, but in fact, he would realize later was a near overdose. After about an hour, Hofmann began to feel a shift in consciousness and asked his lab assistant to take him home. Due to wartime restrictions prohibiting cars, Hofmann and his assistant had to ride their bikes to get there, and Bicycle Day was born.

Hofmann described his wild ride home. "I had great difficulty in speaking clearly, and my field of vision fluctuated and swam like an image in a distorted mirror. . . . I had the feeling that I was not moving from the spot, although my colleague said I was moving at a fast pace." When he got home, he felt decidedly unwell (one might expect that would be the case if you almost overdosed on LSD) and asked his neighbor to call the doctor. Hofmann then began to experience "dizziness, visual disturbance, the faces of those present seemed vividly colored and grimacing; powerful motor disturbances, alternating with paralysis; my head, body, and limbs all felt heavy, as if filled with metal; cramps in the calves, hands cold and without sensation; a metallic taste on the tongue; dry and constricted throat; a feeling of suffocation; confusion alternating with clear recognition of my situation, in which I felt outside myself as a neutral observer as I half-crazily cried or muttered indistinctly." (Sounds about as harrowing as Arunja's vision from Krishna.) But after a while, he began to enjoy the visuals of "kaleidoscopic, fantastic images . . . alternating, variegated, opening, and then closing themselves in circles and spirals, exploding in colored fountains." And in the morning, he awoke with "a sensation of wellbeing and renewed life. . . . The world was as if newly created."

Hofmann recognized the tremendous therapeutic potential of this compound, so Sandoz began producing it and sending it to researchers worldwide. For the next decade or so, psychedelic research progressed unfettered, leading to some pretty exciting results. Admittedly, some of these were not rigorous peer-reviewed studies, but the anecdotal results alone were encouraging. Things changed, however, when in 1960 a Harvard psychology professor named Timothy Leary began taking LSD with his research subjects, many of them students. Soon the word *psychedelics* became negatively associated with the scandal and Leary's ignominious firing that followed. Within a few years, Leary was pleading to the youth of America to "turn on, tune in, and drop out," just as conscription for the Vietnam War began. Nixon declared Leary public enemy number one, and that political perfect storm ushered in the beginning of the end of psychedelic research. For the next several decades, psychedelics were ejected unceremoniously from the tent and have only been cautiously invited back in recent years. Several new names are synonymous with this psychedelics renaissance, like Robin Carhart-Harris and David Yaden, but in a way, these younger researchers are taking the final opening twist of a jar that scientists like David Nutt have been bashing at and loosening since the late 1980s. And in the process, Nutt has taken his own bashing as well, for simply telling the truth.

A bad day for science

There is nothing about David Nutt that screams "counterculture" other than the fact that he advocates for psychedelic research. He isn't wearing tie-dyes and living in a yurt (not that there's anything wrong with that). He didn't change his name like yoga guru Ram Dass or quit his profession and join the counterculture like Timothy Leary. He is simply an incredibly qualified, long-serving psychopharmacology researcher who was asked to research drugs by his government and then was pilloried when he presented data that didn't align with the political narrative of the time.

Nutt's curriculum vitae reads like the greatest hits of pharmacology experience: graduated from Cambridge University, lecturer at Oxford, Fogarty Visiting Scientist at the NIH, Director of Psychopharmacology at the University of Bristol, Fellow of the Royal College of Physicians, the Royal College of Psychiatrists, and the Academy of Medical Scientists, a stint as president of both the British Neuroscience Association and the European Brain Council, as well as a handful of various advisory positions to the UK's Ministry of Defence, Home Office, and Department of Health.

Given this impressive and unassailable background, his appointment in 2008 as the chairman of the UK's Advisory Council on the Misuse of Drugs (ACMD) was roundly applauded. But his subsequent findings were not. "I started doing systematic assessments of the harms of drugs and exposed that basically, drugs like alcohol, tobacco, were clearly as harmful, if not more harmful, than many of the drugs which are illegal. The legality or illegality argument is completely arbitrary, and therefore it is political." Nutt's biggest shot across the bow of the "completely arbitrary" system was a paper he published in the highly respected The Journal of Psychopharmacology titled "Equasy—An Overlooked Addiction with Implications for the Current Debate on Drug Harms." In the admittedly cheekily titled paper, Nutt illustrated that horseback riding led to one serious incident every 350 exposures, whereas the drug Ecstasy resulted in only one serious incident every 10,000 exposures. And yet there were no restrictions on the former. Suffice to say, that paper went over like a skunk at a garden party and led to a protracted exchange between Nutt and his bosses played out in the newspapers and the Houses of Parliament. As one newspaper printed at the time, "Most drug experts believe his analysis is right. But ministers did not want to hear the truth or at least to be reminded of it repeatedly."

Nutt was asked to resign from his position with the ACMD, but the scientific community immediately rallied around him and decried his dismissal, one calling it "a bad day for science and for the cause of evidence-informed policymaking." In a press interview at the time of his sacking, Nutt shared, "My view is policy should be based on evidence. It's a bit odd to make policy that goes in the face of evidence." Given his commitment to following the science, he found the lack of logic regarding drug prohibition maddening.

When I talked to David Nutt, I felt a sense of urgency, as if he wants to make up for lost time. "The bottom line is that people have realized they've been lied to. . . . People have now discovered that cannabis isn't going to lead to a complete annihilation of society. They're wanting to explore other drugs which have also been irrationally abandoned."*

Psychedelics, like so many other topics we're covering, deserve a book in their own right, and many have been written, covering everything from the history of psychedelics in rituals

---

* The root of this irrational abandonment is the UN Convention on Psychotropic Substances of 1971, which effectively banned psychedelics, marking a milestone in international drug policy and the functional end of psychedelic research until very recently.

through time to the battle for prohibition, the battle against prohibition, and now, the multitudinous ways that psychedelics support improved mental health.* When researchers talked about psychedelics prior to the 1990s, they were generally referring to psilocybin (found in as many as one hundred species of mushrooms) and LSD. There are, however, other ancient psychedelics like peyote and mescaline (from cacti), which have a similar neural effect to psilocybin and LSD, and newer "designer drugs" like MDMA (also known as Ecstasy or Molly), DMT (a short-acting chemical found on the skin of *Bufo alvarius* toads, and also found in the shrub *Psychotria viridis*, an ingredient in the ancient psychedelic brew *ayahuasca* that can also be produced synthetically), and ketamine (originally used as a veterinary tranquilizer). As described in an academic paper about these types of drugs, "classic psychedelics are a class of hallucinogens, which act primarily as agonists of the 5-HT2A receptor and are capable of producing profound changes in sensory perceptions, mood, and cognition." Although LSD was the most studied psychedelic before prohibition, recent clinical research is primarily focused on psilocybin, which is very close pharmacologically to LSD. While all these drugs have been found to have various therapeutic benefits, we'll focus primarily on psilocybin and LSD and their association with wonder.

How do psychedelics work?

How and why psychedelic therapy works and the way it varies across treatments is still being studied, as it is such a nascent field. In its simplest terms, what would appear to be at play is

---

* Nutt has since been honored for his tenacity, being given in 2013 the John Maddox Prize, an award granted "to researchers who have shown great courage and integrity in standing up for science and scientific reasoning against fierce opposition and hostility" (an honor he shares with 2020's recipient, chief medical advisor to the US president during the COVID crisis, Anthony Fauci).

that psychedelics lead to a drug-induced self-transcendent experience, characterized by the wonder elements of openness, inward curiosity, absorption, and awe. This subjective experience then creates a period of psychic malleability in which previously intractable cognitive changes can be made.

Psychedelics, even just a single dose, create an "acute destabilization of brain networks." This destabilization prompts increased openness, followed by a pliable, small-self awe state, preparing the mind for behavior change. Then, in this plastic state, once a "therapeutic window" has been opened by the drugs, traditional psychotherapy helps move the patient away from self-focused anxiety, trauma, and rumination toward a broader, more connected psyche, thus solidifying enduring behavior change. The support angle is vital here and serves as a gentle reminder, dear reader, that just going out and dropping acid for an afternoon is unlikely to give you the therapeutic benefits these patients have experienced. There are several critical elements of a successful therapeutic trip, like set and setting, context, preparation prior, guidance during, and integration (processing the experience) after—not to mention the potency of the "heroic dose" administered to patients to achieve these results.

Psychedelics, like wonder, create a degree of mental plasticity that has the power to shift elements of your personality. You become more open, more cognitively flexible, and higher in divergent thinking. The drugs also increase oxytocin, bonding, empathy, and feelings of closeness, trust, and happiness. When discussing how psychedelics appear to make us better, kinder, more balanced people, the question always arises: If terrorists took LSD, would they drop their weapons and sing "Kumbaya"? "The answer is no. It might make it worse," shares Nutt. "We know you can't fundamentally change people's political leanings. MKUltra tried that. It failed." (MKUltra being the CIA's clandestine program of human experiments intended to find ways to manipulate people's mental state, which included, among other reprehensible activities, dosing them with LSD without their knowledge.)

Psychedelics can't create a new human out of whole cloth, but the malleability that psychedelics induce is incredibly potent and therapeutically efficacious. One of the most illustrative images of how one's neural patterns change while under the influence of psychedelics is this representation of a brain operating under typical conditions and one while on psilocybin.

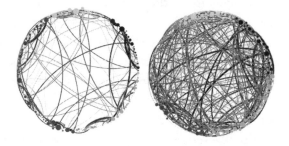

The image on the left shows a brain in a normal active state. Connections are minimum, short, highly efficient, and primarily made along the periphery. The image on the right shows a brain on psilocybin. It looks something like an abstract dream catcher, with heaps of connections shooting straight through the middle, bouncing from one part of the brain to another, from one association to another.

As I looked at this image with Nutt, he explained, "[The picture on the left] is the normal brain and the 7,200 statistical maps of synchronized activity. And in the normal brain, most of the synchronicity is around the edges, called a small brain network. There's a bit of cross talk—you know, if you see a tiger, you've got to move your arms and legs to run—but mostly, it's around [the edges], because this is the most efficient way of doing it." But the image on the right shows a more active, more frenetic brain. "Under psychedelics, because the default mode is disrupted, you get this massive amount of cross talk. And this is like a baby's brain—this is how the brain starts—and eventually over decades, it gets ground down to this kind of constraint."

Echoing what Drs. Lotto, Eagleman, and others have said about how heuristics and shortcuts filter our perspective of the world, Nutt explains that psychedelics don't so much alter our perception as release it by lifting those filters. "It's hard and energy expensive to—in real time—decode every single thing because every sixteen milliseconds, you'd be uploading gigabytes of information. So, your brain predicts. It's very efficient. The brain actually constrains what you see," he says. "But you can loosen up. You can make these connections so you can understand things about yourself that you've forgotten or never knew. And you can also come up with new solutions because you can put bits of the big puzzle together." Nutt explains that with the default mode network disarmed, there is no governor on the associations our brain makes or the changes it becomes capable of creating. "That disorganization allows us to break free. You break down your traditional sense of self, your ego. We believe that's why people can both see things differently but also come back with a longer-term, more rational, and more adaptive perspective on life. They've actually escaped [their old way of thinking]."

Addiction

As early as the 1950s, researchers were already testing LSD for the treatment of addiction. The drug was initially being trialed for its aversive effect, thinking that the hallucinations of LSD might mimic the severe symptoms of alcohol withdrawal called *delirium tremens* (i.e., the DTs) and repel addicts into sobriety. What emerged, however, was that it was not the aversion but rather the insight from a psychedelic experience that appeared to induce sobriety. This effect inspired researcher Humphry Osmond to choose the term psychedelic, meaning "mind-manifesting," to describe this class of drugs.

The Deep South isn't a place one might expect to find psychedelic research, but the University of Alabama, Birmingham, is home to one of the modern-day researchers testing psychedelics for addiction treatment, Peter Hendricks. "There is a heightened political lens around this, and we are in a state that tends to be rather conservative, but the famed Humphry Osmond who coined the term psychedelic—his last academic home was here at UAB," Hendricks shares. He adds by way of further explanation, with perhaps a tiny whiff of pride, "Timothy Leary graduated from Alabama."

Hendricks became interested in the field while flipping through a journal looking for his own first academic publication, his PhD dissertation. He came across an article by one of David Nutt's contemporaries, Roland Griffiths, that shared the results of Griffiths's 2006 landmark study of psychedelics. Hendricks found it fascinating. As he began to research the topic, he discovered a study that showed self-reported hallucinogen use was associated with lower recidivism, and he could immediately see the potential for psychedelics in addiction treatment. "I work in addiction, and most of our treatments are pretty disappointing. The idea that we could have something a whole lot more effective was really exciting to me." For Hendricks, the connection between a mystical psychedelic experience and a profound shift in behavior made sense. "I would describe myself as a person of faith—I come from a faith background—so the idea that a spiritual-type experience could be profoundly life-changing and could motivate behavior was intuitive to me. I think Timothy

Leary actually was not far off when he described [psychedelic experiences] as sort of religious conversion events."

In study after study, the results were not just significant and reliable, but enduring. In one meta-analysis of more than five hundred participants, researchers found those given psychedelics were almost twice as likely to see a reduction in alcohol misuse over the control group—and those improvements lasted at least one month after treatment. In another study of alcoholics treated with a single psilocybin session, participants' drinking had dropped by half or more at the follow-up nine months later. Bill Wilson, cofounder of Alcoholics Anonymous, found psychedelics so promising for treating alcoholism that he therapeutically used LSD himself and became an early proponent. Wilson hoped to integrate it into the broader Alcoholics Anonymous protocol, as he found the psychedelic experience to be very similar to the spiritually transcendent experience that was the catalyst for his own sobriety.

Psychedelics can support treatment for other types of addiction, too. In the United States, cigarette smoking is responsible for almost half a million deaths a year, and Americans spend about $225 billion a year in direct medical care for smokers. And yet, the success rate of America's leading smoking cessation drug is a mere 19 percent. By comparison, psychedelics are more than three times more effective. In a psilocybin experiment for smoking cessation, 75 percent of participants quit smoking and were still smoke-free at a follow-up two and a half years later. In these studies, not only did the intensity of the mystical experience determine who relapsed and who didn't, but those with more intense experiences also had fewer cravings and reported less severe withdrawal symptoms when compared with how they had felt other times they had tried to quit using non-psychedelic interventions.

Addiction, OCD, and mood disorders like depression and anxiety share a central feature: a narrow self-focus and intrusive rumination. For addiction, that rumination is cyclical, quieted only temporarily by the object of the given addiction—whether it is a substance or a behavior—and then it is set in motion again as soon as the object fades from focus. For OCD and eating disorders, that rumination manifests in uncontrollable compulsive behavior. For depression, it manifests as a sense of failing, catastrophization, and guilt. Hendricks sees this short-circuiting of rumination as the most significant potential benefit of psychedelics. "You think of somebody who's addicted to a drug, and they're almost spinning their wheels, thinking about how am I going to get it next? And if you can have an experience in which you're suddenly thinking outside of yourself, you break from these self-nagging thoughts. Suddenly, you're not even thinking about your desire, your craving, for that drug. You're focusing on something else." Psychedelics appear to interrupt that rumination, but how?

When he read the research that showed the rationale for psychedelics' efficacy as "some sort of normalization of the default mode network," Hendricks found it interesting but didn't feel that offered enough from a psychological point of view. "That's all lovely, but as a psychologist, I was really interested in understanding things at a psychological level, right? And to just say to somebody, well, your default mode network is normalizing, is not really helpful." Hendricks wanted to identify the emotions associated with the *subjective* experience of psychedelics, and not just the neuroscience behind it, believing that a broader perspective was critical to telling the whole therapeutic story.

This exploration inspired him to begin connecting the dots between what he knew he was observing from his research with psychedelics and Dacher Keltner's experiments with awe.

"Here's awe defined; here are the elicitors of awe; here's subjectively what awe looks like—and, boy, this sounds exactly like a mystical-type experience on a psychedelic." He laughs, reflecting on how evident the connection appears to him now. "So maybe my claim to fame will be being the first person to make a very obvious connection. And that'll be fine with me."

Hendricks is too humble. When the path is clearly illuminated, it makes intuitive sense. But his insight has now linked the very concrete and measurable benefits of psychedelics to the sometimes more subtle benefits of awe—benefits like a reduced focus on our own needs and more focus on the needs of others. "If part of [a psychedelic] experience also involves taking a new perspective and realizing the pain you may have caused others in pursuit of the addictive substance—in the same way that Ebenezer Scrooge experienced pain when he realized how his pursuit of wealth hurt people around him—then there also could be this desire to really change that behavior. Because you want to be a better family member, a better husband or wife or daughter or son."

He's concerned that some scientists, both inside and outside the psychedelic community, try to hide behind the neuroscience because they are uncomfortable with the idea that the subjective effects, like transcendence and small-self, are the root cause of the benefits. "All the research shows that the self-reported subjective effects are strong predictors of these therapeutic outcomes. Why are you trying to take away the transcendent part of this? What is the problem? I mean, why do we describe that as problematic?" Hendricks doesn't feel any dissonance in embracing both the science and the soul of this therapy. "There's also this pushback that perhaps we shouldn't be manufacturing a mystical-type experience in a research lab or in a clinic setting. Then I'd say, well, if indeed there is a God, then God has given you a nervous system capable of having these experiences, and creating them with a drug certainly doesn't explain them away."

Depression, anxiety, and obsessive-compulsive disorder

We, or at least a great many of us, don't deal with death very well. Honestly, we don't deal with death at all if we can help it. For something that binds us so elementally to the entirety of the human race—none of us are getting out of here alive—we generally try to avoid the topic of death until it is thrust upon us. Then, when it is, grace and equanimity seem distant acquaintances and wonder a stranger. And what of the ones, most of us in fact, who will know of our death ahead of time? Not from a psychic with her crystal ball telling us to avoid falling pianos. Much more pedestrian, like from a diagnosis of cancer or liver failure or heart disease or any of the other myriad ways we learn, "This is basically what's going to kill you."

We should all be so lucky to go like my eighty-something-year-old Pawpaw. He was at a Mardi Gras parade with family, complained of a slight headache, and died napping on the car ride home—his last memory a glittering cavalcade. But only about 10 percent of people will have a sudden death. The rest of us will be diagnosed with some terminal or chronic illness that will lead to our demise, the majority of us drawing our last breath in some sort of medical institution. That means a great many of us will have to face our own impending death, knowledge that can leave an individual, just as Pam Sakuda was, riddled with depression and anxiety, robbing them of the joy in what time they do have left. This sort of existential depression can be incredibly challenging to treat. Sadly, because of the potentially limited time for treatment and the nature of these life-threatening diagnoses, experimentation with various approaches is often not feasible. The speed and efficacy of psychedelics make them a particularly suitable treatment paradigm for people faced with this arduous journey.

In a randomized, double-blind, placebo-controlled study of patients with life-threatening cancer diagnoses, a single dose of psilocybin led to participants experiencing dramatic reductions in depression and anxiety at each follow-up. The more intense and "mystical" the trip, the more enduring the benefits, which were most evident at the day one assessment. However, patients still had significant antidepressant and anxiolytic (anti-anxiety) benefits at the seven-week follow-up, with 83 percent showing a reduction in depression and 58 percent in anxiety. While these beneficial outcomes did reduce somewhat over time, of those who survived, 60 to 80 percent of patients showed significant reductions in hopelessness, demoralization, and death anxiety, with the results being sustained up to the four-and-a-half-year mark.

In the randomized, double-blind Johns Hopkins study mentioned earlier, scientists were exploring dosage effects (to reinforce the research showing the intensity of the psychedelic subjective experience was the root cause of the antidepressant and anxiolytic effects). Patients were given both a low dose and a high dose at different times, and significant antidepressant and anxiolytic effects were seen immediately after the high dose. At the six-month assessment, effects were also sustained, with a reduction of 78 percent in depression and 83 percent in anxiety, and complete palliation of 65 percent and 57 percent, respectively. In a study from 2018 of people with treatment-resistant depression, patients again showed marked improvement after treatment with psychedelics, with almost half of them reporting significant antidepressant effects at the six-month follow-up.

There are several studies with similar results and more being published regularly, and in each of these, there were no serious adverse effects.*

Researchers have also been trialing psychedelics for obsessive-compulsive disorder (OCD), believing the disorder's ruminative and self-focused nature would also respond well to the insight and perspective of the psychedelic experience. While the results are not as enduring as those from studies of people with depression and anxiety, they show promise for larger-scale studies. In one small study, subjects reported a significant reduction in OCD symptoms after psilocybin treatment, with all patients experiencing a decrease in symptoms ranging between 23 and 100 percent, and almost 70 percent had their symptoms reduced by half or more the day following treatment. With results like these, David Nutt sees incredible potential for the use of psychedelics to treat neurological and mood disorders. "Our current hypothesis is that psychedelics will work on disorders where there is a great deal of internalized thinking. Rumination, whether it's about depressive thoughts, whether it's about alcohol, whether it's about heroin, whether it's about cleanliness and OCD, whether it's about body shape as in anorexia, I think those disorders will respond."

Psychedelics are also being explored for the treatment of brain injury. The neuroplasticity of psychedelics is one reason, as it supports rerouting of certain neural pathways around injured areas. But researchers have also found psychedelics have anti-inflammatory characteristics, just as Jennifer Stellar established with awe. Those characteristics could provide a powerful

---

* This is not to say there has never been an adverse effect in a psychedelics study, but they are not common. Of course, as more studies are run, there may be further findings of adverse effects. These are incredibly powerful drugs, and some people are not suitable for the treatment, which is why therapeutic use is managed by psychological professionals.

neuroregenerative and neuroprotective benefit. For example, after a stroke, the brain is flooded with cytokines in an effort to promote healing, but this same immune response also exacerbates brain inflammation. Standard steroid treatment reduces that inflammation, but also reduces the body's total immune response, putting patients at increased risk for infection. Psychedelics produce a "unique pattern of cytokine expression" that successfully reduces those target areas of inflammation without exposing the body to the risk associated with total immune suppression. Further exploring this relationship between cytokines and wonder could offer insights into the physiology of the brain-body connection with profound implications for the treatment of neuroinflammatory conditions like Alzheimer's and Parkinson's. In the words of one study author, "Psychedelics may represent a fourth class of anti-inflammatory drug." Given how this aligns with Stellar and Anderson's research on wonder's effect on proinflammatory cytokines, we may find wonder also has a "unique pattern of cytokine expression" and is an efficacious treatment for inflammation.

Though the pharmacological effects of these drugs fully clear the body within hours, the therapeutic effects of psychedelics typically remain long after the drug effects have subsided. It's clear that the psychological nature of the subjective experience makes this treatment approach different and more effective than conventional pharmacological treatment of these conditions. It's also clear that the magnitude of the mystical experience (but not the magnitude of the hallucinations) appears to be the strongest predictor of enduring outcomes. The greater the transcendence, ineffability, sacredness, or noetic quality, the greater the benefit derived, emphasizing once again the psychedelic (i.e., mind-revealing) effects, rather than the hallucinogenic effects of the treatment.

Studying psychedelics

Admittedly, the studies looking at the therapeutic potential for psychedelics aren't perfect, but they paint a very compelling picture of the significant and enduring benefits of psychedelic therapy. Within the current legal framework, difficulty in running psychedelic research remains; hence many of these studies are either very small or not randomized and blinded. But the size and quality of research studies are rapidly improving. And some, like the two cancer diagnosis depression studies, are the gold standard of research, featuring randomized, double-blind, placebo-controlled experiments. The more of these sorts of studies that are run, the bigger the data set for future meta-analyses to further support psychedelics' efficacy in treating addiction, OCD, and mood disorders.

There is another complication in studying the therapeutic benefits of psychedelics. Some regulators, such as the Food and Drug Administration (FDA) in the United States, are of the opinion that if a drug derives its benefit from the subjective experience it facilitates, then that drug isn't actually efficacious. On the contrary, it's not a drug but rather an *experience*, which means the drug is just a placebo. How does the FDA suggest that researchers prove it's a "real" drug? David Nutt explains, "The FDA have said to researchers like us, the only way to prove whether these drugs work is to give them under anesthesia, which I think is both unethical and absolutely stupid." Nutt finds the pushback against the emotionally therapeutic experience of psychedelics absurd. "It's the negative emotional experiences that fucks their brains up for decades. I think it would be kind of bizarre if the emotional experience [of psychedelics] didn't have some bearing [on fixing them]."

As we learned in Chapter 3, David Yaden began his academic career studying religious callings, STEs, and awe. Over time, however, he became frustrated by how fleeting some of the benefits of experimentally induced awe were, eventually landing on psychedelics as the most reliable conduit to gather insight into awe. "Basically, psychedelics are, I think, the only real game in town to induce reliably very strong experiences of awe." Yaden now works exclusively in psychedelics and has transferred to Johns Hopkins University School of Medicine's Center for Psychedelic and Consciousness Research, so he has greater freedom to do so. He believes the long-lasting, mind-altering power of wonder is best unleashed by the psychedelic experience. "Going up and looking at a scenic, really awe-inspiring, wonder-inducing overlook—I don't think we know how long we can expect those effects to last. . . . Whereas psychedelics I believe are enduring."

For her part, Lani Shiota is apprehensive about the allure of psychedelics as a speed train to awe, cautioning, "Speed is not always the solution." She sees a higher benefit in slow science. Shiota recognizes the potential for using psychedelics as a therapy adjunct that primes the patient with cognitive malleability and is then followed up with traditional therapy to change the self-schema, but she warns against overexuberance and wants to see more rigorous research to back it up. "That mechanism-level, randomized-control trial work is simply not being done. And it needs to because there's so much potential here. But it's expensive work. It's hard work. It's longitudinal work. You've got to let it play out over time and not be overly ambitious in what you expect with a single-shot intervention."

Shiota is confident, however, that small doses of wonder over time can have benefits, even if she is still withholding judgment about psychedelics. "So, if we just want to make the claim that small doses, on a regular basis, can help us settle ourselves, reduce some stress, put our personal problems into perspective, and calm us down? Well, there's plenty of evidence for that." And she is hopeful, *cautiously*, that future research will yield evidence that further supports psychedelic wonder's broader impacts. "I think the jury's still out. It's a good hypothesis, so there's good evidence to try to do the really rigorous, randomized controlled trials with strong control conditions that would ask, 'Does this work and why?'"

Walking through the doors of perception

Answering the question of how psychedelics are so effective is the crux of psychedelic medicine. Assuming it isn't chemistry and pharmacology but rather the subjective experience of tripping that creates enduring impacts, what exactly is happening to one's psyche during that subjective experience? When I ask any of the people who work in psychedelics that question, they usually respond by saying there is far more that we don't understand about the brain and consciousness than we do. "It's very interesting," says Nutt. "It just shows the power of the mind, which we need to explore." He hopes to understand the phenomenon of shared hallucinations, believing that may offer some new insight into how we subconsciously communicate with one another. "We're very interested to see whether we can link people up through the EEGs and see if we can see synchronicity. It's going to be a while before we do that, but it's a very interesting concept."

Psychedelic researchers are a bit—no, they are *very*—cautious about bringing in any hint of parapsychology when discussing psychedelics. They will dance around the topic of consciousness and admit that there is much we don't quite know, but the metaphysical becomes an unseemly matter. That's not to say that they aren't open to the idea of the inexplicable, but they prefer to be precise. "I find being able to stay in a state of mystery keeps me in wonder," says Yaden. "And I find that a lot of people are too quick to collapse their unknowing into a false sense of certainty. . . . And I'm comfortable with staying in a state of unknowing."

David Luke, senior lecturer for psychology at the University of Greenwich, however, is happy to broach the subject. "There is a huge amount of speculation. Even the way in which we do science and the kind of answers we can get is determined by the questions we ask, so we only ask questions which fit within our reality tunnel." He sees scientific and societal norms colluding in a sense to keep parapsychology out of the conversation. "That's why we don't see much parapsychology, let alone psychedelic parapsychology. Because even asking those kinds of questions is taboo and an anathema to the foundations of scientism, which is that there's this kind of materialist reductionist reality." While most of the psychologists I have spoken to would agree with Luke's concerns about reductionism, they are reluctant to explore this aspect of psychedelic science. "Even to explore possible alternatives to brain-based consciousness is kind of like taboo, so it becomes ridiculed, it becomes ostracized, and therefore there's not much of a kind of scientific attention paid to it, and so we just carry on reinforcing our own particular world views about the nature of reality and the brain and consciousness."

In the spring of 1953, supervised by Humphry Osmond, author Aldous Huxley took four-tenths of a gram of mescaline, and this experience became the fodder for his autobiographical book The Doors of Perception. The publication became a counterculture hit and was the inspiration for the name of Jim Morrison's band, the Doors. Most well known for his dystopian novel Brave New World, Huxley became fascinated by the potential of psychedelics to expand our thinking, coming to believe that they open a door in our mind to places that are always there, always accessible, but that our psyches suppress. (And you can count Huxley as an early adopter of psychedelics for easing the fear of death, as he requested LSD on his deathbed, which his wife obligingly injected.) David Nutt sees Huxley's perspective as valid. "Why would people's perceptions of the world become much more powerful and relevant and awesome under psychedelics? Because psychedelics break down your brain. The brain just dampens down things it doesn't want you to be bothered with. And the fact that it can be brought back to consciousness by psychedelics is proof of Huxley's theory of the brain."

Regardless of the cause, these psychedelic experiences are extraordinary to the participants. David Yaden's research revealed that about two-thirds of study participants who took psilocybin reported a mystical experience that ranked among the top five most meaningful moments in their lives, and more than 10 percent said it was the *single* most meaningful experience of their lives. Nutt calls this last statistic "one of the most important figures in the last twenty years of psychology." In one of the most famous psychedelic experiments, psychologist Walter Pahnke's 1962 Good Friday experiment, researchers had divinity students take psilocybin or a placebo before attending a Good Friday church service. The participants who took the psilocybin unanimously rated the event as one of the most meaningful experiences of their spiritual lives—*a full twenty-five years later.* Bill Richards, a colleague of Yaden's at Johns Hopkins, put it this way: "You go deep enough or far out enough in consciousness and you will bump into the sacred. It's not something we generate; it's something out there waiting to be discovered. And this reliably happens to non-believers as well as believers."

But, as Yaden notes, people also consider these their most daunting experiences. "People will say that their psychedelic experience was not only highly meaningful, highly positive, and sometimes, if they're religious or spiritual, they'll say it's highly spiritually significant, but they'll also say it was extremely challenging." Yaden believes this dichotomy is part of its potency. "I think awe and wonder—these self-transcendent experiences—challenge our cultural reflex to see things as purely positive or purely negative. It's a little bit of both. It's difficult, but it's ultimately profound."

Scientists are also looking at alternatives to psychedelics that may generate the same level of self-transcendent benefit. David Nutt has seen promising research with two such candidates—holotropic breathwork and meditation. Still, there is a recognition that while they may create some similar effects *eventually*, the rigor and time it takes to become proficient enough at either is a stumbling block to practicality. "These drugs facilitate access to the mind in a way that nothing else does as easily," acknowledges Nutt. "And the similarities between deep meditation and psychedelics—the point is, it takes you twenty years to get there, whereas we can get there with psilocybin in about twenty seconds." Of course, this may not be entirely accurate. As we learned in Chapter 15, a master yogi's mind has undergone a fundamental shift in consciousness that may be more profound than that of a single psychedelic dose. (Although there could be some Olympic-level psychedelic users who have yet to be tested, so it's possible they have similar attributes.)

There has been a massive shift in public sentiment toward psychedelics. In 2020, Oregon became the first state to legalize psilocybin for therapeutic use, and nine more are considering active legislation to loosen restrictions. (You know it's gone mainstream when the *Today* show and *Good Housekeeping* are covering the research.) There is still a long way to go, and there exists the ever-present risk of overstating the benefits or hysteria taking hold again in violation of the science, but it would appear we have reached a tipping point in the war against psychedelics.

It might seem odd to include psychedelics in a section about living in wonder—it's not exactly an approach that many of us will have occasion to experience. But psychedelics are a conduit between the science and soul of wonder. On one side of the door of perception sits the chemistry, the pharmacology, the neuroscience. Receptors and statistical maps. The small brain network and the default mode network. And then, on the other side of the door is the ineffable, the mysterious, the mystical, the magical. Psychedelics don't open that door. They're merely one key of many. Wonder opens that door. It's our choice to walk through it. And choosing to walk through the door that separates our daily reality from the magic that resides on the other side is a decision we can make every day—a decision to live in wonder.

WONDER WRAP-UP

- Psychedelics have been used in rituals and healing for millennia. In the mid-1940s, Albert Hofmann discovered LSD, and it showed great promise for the treatment of several conditions. In the 1960s, however, psychedelics' association with the counterculture forced them into the fringe, and research on them was made illegal. Because of this prohibition, there is a lingering stigma to psychedelics, and studying them remains challenging.

- The term *psychedelics*, coined by Humphry Osmond, means "mind-manifesting," which speaks to the changes within the mind, not just the hallucinations that may accompany them. There are a number of psychedelics, but LSD and psilocybin are the ones most associated with studying wonder.

- Psychedelics appear to work by causing a disruption in the default mode network such that the filters that naturally constrain our thinking are lifted. This period of destabilization creates a window of wonder-induced malleability that can then be harnessed with psychotherapy.

• Psychedelics can help reduce the symptoms of addiction, depression, anxiety, and OCD primarily by quieting rumination. These results can be realized in as little as one dose. The effect is not pharmacological but subjective, meaning it is the experience of the trip that changes mental schemas, not chemical effects like those found in antidepressants.

• There need to be more randomized controlled trials, and caution is needed to not overhype the benefits, but the current findings are incredibly encouraging.

• These drugs' inexplicable, ineffable nature invites a metaphysical or parapsychological perspective. Scientists are cautious about entering this discussion, but given the unfathomable mystery of experiences with psychedelics, what we know about consciousness appears insufficient to illuminate their profundity and wonder.

17

Overtone

Some of the earliest composed group vocal performances are the pre-polyphonic religious chants from the ninth and tenth centuries. Credited to Pope Gregory I, who ruled some three hundred years prior in AD 590, and hence called Gregorian chants, the monophonic masterpieces were shared and transmitted orally as early as 800, and the first written example dates to 930. Known for their uniform and unison style, they were sung with no harmony, as the polyphonic style had not yet been developed. Perhaps, however, it is better said that harmony always existed but was yet to be discovered.

Monks performed these pieces in grand churches built with a keen ear toward amplifying sound. When the groups sang their singular tones in perfect pitch, a happy accident of aural physics occurred—the overtone, a psychoacoustic phenomenon in which tonal frequency and acoustic design marry in such a way that the single tone being sung splits into harmony. It is thought that hearing the overtone of their own voices in third and fifth harmonics provided the creative impetus to compose polyphonic music, mimicking what the monks heard resonate in the church. Always there and ready to be heard, harmonies revealed themselves as a peculiarity of pure absorption in single tonality.

Tibetan monk throat singers, however, have learned how to simultaneously produce primary tone and overtone through the manipulation of their vocal folds. They reshape their own oral cavity to create resonance. Compare these two groups—both using music to communicate and worship, with one discovering overtone by happenstance and the other creating it through intentional manipulation. One stumbled upon by chance when the conditions were ideal, and the other developed as a practice.

The summer between my senior year in high school and my freshman year in college, I toured Europe with my high school choir. It was a very Up with People sort of vibe. The trip involved homestays and hostels, no internet or mobile phones, fifty of your closest friends packed onto a bus, traveling around, singing in town squares and church halls. That summer remains the source of some of my most wonder-filled memories.

While the time with friends and the adventure of new cultures was undoubtedly an enormous part of the experience, what was most memorable was the music. I recall one particularly stirring concert where we performed in the same church Mozart had as a seven-year-old boy. His breath seemed to still hang in the air. And when we sang, our voices mingled with the lingering spirits of everyone who had ever performed in that space before us. Like the patina on an old piece of furniture, layers and layers of musical history fused into the structure of the cathedral seemed to shine again when burnished with our contribution.

What stands out in my memory of that performance was the overtone we created that night. It was otherworldly. The acoustics in the space made our choir sound twice the size, with notes hanging magically above and below our own voices. It's one thing to hear music like this, but another altogether to *make* it; to feel it reverberate in your chest, your heart, and inch its way up your spine until you feel like your whole body is vibrating. It still moves me. But to achieve this frisson took years of rehearsals, the acoustic embrace of a sonorous space, and an alchemical consequence of how our brain interprets the phonic environment. Wonder is like this—experiencing it is a synthesis of practice, design, and magic.

Imagine the exhilaration, the pure sensorial perception the overtone must have seemed to those monks when they heard it for the first time. Or when the earliest humans glimpsed an eclipse or phosphorescence or a murmuration. For millennia we viewed stars with our naked eye, but before the first telescope was invented in the 1600s, the true vastness of the cosmos was more a matter of imagination than science. Prior to the microscope, we couldn't even conceive of the mysterious quantum dance that resides within all matter. But it existed nonetheless. Perhaps wonder is our psychoscope—the device that allows us to peer inside our consciousness and see beyond our current conception of ourselves, no longer constrained by just mystery and our imagination.

Maybe, like the monks who heard the harmonies, or Hofmann, who discovered LSD, wonder skims its hand ever so gently across the filmy ethereal veil that separates us from some other consciousness, causing the veil to flutter, to become disturbed, and every so often perhaps coaxing it to fall back for a moment such that we can see the realm beyond. And what do we see beyond the veil? Hope? Healing? Peace? Empathy? Grace? Solidarity? Oneness? Maybe just possibilities. I can't be sure, but I have to believe that perhaps there lie some of the angels of our better nature. The part of us—that each has hidden somewhere—that wants to find connection rather than discord.

I am not a Pollyanna. Sometimes life sucks. And seeking wonder means sending an invitation to all experience. Invariably, when we invite Good to the party, Bad is sure to be her plus one. (Why she won't dump that creep, I'll never know, but opposites attract.) With wonder, we can entertain them both. Happiness is a fickle friend, so warm in his sun and yet so cold in his shadow. Wonder finds us in all shades of light and dark. In grief and pain. In joy and laughter. In bittersweet longing and transition and loss. I guess it takes some sort of hope to seek wonder, but in that hope there is bravery, too. Because by seeking it, we are expressing that we are open to change, curious for connection, willingly vulnerable in the presence of transcendence.

If you look for wonder and think there is none to be found, look again. It may not come packaged in sunsets and dolphins and rainbows. Sometimes there is violence in wonder. Consider birth, or the struggle of a butterfly as it wriggles free of its chrysalis. Wonder is woven into our life out of whole cloth, so it can't be free of darkness. Look inward. Find the pure, clear tone that resonates within. Allow its crystalline vibration to ripple from you. Watch as it caroms off life's hard, rough surfaces, softening them, and returning to you as wonder.

A thread throughout this book is that there exists a magic crackle, a sacred thrum, found at the threshold between two states. Liminal space has its own tantalizing quality to it. Like the overtone, these moments are our indication that we are at the cusp of more. It's the voice heard through the wall. Indistinct, discarnate, but undeniable. If you take nothing from this book, take that. *There is more.* This chaotic, insane, baffling, lush, enchanting, intricate, tender, fragile earthly plane hurtling through space is not all there is. Even this corporeal being— creaky knees and restless minds and full hearts—is just the smallest snicket of our essence.

This world that we experience. That gives us stress and agita and angst. That seems some days to be fueled by nothing more than caffeine and vitriol. It's just an illusion. Your money, your stuff, your KPIs. That's an illusion, too. And I know some days this illusion trope is hard to swallow because the looming deadlines and the co-pays and the cranapple juice stain on the new carpet seem pretty f*cking real. But I'm just saying it's not *all* there is. *There is more.* And like the overtone, when we become attuned to more, when we cross over the threshold and walk through the door of perception, the magnitude of this illusory world shrinks in relation to the wonder we find on the other side.

In the spirit of full disclosure, I have to divulge—this whole "follow a wonder practice every day and become a higher-consciousness human" thing? *I am not good at it.* Lest you think that I am some sort of Jedi wonder master, allow me to disabuse you of that notion. I am not. I am a bundle of anxiety and self-doubt, terrified of screwing up, a bit standoffish because I'm actually an introvert but no one believes me, and someone who wore the same pair of leggings for two straight weeks in the autumn of 2020.*

But I continue to try. Because I believe. I believe there is more—untapped, unseen. I believe we came into the world made of stardust and inherent goodness, and we all yearn to return, even if we don't know how. I believe relentless reality breaks us, and magical wonder can make us whole. Maybe not perfectly whole, not pristine, but a sort of kintsugi of the soul. Wonder is the precious metal we pour into the fissures of our broken selves, and it fuses us back together, perfectly imperfect.

I believe in wonder when I don't believe in myself. I believe in wonder when I don't believe in the goodness of the world. I believe in wonder when I don't believe that the lovely waiter will

---

* I referred to these as my "space pants" because when I was researching the Overview Effect, I learned that astronauts wear their clothes until they are filthy and then jettison them into space. It was my attempt at method writing.

remember my neurotically complex order without writing it down. Because we all have to believe in something or the magic inside us dies. And wonder, to me, is both tangible *and* magical. It's like Avalon dropped a rope down to us and said, *Climb up.*

I also believe we can be better. As individual humans. As families and communities and businesses and governments. As first-timers and old-timers. As students and teachers. As friends and lovers and parents and complete strangers.

What might the world be if we met one another in wonder? With nonjudgmental openness, with empathetic curiosity, with our minds willing to be filled and changed, with the focus and attention that reflect our gratitude for that moment, in awe of the very nature of existence. If we did that, we might be able to pull this veil back together.

And I believe if we approach our day and one another with wonder, if we approach life like a beginner, if we open ourselves to the f*cking magic, we will become better. I'm not talking change-the-world-tomorrow better, but marginal gains. Let's start there. It takes time. Even the starlight we see today took hundreds of years to reach us. Let's make the small changes in ourselves that cascade outward. We can change the world next year. Today let's just breathe, believe, and follow wonder.

Acknowledgments

Writing this book has been one of the most wonder-filled explorations of my life. Terrifying yet exhilarating. Profound gratitude to those who encouraged me, challenged me, and just made me feel capable. I was a stranger to many of you, yet you shared your time, support, contacts, and knowledge so freely. It is my privilege to thank you for your role in making this book possible.

First, if you've made it this far, dear reader, thank you! Allen Ginsberg said, "Follow your inner moonlight." I hope you follow your inner wonder and share your glow with the world.

Steve Harris, my manager, what a mensch you are in every sense of the word. Thank you for taking a chance on me and for your wisdom, patience, and positivity—what a guy.

My editor, Sara Carder, meeting you was kismet. You are a magical combination of warm, expressive, nerdy, and simply brilliant at your job. Your contributions to the manuscript and to me as an author are immeasurable.

Debbie Reber, my book coach, you can make a silk purse out of a sow's ear. Your deft guidance and compassion drew out the best in me. You are a special soul.

I'm grateful to everyone at Penguin Random House and TarcherPerigee, including Lindsay Gordon for your fierce protection of authors; Ashley Alliano, Anne Kosmoski, Sara Johnson, and Katie Macleod-English for your instant enthusiasm about the book; Caroline Johnson for your beautiful jacket design; and Kim Lewis for your dogged attention to detail. And, of course, that extends to the dozens of PRH folk unseen by me who perfected the book and ushered it into the hands of readers.

To Peter, Alana, Brian, and Margaret, my trusted guides to the wild, wacky world of publishing, you make me feel like a superstar.

I love scientists, and I hope that is apparent in my writing. Particular thanks to those who made time to speak to me, including Dayna Johnson, Melanie Rudd, Lani Shiota, Jennifer Stellar, Tierney Thys, Jim Garrison, Scott Barry Kaufman, Dacher Keltner, John Leach, Beau Lotto, David Nutt, Kirk Schneider, Azizi Seixas, and David Yaden. You are rock stars, and it is my absolute honor to amplify your work.

Additional thanks to others who contributed, including Betty Bienert, Alison Levine, Kruti Parekh, Madelyn Willis, Jason Burton, Steven Callahan, Chris Johnston, David Pearl, and Nathan Sawaya. Your expertise and stories of wonder gave the book depth and humanity.

Humble gratitude to Daniel Pink and David Eagleman. My little nerd heart is full from your support.

Anne Lamott, on some long nights, Bird by Bird became like a prayer to me.

Ann O'Dea, the pied piper of amazing humans, meeting you has changed the trajectory of my life. The phenomenal community you've built made this possible.

Carol Franco, you once said to me, "I live in service of authors." You've proven that beyond question. Nilofer Merchant, your intro to Carol was a small gesture that has had a monumental impact. I am in both your debts.

To my Wonder Women, thank you for being there. Special thanks to Elena Rossini for my stunning headshots and to Anne Ravanona, my impostor-syndrome slayer.

Kelly Hoey, my book cheerleader, partner-in-dreams, and ego-boost champion, may our lives be forever entwined. "Celebrate every milestone!" Thank you for this constant reminder, and for your true and steadfast friendship.

Mom, the woman who continues to teach me the power of positive thinking (despite my best efforts), thank you for showing me that science and soul can and should coexist.

Dad, who's fond of saying, "I'd rather be lucky than smart." As it turns out, you're both. Thank you for imparting to me your love of words, and for a superlative education that's granted me a life of opportunity.

My brother, Phil, whose love language is snark, thanks for supporting every twist and turn I have taken in life, while mocking me as only a big brother can.

I appreciate the many family and friends who listened to me talk about wonder nonstop and politely feigned interest, especially Zoe and Mirabel, the brightest stars in my firmament. I wish you a lifetime of wonder. Thanks also to Georgine, Maggie, Buzz, Jacque, Sarah, Sue, Laura, Evan, Joel, Ashley, Craig, Trisha, Meagan, Arthur, and PK.

And to those who I feel supporting me from beyond the veil, especially Dr. Selwyn Hartley, a man of so few words, and yet every one you uttered was a rapier. Your pen is being put to good use.

Jude, thank you for your patience, for keeping Dad occupied, and for your creative Easter egg contributions. I hope you see little bits of yourself here.

Last, but certainly not least, Julian, this book is yours. I would never have had the guts, the stamina, the faith to make it. From living with a vampire to constructing my homemade pandemic desk ("made with love and Dettol"), any success I have is because of your unalloyed commitment to me, to us. The truth is, I don't have the words to express what you mean to me. They should have sent a poet.

Notes

Introduction

4   **Automation:** Manyika, James, Susan Lund, Michael Chui, Jacques Bughin, Jonathan Woetzel, Parul Batra, Ryan Ko, and Saurabh Sanghvi. 2017. "Jobs Lost, Jobs Gained: What the Future of Work Will Mean for Jobs, Skills, and Wages." n.d. *McKinsey & Company.* https://www.mckinsey.com/featured-insights/future-of-work/jobs-lost-jobs-gained-what-the-future-of-work-will-mean-for-jobs-skills-and-wages.

5   **Stress-related illness:** Krebs, K. 2007. "Stress Management, CAM Approach." *Encyclopedia of Stress,* 2nd ed. Edited by George Fink, 636–40. New York: Academic Press. doi:10.1016/B978012373947-6.00363-9.

5   **Empathy levels dropping:** Konrath, S. H., E. H. O'Brien, and C. Hsing. 2010. "Changes in Dispositional Empathy in American College Students over Time: A Meta-Analysis." *Personality and Social Psychology Review* 15 (2): 180–98. doi:10.1177/1088868310377395.

7   **Health and well-being benefits of curiosity:** Sakaki, Michiko, Ayano Yagi, and Kou Murayama. 2018. "Curiosity in Old Age: A Possible Key to Achieving Adaptive Aging." *Neuroscience & Biobehavioral Reviews* 88 (May): 106–16. doi:10.1016/j.neubiorev.2018.03.007.

7   **Cancer and cytokines:** Kabel, Ahmed M. 2014. "Relationship Between Cancer and Cytokines." *Journal of Cancer Research and Treatment* 2 (2): 41–3. doi:10.12691/jcrt-2-2-3.

7   **"biological pathway":** Stellar, Jennifer E., Neha John-Henderson, Craig L. Anderson, Amie M. Gordon, Galen D. McNeil, and Dacher Keltner. 2015. "Positive Affect and Markers of Inflammation: Discrete Positive Emotions Predict Lower Levels of Inflammatory Cytokines." *Emotion* 15 (2): 129–33. doi:10.1037/emo0000033.

7 **"Man is the only animal that blushes":** Twain, Mark. 1970. *Man Is the Only Animal That Blushes . . . or Needs To: the Wisdom of Mark Twain.* Los Angeles: Stanyan Books.

8 **Universal facial expressions:** Ekman, Paul. 1992. "Facial expressions of emotion: an old controversy and new findings." *Philosophical Transactions of the Royal Society of London. Series B: Biological Sciences* 335, no. 1273: 63–69; Ekman, Paul. 1982. "Methods for measuring facial action." *Handbook of Methods in Nonverbal Behavior Research:* 45–90.

8 **Intersubjectivity:** Rochat, Philippe, Cláudia Passos-Ferreira, and Pedro Salem. 2009. "Three Levels of Intersubjectivity in Early Development." *Enacting Intersubjectivity: Paving the Way for a Dialogue Between Cognitive Science, Social Cognition and Neuroscience.* Edited by Antonella Carassa, Francesca Morganti, and Giuseppe Riva, 73–190. Lugano, Switzerland: Università Svizzera Italiana.

8 **Fifty words for snow:** Boas, Franz. 1938. *Handbook of American Indian Languages.* No. 40. US Government Printing Office.

8 **Great Eskimo vocabulary hoax:** This is a somewhat controversial factoid. You can find more about anthropologist Franz Boas and Inuit languages here: Krupnik, Igor. 2010. *SIKU: Knowing Our Ice: Documenting Inuit Sea Ice Knowledge and Use.* London: Springer.

9 **Definition of wonder (noun):** "Wonder, n." n.d. OED Online. Oxford University Press. https://www.oed.com/view/Entry/229936?result=1&rskey=emnGCf&.

9 **Definition of wonder (verb):** "Wonder, v." n.d. OED Online. Oxford University Press. https://www.oed.com/view/Entry/229938?rskey=aFwJPj&result=3.

9 **Wonder as an "umbrella term":** Paulson, Steve, Lisa Sideris, Jennifer Stellar, and Piercarlo Valdesolo. 2021. "Beyond Oneself: The Ethics and Psychology of Awe." *Annals of the New York Academy of Sciences* 1501 (1): 30–47. doi:10.1111/nyas.14323.

9 **Chinese characters for wonder:** Betty Bienert, communication with author, 2021.

9 **"Eyelashes are slightly curved":** Muni, Bharata, and Manomohan Ghosh. 2016. *Nāṭyaśāstram: A Treatise on Ancient Indian Dramaturgy and Histrionics.* Varanasi: Chaukhamba Surbharati Prakashan.

10 **William Whewell and scientist:** "How the Word 'Scientist' Came to Be." n.d. NPR.org. https://www.npr.org/2010/05/21/127037417/how-the-word-scientist-came-to-be.

11 **Randomized controlled trial:** There is some pushback to this assumption, as some say there are limitations with the randomized

control trial, and that it is not always the best experimental design in all circumstances. Grossman, Jason, and Fiona J. Mackenzie. 2005. "The Randomized Controlled Trial: Gold Standard, or Merely Standard?" *Perspectives in Biology and Medicine* 48 (4): 516–34. doi:10.1353/pbm.2005.0092.

11 **Complexity of the brain:** Herculano-Houzel, Suzana. 2009. "The Human Brain in Numbers: A Linearly Scaled-Up Primate Brain." *Frontiers in Human Neuroscience* 3 (31). doi:10.3389/neuro.09.031.2009.

11 **Energy expenditure of the brain:** Herculano-Houzel, S. 2012. "The Remarkable, Yet Not Extraordinary, Human Brain as a Scaled-Up Primate Brain and Its Associated Cost." *Proceedings of the National Academy of Sciences* 109 (Supplement_1): 10661–68. doi:10.1073/pnas.1201895109.

13 **Mind-body dualism:** Rossano, Matt J. 2006. "The Religious Mind and the Evolution of Religion." *Review of General Psychology* 10 (4): 346–364. doi:10.1037/1089-2680.10.4.346.

13 **Supraphysical:** *Supraphysical* isn't really a word used very often, and by their strict definitions, you could use the words *supernatural* or *metaphysical*. But their connotation has been co-opted to mean "fantastical" and "not real," so this felt most apt.

14 **Depression and anxiety statistics:** "Depression." 2021. World Health Organization. https://www.who.int/news-room/fact-sheets/detail/depression.

14 **Anxiety statistics:** "Facts & Statistics." 2021. Anxiety and Depression Association of America (April 21). https://adaa.org/understanding-anxiety/facts-statistics.

15 **Cost of mental illness:** Roehrig, Charles. 2016. "Mental Disorders Top the List of the Most Costly Conditions in the United States: $201 Billion." *Health Affairs* 35 (6): 1130–35. doi:10.1377/hlthaff.2015.1659.

15 **Etymology of happiness:** "Happy, Adj. and n." n.d. OED Online. Oxford University Press. https://www.oed.com/view/Entry/84074.

15 **Aristippus's parenting style:** By all accounts, Aristippus was quite a piece of work. Reportedly, when he was admonished for failing to protect his son from harm, he retorted that "phlegm and vermin are also of our own begetting, but we still cast them as far away from us as possible because they are useless." Charming. "Aristippus." n.d. *Internet Encyclopedia of Philosophy.* https://iep.utm.edu/aristippus/.

15 **Aristippus and hedonism:** Lampe, Kurt. 2014. "The Birth of Hedonism." *The Birth of Hedonism.* Princeton: Princeton University Press.

16 **Aristotle and eudaimonia:** Aristotle, W. D. Ross, and Lesley Brown. 2009. *The Nicomachean Ethics.* Oxford: Oxford University Press.

17 **Awe oppositional to money:** Jiang, Libin, Jun Yin, Dongmei Mei, Hong Zhu, and Xinyue Zhou. 2018. "Awe Weakens the Desire for Money." *Journal of Pacific Rim Psychology* 12. Cambridge University Press: e4. doi:10.1017/prp.2017.27.

17 **"wonder-amazement of living":** Schneider, Kirk J. 2009. *Awakening to Awe: Personal Stories of Profound Transformation.* Lanham, MD: Jason Aronson.

17 **"I would say it adds to the vitality":** Kirk Schneider, interview with author, 2021.

17 **"we're all so bad at pursuing happiness":** Melanie Rudd, interview with author, 2021.

17 **Affective forecasting:** Wilson, Timothy D., and Daniel T. Gilbert. 2003. "Affective Forecasting." *Advances in Experimental Social Psychology* 35: 345–411. doi:10.1016/s0065-2601(03)01006-2.

18 **Emodiversity improves coping:** Tugade, Michele M., Barbara L. Fredrickson, and Lisa Feldman Barrett. 2004. "Psychological Resilience and Positive Emotional Granularity: Examining the Benefits of Positive Emotions on Coping and Health." *Journal of Personality* 72 (6): 1161–90. doi:10.1111/j.1467-6494.2004.00294.x.

19 **Psychological richness:** Oishi, Shigehiro, and Erin C. Westgate. 2021. "A Psychologically Rich Life: Beyond Happiness and Meaning." *Psychological Review.* doi:10.1037/rev0000317.

19 **"You're either a lumper":** David Yaden, interview with author, 2021.

20 **"family resemblances":** McLachlan, Hugh V. 1981. "Wittgenstein, Family Resemblances and the Theory of Classification." *International Journal of Sociology and Social Policy* 1 (1): 1–16. doi:10.1108/eb012920.

Chapter 1: Watch

24 **William James's background:** Richardson, Robert D. 2007. *William James: In the Maelstrom of American Modernism: A Biography.* Boston: Houghton Mifflin Company.

25 **"at sea in a dense fog":** Sullivan, Annie, and Helen Keller. 1905. *The Story of My Life.* United States: Grosset and Dunlap.

25 **"When I was a little girl":** Keller, Helen. 1929. *Midstream: My Later Life.* Garden City, NY: Doubleday, Doran & Company, Inc.

25 **Keller and eugenics:** One of Keller's regrettably less progressive ideas, eugenics, was made public during a 1915 controversy regarding

"Baby Bollinger," in which Keller came out in support of medical professionals who allowed the death of an infant with significant, but treatable, disabilities. Gerdtz, John. 2006. "Disability and Euthanasia: The Case of Helen Keller and the Bollinger Baby." *Life and Learning* 16 (15): 491–500.

25 **"Perhaps because she was blind":** Du Bois, William Edward Burghardt. 1982. *Writings by W.E.B. Du Bois in Non-periodical Literature Edited by Others.* Millwood, NY: Kraus-Thomson.

26 **Keller FBI file:** Keller's FBI file can be viewed at https://vault.fbi .gov/Helen%20Keller/Helen%20Keller%20Part%201%20of%201 /view.

26 **"You have escaped from your prison-house":** Keller, Helen A. Letter to Joseph E. Chamberlin. September 10, 1930. "Letter from Helen Keller to J. E. Chamberlin with Accompanying Article Entitled 'My Recollections of . . .'" Helen Keller Archive, American Foundation for the Blind. https://www.afb.org/HelenKellerArchive?a=d&d=A-HK01 -03-B050-F08-007&e=-------en-20--1--txt--------3------------------0-1.

27 **High in openness attributes:** McCrae, Robert R. 2004. "Openness to Experience." *Encyclopedia of Applied Psychology,* 707–9. doi:10.1016/b0 -12-657410-3/00068-4.

27 **World War I personality tests:** Gibby, Robert E., and Michael J. Zickar. 2008. "A History of the Early Days of Personality Testing in American Industry: An Obsession with Adjustment." *History of Psychology* 11 (3): 164–84. doi:10.1037/a0013041.

28 **Mixed results of Enneagram:** The Enneagram has shown "mixed evidence of reliability and validity" but it is "helpful for personal/ spiritual growth." Hook, Joshua N., Todd W. Hall, Don E. Davis, Daryl R. Van Tongeren, and Mackenzie Conner. 2020. "The Enneagram: A Systematic Review of the Literature and Directions for Future Research." *Journal of Clinical Psychology* 77 (4): 865–83. doi:10.1002/jclp.23097.

28 **Accuracy of the MBTI:** The unreliability of the MBTI is disputed by the company that publishes the tool, but as of this writing, there has been no academic validity of the tool established. Pittenger, David J. 2005. "Cautionary Comments Regarding the Myers-Briggs Type Indicator." *Consulting Psychology Journal: Practice and Research* 57 (3): 210. doi:10.1037/1065-9293.57.3.210.

28 **Big Five personality inventory:** The Big Five was first developed in 1884 by Sir Francis Galton using a unique "lexical hypothesis." The theory was, if people have different characteristics, and understanding and communicating those characteristics is primary

to functioning as a society, then humans must have also developed language to describe them. So researchers studied personality traits through the lens of our own language. Goldberg, Lewis R. 1990. "An Alternative 'Description of Personality': The Big-Five Factor Structure." *Journal of Personality and Social Psychology* 59 (6): 1216–29. doi:10.1037//0022-3514.59.6.1216.

29 **Big Five is predictive:** Cobb-Clark, Deborah A., and Stefanie Schurer. 2012. "The Stability of Big-Five Personality Traits." *Economics Letters* 115 (1): 11–15. doi:10.1016/j.econlet.2011.11.015.

29 **People high in openness are more wonderprone—curiosity:** Kashdan, Todd B., Matthew W. Gallagher, Paul J. Silvia, Beate P. Winterstein, William E. Breen, Daniel Terhar, and Michael F. Steger. 2009. "The Curiosity and Exploration Inventory-II: Development, Factor Structure, and Psychometrics." *Journal of Research in Personality* 43 (6): 987–98. doi:10.1016/j.jrp.2009.04.011.

29 **People high in openness are more wonderprone—absorption:** Tellegen, Auke, and Gilbert Atkinson. 1974. "Openness to Absorbing and Self-Altering Experiences ('Absorption'), a Trait Related to Hypnotic Susceptibility." *Journal of Abnormal Psychology* 83 (3): 268–77. doi:10.1037/h0036681.

29 **People high in openness are more wonderprone—awe:** Dong, Rui, and Shi G. Ni. 2020. "Openness to Experience, Extraversion, and Subjective Well-Being Among Chinese College Students: The Mediating Role of Dispositional Awe." *Psychological Reports* 123 (3): 903–28. doi:10.1177/0033294119826884.

29 **"It is as though":** Smillie, Luke. 2017. "Openness to Experience: The Gates of the Mind." *Scientific American* (August 15). https://www .scientificamerican.com/article/openness-to-experience-the-gates -of-the-mind/.

30 **"People high in openness":** Silvia, Paul J., Kirill Fayn, Emily C. Nusbaum, and Roger E. Beaty. 2015. "Openness to Experience and Awe in Response to Nature and Music: Personality and Profound Aesthetic Experiences." *Psychology of Aesthetics, Creativity, and the Arts* 9 (4): 376–84. doi:10.1037/aca0000028.

30 **Twin studies and personality:** Nature-versus-nurture twin studies can be traced back to 1875 and British scientist Sir Francis Galton. The most well-known twin study is from 1990 by Thomas J. Bouchard Jr. of the University of Minnesota, in which Bouchard found eerily similar results (same spouse name, same career, etc.) across separated twins. Dixon, Travis. 2019. "Key Study: The Minnesota Twin Study of Twins Reared Apart." *IB Psychology*

(February). https://www.themantic-education.com/ibpsych/2019
/02/11/key-study-the-minnesota-twin-study-of-twins-reared-apart/.

31   **"grow and learn":** Dweck, Carol S. 2008. "Can Personality Be
Changed? The Role of Beliefs in Personality and Change." *Current
Directions in Psychological Science* 17 (6): 391–94. doi:10.1111/j.1467
-8721.2008.00612.x.

32   **"the sole cause":** Pascal, Blaise, and A. J. Krailsheimer (1670). 1995.
Pensées. London; New York: Penguin Books.

32   **"the existential vacuum":** Frankl, Viktor E. (1946). 2017. *Man's Search
for Meaning.* Boston: Beacon Press.

32   **"We are less bored":** Russell, Bertrand, and Daniel C. Dennett. 2013.
The Conquest of Happiness. New York: Liveright.

33   **Listen to boring newscasts for stimuli:** Loewenstein, George. 1994.
"The Psychology of Curiosity: A Review and Reinterpretation."
Psychological Bulletin 116 (1): 75. doi:10.1037/0033-2909.116.1.75.

33   **Rats take novel route:** Loewenstein, "The Psychology of Curiosity."

33   **Percentage of time mind-wandering:** Killingsworth, Matthew A.,
and Daniel T. Gilbert. 2010. "A Wandering Mind Is an Unhappy
Mind." *Science* 330 (6066): 932. doi:10.1126/science.1192439.

33   *Psychology of Day-Dreams:* Varendonck, J. 1921. *The Psychology of Day-
dreams.* London: George Allen & Unwin.

34   **"a cognitive control failure":** McMillan, Rebecca L., Scott
Barry Kaufman, and Jerome L. Singer. 2013. "Ode to Positive
Constructive Daydreaming." *Frontiers in Psychology* 4: 1–9. doi:10.3389
/fpsyg.2013.00626.

34   **Poor attentional control:** Mooneyham, Benjamin W., and Jonathan
W. Schooler. 2013. "The Costs and Benefits of Mind-Wandering: A
Review." *Canadian Journal of Experimental Psychology/Revue canadienne de
psychologie expérimentale* 67m (1): 11. doi:10.1037/a0031569.

34   **Positive constructive daydreaming associated with openness and
curiosity:** Zhiyan, Tang, and Jerome L. Singer. 1997. "Daydreaming
Styles, Emotionality and the Big Five Personality Dimensions."
Imagination, Cognition and Personality 16 (4): 399–414. doi:10.2190/ATEH
-96EV-EXYX-2ADB

34   **Positive constructive daydreaming associated with absorption:**
Roche, Suzanne M., and Kevin M. McConkey. 1990. "Absorption:
Nature, Assessment, and Correlates." *Journal of Personality and Social
Psychology* 59 (1): 91. doi:10.1037/0022-3514.59.1.91.

34   **Positive constructive daydreaming associated with awe:** Fox, Kieran

C. R., Jessica R. Andrews-Hanna, Caitlin Mills, Matthew L. Dixon, Jelena Markovic, Evan Thompson, and Kalina Christoff. 2018. "Affective Neuroscience of Self-Generated Thought." *Annals of the New York Academy of Sciences* 1426 (1): 25–51. doi:10.1111/nyas.13740.

34   **Benefits of positive constructive daydreaming:** McMillan et al., "Ode to Positive Constructive Daydreaming."

35   **Scott Barry Kaufman's childhood:** "Former 'Special Ed' Student's Book Shows Why It's Wrong to Label Kids." n.d. Today.com. https://www.today.com/parents/former-special-ed-students-book-shows-why -its-wrong-label-6C10415044.

36   **Canonical networks:** Thomas Yeo, B. T., Fenna M. Krienen, Jorge Sepulcre, Mert R. Sabuncu, Danial Lashkari, Marisa Hollinshead, Joshua L. Roffman et al. 2011. "The Organization of the Human Cerebral Cortex Estimated by Intrinsic Functional Connectivity." *Journal of Neurophysiology* 106 (3): 1125–65. doi:10.1152 /jn.00338.2011.

36   **The brain at "rest" and the default mode network:** Andrews-Hanna, Jessica R. 2011. "The Brain's Default Network and Its Adaptive Role in Internal Mentation." *The Neuroscientist* 18 (3): 251–70. doi:10.1177/1073858411403316.

36   **Role of the default mode network:** Fair, D. A., A. L. Cohen, N. U. F. Dosenbach, J. A. Church, F. M. Miezin, D. M. Barch, M. E. Raichle, S. E. Petersen, and B. L. Schlaggar. 2008. "The Maturing Architecture of the Brain's Default Network." *Proceedings of the National Academy of Sciences* 105 (10): 4028–32. doi:10.1073/pnas.0800376105.

37   **Benefits of a healthy DMN:** Mevel, Katell, Gaël Chételat, Francis Eustache, and Béatrice Desgranges. 2011. "The Default Mode Network in Healthy Aging and Alzheimer's Disease." *International Journal of Alzheimer's Disease* 2011: 1–9. doi:10.4061/2011/535816.

37   **"perception of what passes":** Locke, John, Alexander Campbell Fraser. 1894. *An Essay Concerning Human Understanding.* United Kingdom: Clarendon Press.

37   **Coining the term *consciousness*:** Some say Ralph Cudworth coined the term in his *The True Intellectual System of the Universe.* Carter, Benjamin. 2010. "Ralph Cudworth and the Theological Origins of Consciousness." *History of the Human Sciences* 23, no. 3 (July): 29–47. doi:10.1177/0952695110363354.

37   **The Zürau Aphorisms:** The manuscript containing these aphorisms, since published as *The Zürau Aphorisms*, was meant to be burned upon Kafka's death at his request, along with all his other

unpublished masterpieces. His friend Max Brod, who was charged with this task, refused. Find you a friend who loves you and your work as much as Max Brod loved Kafka's. Kafka, Franz, Roberto Calasso, Geoffrey Brock, and Michael Hofmann (1931). 2006. *The Zürau Aphorisms of Franz Kafka*. New York: Schocken Books.

37 **"You do not need to leave":** Kafka et al., *The Zürau Aphorisms of Franz Kafka*.

Chapter 2: Wander

41 **Dog poop pics experiment:** Hsee, Christopher, and Bowen Ruan. 2015. "Curiosity Kills the Cat." Association for Consumer Research North American Advances NA-43. http://www.acrwebsite.org /volumes/1019134/volumes/v43/NA-43.

42 **Higher engagement of negative posts:** Rathje, Steve, Jay J. Van Bavel, and Sander van der Linden. 2021. "Out-Group Animosity Drives Engagement on Social Media." *Proceedings of the National Academy of Sciences* 118 (26). doi:10.1073/pnas.2024292118.

42 **Ian Leslie on curiosity:** Leslie, Ian. 2015. *Curious: The Desire to Know & Why Your Future Depends on It*. London: Quercus.

43 **"impulse towards better cognition":** James, William. 2020. *Talks to Teachers on Psychology and Other Writings*. Edited by Graphyco Editions. Independently published.

43 **"I have no special talents":** Einstein, Albert. Letter to Carl Seelig, March 11, 1952. Einstein Archives 39-013.

43 **Curiosity in animals:** Pavlov, Ivan Petrovich. 1927. "Conditioned Reflexes: An Investigation of the Physiological Activity of the Cerebral Cortex." *Annals of Neurosciences* 17(3). doi:10.5214/ans.0972-7531.1017309.

43 **"exploration-exploitation trade-off":** Westfall, Chris. 2021. "Creative Solutions for Coping with Change at Work: A Conversation with David Eagleman." *Forbes* (August 9). https:// www.forbes.com/sites/chriswestfall/2021/08/09/creative-solutions -for-coping-with-change-at-work-a-conversation-with-david -eagleman/?sh=338bb66ceb98.

43 **Different types of curiosity:** Kashdan, Todd B., and Paul J. Silvia. 2009. "Curiosity and Interest: The Benefits of Thriving on Novelty and Challenge." Edited by Shane J. Lopez and C. R. Snyder. *The Oxford Handbook of Positive Psychology* (July), 366–74. doi:10.1093 /oxfordhb/9780195187243.013.0034.

43 **Caudate nucleus:** Villablanca, Jaime R. 2010. "Why Do We Have a Caudate Nucleus?" *Acta Biologiae Experimentalis* (Wars) 70 (1): 95–105.

44   **Models of curiosity:** Scrivner, Coltan. 2021. "Curiosity: A Behavioral Biology Perspective." doi:10.31234/OSF.IO/RQA5B.

44   **James's sensational/theoretic curiosity model:** James, *Talks to Teachers on Psychology and Other Writings.*

44   **Berlyne's perceptual/epistemic curiosity model:** Berlyne, D. E. 1954. "A Theory of Human Curiosity." *British Journal of Psychology.* General Section 45 (3): 180–91. doi:10.1111/j.2044-8295.1954.tb01243.x.

44   **Kashdan's five-factor model of curiosity:** Kashdan, Todd B., Melissa C. Stiksma, David J. Disabato, Patrick E. McKnight, John Bekier, Joel Kaji, and Rachel Lazarus. 2018. "The Five-Dimensional Curiosity Scale: Capturing the Bandwidth of Curiosity and Identifying Four Unique Subgroups of Curious People." *Journal of Research in Personality* 73: 130–49. doi:10.1016/j.jrp.2017.11.011.

45   **Purpose of curiosity:** Kashdan and Silvia, "Curiosity and Interest."

45   **Different motivations for curiosity:** Litman, Jordan A. 2007. "Curiosity as a Feeling of Interest and Feeling of Deprivation: The I/D Model of Curiosity. *Issues in the Psychology of Motivation* 149: 156.

45   **Kashdan's social curiosity:** Kashdan later modified this subtrait to reflect overt and covert social curiosity, differentiating between those who gossip and those with more positive interpersonal skills. Kashdan, Todd B., David J. Disabato, Fallon R. Goodman, and Patrick E. McKnight. 2020. "The Five-Dimensional Curiosity Scale Revised (5DCR): Briefer Subscales While Separating Overt and Covert Social Curiosity." *Personality and Individual Differences* 157: 1–10.

45   **Benefits of curiosity:** Kashdan, Todd B., and Michael F. Steger. 2007. "Curiosity and Pathways to Well-Being and Meaning in Life: Traits, States, and Everyday Behaviors." *Motivation and Emotion* 31 (3): 159–73. doi:10.1007/s11031-007-9068-7. Kashdan and Silvia, "Curiosity and Interest."

45   **Low exploratory behavior and body dysmorphia:** Klump, Kelly L., Michael Strober, Cynthia M. Bulik, Laura Thornton, Craig Johnson, Bernie Devlin, Manfred M. Fichter et al. 2004. "Personality Characteristics of Women Before and After Recovery from an Eating Disorder." *Psychological Medicine* 34 (8): 1407–18. doi:0.1017/s0033291704002442.

46   **Low exploratory behavior and bias, groupthink:** Kahan, Dan M., Asheley Landrum, Katie Carpenter, Laura Helft, and Kathleen Hall Jamieson. 2017. "Science Curiosity and Political Information Processing: Curiosity and Information Processing." *Political Psychology* 38 (February): 179–99. doi:10.1111/pops.12396.

46   **Need for cognition and need for cognitive closure:** Fortier,

Alexandre, and Jacquelyn Burkell. 2014. "Influence of Need for Cognition and Need for Cognitive Closure on Three Information Behavior Orientations." *Proceedings of the American Society for Information Science and Technology* 51 (1): 1–8. doi:10.1002 /meet.2014.14505101066.

46   **Need for cognition:** Lins de Holanda Coelho, Gabriel, Paul H. P. Hanel, and Lukas J. Wolf. 2020. "The Very Efficient Assessment of Need for Cognition: Developing a Six-Item Version." *Assessment* 27 (8): 1870–85. doi:10.1177/1073191118793208.

46   **NFC in relation to NFCC:** Webster, Donna M., and Arie W. Kruglanski. 1994. "Individual Differences in Need for Cognitive Closure." *Journal of Personality and Social Psychology* 67 (6): 1049.

46   **NFC and openness:** Sadowski, Cyril J., and Helen E. Cogburn. 1997. "Need for Cognition in the Big-Five Factor Structure." *Journal of Psychology* 131 (3): 307–12.

46   **NFCC and openness:** Onraet, Emma, Alain Van Hiel, Arne Roets, and Ilse Cornelis. 2011. "The Closed Mind: 'Experience' and 'Cognition' Aspects of Openness to Experience and Need for Closure as Psychological Bases for Right-Wing Attitudes." *European Journal of Personality* 25 (3): 184–97. doi:10.1002/per.775.

46   **NFC and curiosity:** Olson, Kenneth, Cameron Camp, and Dana Fuller. 1984. "Curiosity and Need for Cognition." *Psychological Reports* 54 (1): 71–4. doi:10.2466/pr0.1984.54.1.71.

46   **NFCC and curiosity:** Litman, Jordan A. 2010. "Relationships Between Measures of I- and D-Type Curiosity, Ambiguity Tolerance, and Need for Closure: An Initial Test of the Wanting-Liking Model of Information-Seeking." *Personality and Individual Differences* 48 (4): 397–402. doi:10.1016/j.paid.2009.11.005.

46   **NFC and absorption:** Li, Dahui, and Glenn J. Browne. 2006. "The Role of Need for Cognition and Mood in Online Flow Experience." *Journal of Computer Information Systems* 46 (3): 11–7.

46   **NFC and awe:** Pilgrim, Leanne, J. Ian Norris, and Jana Hackathorn. 2017. "Music Is Awesome: Influences of Emotion, Personality, and Preference on Experienced Awe." *Journal of Consumer Behaviour* 16 (5): 442–51. doi:10.1002/cb.1645.

46   **NFCC and awe:** Pilgrim, Norris, and Hackathorn, "Music Is Awesome."

46   **"try to love the questions themselves":** Rilke, Rainer Maria (1929). 2021. *Letters to a Young Poet: A New Translation and Commentary.* Translated by Anita Barrows and Joanna Macy. United States: Shambhala.

47 "it completely transformed my life": "DIY Street Wisdom." 2014. *Street Wisdom* (June 22). https://www.streetwisdom.org/2014/06/23/diy-street-wisdom/.

48 **Jungian synchronicities:** Jung, C. G., and Sonu Shamdasani (1960). 2010. *Synchronicity: An Acausal Connecting Principle.* Translated by R. F. C. Hull. Princeton, NJ: Princeton University Press.

48 **"I am a musician":** David Pearl, interview with author, 2021.

Chapter 3: Whittle

52 **Tellegen on absorption:** Tellegen, A., and G. Atkinson. 1974. "Openness to Absorbing and Self-Altering Experiences ('Absorption'), a Trait Related to Hypnotic Susceptibility." *Journal of Abnormal Psychology* 83 (3): 268–77. doi:10.1037/h0036681.

53 **Absorption and explorers:** Tellegen and Atkinson, "Openness to Absorbing and Self-Altering Experiences."

53 **Absorption and cannabis:** Fabian, William D., and Steven M. Fishkin. 1981. "A Replicated Study of Self-Reported Changes in Psychological Absorption with Marijuana Intoxication." *Journal of Abnormal Psychology* 90 (6): 546.

53 **Absorption and lower blood pressure:** Zawadzki, Matthew J., Joshua M. Smyth, Marcellus M. Merritt, and William Gerin. 2013. "Absorption in Self-Selected Activities Is Associated with Lower Ambulatory Blood Pressure but Not for High Trait Ruminators." *American Journal of Hypertension* 26 (11): 1273–79. doi:10.1093/ajh/hpt118.

53 **Mihály Csíkszentmihályi background:** "Csikszentmihalyi, Mihaly." 2020. Encyclopedia.com. https://www.encyclopedia.com/history/encyclopedias-almanacs-transcripts-and-maps/csikszentmihalyi-mihaly.

54 **"I tried to understand":** Csíkszentmihályi, Mihály. 2004. "Flow, the Secret to Happiness." TED2004. 18:42. https://www.ted.com/talks/mihaly_csikszentmihalyi_flow_the_secret_to_happiness.

54 **"flow from them":** Csíkszentmihályi, Mihály. 1990. *Flow: The Psychology of Optimal Experience.* New York: Harper and Row.

54 **Sweet spot of flow:** Csíkszentmihályi, *Flow.*

55 **"Enjoyment appears at the boundary between boredom and anxiety":** Csíkszentmihályi, *Flow.*

55 **"There's been moments":** Nathan Sawaya, interview with author, 2021.

56 **Nathan Sawaya and eighty thousand pieces:** Karlin, Susan. 2013. "Making Lego into Art: Nathan Sawaya's Impossible Brick

Sculptures." *Fast Company* (January 3). https://www.fastcompany
.com/1682144/making-lego-into-art-nathan-sawayas-impossible
-brick-sculptures.

56 **Flow as a self-transcendent experience (STE):** While flow shares some
characteristics with other self-transcendent experiences (like awe), the
effect of the experience is not enduring like with other STEs. Outside
of some personal growth benefits from the stretching of capabilities,
flow is really only enjoyed in the moment. And while flow does a good
job of taking us out of ourselves, there is less connectivity to others
seen in typical STEs, hence the debate. Schouten, John W., James H.
McAlexander, and Harold F. Koenig. 2007. "Transcendent Customer
Experience and Brand Community." *Journal of the Academy of Marketing
Science* 35 (3): 357. doi:10.1007/s11747-007-0034-4.

57 **"I realized I could no longer define":** "A Brain Scientist's Insight."
n.d. Oprah.com. https://www.oprah.com/health/dr-jill-bolte-taylor
-explains-her-stroke-of-genius/all.

57 **STE range:** Yaden, David B., Jonathan Haidt, Ralph W. Hood, David
R. Vago, and Andrew B. Newberg. 2017. "The Varieties of Self-
Transcendent Experience." *Review of General Psychology* 21 (2): 143–60.
doi:10.1037/gpr0000102.

58 **James versus Freud on STEs:** Yaden et al., "Varieties of Self-
Transcendent Experience."

58 **"This was during my college years":** Kaufman, Scott Barry. 2020.
"192: David Yaden on the Science of Self-Transcendent Experiences."
The Psychology Podcast (April 14). 58:23. https://scottbarrykaufman
.com/podcast/the-science-of-self-transcendent-experiences-with
-david-yaden/.

59 **Types of STEs:** Yaden et al., "Varieties of Self-Transcendent
Experience."

59 **"regression in the service of the ego":** Tellegen and Atkinson,
"Openness to Absorbing and Self-Altering Experiences."

59 **Maslow and peak experiences:** Like many STE researchers, Maslow
also believed peak experiences would be fleeting and rare. Yaden et
al., "Varieties of Self-Transcendent Experience."

59 **Gallup and Pew STE research:** This statistic has increased steadily
through the years as similar studies have been run by both Pew and
polling firm Gallup, with Pew's 2009 statistic of 49 percent being
more than double that of a Gallup poll from 1962 at 22 percent. A
hopeful counterpoint to a world seeking wonder. Heimlich, Russell.
n.d. "Mystical Experiences." Pew Research Center. https://www
.pewresearch.org/fact-tank/2009/12/29/mystical-experiences/.

59   **"importance and intimacy":** Tellegen and Atkinson, "Openness to Absorbing and Self-Altering Experiences."

60   **Flow and wonder:** Scott Barry Kaufman, interview with author, 2021.

60   **People high in absorption enjoy the arts:** Hall, Sarah E., Emery Schubert, and Sarah J. Wilson. 2016. "The Role of Trait and State Absorption in the Enjoyment of Music." Edited by Lutz Jaencke. *PLoS ONE* 11 (11): e0164029. doi:10.1371/journal.pone.0164029.

60   **Absorption enhances awe:** Van Elk, Michiel, Annika Karinen, Eva Specker, Eftychia Stamkou, and Matthijs Baas. 2016. "'Standing in Awe': The Effects of Awe on Body Perception and the Relation with Absorption." *Collabra* 2 (1): 4. doi:10.1525/collabra.36.

61   **Alison Levine's background:** "About Alison." n.d. Alison Levine. https://alisonlevine.com/about-alison/.

Chapter 4: Compression and Release

63   **Frank Lloyd Wright and Taliesin West:** "Taliesin West." 2017. Frank Lloyd Wright Foundation. https://franklloydwright.org/taliesin-west/.

63   **Frank Lloyd Wright design approach:** Hildebrand, Grant. 1994. *The Wright Space: Pattern and Meaning in Frank Lloyd Wright's Houses.* Seattle: University of Washington Press.

64   **Compression and release:** "Compression and Release." n.d. Elizabeth Murphy House. https://elizabethmurphyhouse.com/tag/compression-and-release/.

65   **Number of stimuli per second:** Markowsky, George. 2019. "Information Theory—Physiology." *Encyclopædia Britannica.* https://www.britannica.com/science/information-theory/Physiology.

66   **Troxler effect:** Clarke, F. J. J. 1960. "A Study of Troxler's Effect." *Optica Acta: International Journal of Optics* 7 (3): 219–36. doi:10.1080/713826335.

66   **Sea legs:** Gordon, Carlos R., Orna Spitzer, Ilana Doweck, Yehuda Melamed, and Avi Shupak. 1995. "Clinical Features of Mal de Debarquement: Adaptation and Habituation to Sea Conditions." *Journal of Vestibular Research* 5 (5): 363–9.

66   **Underdogs and expectation violation:** Vandello, Joseph A., Nadav Goldschmied, and Kenneth Michniewicz. 2016. "Underdogs as Heroes." *Handbook of Heroism and Heroic Leadership.* Edited by Scott T. Allison, George R. Goethals, and Roderick M. Kramer, 361–77. New York: Routledge.

67   **Latent inhibition and creativity:** Carson, Shelley H., Jordan B. Peterson, and Daniel M. Higgins. 2003. "Decreased Latent Inhibition Is Associated with Increased Creative Achievement

in High-Functioning Individuals." *Journal of Personality and Social Psychology* 85 (3): 499–506. doi:10.1037/0022-3514.85.3.499.

67   **ADD/ADHD and latent inhibition:** Low latent inhibition (LLI) is separate from ADD/ADHD, although people with LLI may be misdiagnosed with ADD/ADHD as the features may be similar. Further, not all people who have LLI are distractible, but the combo can compound the features of each condition. Lorca Garrido, Antonio José, Olivia López-Martínez, and María Isabel de Vicente-Yagüe Jara. 2021. "Latent Inhibition as a Biological Basis of Creative Capacity in Individuals Aged Nine to 12." *Frontiers in Psychology* 12. doi:10.3389/fpsyg.2021.650541.

68   **"mad genius":** Fink, Andreas, Mirjam Slamar-Halbedl, Human F. Unterrainer, and Elisabeth M. Weiss. 2012. "Creativity: Genius, Madness, or a Combination of Both?" *Psychology of Aesthetics, Creativity, and the Arts* 6 (1): 11–8. doi:10.1037/a0024874.

68   **IQ and low latent inhibition:** Those with lower IQs appear to be more susceptible to the negative aspects of low latent inhibition, whereas those with high IQ are more likely to experience divergent thinking and creativity. Fink et al., "Creativity."

68   **Improving inhibitory control—music:** Moreno, Sylvain, and Faranak Farzan. 2015. "Music Training and Inhibitory Control: A Multidimensional Model." *Annals of the New York Academy of Sciences* 1337 (1): 147–52.

68   **Improving inhibitory control—cycling:** Martin, Kristy, Walter Staiano, Paolo Menaspà, Tom Hennessey, Samuele Marcora, Richard Keegan, Kevin G. Thompson, David Martin, Shona Halson, and Ben Rattray. 2016. "Superior Inhibitory Control and Resistance to Mental Fatigue in Professional Road Cyclists." *PLoS ONE* 11 (7): e0159907.

69   **Echolocation neural implants:** "These Inventors Want to Give Humans the Sense of Echolocation." 2021. Neosensory (April 1). https://neosensory.com/blog/echolocation-for-humans/.

71   **"You're in the presence of something novel":** Paulson, Steve, Lisa Sideris, Jennifer Stellar, and Piercarlo Valdesolo. 2021. "Beyond Oneself: The Ethics and Psychology of Awe." *Annals of the New York Academy of Sciences* 1501 (1): 30–47. doi:10.1111/nyas.14323.

72   **Einstein's expectation violation:** Einstein, Albert, and Paul Arthur Schilpp. (1979). 1996. *Autobiographical Notes.* La Salle, IL: Open Court Printing.

73   **"The brain is only looking at relationships":** Beau Lotto, interview with author, 2021.

74   **"When our first encounter with some object":** Descartes, René,

and Michael Moriarty. 2015. *The Passions of the Soul: And Other Late Philosophical Writings*. Oxford: Oxford University Press.

Chapter 5: Wow and Whoa

77 **Earthrise:** "The Story Behind Apollo 8's Famous Earthrise Photo." n.d. NASA Solar System Exploration. https://solarsystem.nasa.gov /resources/2234/the-story-behind-apollo-8s-famous-earthrise-photo.

77 **"No amount of prior study":** Sullivan, Kathryn D. 1991. "An Astronaut's View of Earth." *Update* (newsletter of the National Geographic Society's Geography Education Program) 1 (Fall): 12–4.

77 **"it was as if time stood still":** Garan, Ron. 2015. *The Orbital Perspective: An Astronaut's View*. London: Metro.

77 **"From the moon":** White, F. 1987. *The Overview Effect: Space Exploration and Human Evolution*. Boston: Houghton Mifflin.

77 **Overview Effect:** White, *Overview Effect*.

77 **"truly transformative experiences":** Vakoch, Douglas A., ed. 2011. *Psychology of Space Exploration: Contemporary Research in Historical Perspective*. Vol. 4411. US Government Printing Office.

78 **"an instant global consciousness":** "Edgar Mitchell's Strange Voyage." April 8, 1974. *People*. https://people.com/archive/edgar-mitchells -strange-voyage-vol-1-no-6/.

78 **"I felt the power of God":** Wilford, John Noble. 1991. "James B. Irwin, 61, Ex-Astronaut; Founded Religious Organization." *New York Times*, August 10, 1991. https://www.nytimes.com/1991/08/10/us /james-b-irwin-61-ex-astronaut-founded-religious-organization.html.

78 **"It was when I took a picture":** Tayag, Yasmin. "NASA Astronauts Describe the 'Overview Effect' in Their Own Words." *Inverse*. https:// www.inverse.com/article/42902-nasa-astronauts-describe-overview -effect-everything-changed.

79 **"deep states of unity":** Kaufman, Scott Barry. 2020. "192: David Yaden on the Science of Self-Transcendent Experiences." *The Psychology Podcast* (April 14). 58:23. https://scottbarrykaufman.com/podcast/the -science-of-self-transcendent-experiences-with-david-yaden/.

79 **Yaden and Newberg on the Overview Effect:** Yaden, David B., Jonathan Iwry, Kelley J. Slack, Johannes C. Eichstaedt, Yukun Zhao, George E. Vaillant, and Andrew B. Newberg. 2016. "The Overview Effect: Awe and Self-Transcendent Experience in Space Flight." *Psychology of Consciousness: Theory, Research, and Practice* 3 (1): 1–11. doi:10.1037/cns0000086.

79 **Keltner and Haidt on awe:** Keltner, Dacher, and Jonathan Haidt.

2003. "Approaching Awe, a Moral, Spiritual, and Aesthetic Emotion." *Cognition and Emotion* 17 (2): 297–314. doi:10.1080/02699930302297.

80 **"I was raised by kind of countercultural types":** Dacher Keltner, interview with author, 2021.

80 **Seligman and positive psychology:** Seligman, Martin E. P. 2019. "Positive Psychology: A Personal History." *Annual Review of Clinical Psychology* 15: 1–23. doi:10.1146/annurev-clinpsy-050718-095653.

81 **Greater Good Science Center:** "Greater Good: The Science of a Meaningful Life." n.d. Greater Good Science Center. https://www .greatergood.berkeley.edu/.

82 **Schemas:** Piaget, Jean. 1970. *Genetic Epistemology.* New York: W. W. Norton.

84 **"sphere of magical power":** Flowers, Stephen. 1989. *The Galdrabók: An Icelandic Grimoire.* York Beach, ME: Samuel Weiser.

84 **Poetic Edda:** Crawford, Jackson. 2015. *The Poetic Edda: Stories of the Norse Gods and Heroes.* Cambridge, MA: Hackett Publishing Company.

85 **Rumi poem:** Jalāl Al-Dīn Rūmī, Maulana, Coleman Barks, A. J. Arberry, and John Moyne. 2004. *The Essential Rumi.* New York: Harper One.

86 **Shape-shifting *awe* meaning:** Bonner, Edward T., and Harris L. Friedman. 2011. "A Conceptual Clarification of the Experience of Awe: An Interpretative Phenomenological Analysis." *Humanistic Psychologist* 39 (3): 222–35. doi:10.1080/08873267.2011.593372.

87 **"I am absolutely not someone":** Michelle Shiota, interview with author, 2021.

88 **T. rex awe experiment:** Shiota, Michelle N., Dacher Keltner, and Amanda Mossman. 2007. "The Nature of Awe: Elicitors, Appraisals, and Effects on Self-Concept." *Cognition and Emotion* 21 (5): 944–63. doi:10.1080/02699930600923668.

89 **"We went to Las Vegas":** Lotto, Beau, and Cirque du Soleil. 2019. "Beau Lotto and Cirque Du Soleil: How We Experience Awe—and Why It Matters." TED2019. 14:39. https://www.ted.com/talks/beau_lotto_and _cirque_du_soleil_how_we_experience_awe_and_why_it_matters.

89 **Cirque du Soleil awe experiment:** Lotto and Cirque Du Soleil, "Beau Lotto and Cirque Du Soleil."

90 **"It's not like a reality TV show":** Michelle Shiota, interview with author, 2021.

91 **Emotions in collectivist vs. individualistic cultures:** Lim, Nangyeon. 2016. "Cultural Differences in Emotion: Differences in Emotional Arousal Level Between the East and the West." *Integrative Medicine Research* 5 (2): 105–9. doi:10.1016/j.imr.2016.03.004.

91 **Cultural variations of awe:** Chen, Enna Yuxuan. 2020. "Cultural Variations in the Appraisals of Awe." Escholarship.org (April). https://escholarship.org/uc/item/0dh4s9j3. (This research was performed as part of an undergraduate degree supervised by Dacher Keltner and Yang Bai.)

91 **Yaden on the Overview Effect across cultures:** David Yaden, interview with author, 2021.

91 **"We've done one cross-cultural study":** Jennifer Stellar, interview with author, 2021.

92 **Percentage of positive awe experiences:** Gordon, Amie M., Jennifer E. Stellar, Craig L. Anderson, Galen D. McNeil, Daniel Loew, and Dacher Keltner. 2017. "The Dark Side of the Sublime: Distinguishing a Threat-Based Variant of Awe." *Journal of Personality and Social Psychology* 113 (2): 310–28. doi:10.1037/pspp0000120.

92 **Evolution of awe:** Bonner et al., "A Conceptual Clarification of the Experience of Awe: An Interpretative Phenomenological Analysis."

93 **Chinese *awe* translation:** Betty Bienert, communication with author, 2021.

Chapter 6: Wonder Mindset

97 **Magic Eye as a transcendent experience:** "The Hidden History of Magic Eye, the Optical Illusion That Briefly Took Over the World." n.d. *Eye on Design.* https://web.archive.org/web/20220403060836 /https://eyeondesign.aiga.org/the-hidden-history-of-magic-eye-the -optical-illusion-that-briefly-took-over-the-world/.

98 **"It's actually a way of looking":** Beau Lotto, interview with author, 2021.

99 **Thresholds:** Feist, Gregory J. 2017. "Personality, Behavioral Thresholds, and the Creative Scientist." *The Cambridge Handbook of Creativity and Personality Research.* Edited by Gregory J. Feist, Roni Reiter-Palmon, and James C. Kaufman. Cambridge: Cambridge University Press: 64–83. doi:10.1017/9781316228036.005.

99 **Survey for determining wonderproneness:** You can take this survey at https://Monica-Parker.com/wonderprone to see how wonderprone you are and learn what areas you may want to boost.

100 **"Openness to experience" questions:** Goldberg, Lewis R. 1999. "A Broad-Bandwidth, Public Domain, Personality Inventory Measuring the Lower-Level Facets of Several Five-Factor Models." *Personality Psychology in Europe* 7 (1): 7–28.

100 **"creativity, authenticity, IQ":** Kaufman, Scott Barry. 2018. "What

Happens When People Are Intentionally More Open to New Experiences?" *Scientific American* (November 21). https://blogs .scientificamerican.com/beautiful-minds/what-happens-when -people-are-instructed-to-be-more-open-to-new-experiences/.

100 **"If we view traits as 'thresholds'":** Silvia, Paul J., Kirill Fayn, Emily C. Nusbaum, and Roger E. Beaty. 2015. "Openness to Experience and Awe in Response to Nature and Music: Personality and Profound Aesthetic Experiences." *Psychology of Aesthetics, Creativity, and the Arts* 9 (4): 376–84. doi:10.1037/aca0000028.

101 **"If I'm somebody who's particularly open":** Jennifer Stellar, interview with author, 2021.

101 **Increasing openness to experience:** "Enhancing Cognition in Older Adults Also Changes Personality." n.d. EurekAlert! https://www .eurekalert.org/news-releases/794085.

102 **"While we didn't explicitly test this":** "Enhancing Cognition in Older Adults Also Changes Personality."

103 **Changing your personality:** Jarrett, Christian. 2021. *Be Who You Want: Unlocking the Science of Personality Change.* New York: Simon & Schuster.

103 **Curiosity questions:** Litman, Jordan A., and Charles D. Spielberger. 2003. "Measuring Epistemic Curiosity and Its Diversive and Specific Components." *Journal of Personality Assessment* 80 (1): 75–86.

104 **"your brain is rewiring":** Paulson, Steve. 2020. "Review of Your Brain Makes You a Different Person Every Day." *Nautilus.* Science Connected (October 14). https://nautil.us/your-brain-makes-you-a-different -person-every-day-9326/.

104 **Curiosity decreases with age:** Chu, Li, and Helene H. Fung. 2021. "Age Differences in State Curiosity: Examining the Role of Personal Relevance." *Gerontology* (June): 1–9. doi:10.1159/000516296; Sakaki, Michiko, Ayano Yagi, and Kou Murayama. 2018. *Neuroscience & Biobehavioral Reviews* 88 (May): 106–16. doi:10.1016/j .neubiorev.2018.03.007. "Curiosity in Old Age: A Possible Key to Achieving Adaptive Aging." *Neuroscience & Biobehavioral Reviews* 88 (May): 106–16. doi:10.1016/j.neubiorev.2018.03.007.

104 **"actively seek out wonder":** David Yaden, interview with author, 2021.

104 **Neuroscience of novelty:** Bunzeck, Nico, and Emrah Düzel. 2006. "Absolute Coding of Stimulus Novelty in the Human Substantia Nigra/VTA." *Neuron* 51 (3): 369–79. doi:10.1016/j.neuron.2006.06.021.

105 **"When we see something new":** University College London. 2006.

"Novelty Aids Learning." *UCL News* (August 2). https://www.ucl
.ac.uk/news/2006/aug/novelty-aids-learning.

106 **Wear your watch on a different wrist:** David Eagleman, interview
with author, 2021.

106 **"to be always beginning":** Rilke, Rainer Maria (1929). 2021. *Letters
to a Young Poet: A New Translation and Commentary.* Translated by Anita
Barrows and Joanna Macy. United States: Shambhala.

107 **Stress increases need for certainty:** White, Holly A. 2022. "Need for
Cognitive Closure Predicts Stress and Anxiety of College Students
During COVID-19 Pandemic." *Personality and Individual Differences* 187:
111393. doi:10.1016/j.paid.2021.111393.

107 **Absorption questions:** Tellegen, A. 1982. Brief Manual for the
Multidimensional Personality Questionnaire. Unpublished
manuscript, University of Minnesota, Minneapolis.

108 **Self-conscious emotions and anxiety:** Gaydukevych, Darya, and
Nancy L. Kocovski. 2012. "Effect of Self-Focused Attention on Post-
Event Processing in Social Anxiety." *Behaviour Research and Therapy* 50
(1): 47–55. doi:10.1016/j.brat.2011.10.010.

108 **Self-conscious emotions and OCD:** Stewart, S. Evelyn, and L.
Shapiro. 2011. "Pathological Guilt: A Persistent Yet Overlooked
Treatment Factor in Obsessive-Compulsive Disorder." *Annals of
Clinical Psychiatry* 23 (1): 63–70.

109 **Purpose of boredom:** Bench, Shane, and Heather Lench. 2013.
"On the Function of Boredom." *Behavioral Sciences* 3 (3): 459–72.
doi:10.3390/bs3030459.

109 **"When you have closure, you don't look for information":**
Kruglanski, Arie, and Julianna Photopoulos. 2021. "A Scientist's
Opinion: Interview with Professor Arie Kruglanski About Our Need
for Cognitive Closure during COVID-19." European Science-Media
Hub. https://sciencemediahub.eu/2021/04/14/a-scientists-opinion
-interview-with-professor-arie-kruglanski-about-our-need-for
-cognitive-closure-during-covid-19/.

110 **Awe questions:** Yaden, David B., Scott Barry Kaufman, Elizabeth
Hyde, Alice Chirico, Andrea Gaggioli, Jia Wei Zhang, and Dacher
Keltner. 2019. "The Development of the Awe Experience Scale
(AWE-S): A Multifactorial Measure for a Complex Emotion." *Journal of
Positive Psychology* 14 (4): 474–88. doi:10.1080/17439760.2018.1484940.

111 **Nudge theory and priming nudges:** There have been some
concern of replication (reproducing the same results) in priming

experiments. Friis, Rasmus, Laurits Rohden Skov, Annemarie Olsen, Katherine Marie Appleton, Laure Saulais, Caterina Dinnella, Heather Hartwell, et al. 2017. "Comparison of Three Nudge Interventions (Priming, Default Option, and Perceived Variety) to Promote Vegetable Consumption in a Self-Service Buffet Setting." *PLoS ONE* 12 (5): e0176028. doi:10.1371/journal.pone.0176028.

112 **Goal priming:** Papies, Esther K. 2016. "Goal Priming as a Situated Intervention Tool." *Current Opinion in Psychology* 12 (December): 12–6. doi:10.1016/j.copsyc.2016.04.008.

112 **"The tree which moves some":** Blake, William. 1977. *The Portable William Blake.* New York: Penguin Publishing Group.

Chapter 7: Identifying a Wonderbringer

114 **Seven Wonders of the World:** The original Seven Wonders of the World were the Hanging Gardens of Babylon, the Great Pyramid of Giza, the Statue of Zeus at Olympia, the Temple of Artemis at Ephesus, the Mausoleum of Halicarnassus, the Colossus of Rhodes, and the Lighthouse of Alexandria, Egypt. Some say, however, that the Hanging Gardens were mere poetry, not reality. "Seven Wonders of the World | List & Pictures." 2019. *Encyclopædia Britannica.* https://www.britannica.com/topic/Seven-Wonders-of -the-World.

115 **"awe is part of human nature":** Michelle Shiota, interview with author, 2021.

115 **Innate features of wonderbringers:** Shiota, Michelle N., Dacher Keltner, and Amanda Mossman. 2007. "The Nature of Awe: Elicitors, Appraisals, and Effects on Self-Concept." *Cognition and Emotion* 21 (5): 944–63. doi:10.1080/02699930600923668.

115 **Why fractals are wonderbringers:** Aeon, Florence Williams. 2017. "Why Fractals Are So Soothing." *The Atlantic* (January 26). https:// www.theatlantic.com/science/archive/2017/01/why-fractals-are-so -soothing/514520/.

115 **"Your visual system":** Aeon, "Why Fractals Are So Soothing."

116 **"pertaining to sense perception":** "Aesthetic, n. and adj." n.d. OED Online. Oxford University Press. https://www.oed.com/view /Entry/3237.

116 **Mundane aesthetics:** The word *aesthetics* is more commonly used to refer to the design or style of something—like the aesthetic of someone's new kitchen—and this is known as mundane aesthetics. Whitfield, T. W., and Lucila R. de Destefani. 2011. "Mundane Aesthetics." *Psychology of Aesthetics, Creativity, and the Arts* 5 (3): 291.

117   **"get our head around":** Burnham, Douglas. n.d. "Kant, Immanuel: Aesthetics." *Internet Encyclopedia of Philosophy.* https://iep.utm.edu /kantaest/.

117   **Kant and Theory of Mind:** One of Kant's greatest contributions to general philosophy was the idea of the Theory of Mind (ToM). Within the context of ToM, Kant saw the mind as "an organ that soaked up sensory experiences and turned them into ideas." Much like Otto's numinous and James's self-transcendent experiences, the sublime appears to be an overlap between aesthetics and wonder. Burnham, "Kant, Immanuel."

117   **"The sublime is limitless":** Kant, Immanuel, N. Marcus Weigelt (1781). 2007. *Critique of Pure Reason.* London: Penguin Books.

117   **Schopenhauer and the sublime continuum:** Schopenhauer saw the sublime as sitting on a continuum, with beauty at the weakest end and "fullest sublime" at the other, but still a mixture of pleasure with a tinge of threat. Not unlike Burke's description, which was astonishment, absorption, a bit of horror, and a sense in which "all motions are suspended [and] the mind is so entirely filled with its object, that it cannot entertain any other." Burke, Edmund, and James T. Boulton (1757). 1986. *A Philosophical Enquiry into the Origin of Our Ideas of the Sublime and Beautiful.* Notre Dame: University of Notre Dame Press.

117   **Comparing awe and the sublime:** Clewis, Robert R., David B. Yaden, and Alice Chirico. 2021. "Intersections Between Awe and the Sublime: A Preliminary Empirical Study." *Empirical Studies of the Arts* 40 (2): 143–73. doi:10.1177/0276237421994694.

118   **Features of the sublime:** Seibt, Beate, Thomas W. Schubert, Janis H. Zickfeld, and Alan Page Fiske. 2017. "Interpersonal Closeness and Morality Predict Feelings of Being Moved." *Emotion* 17 (3): 389–94. doi:10.1037/emo0000271.

118   **Heartwarming feeling:** This feeling is thought to be brought about by an increase in vagal activity. Zickfeld, Janis H., Patrícia Arriaga, Sara Vilar Santos, Thomas W. Schubert, and Beate Seibt. 2020. "Tears of Joy, Aesthetic Chills and Heartwarming Feelings: Physiological Correlates of Kama Muta." *Psychophysiology* 57 (12): e13662. doi:10.1111 /psyp.13662.

118   **tears of "wonder-joy":** Braud, William. 2001. "Experiencing Tears of Wonder-Joy: Seeing with the Heart's Eye." *Journal of Transpersonal Psychology* 33 (2): 992013–112.

118   **William James and chills:** William James described them as a "cutaneous shiver which like a sudden wave flows over us,"

accompanied by "heart-swelling" and "lachrymal effusion." This sense of "being moved" was observed by Darwin when he wrote of the "tender" feelings that were unique to humans. James, William. 1890. *The Principles of Psychology*. New York: H. Holt.

118   **Role of aesthetic chills:** Schurtz, David R., Sarai Blincoe, Richard H. Smith, Caitlin A. J. Powell, David J. Y. Combs, and Sung Hee Kim. 2011. "Exploring the Social Aspects of Goose Bumps and Their Role in Awe and Envy." *Motivation and Emotion* 36 (2): 205–17. doi:10.1007/s11031-011-9243-8.

118   **Thrills:** "Thrills" was used to also differentiate from chills of fear, although they may be closely connected. Some studies using skin sensors found that the physical process of piloerection did not appear to be correlated to experimentally generated awe. This makes some sense, as piloerection is a response of the sympathetic nervous system, whereas awe is associated with both a decrease in the sympathetic response and an increase in parasympathetic activation, so you wouldn't necessarily expect to see them occur together. However, there have been recorded instances of awe-related piloerection as well as other sympathetic reactions such as freezing response. One possible explanation is that the impact of some types of experimentally induced awe is not intense enough to produce piloerection. The other is that people associate subjective frisson with physical piloerection and therefore conflate the two in their self-reporting. Harrison, Luke, and Psyche Loui. 2014. "Thrills, Chills, Frissons, and Skin Orgasms: Toward an Integrative Model of Transcendent Psychophysiological Experiences in Music." *Frontiers in Psychology* 5: 790. doi:10.3389/fpsyg.2014.00790.

119   **Emotional prosthesis for goose bumps:** "AWElectric." Sensoree. n.d. https://www.sensoree.com/artifacts/awelectric/; Haar, A. J. H., A. Jain, F. Schoeller, and P. Maes. 2020. "Augmenting Aesthetic Chills Using a Wearable Prosthesis Improves Their Downstream Effects on Reward and Social Cognition." *Scientific Reports* 10 (1): 21603.

119   **Sachs music formula:** Sachs, Matthew E., Robert J. Ellis, Gottfried Schlaug, and Psyche Loui. 2016. "Brain Connectivity Reflects Human Aesthetic Responses to Music." *Social Cognitive and Affective Neuroscience* 11 (6): 884–91. doi:10.1093/scan/nsw009.

119   **Percentage of people who don't get goose bumps:** Neidlinger, Kristin, Lianne Toussaint, Edwin Dertien, Khiet P. Truong, Hermie Hermens, and Vanessa Evers. 2019. "Emotional Prosthesis for Animating Awe Through Performative Biofeedback." *Proceedings of the 23rd International Symposium on Wearable Computers* (September). doi:10.1145/3341163.3346939.

119 **Aesthetic chills as a somatic marker:** Bignardi, Giacomo, Rebecca Chamberlain, Sofieke T. Kevenaar, Zenab Tamimy, and Dorret I. Boomsma. 2002. "On the Etiology of Aesthetic Chills: A Behavioral Genetic Study." *Scientific Reports* 12, no. 1: doi:10.1038/s41598-022 -07161-z.

120 **"You can divide the human brain":** Richardson, Michael W. 2019. "What Causes Goosebumps?" BrainFacts.org. https://www.brainfacts .org/brain-anatomy-and-function/body-systems/2019/what-causes -goosebumps-120619.

120 **Aesthetic chills as a cross-cultural marker of openness:** According to researcher Robert McCrae and data from the Personality Profiles of Cultures Project, a person's propensity toward chills is highly correlated with their openness to experience. McCrae, Robert R. 2007. "Aesthetic Chills as a Universal Marker of Openness to Experience." *Motivation and Emotion* 31 (1): 5–11. doi:10.1007/s11031 -007-9053-1.

121 **Chills and openness to ideas:** Colver, Mitchell C., and Amani El-Alayli. 2016. "Getting Aesthetic Chills from Music: The Connection Between Openness to Experience and Frisson." *Psychology of Music* 44 (3): 413–27. doi:10.1177/0305735615572358.

121 **Global expressions for aesthetic chills:** McCrae, "Aesthetic Chills as a Universal Marker of Openness to Experience."

123 **"Our normal waking consciousness":** James, *The Principles of Psychology.*

124 **"Philosophers do this annoying thing":** Fridman, Lex. 2020. "David Chalmers: The Hard Problem of Consciousness." *Lex Fridman Podcast #69* (January 19). 1:38:48. https://www.youtube.com /watch?v=LW59lMvxmY4.

Chapter 8: Wonderbringers

126 **"It is not half so important":** Carson, Rachel, Nick Kelsh, and Linda J. Lear (1965). 2017. *The Sense of Wonder: A Celebration of Nature for Parents and Children.* New York: Harper Perennial.

126 **"I can remember no time":** Carson, Kelsh, and Lear, *Sense of Wonder.*

126 **"affluent chemical industry":** "Rachel Carson Dies of Cancer." 1964. *New York Times* (April 15). https://www.nytimes.com/1964/04/15 /rachel-carson-dies-of-cancer.html.

127 **"The more clearly we can focus":** Carson biography. 2021. Rachel Carson National Wildlife Refuge. https://web.archive.org /web/20210212013149/https://www.fws.gov/northeast/rachelcarson /writings.html.

127 **"Drink in the beauty and wonder":** Carson, Kelsh, and Lear, *Sense of Wonder.*

127 **"A child's world is fresh":** Carson, Kelsh, and Lear, *Sense of Wonder.*

127 **Carson hid being a female author:** Carson wrote under the name R. L. Carson early in her career because "she knew a woman would never be heard. Women weren't in science unless they were secretaries to scientists," said Linda Lear, her biographer. Thomson, Candus. 2007. "Love, Dread Drove Carson." *Baltimore Sun.* https://web.archive.org/web/20210625015410/www.baltimoresun.com/news/bs-xpm-2007-04-22-0704220034-story.html.

129 **"quintessentially collective emotion":** Awe generates a connection with other people and has been found to increase collective engagement across individualist as well as collectivist cultures. Bai, Yang, Laura A. Maruskin, Serena Chen, Amie M. Gordon, Jennifer E. Stellar, Galen D. McNeil, Kaiping Peng, and Dacher Keltner. 2017. "Awe, the Diminished Self, and Collective Engagement: Universals and Cultural Variations in the Small Self." *Journal of Personality and Social Psychology* 113 (2): 185–209. doi:10.1037/pspa0000087.

131 **"without art, the crudeness of reality":** Shaw, Bernard (1921). 1990. *Back to Methuselah: A Metabiological Pentateuch.* London: Penguin Books.

131 **"means of union":** Tolstoy, Leo. 1975. *What Is Art? And Essays on Art.* London: Oxford University Press.

131 **"evokes the mystery":** Wargo, Eric. 2002. "Infinite Recess: Perspective and Play in Magritte's La Condition Humaine." *Art History* 25 (1): 47–67. doi:10.1111/1467-8365.00302.

131 **"music . . . you can't destroy it":** "Saved by Music: A Holocaust Survivor's Story." 2019. CBS News. https://www.cbsnews.com/news/saved-by-music-a-holocaust-survivors-story-60-minutes-2019-12-15/.

132 **"The people who weep":** Rodman, Selden. 1961. *Conversations with Artists.* New York: Capricorn Books.

132 **"empathy gym":** "Fighting the Empathy Deficit: How the Arts Can Make Us More Compassionate." n.d. KQED. https://www.kqed.org/arts/10933932/fighting-the-empathy-deficit-how-the-arts-can-make-us-more-compassionate.

132 **Art evokes openness and curiosity:** Rollins, Judy Ann. 2011. "Arousing Curiosity: When Hospital Art Transcends." *HERD: Health Environments Research & Design Journal* 4 (3): 72. https://www.academia.edu/4439829/Arousing_Curiosity_When_Hospital_Art_Transcends.

132 **Art schema:** Wagner, Valentin, Winfried Menninghaus, Julian Hanich, and Thomas Jacobsen. 2014. "Art Schema Effects on

Affective Experience: The Case of Disgusting Images." *Psychology of Aesthetics, Creativity, and the Arts* 8 (2): 120–9. doi:10.1037/a0036126.

132 **Art, awe, and increased patience and tolerance:** Researchers are even trialing art in the workplace as a catalyst to increase patience and kindness, and some are piloting the use of awe-inspiring art to increase tolerance and decrease outgrouping bias. Beau Lotto, interview with author, 2021.

132 **Design attributes of wonder:** Ke, Jialin, and Jung Kyoon Yoon. 2020. "Design for Breathtaking Experiences: An Exploration of Design Strategies to Evoke Awe in Human–Product Interactions." *Multimodal Technologies and Interaction* 4 (4): 82. doi:10.3390/mti4040082.

132 **Fractals and Jackson Pollock:** Williams, "Why Fractals Are So Soothing."

133 **Food as a wonderbringer:** Angela Hartnett, meal served to author, 2019.

133 **Features of wonderbringing architecture:** An example of a design feature using "safe threat" might be a dark area on the perimeter and light in the center, creating a campfire effect that draws people to the light. Yan, Wendi. 2019. "Neuroscience Informs Design, Now What? Towards an Awe-Inspiring Spatial Design." The Centre for Conscious Design. https://theccd.org/article/17/neuroscience-informs-design-now-what-towards-an-awe-inspiring-spatial-design/.

133 **Features of wonderbringing design:** Negami, Hanna R., and Colin G. Ellard. 2021. "How Architecture Evokes Awe: Predicting Awe Through Architectural Features of Building Interiors." *Psychology of Aesthetics, Creativity, and the Arts.* Advance online publication. doi:10.1037/aca0000394.

133 **Wonder in museum design:** Price, C. Aaron, Jana Nicole Greenslit, Lauren Applebaum, Natalie Harris, Gloria Segovia, Kimberly A. Quinn, and Sheila Krogh-Jespersen. 2021. "Awe & Memories of Learning in Science and Art Museums." *Visitor Studies* (April): 1–50. doi:10.1080/10645578.2021.1907152.

134 **United States Holocaust Memorial Museum:** The architect, James Ingo Freed, described his approach, saying, "All the survivors I spoke to said that everything was taken away from them—their families, their identity, their dignity—and the only thing they held on to was a shaft of light. So I played the sun." Freed later said of how it felt to be able to produce evocative architecture, "The ability to see space is like the ability, in a way, to hear music." Giovanni, Joseph. 1993. "The Architecture of Death: To Design the U.S. Holocaust Museum, James Freed had to Challenge the Values That Had Guided His Work—and

Confront Old Horrors." *Los Angeles Times* (April 18). https://www
.latimes.com/archives/la-xpm-1993-04-18-tm-24163-story.html.

134 **Architecture facilitates social cohesion:** Joye, Yannick, and Jan
Verpooten. 2013. "An Exploration of the Functions of Religious
Monumental Architecture from a Darwinian Perspective." *Review of
General Psychology* 17 (1): 53–68. doi:10.1037/a0029920.

134 **"with expectations to see wondrous things":** Smith, J. K. 2014. *The
Museum Effect: How Museums, Libraries, and Cultural Institutions Educate
and Civilize Society.* Lanham, MD: Rowman & Littlefield.

135 **Awe in museum design:** Negami and Ellard, "How Architecture
Evokes Awe."

134 **Office design lacks biophilia:** "Global Study Connects Levels of
Employee Productivity and Well Being to Office Design." 2015. PR
Newswire (March 31). https://www.prnewswire.com/news-releases
/global-study-connects-levels-of-employee-productivity-and-well
-being-to-office-design-300058034.html.

134 **Natural light reduces eyestrain, headaches, fatigue:** Edwards, L.,
and P. Torcellini. 2002. "Literature Review of the Effects of
Natural Light on Building Occupants" (July 1). OSTI.gov (July 1).
doi:10.2172/15000841. Golden, CO: National Renewable Energy
Laboratory.

134 **Air quality and illness:** "How Can Facility Managers Protect Their
Buildings and Avoid Being a Sick Building Statistic?" 2018. Global
Wellness Institute. https://globalwellnessinstitute.org/wp-content
/uploads/2018/12/sick-building-syndrome-factsheet.pdf.

135 **Indoor air quality:** "The Inside Story: A Guide to Indoor Air
Quality." 2014. US Environmental Protection Agency. https://www
.epa.gov/indoor-air-quality-iaq/inside-story-guide-indoor-air-quality.

135 **Music in the Pentecostal Church:** Miller, Mandi M., and
Kenneth T. Strongman. 2022. "The Emotional Effects of Music
on Religious Experience: A Study of the Pentecostal-Charismatic
Style of Music and Worship." *Psychology of Music* 30, (1): 8–27.
doi:10.1177/0305735602301004.

135 **African Igbo and music:** Becker, Judith. 2001. "Anthropological
Perspectives on Music and Emotion." In *Music and Emotion: Theory
and Research.* Edited by P. N. Juslin and J. A. Sloboda, 135–60. Oxford:
Oxford University Press.

135 **Singing together improves vagal tone:** Vickhoff, Björn, Helge
Malmgren, Rickard Åström, Gunnar Nyberg, Seth-Reino Ekström,
Mathias Engwall, Johan Snygg, Michael Nilsson, and Rebecka

Jörnsten. 2013. "Music Structure Determines Heart Rate Variability of Singers." *Frontiers in Psychology* 4: 334.

135 **Universality of music:** Mehr, Samuel A., Manvir Singh, Dean Knox, Daniel M. Ketter, Daniel Pickens-Jones, Stephanie Atwood, Christopher Lucas, et al. 2019. "Universality and Diversity in Human Song." *Science* 366, no. 6468: eaax0868.

135 **Music increases social bonding:** Savage, Patrick E., Psyche Loui, Bronwyn Tarr, Adena Schachner, Luke Glowacki, Steven Mithen, and W. Tecumseh Fitch. 2021. "Music as a Coevolved System for Social Bonding." *Behavioral and Brain Sciences* 44: e59. doi:10.1017 /S0140525X20000333.

135 **Nonmusical causes of chills:** Autonomous sensory meridian response, or ASMR, is one nonmusical trigger for these chills, too, but likely outside the scope of wonder. Barratt, E. L., and N. J. Davis. 2015. "Autonomous Sensory Meridian Response (ASMR): A Flow-Like Mental State." *PeerJ* 3: e851.

135 **Music causes aesthetic chills:** McCrae, Robert R. 2007. "Aesthetic Chills as a Universal Marker of Openness to Experience." *Motivation and Emotion* 31 (1): 5–11. doi:10.1007/s11031-007-9053-1.

135 **Charles Darwin and chills:** Charles Darwin remarked on chills, saying, "I acquired a strong taste for music, and used very often to time my walks so as to hear on weekdays the anthem in King's College Chapel. This gave me intense pleasure, so that my backbone would sometimes shiver." Browne, Janet, ed. 2017. *The Quotable Darwin.* Princeton: Princeton University Press.

136 **Aesthetic chills and transitional points in music:** Sloboda, John A. 1991. "Music Structure and Emotional Response: Some Empirical Findings." *Psychology of Music* 19 (2): 110–20. doi:10.1177/0305735691192002.

135 **Aural expectation violation:** Huron, D., and E. H. Margulis. 2010. "Music, Expectation and Frission." *Handbook of Music and Emotion: Theory, Research, Applications.* Edited by Patrik N. Juslin and John Sloboda, 575–604. Oxford: Oxford University Press.

136 **Neuroscience of musical chills:** Williams, Paula G., Kimberley T. Johnson, Brian J. Curtis, Jace B. King, and Jeffrey S. Anderson. 2018. "Individual Differences in Aesthetic Engagement Are Reflected in Resting-State fMRI Connectivity: Implications for Stress Resilience." *NeuroImage* 179 (October): 156–65. doi:10.1016/j .neuroimage.2018.06.042.

136 **"Hoppipolla":** Just as researchers have a tried-and-true video they

show subjects to elicit awe (BBC's *Planet Earth*), they also have a favorite song—"Hoppipolla," by Sigur Rós. Researchers say the Icelandic band is obscure enough that there is no personal nostalgic connection to the music, and while this song does have lyrics, they are in Icelandic, which is a less commonly spoken language, so there are no emotional associations from lyrics. (Not a ton of native Icelandic speakers on North American university campuses.) Silvia, Paul J., Kirill Fayn, Emily C. Nusbaum, and Roger E. Beaty. 2015. "Openness to Experience and Awe in Response to Nature and Music: Personality and Profound Aesthetic Experiences." *Psychology of Aesthetics, Creativity, and the Arts* 9 (4): 376–84. doi:10.1037/aca0000028.

136 **Personality and preference in aesthetic chills:** Pilgrim, Leanne, J. Ian Norris, and Jana Hackathorn. 2017. "Music Is Awesome: Influences of Emotion, Personality, and Preference on Experienced Awe." *Journal of Consumer Behaviour* 16 (5): 442–51. doi:10.1002/cb.1645.

136 **DMN activated during improv music:** Vergara, Victor M., Martin Norgaard, Robyn Miller, Roger E. Beaty, Kiran Dhakal, Mukesh Dhamala, and Vince D. Calhoun. 2021. "Functional Network Connectivity During Jazz Improvisation." *Scientific Reports* 11 (1): 19036. doi:10.1038/s41598-021-98332-x.

137 **"an island of remembrance":** "Music Activates Regions of the Brain Spared by Alzheimer's Disease." 2018. Utah University. https://healthcare.utah.edu/publicaffairs/news/2018/04/alzheimer.php.

137 **Role of the insula:** Craig, Arthur D. 2009. "How Do You Feel—Now? The Anterior Insula and Human Awareness." *Nature Reviews. Neuroscience* 10 (1): 59–70. doi:10.1038/nrn2555.

137 **Insula and the lateral sulcus:** Uddin, Lucina Q., Jason S. Nomi, Benjamin Hébert-Seropian, Jimmy Ghaziri, and Olivier Boucher. 2017. "Structure and Function of the Human Insula." *Journal of Clinical Neurophysiology* 34 (4): 300.

138 **"Love is the sublime crucible":** Hugo, Victor, and Christine Donougher (1862). 2018. *Les Misérables.* London: BBC Books.

138 **"Bridegroom, dear to my heart":** Kramer, Samuel Noah. 1990. *History Begins at Sumer: Thirty-Nine Firsts in Man's Recorded History.* Philadelphia: University of Pennsylvania Press.

138 **Empathy as a precursor to love:** Allott, Robin. 1992. "Evolutionary Aspects of Love and Empathy." *Journal of Social and Evolutionary Systems* 15 (4): 353–70. doi:10.1016/1061-7361(92)90023-7.

138 **Hypothalamus, dopamine, and lust:** Wu, Katherine. 2017. "Love, Actually: The Science Behind Lust, Attraction, and Companionship." *Science in the News* (February 14). Harvard University. https://sitn.hms .harvard.edu/flash/2017/love-actually-science-behind-lust-attraction -companionship/.

139 **"being able to attain long-lasting":** Sayin, H. Ümit. 2012. "Doors of Female Orgasmic Consciousness: New Theories on the Peak Experience and Mechanisms of Female Orgasm and Expanded Sexual Response." *NeuroQuantology* 10 (4): 692–714.

139 **orgasm as a portal to a transcendent state:** Tantric orgasm has also been associated with several benefits, including a decrease in depression. Sayin, H. Ümit. 2017. "Tantra, ESR and the Limits of Female Potentials." *Sexus Journal* 2 (3): 55–74.

140 **"soul orgasm":** Lousada, Mike, and Elena Angel. 2011. "Tantric Orgasm: Beyond Masters and Johnson." *Sexual and Relationship Therapy* 26 (4): 389–402. doi:10.1080/14681994.2011.647903.

141 **Openness to experience, curiosity, awe, and sensation seeking:** Chen, Susan K., and Myriam Mongrain. 2021. "Awe and the Interconnected Self." *Journal of Positive Psychology* 16 (6): 770–8. doi:10 .1080/17439760.2020.1818808.

141 **Sex as a wonderbringer:** Jamea, Emily. 2020. "The Role of Sensuality, Imagination, and Curiosity in High and Optimal Sexual Satisfaction." *Sexual and Relationship Therapy* (February): 1–20. doi:10.10 80/14681994.2020.1714023.

141 **Health benefits of friendships:** Holt-Lunstad, Julianne, Timothy B. Smith, and J. Bradley Layton. 2010. "Social Relationships and Mortality Risk: A Meta-Analytic Review." Edited by Carol Brayne. *PLoS Medicine* 7 (7). doi:10.1371/journal.pmed.1000316.

141 **Challenge with adult friendships:** Paul, Marla. 2004. *The Friendship Crisis: Finding, Making, and Keeping Friends When You're Not a Kid Anymore.* Emmaus, PA: Rodale.

142 **Sharing wonderbringers:** Kashdan, Todd B., and Paul J. Silvia. 2009. "Curiosity and Interest: The Benefits of Thriving on Novelty and Challenge." In *The Oxford Handbook of Positive Psychology*, 366–74. Edited by Shane J. Lopez and C. R. Snyder. Oxford: Oxford University Press.

142 **"When you see other people":** Alison Levine, interview with author, 2021.

143 **Wonder and friendships:** Piff, Paul K., Pia Dietze, Matthew Feinberg, Daniel M. Stancato, and Dacher Keltner. 2015. "Awe, the

Small Self, and Prosocial Behavior." *Journal of Personality and Social Psychology* 108 (6): 883–99. doi:10.1037/pspi0000018.

143 **Communal engagement:** Silvia et al., "Openness to Experience and Awe in Response to Nature and Music."

143 **Wonder consolidates collective identity:** Bai et al., "Awe, the Diminished Self, and Collective Engagement."

143 **Awe connects groups more than pride:** Shiota, Michelle N., Dacher Keltner, and Amanda Mossman. 2007. "The Nature of Awe: Elicitors, Appraisals, and Effects on Self-Concept." *Cognition and Emotion* 21 (5): 944–63. doi:10.1080/02699930600923668

143 **"mind-body nexuses":** Keltner, Dacher. 2012. "The Compassionate Species." *Greater Good Magazine* (July 31). https://greatergood.berkeley .edu/article/item/the_compassionate_species.

143 **"social engagement behaviors":** "Love's Brain: A Conversation with Stephen Porges." 2018. Nalanda Institute. https://nalandainstitute .org/2018/04/17/loves-brain-a-conversation-with-stephen-porges/.

144 **Vagus nerve background:** Porges, Marcus. 2019. *Vagus Nerve: Activate the Power of the Vagus Nerve and Heal Yourself.* Independently Published.

144 **Vagus nerve stimulation:** Mayo Clinic. 2018. "Vagus Nerve Stimulation." https://www.mayoclinic.org/tests-procedures/vagus -nerve-stimulation/about/pac-20384565.

144 **Vagus nerve and prosocial emotions:** Quintana, Daniel S., Adam J. Guastella, Tim Outhred, Ian B. Hickie, and Andrew H. Kemp. 2012. "Heart Rate Variability Is Associated with Emotion Recognition: Direct Evidence for a Relationship Between the Autonomic Nervous System and Social Cognition." *International Journal of Psychophysiology* 86 (2): 168–72. doi:10.1016/j.ijpsycho.2012.08.012.

144 **Nostalgia and the vagus nerve:** Fleury, Julie, Constantine Sedikides, Tim Wildschut, David W. Coon, and Pauline Komnenich. 2022. "Feeling Safe and Nostalgia in Healthy Aging." *Frontiers in Psychology* 13 (April): 843051. doi:10.3389/fpsyg.2022.843051.

145 **VR AWE project:** Quesnel, Denise, Ekaterina R. Stepanova, Ivan A. Aguilar, Patrick Pennefather, and Bernhard E. Riecke. 2018. "Creating AWE: Artistic and Scientific Practices in Research-Based Design for Exploring a Profound Immersive Installation." *IEEE Xplore* (August 1). doi:10.1109/GEM.2018.8516463.

146 **Video footage and awe:** Rudd, Melanie, Kathleen D. Vohs, and Jennifer Aaker. 2012. "Awe Expands People's Perception of Time, Alters Decision Making, and Enhances Well-Being." *Psychological Science* 23 (10): 1130–36. doi:10.1177/0956797612438731.

Chapter 9: Time

148   **"Americans are so restless":** de Tocqueville, Alexis, and Gerald Bevan. 2003. *Democracy in America and Two Essays on America.* London: Penguin.

148   **Americans and vacation time:** "State of American Vacation 2018." 2019. U.S. Travel Association. https://www.ustravel.org/research /state-american-vacation-2018.

149   **"Time is money" tied to Franklin:** This was written by Franklin in a 1748 essay titled "Advice to a Young Tradesman." It was, however, printed by another author thirty years prior in the 1719 periodical *The Free-Thinker.* There are further examples of similar phraseology going back to the Greeks. But fair to say, Franklin popularized it. Villers, Damien, and Wolfgang Mieder. 2017. "Time Is Money: Benjamin Franklin and the Vexing Problem of Proverb Origins." *Proverbium: Yearbook of International Proverb Scholarship* 34 (1): 391–404.

149   **Opera and money experiment:** DeVoe, Sanford E., and Julian House. 2012. "Time, Money, and Happiness: How Does Putting a Price on Time Affect Our Ability to Smell the Roses?" *Journal of Experimental Social Psychology* 48 (2): 466–74.

149   **Saint Augustine and the philosophy of time:** Le Poidevin, Robin. 2019. "The Experience and Perception of Time." *Stanford Encyclopedia of Philosophy.* Stanford University. https://plato.stanford.edu/entries /time-experience/.

150   **"Sitting with a pretty girl":** Winchell, Walter. 1938. "On Broadway." *Bradford Evening Star and Daily Record* (December 8). Bradford, PA. https://www.newspapers.com/newspage/75939706/.

150   **"He made a one-point landing":** Bilger, Burkhard. 2011. "The Possibilian." *The New Yorker* (April 25). https://www.newyorker.com /magazine/2011/04/25/the-possibilian.

150   **"I was thinking about *Alice in Wonderland*":** "Falling." 2020. *Radiolab* (September 17). WNYC Studios. 56:27. https://www.wnycstudios.org /podcasts/radiolab/episodes/91726-falling.

151   **Eagleman named best dressed:** Schmal, Jody. 2011. Going Global. *Houston* (April). https://digital.modernluxury.com/publication/?m=3 621&i=65156&p=80&ver=html5.

151   **Eagleman and plasticity:** It is worth noting that Eagleman does not care for the term *plasticity.* Rather, he prefers the term *livewired,* which is also the name of his bestselling book. His argument is that plasticity implies our brain becomes hard again after a brief period of malleability, like plastic, rather than constantly creating new connections. I use *plasticity* because it is understood by a broader

audience. Eagleman, David. 2020. *Livewired: The Inside Story of the Ever-Changing Brain*. New York: Pantheon.

153 **Eagleman time study:** Stetson, Chess, Matthew P. Fiesta, and David M. Eagleman. 2007. "Does Time Really Slow Down during a Frightening Event?" PLoS ONE 2 (12): e1295. doi:10.1371/journal .pone.0001295.

155 **"facilitate the encoding of vivid episodic memory":** Michelle Shiota, interview with author, 2021.

155 **Time cells and the hippocampus:** Reddy, Leila, Benedikt Zoefel, Jessy K. Possel, Judith Peters, Doris E. Dijksterhuis, Marlene Poncet, Elisabeth C. W. van Straaten, Johannes C. Baayen, Sander Idema, and Matthew W. Self. 2021. "Human Hippocampal Neurons Track Moments in a Sequence of Events." *Journal of Neuroscience* 41 (31): 6714–25. doi:10.1523/JNEUROSCI.3157-20.2021.

155 **"When you ask a question in the context of your curiosity":** David Eagleman, interview with author, 2021.

156 **"If you don't feel you have time":** Melanie Rudd, interview with author, 2021.

156 **Awe stretches time:** Rudd, Melanie, Kathleen D. Vohs, and Jennifer Aaker. 2012. "Awe Expands People's Perception of Time, Alters Decision Making, and Enhances Well-Being." *Psychological Science* 23 (10): 1130–36. doi:10.1177/0956797612438731.

156 **"The more you encode along with an experience":** Melanie Rudd, interview with author, 2021.

158 **Awe makes people more generous and less materialistic:** Rudd et al., "Awe Expands People's Perception of Time."

158 **Experiences over stuff for eudaemonia:** One of the theories behind this is that a material object is a quickly achievable benefit, whereas the experiential one requires an investment of time. Kumar, Amit, Matthew A. Killingsworth, and Thomas Gilovich. 2020. "Spending on Doing Promotes More Moment-to-Moment Happiness Than Spending on Having." *Journal of Experimental Social Psychology* 88 (May): 103971. doi:10.1016/j.jesp.2020.103971.

158 **Other benefits of awe:** Researchers from California found that awe mitigated the anxiety and discomfort of waiting for stressful news, like an exam grade or the result of a medical test, supporting Rudd's patience and well-being findings. An interesting adjunct to this is research that shows awe prompts more positive food choices via increased critical thinking. We know that people who feel time-pressured make less healthy food decisions, so, while

this was not tested specifically, perhaps time perception could be a factor here as well. Cao, Fei, Xia Wang, and Ze Wang. 2020. "Effects of Awe on Consumer Preferences for Healthy Versus Unhealthy Food Products." *Journal of Consumer Behaviour* 19 (3): 264–76. doi:10.1002/cb.1815; Prade, Claire, and Vassilis Saroglou. 2016. "Awe's Effects on Generosity and Helping." *Journal of Positive Psychology* 11 (5): 522–30. doi:10.1080/17439760.2015.1127992; Rankin, Kyla, Sara E. Andrews, and Kate Sweeny. 2019. "Awe-Full Uncertainty: Easing Discomfort During Waiting Periods." *Journal of Positive Psychology* (May): 1–10. doi:10.1080/17439760.2019.1615106; Zhou, Chan, Michael Shengtao Wu, Buxin Han, and Chongde Lin. 2014. "Connecting Awe with Virtues: Evidence from Beneficiary Sensitivity and Consumption Behaviors." http://asbbs.org/files /ASBBS2014/PDF/Z/Zhou_Wu_Han_Lin(P731-738).pdf.

158   **"A small dose of awe":** Friedman, Amy. 2012. "The Awe Effect: How Visions of Awe Can Improve Your Health." *Time* (July 26). https:// newsfeed.time.com/2012/07/26/the-awe-effect-how-visions-of-awe -can-improve-your-health/.

158   **Awe and tourism:** It's worth noting that based on what we know about novelty, the wonder effect will likely become less intense with time, but assuming these visits are occasional, place attachment venues can still be dependable wonderbringers. Wang, Lili, and Jiaying Lyu. 2019. "Inspiring Awe Through Tourism and Its Consequence." *Annals of Tourism Research* 77 (July): 106–16. doi:10.1016/j.annals.2019.05.005.

159   **"I'm not going to change the world":** Melanie Rudd, interview with author, 2021.

Chapter 10: Learning

161   **India's first test-tube baby:** This distinction isn't without controversy. Kruti's insemination occurred in the UK, with the birth occurring in India, so some say her claim is incorrect. Harsha Chawda was the first person who was both inseminated *and* born in India. I will leave it to folks to decide who holds this record.

161   **"magic is my birthright":** Kruti Parekh, interview with author, 2021.

162   **"a liminal experience":** Pearce, Cathie, and Maggie MacLure. 2009. "The Wonder of Method." *International Journal of Research & Method in Education* 32 (3): 249–65. doi:10.1080/17437270903259733.

162   **"a sudden surprise":** Descartes, René, and Michael Moriarty. 2015. *The Passions of the Soul: And Other Late Philosophical Writings.* Oxford: Oxford University Press.

164 **Deep and surface learning:** "Characteristics of Deep and Surface Approaches to Learning." n.d. https://teaching.unsw.edu.au/sites /default/files/upload-files/deep_and_surface_learning.pdf.

164 **Openness and deep learning:** Chamorro-Premuzic, Tomas, and Adrian Furnham. 2009. "Mainly Openness: The Relationship Between the Big Five Personality Traits and Learning Approaches." *Learning and Individual Differences* 19 (4): 524–29. doi:10.1016/j .lindif.2009.06.004.

164 **"The most vital and significant factor":** Dewey, John (1933.) 1997. *How We Think.* Mineola, NY: Dover Publications.

165 **Curiosity and motivation:** Deci, E. L., R. Koestner, and R. M. Ryan. 2001. "Extrinsic Rewards and Intrinsic Motivation in Education: Reconsidered Once Again." *Review of Educational Research* 71 (1): 1–27. doi:10.3102/00346543071001001.

165 **"ten important dates in Mongolian history":** David Eagleman, interview with author, 2021.

166 **"Curiosity may put the brain":** "The Secret Benefits of a Curious Mind." 2014. https://www.psychologytoday.com/us/blog /thriving101/201410/the-secret-benefits-curious-mind.

166 **Awe and experiential learning:** Rudd, Melanie, Christian Hildebrand, and Kathleen D. Vohs. 2018. "Inspired to Create: Awe Enhances Openness to Learning and the Desire for Experiential Creation." *Journal of Marketing Research* 55 (5): 766–81.

166 **"openness to learning and curiosity":** Melanie Rudd, interview with author, 2021.

166 **"an impact for learning environments":** Rudd, interview.

167 **Monotony inhibits learning:** Stahn, Alexander C., Hanns-Christian Gunga, Eberhard Kohlberg, Jürgen Gallinat, David F. Dinges, and Simone Kühn. 2019. "Brain Changes in Response to Long Antarctic Expeditions." *New England Journal of Medicine* 381 (23): 2273–75. doi:10.1056/nejmc1904905.

167 **Curiosity and expectation violation for learning:** Price, C. Aaron, Jana Nicole Greenslit, Lauren Applebaum, Natalie Harris, Gloria Segovia, Kimberly A. Quinn, and Sheila Krogh-Jespersen. 2021. "Awe & Memories of Learning in Science and Art Museums." *Visitor Studies* 24 (2): 137–65. doi:10.1080/10645578.2021.1907152.

168 **Broaden-and-build:** Fredrickson, Barbara L. "The Broaden-and-Build Theory of Positive Emotions." 2004. *Philosophical Transactions of the Royal Society of London. Series B: Biological Sciences* 359 (1449): 1367–77.

168 **Diane Ackerman:** Carl Sagan was Ackerman's doctoral advisor.

168 **"Deep play is a fascinating hallmark":** Ackerman, Diane. 2000. *Deep Play.* New York: Vintage Books.

168 **"Wonder is the heaviest element":** Zinsser, W. 2011. *Going on Faith: Writing as a Spiritual Quest.* Eugene, OR: Wipf and Stock.

168 **Play and learning:** Hirsh-Pasek, Kathy, and Roberta Michnick Golinkoff. 2008. "Why Play = Learning." *Encyclopedia on Early Childhood Development* 1: 1–7. Montreal: CEECD.

168 **"We may think of play as optional":** Ackerman, *Deep Play.*

169 **Ancient play:** Gray, Peter. 2012. "The Value of a Play-Filled Childhood in Development of the Hunter-Gatherer Individual." In *Evolution, Early Experience and Human Development.* Edited by Darcia Narvaez, Jaak Panksepp, Allan N. Schore, and Tracy R. Gleason, 352–70. New York: OUP USA.

169 **History of education:** Mulhern, James. 1959. *A History of Education: A Social Interpretation.* New York: Ronald Press.

170 **Blue School:** "Blue School—Independent School in New York City, Preschool, Elementary School, Middle School." n.d. https://www.blueschool.org/.

170 **The Innovative Schools Cooperative:** "The Innovative Schools Cooperative." n.d. https://theinnovativeschools.com/welcome.

170 **"play begins with wonder":** Beau Lotto, interview with author, 2021.

171 **Highly curious children have higher IQs:** Raine, Adrian, Chandra Reynolds, Peter H. Venables, and Sarnoff A. Mednick. 2002. "Stimulation Seeking and Intelligence: A Prospective Longitudinal Study." *Journal of Personality and Social Psychology* 82 (4): 663.

171 **"Gifted curiosity":** Gottfried, Allen W., Adele Eskeles Gottfried, and Diana Wright Guerin. 2006. "The Fullerton Longitudinal Study: A Long-Term Investigation of Intellectual and Motivational Giftedness." *Journal for the Education of the Gifted* 29 (4): 430–50. doi: 10.4219/jeg-2006-244.

171 **Novelty and plasticity in the hippocampus:** Bunzeck, Nico, and Emrah Düzel. 2006. "Absolute Coding of Stimulus Novelty in the Human Substantia Nigra/VTA." *Neuron* 51 (3): 369–79. doi:10.1016/j.neuron.2006.06.021.

171 **William James and genius:** William James maintained that genius "means little more than the faculty of perceiving in an unhabitual way," so it's easy to see why novelty has been called "the motivation that drives explorers and scientists alike." James, William, and John

J. Mcdermott. 1977. *The Writings of William James: A Comprehensive Edition, Including an Annotated Bibliography Updated Through 1977.* Chicago: University of Chicago Press.

172 **Children write peer-reviewed paper:** Blackawton, P. S., S. Airzee, A. Allen, S. Baker, A. Berrow, C. Blair, M. Churchill, et al. 2010. "Blackawton Bees." *Biology Letters* 7 (2): 168–72. doi:10.1098 /rsbl.2010.1056.

172 **Experiential learning leads to better outcomes:** Burch, Gerald F., Robert Giambatista, John H. Batchelor, Jana J. Burch, J. Duane Hoover, and Nathan A. Heller. 2019. "A Meta-Analysis of the Relationship Between Experiential Learning and Learning Outcomes." *Decision Sciences Journal of Innovative Education* 17 (3): 239–73. doi:10.1111/dsji.12188.

172 **"He mirrored the Buddha":** Jim Garrison, interview with author, 2021.

173 **Eighteen jobs in six industries:** McCrindle, Mark. 2019. *McCrindle Insights.* https://mccrindle.com.au/wp-content/uploads/reports /McCrindle-Magazine-Issue-2.pdf.

174 **"what will definitely happen":** Doidge, Norman. 2008. *The Brain That Changes Itself: Stories of Personal Triumph from the Frontiers of Brain Science.* London: Penguin.

174 **Brain likes shortcuts:** Doidge, *The Brain That Changes Itself.*

175 **"Learning what to ignore is critical":** Smillie, Luke. 2017. "Openness to Experience: The Gates of the Mind." *Scientific American* (August 15). https://www.scientificamerican.com/article/openness-to-experience -the-gates-of-the-mind/.

175 **Lewin's three-step model of change:** Burnes, Bernard. 2020. "The Origins of Lewin's Three-Step Model of Change." *Journal of Applied Behavioral Science* 56 (1): 32–59. doi:10.1177/0021886319892685.

176 **"The illiterate of the 21st-century":** Toffler, Alvin. 1970. *Future Shock.* New York: Bantam Books.

176 **"they've got to eliminate curiosity":** Jim Garrison, interview with author, 2021.

176 **Percentage of children with anxiety:** "Children and Teens." 2021. Anxiety and Depression Association of America. https://adaa.org /find-help/by-demographics/children/children-teens.

176 **Children with anxiety more likely to drop out:** "Social Consequences of Psychiatric Disorders, I: Educational Attainment." 1995. *American Journal of Psychiatry* 152 (7): 1026–32. doi:10.1176/ajp.152.7.1026.

177 **Music and test anxiety:** Presence of music ameliorates some of this anxiety. The scores of high-test-anxiety subjects were significantly

enhanced by the presence of unobtrusive classical music during the test. In contrast, the scores of low-test-anxiety students were depressed in the presence of music. Hembree, Ray. 1988. "Correlates, Causes, Effects, and Treatment of Test Anxiety." *Review of Educational Research* 58 (1): 47–77. doi:10.3102/00346543058001047.

177   **Anxiety and educational outcomes:** Kessler, R. C., C. L. Foster, W. B. Saunders, and P. E. Stang. 1995. "Social Consequences of Psychiatric Disorders, I: Educational Attainment." *American Journal of Psychiatry* 152 (7): 1026–32.

177   **"wonder is inherently a social enterprise":** Jim Garrison, interview with author, 2021.

178   **"destruction of brain tissue":** Tomkins, Silvan. 1962. *Affect Imagery Consciousness, Volume I: The Positive Affects.* New York: Springer.

178   **Peak awe periods:** Dacher Keltner, interview with author, 2021.

178   **"There's probably a pedagogical philosophy":** Keltner, interview.

179   **"how do you design a learning system":** Garrison, interview.

179   **Learners with purpose perform better:** Yeager, David S., Marlone D. Henderson, David Paunesku, Gregory M. Walton, Sidney D'Mello, Brian J. Spitzer, and Angela Lee Duckworth. 2014. "Boring but Important: A Self-Transcendent Purpose for Learning Fosters Academic Self-Regulation." *Journal of Personality and Social Psychology* 107 (4): 559–80. doi:10.1037/a0037637.

179   **"In my view, students":** Piersol, Laura. 2013. "Our Hearts Leap Up: Awakening Wonder Within the Classroom." In *Wonder-Full Education.* Edited by Kieran Egan, Annabella I. Cant, Gillian Judson, 11–29. New York: Routledge.

179   **"the importance of questions":** Garrison, interview.

179   **"most worrying part about the lack of wonder":** Piersol, "Our Hearts Leap Up."

180   **"It's a profound tragedy":** Kirk Schneider, interview with author, 2021.

181   **"Differently wired children frequently struggle":** Deborah Reber, communication with author, 2021.

181   **Psychiatric drugs:** Psychiatric drugs have a way of reframing the landscape in which we view behavior. The approval of lithium for manic depression, for example, led to a dramatic increase in diagnoses of manic depression. Prozac had the same effect on depression diagnoses. In other words, once a "fix" emerged, so did a lot of people in need of fixing. Adderall is on this same usage trajectory. Cruz, Noelia de la. 2012. "Infographic: America Is Over-

Medicated." https://www.businessinsider.com/infographic-america
-is-over-medicated-2012-2?op=1.

182 **Neuroscience of ADD/ADHD:** There are also other elements at play
with ADD/ADHD, including serotonin, hormones, and certain
neurological features. Konopka, Lukasz M. 2014. "Understanding
Attention Deficit Disorder: A Neuroscience Prospective." *Croatian
Medical Journal* 55 (2): 174–6. doi:10.3325/cmj.2014.55.174.

183 **Psychedelics and autism:** Both historical research using LSD and
current research using MDMA show the potential for these drugs
to be used therapeutically for those on the autism spectrum as well
as those with ADHD. More important though, these psychedelic
discoveries open the door to possible nonpharmaceutical wonder-
based therapies in the future. Markopoulos, Athanasios, Antonio
Inserra, Danilo De Gregorio, and Gabriella Gobbi. 2021. "Evaluating
the Potential Use of Serotonergic Psychedelics in Autism Spectrum
Disorder." *Frontiers in Pharmacology* 12.

183 **Green views improve attention:** Li, Dongying, and William C.
Sullivan. 2016. "Impact of Views to School Landscapes on Recovery
from Stress and Mental Fatigue." *Landscape and Urban Planning* 148
(April): 149–58. doi:10.1016/j.landurbplan.2015.12.015.

183 **Green walks improve ADHD symptoms:** Kuo, Frances E., and
Andrea Faber Taylor. 2004. "A Potential Natural Treatment for
Attention-Deficit/Hyperactivity Disorder: Evidence from a National
Study." *American Journal of Public Health* 94 (9): 1580–86. doi:10.2105
/ajph.94.9.1580.

183 **Green advantage and attention in children:** Bakir-Demir,
Tugce, Sibel Kazak Berument, and Basak Sahin-Acar. 2019. "The
Relationship Between Greenery and Self-Regulation
of Children: The Mediation Role of Nature Connectedness."
Journal of Environmental Psychology 65 (October): 101327. doi:10.1016/j
.jenvp.2019.101327.

184 **"constructive internal reflection":** Immordino-Yang, Mary Helen,
Joanna A. Christodoulou, and Vanessa Singh. 2012. "Rest Is Not
Idleness: Implications of the Brain's Default Mode for Human
Development and Education." *Perspectives on Psychological Science* 7 (4):
352–64. doi:10.1177/1745691612447308.

184 **"I would tell the teachers":** Kushner, *Nine Essential Things.*

184 **"the wonder and beauty of God's world":** Kushner, Harold S. 2015.
Nine Essential Things I've Learned About Life. New York: Alfred A. Knopf.

184 **Parents model questioning behavior:** In a study of differences
between working-class families' and middle-class families' child-

rearing styles, researcher Annette Lareau from the University of Pennsylvania found that working-class children weren't less curious, but they were not as proficient at asking openly curious questions. Middle-class children were asked more openly curious questions by their parents, so they modeled this. But they also observed their parents use questions to confidently challenge those in authority, meaning they felt more confident to ask doctors or teachers to clarify statements. We know children whose parents read to them at an early age have increased verbal proficiency compared to those whose parents do not. Even providing children with a richer emotional vocabulary resulted in improved behavior and better grades. These subtle differences in questioning behavior are certain to impact a child's tendencies toward a deeper kind of curiosity. Lareau, Annette. 2011. *Unequal Childhoods: Class, Race, and Family Life*. Berkeley: University of California Press.

184 **"Stop fucking worrying":** Keltner, interview.

Chapter 11: Wonder at Work

188 **Oude Kerk experiment:** While these results showed a low but significant correlation between body size and awe, the results have been replicated in several subsequent studies, with people estimating their physical size smaller in relation to room size and even in relation to distances between objects. Van Elk, Michiel, Annika Karinen, Eva Specker, Eftychia Stamkou, and Matthijs Baas. 2016. "'Standing in Awe': The Effects of Awe on Body Perception and the Relation with Absorption." *Collabra* 2 (1): 4. doi:10.1525/collabra.36.

188 **Empathy and power:** According to researchers, power and empathy have an inverse relationship. The more powerful a person is, the less help they need from others, and thus the less they put themselves in the shoes of others. Perhaps empathy is the difference between the charisma of a cult and the charisma of a transformational leader. Stellar, Jennifer E., Vida M. Manzo, Michael W. Kraus, and Dacher Keltner. 2012. "Class and Compassion: Socioeconomic Factors Predict Responses to Suffering." *Emotion* 12 (3): 449–59. doi:10.1037/a0026508.

188 **Manager impact on employee engagement:** "People Management Survey 2018." 2018. The Predictive Index. https://www.predictiveindex.com/learn/inspire/resources/surveys-reports/people-management-survey-2018/.

190 **Salary cut for empathetic leadership:** "Businessolver Empathy Executive Summary Whitepaper." 2020. Businessolver. https://

info.businesssolver.com/en-us/empathy-2020-exec-summary
-ty?submissionGuid=42cfac5c-13f6.

190 **Empathetic companies perform better:** This research carries a
caveat, given it was conducted by a consulting firm in, you guessed it,
empathy; however, the results are intriguing. Growth was defined by
market capitalization. Parmar, Belinda. 2016. "The Most Empathetic
Companies, 2016." *Harvard Business Review* (December 1). https://hbr
.org/2016/12/the-most-and-least-empathetic-companies-2016.

190 **ToM and empathy:** Singer, Tania, and Anita Tusche. 2014.
"Understanding Others: Brain Mechanisms of Theory of Mind and
Empathy." *Neuroeconomics.* Edited by Paul W. Glimcher and Ernst Fehr,
513–32. Cambridge, MA: Academic Press.

190 **Types of empathy:** Generally, empathy falls into one of three
categories. The first category is *contagious* or *emotional empathy*, the
kind in which someone "catches feelings" and experiences the same
emotions as another person. The second is *cognitive empathy*, which
is more rational than emotional empathy and is more influenced by
social norms. The last category is *compassionate empathy*, which is the
kind that compels the empathizer into action.

190 **ToM and neurodiversity:** It is believed that certain neurodiverse
people, who sometimes have challenges with social cues and
empathetic responsiveness, may have a deficit in this area. In a
standard test used to measure ToM, 85 percent of developmentally
typical children and 86 percent of children with Down syndrome
answered the test question correctly, whereas 80 percent of children
with autism spectrum disorder (ASD) did not. This is further
supported by brain scans, in which the area of the brain responsible
for ToM is less active in people with ASD. Yirmiya, Nurit, Osnat
Erel, Michal Shaked, and Daphna Solomonica-Levi. 1998. "Meta-
Analyses Comparing Theory of Mind Abilities of Individuals with
Autism, Individuals with Mental Retardation, Normally Developing
Individuals." *Psychological Bulletin* 124 (3): 283.

191 **Mirror neurons:** While many animal species depend on one another
and work together in cooperative ways, primates are unique in their
possession of mirror neurons. These were discovered unexpectedly
while studying the grasp response of macaque. Researchers observed
that while one monkey watched another monkey grasp an object, the
area of the brain associated with the action was activated in both
the doer and the watcher (although in the watcher to a lesser extent,
because it was just the watcher's mirror neuron system that was
activated, not the whole area responsible for movement). Rizzolatti,
Giacomo, and Laila Craighero. 2004. "The Mirror-Neuron System."

Annual Review of Neuroscience 27 (1): 169–92. doi:10.1146/annurev .neuro.27.070203.144230.

191 **"a chronic and growing empathy deficit":** Krznaric, Roman. 2015. *Empathy: Why It Matters, and How to Get It.* New York: Perigee.

191 **Drop in empathy levels of college students:** Konrath et al., "Changes in Dispositional Empathy in American College Students over Time: A Meta-Analysis"; "The Decline of Empathy and the Rise of Narcissism with Sara Konrath, PhD." 2019. *Speaking of Psychology* (December 4). 45:34. https://www.youtube.com/watch?v= UaZeDKwnvg8.

191 **"Digital culture has created an epidemic":** "Empathy Erosion: 5 Strategies to Rebuild Yours." 2020. *TalentSmart* (October 27). https:// www.talentsmarteq.com/blog/empathy-erosion-5-strategies-to -rebuild-yours/.

191 **"homo empathicus":** Krznaric, Roman. 2012. "Six Habits of Highly Empathic People." *Greater Good Magazine.* https://greatergood .berkeley.edu/article/item/six_habits_of_highly_empathic_people1.

192 **"Empathy is like a skill":** "How Power Erodes Empathy, and the Steps We Can Take to Rebuild It." 2020. WBUR. https://www.wbur .org/hereandnow/2020/07/09/jamil-zaki-empathy-power.

192 **"Curiosity expands our empathy":** Krznaric, "Six Habits of Highly Empathic People."

192 **"Be curious, not judgmental":** Actually, I do know. Although often falsely attributed to Walt Whitman, in this case it was Coach Lasso.

192 **"Highly empathic people":** Krznaric, "Six Habits of Highly Empathic People."

192 **Absorption, mimicry, and empathy:** Wickramasekera, Ian E., and Janet P. Szlyk. 2003. "Could Empathy Be a Predictor of Hypnotic Ability?" *International Journal of Clinical and Experimental Hypnosis* 51 (4): 390–9. doi:10.1076/iceh.51.4.390.16413.

193 **Absorption and empathy:** Rivers, Anissa, Ian E. Wickramasekera, Ronald J. Pekala, and Jennifer A. Rivers. 2015. "Empathic Features and Absorption in Fantasy Role-Playing." *American Journal of Clinical Hypnosis* 58 (3): 286–94. doi:10.1080/00029157.2015.1103696.

193 **Humility and moral character:** Cohen, Taya R., A. T. Panter, Nazlı Turan, Lily Morse, and Yeonjeong Kim. 2014. "Moral Character in the Workplace." *Journal of Personality and Social Psychology* 107 (5): 943–63. doi:10.1037/a0037245.

193 **Humility and sense of self:** Chancellor, Joseph, and Sonja Lyubomirsky. 2013. "Humble Beginnings: Current Trends, State

Perspectives, and Hallmarks of Humility." *Social and Personality Psychology Compass* 7 (11): 819–33. doi:10.1111/spc3.12069.

193 **Humble CEOs more effective:** Ou, Amy Y., David A. Waldman, and Suzanne J. Peterson. 2015. "Do Humble CEOs Matter? An Examination of CEO Humility and Firm Outcomes." *Journal of Management* 44 (3): 1147–73. doi:10.1177/0149206315604187.

193 **Humble CEOs have empowering leadership behaviors:** Ou, Amy Y., Anne S. Tsui, Angelo J. Kinicki, David A. Waldman, Zhixing Xiao, and Lynda Jiwen Song. 2014. "Humble Chief Executive Officers' Connections to Top Management Team Integration and Middle Managers' Responses." *Administrative Science Quarterly* 59 (1): 34–72. doi:10.1177/0001839213520131.

194 **"Emotions not only function":** Stellar, Jennifer E., Amie Gordon, Craig L. Anderson, Paul K. Piff, Galen D. McNeil, and Dacher Keltner. 2018. "Awe and Humility." *Journal of Personality and Social Psychology* 114 (2): 258–69. doi:10.1037/pspi0000109.

194 **Awe, humility, and negative feedback:** In another study out of China, awe also increased humility and made people more open to negative feedback. Atamba, Cynthia. 2019. "Restorative Effects of Awe on Negative Affect After Receiving Negative Performance Feedback." *Journal of Psychology in Africa* 29 (2): 95–103. doi:10.1111/spc3.12069.

194 **Berkeley eucalyptus grove:** "Eucalyptus | Creeks of UC Berkeley." n.d. http://strawberrycreek.berkeley.edu/tour/08eucalyptus.html.

195 **Awe and small-self experiment:** Piff, Paul K., Pia Dietze, Matthew Feinberg, Daniel M. Stancato, and Dacher Keltner. 2015. "Awe, the Small Self, and Prosocial Behavior." *Journal of Personality and Social Psychology* 108 (6): 883–99. doi:10.1037/pspi0000018.

195 **Honesty as a desirable leadership quality:** Pew Research Center. 2015. "What Makes a Good Leader, and Does Gender Matter?" Pew Research Center's Social & Demographic Trends Project (January 14). https://www.pewresearch.org/social-trends/2015/01/14/chapter-2-what-makes-a-good-leader-and-does-gender-matter/.

196 **Authentic culture gap:** PricewaterhouseCoopers. 2021. *Global Culture Survey 2021 Report*. https://www.pwc.com/gx/en/issues/upskilling/global-culture-survey-2021/global-culture-survey-2021-report.html#content-free-1-817d.

196 **Authenticity at work:** Bosch, Ralph van den, and Toon W. Taris. 2013. "Authenticity at Work: Development and Validation of an Individual Authenticity Measure at Work." *Journal of Happiness Studies* 15 (1): 1–18. doi:10.1007/s10902-013-9413-3.

196 **Authenticity and well-being:** Rivera, Grace N., Andrew G. Christy, Jinhyung Kim, Matthew Vess, Joshua A. Hicks, and Rebecca J. Schlegel. 2019. "Understanding the Relationship Between Perceived Authenticity and Well-Being." *Review of General Psychology* 23 (1): 113–26.

196 **Authenticity and first impressions:** Gino, Francesca, Ovul Sezer, and Laura Huang. 2020. "To Be or Not to Be Your Authentic Self? Catering to Others' Preferences Hinders Performance." *Organizational Behavior and Human Decision Processes* 158: 83–100. doi:10.1016/j.obhdp .2020.01.003.

196 **Awe and authenticity:** Jiang, Tonglin, and Constantine Sedikides. 2021. "Awe Motivates Authentic Self-Pursuit via Self-Transcendence: Implications for Prosociality." *Journal of Personality and Social Psychology*: 1–64. doi:10.17605/OSF.IO/8QYC2.

196 **Curiosity and authentic leadership:** Walker, Allan, and Chen Shuangye. 2007. "Leader Authenticity in Intercultural School Contexts." *Educational Management Administration & Leadership* 35 (2): 185–204. doi:10.1177/1741143207075388.

197 **Ingrouping and outgrouping:** Vaughn, Don A., Ricky R. Savjani, Mark S. Cohen, and David M. Eagleman. 2018. "Empathic Neural Responses Predict Group Allegiance." *Frontiers in Human Neuroscience* 12 (July): 302. doi:10.3389/fnhum.2018.00302.

197 **Best teams are diverse teams:** Page, Scott E. 2007. *The Difference: How the Power of Diversity Creates Better Groups, Firms, Schools, and Societies.* Princeton: Princeton University Press.

198 **Hand-stabbing outgrouping study:** Vaughn et al., "Empathic Neural Responses Predict Group Allegiance."

198 **"just how hardwired we are to make groups":** David Eagleman, interview with author, 2021.

198 **Diverse leadership performs better:** Businesses with diverse management teams perform 35 percent better than those without them. Hunt, Vivian, Dennis Layton, and Sara Prince. 2015. "Why Diversity Matters." *McKinsey & Company* (Jan 1). https://www .mckinsey.com/business-functions/people-and-organizational -performance/our-insights/why-diversity-matters.

198 **Diverse teams are better:** Hunt, Layton, and Prince, "Why Diversity Matters."

199 **Diverse stock pickers:** Levine, Sheen S., Evan P. Apfelbaum, Mark Bernard, Valerie L. Bartelt, Edward J. Zajac, and David Stark. 2014. "Ethnic Diversity Deflates Price Bubbles." *Proceedings of the National Academy of Sciences* 111 (52): 18524–9. doi:10.1073/pnas.1407301111.

199　**Future cooperation and ingrouping bias:** Misch, Antonia, Markus Paulus, and Yarrow Dunham. 2021. "Anticipation of Future Cooperation Eliminates Minimal Ingroup Bias in Children and Adults." *Journal of Experimental Psychology: General* (March). doi:10.1037/xge0000899.

199　**"nothing about us is permanent":** Eagleman, interview.

199　**Curiosity and social rejection:** Kawamoto, Taishi, Mitsuhiro Ura, and Kazuo Hiraki. 2017. "Curious People Are Less Affected by Social Rejection." *Personality and Individual Differences* 105 (January): 264–7. doi:10.1016/j.paid.2016.10.006.

200　**Awe and stereotypes:** Perez, Kenneth A., and Heather C. Lench. 2018. "3. Benefits of awe in the workplace." *Social Functions of Emotion and Talking About Emotion at Work*: 46.

200　**Awe and social cohesion:** Stellar, Jennifer E., Amie M. Gordon, Paul K. Piff, Daniel Cordaro, Craig L. Anderson, Yang Bai, Laura A. Maruskin, and Dacher Keltner. 2017. "Self-Transcendent Emotions and Their Social Functions: Compassion, Gratitude, and Awe Bind Us to Others Through Prosociality." *Emotion Review* 9 (3): 200–7. doi:10.1177/1754073916684557.

200　**STEs and tribal culture:** Yaden, David Bryce, Jonathan Haidt, Ralph W. Hood, David R. Vago, and Andrew B. Newberg. 2017. "The Varieties of Self-Transcendent Experience." *Review of General Psychology* 21 (2): 143–60. doi:10.1037/gpr0000102.

200　**"What if we could use awe":** Lotto, Beau and Cirque du Soleil. 2019. "Beau Lotto and Cirque Du Soleil: How We Experience Awe—and Why It Matters." TED2019. 14:39. https://www.ted.com/talks/beau_lotto_and_cirque_du_soleil_how_we_experience_awe_and_why_it_matters.

201　**"Especially in modern times":** Melanie Rudd, interview with author, 2021.

201　**"tend to prefer an autocratic leadership":** Singal, Jesse. 2015. "How Well Do You Handle Uncertainty? Take This Quiz to Find Out." *The Cut* (December 29). https://www.thecut.com/2015/12/this-quiz-shows-how-well-you-handle-uncertainty.html.

201　**NFCC and conservatism:** People who are high in NFCC also tend to be more conservative politically and religiously. Chirumbolo, Antonio, Alessandra Areni, and Gilda Sensales. 2004. "Need for Cognitive Closure and Politics: Voting, Political Attitudes and Attributional Style." *International Journal of Psychology* 39 (4): 245–53.

202　**Openness and knowledge sharing:** Zhang, Wei, Sunny Li Sun, Yuan

Jiang, and Wenyao Zhang. 2019. "Openness to Experience and Team Creativity: Effects of Knowledge Sharing and Transformational Leadership." *Creativity Research Journal* 31 (1): 62–73. doi:10.1080/10400 419.2019.1577649.

202 **Openness and creativity:** Schilpzand, Marieke C., David M. Herold, and Christina E. Shalley. 2010. "Members' Openness to Experience and Teams' Creative Performance." *Small Group Research* 42 (1): 55–76. doi:10.1177/1046496410377509.

202 **NFCC and creativity:** Chirumbolo, Antonio, Stefano Livi, Lucia Mannetti, Antonio Pierro, and Arie W. Kruglanski. 2004. "Effects of Need for Closure on Creativity in Small Group Interactions." *European Journal of Personality* 18 (4): 265–78. doi:10.1002/per.518.

202 **"better able to sit with uncertainty":** Beau Lotto, interview with author, 2021.

202 **Paradox mindset:** Experimenters used what is known as "the candle problem," an activity in which participants are given a box filled with a candle, a pack of matches, and a box of tacks and they have three minutes to figure out how to affix the candle to the wall without it dripping on the floor when lit, using only the materials provided. The majority of participants fail to recognize that using the box the materials were delivered in offers the solution, by affixing that to the wall. Miron-Spektor, Ella, Amy Ingram, Joshua Keller, Wendy K. Smith, and Marianne W. Lewis. 2018. "Microfoundations of Organizational Paradox: The Problem Is How We Think about the Problem." *Academy of Management Journal* 61 (1): 26–45. doi:10.5465/amj.2016.0594.

Chapter 12: Health

205 **"I am part or particle of God":** Emerson, Ralph Waldo, and Sam Torode. 2003. *Nature and Selected Essays.* Edited by Larzer Ziff. Reissue edition. New York: Penguin Classics.

206 **Emerson as first American philosopher:** Emerson and Trode, *Nature and Selected Essays.*

206 **"Nature itself is the best physician":** It is debated whether Hippocrates said this exact thing; however, he is credited with creating the principle of *vis medicatrix naturae* ("the healing power of nature"), which, translated into Greek, reads "Nature is the healer" or "Nature is the physician." So—and not to put words in Hippocrates's mouth—while he might not have said it, it is credible that he believed it.

206 **History of anesthesia:** "The History of Anaesthesia." 2019. The Royal College of Anaesthetists. https://www.rcoa.ac.uk/about-college /heritage/history-anaesthesia.

206 **History of antibiotics:** "The History of Antibiotics." 2019. Microbiology Society. https://microbiologysociety.org/members -outreach-resources/outreach-resources/antibiotics-unearthed /antibiotics-and-antibiotic-resistance/the-history-of-antibiotics.html.

206 **Sanatorium movement:** "The White Plague in the City of Angels: The Sanatorium Movement in America." n.d. https://scalar.usc .edu/hc/tuberculosis-exhibit/the-sanatorium-movement-in-america.

208 **Qing Li:** de Geus, Sjanett. 2021. "Forest Bathing Cures Covid-19." *Transformation Podcast* (February 11). 1:04:35. https://www.youtube .com/watch?v=vNRZGuY3J6U&t=32s

208 **"Some people study forests":** Livni, Ephrat. 2018. "Japanese 'Forest Medicine' Is the Science of Using Nature to Heal Yourself— Wherever You Are." *Quartz* (February 21). https://qz.com/1208959 /japanese-forest-medicine-is-the-art-of-using-nature-to-heal -yourself-wherever-you-are/.

208 **"stress inhibits immune function":** Das, Deepannita. 2018. "Dr. Qing Li—the Man Behind Forest Bathing and Why You Need It." Life Beyond Numbers (July 3). https://lifebeyondnumbers.com/dr-qing-li -forest-bathing-why-you-need/.

208 **Time spent in the forest and health outcomes:** Li, Qing. 2018. *Forest Bathing: How Trees Can Help You Find Health and Happiness.* New York: Viking.

208 **"[Forest bathing] is like a bridge":** Li, Qing. 2018. " 'Forest Bathing' Is Great for Your Health. Here's How to Do It." *Time* (May 1). https://time.com/5259602/japanese-forest-bathing/.

209 **"I just have a feeling":** de Geus, "Forest Bathing Cures Covid-19."

209 **Shinrin-yoku:** Park, Bum Jin, Yuko Tsunetsugu, Tamami Kasetani, Takahide Kagawa, and Yoshifumi Miyazaki. 2009. "The Physiological Effects of Shinrin-Yoku (Taking in the Forest Atmosphere or Forest Bathing): Evidence from Field Experiments in 24 Forests Across Japan." *Environmental Health and Preventive Medicine* 15 (1): 18–26. doi:10.1007/s12199-009-0086-9.

209 **Percentage of Japanese woodlands:** de Geus, "Forest Bathing Cures Covid-19."

209 **"affiliate with other organisms":** Wilson, Edward O. 1984. *Biophilia.* Cambridge, MA: Harvard University Press.

210 **Ulrich's window research:** Ulrich, R. S. 1984. "View Through a

Window May Influence Recovery from Surgery." *Science* 224 (4647): 420–1. doi:10.1126/science.6143402.

210 **Forest walks:** Park et al., "The Physiological Effects of Shinrin-Yoku."

211 **Natural environments and the brain:** Ulrich, "View Through a Window May Influence Recovery from Surgery."

211 **Percentage of people living in urban environments:** "68% of the World Population Projected to Live in Urban Areas by 2050, Says UN." 2018. United Nations Department of Economic and Social Affairs (May 16). https://www.un.org/development/desa/en/news /population/2018-revision-of-world-urbanization-prospects.html.

211 **"bodies that are still adapted to the natural environment":** Miyazaki, Yoshifumi. 2018. *Shinrin Yoku: The Japanese Art of Forest Bathing.* Portland, OR: Timber Press.

211 **"effortlessly engaging":** Ohly, Heather, Mathew P. White, Benedict W. Wheeler, Alison Bethel, Obioha C. Ukoumunne, Vasilis Nikolaou, and Ruth Garside. 2016. "Attention Restoration Theory: A Systematic Review of the Attention Restoration Potential of Exposure to Natural Environments." *Journal of Toxicology and Environmental Health, Part B* 19 (7): 305–43. doi:10.1080/10937404.2016.1196155.

212 **NK cells and phytoncide essential oil:** This result was reproduced in a hotel room as well. For three nights, people stayed in a hotel room where the phytoncide aroma of Japanese cypress was pumped in via a humidifier. Participants went to work during the day and spent only the evenings in the room. After just that limited exposure, they showed improvement in the activity and number of their NK cells, as well as better sleep quality and lower levels of the stress hormone cortisol. Li, Q., M. Kobayashi, Y. Wakayama, H. Inagaki, M. Katsumata, Y. Hirata, K. Hirata, et al. 2009. "Effect of Phytoncide from Trees on Human Natural Killer Cell Function." *International Journal of Immunopathology and Pharmacology* 22 (4): 951–9. doi:10.1177/039463200902200410.

212 **Healing power of nature:** Forest medicine is now an established therapy in Japan, with more than one thousand certified forest therapists, and other countries are slowly following suit by looking for ways to tap into the healing power of nature. In the US and UK, some doctors are already prescribing nature walks to their patients and, in fact, walks outdoors are listed as a treatment suggestion by the Scottish National Health Service. Hospital gardens are taking root, too, like Prouty Garden at Children's Hospital Boston, where the designers suggest a green-to-built environment ratio of at least seven to three. Thompson, Alexandra. 2020. "Patients Will Be Prescribed Walks in the Great Outdoors on the NHS."

www.yahoo.com (July 20). https://www.yahoo.com/lifestyle/nhs
-prescriptions-george-eustice-walk-nature-115306399.htmlhttps://
www.yahoo.com/lifestyle/nhs-prescriptions-george-eustice-walk
-nature-115306399.html; Franklin, Deborah. 2012. "How Hospital
Gardens Help Patients Heal." *Scientific American* (March 1). https://
www.scientificamerican.com/article/nature-that-nurtures/.

212   **"It wasn't like a love at first sight":** Jennifer Stellar, interview with
author, 2021.

213   **Anger, fear, and cytokines:** Moons, Wesley G., Naomi I. Eisenberger,
and Shelley E. Taylor. 2010. "Anger and Fear Responses to Stress
Have Different Biological Profiles." *Brain, Behavior, and Immunity* 24
(2): 215–9. doi:10.1016/j.bbi.2009.08.009.

213   **Shame and cytokines:** Dickerson, Sally S., Margaret E. Kemeny,
Najib Aziz, Kevin H. Kim, and John L. Fahey. 2004. "Immunological
Effects of Induced Shame and Guilt." *Psychosomatic Medicine* 66 (1):
124–31. doi:10.1097/01.PSY.0000097338.75454.29.

213   **Stress and cytokines:** Kiecolt-Glaser, J. K., K. J. Preacher, R. C.
MacCallum, C. Atkinson, W. B. Malarkey, and R. Glaser. 2003.
"Chronic Stress and Age-Related Increases in the Proinflammatory
Cytokine IL-6." *Proceedings of the National Academy of Sciences* 100 (15):
9090–5. doi:10.1073/pnas.1531903100.

213   **Negative effects of proinflammatory cytokines:** Ramani, Thulasi,
Carol S. Auletta, Daniel Weinstock, Barbara Mounho-Zamora,
Patricia C. Ryan, Theodora W. Salcedo, and Gregory Bannish. 2015.
"Cytokines: The Good, the Bad, and the Deadly." *International Journal
of Toxicology* 34 (4): 355–65. doi:10.1177/1091581815584918.

213   **Awe reduces inflammatory cytokines:** Stellar, Jennifer E., Neha
John-Henderson, Craig L. Anderson, Amie M. Gordon, Galen D.
McNeil, and Dacher Keltner. 2015. "Positive Affect and Markers of
Inflammation: Discrete Positive Emotions Predict Lower Levels of
Inflammatory Cytokines." *Emotion* 15 (2): 129–33. doi:10.1037
/emo0000033.

214   **Awe as an anti-inflammatory:** Castillo, Stephanie. 2015. "Awe May
Be a Natural Anti-Inflammatory." *Medical Daily* (April 3). https://www
.medicaldaily.com/awe-inspiring-moments-lower-inflammation
-marker-cytokines-positively-impact-health-328092.

214   **"Those less intense experiences":** Dacher Keltner, interview with
author, 2021.

214   **Wonder walks:** Sturm, Virginia E., Samir Datta, Ashlin R. K. Roy,
Isabel J. Sible, Eena L. Kosik, Christina R. Veziris, Tiffany E. Chow,
et al. 2020. "Big Smile, Small Self: Awe Walks Promote Prosocial

Positive Emotions in Older Adults." *Emotion* (September). Advance online publication. doi:10.1037/emo0000876.

216 **"I am glad to the brink of fear":** Emerson, *Nature and Selected Essays.*

Chapter 13: Resilience

221 **Florida's death row:** "Florida." 2016. Death Penalty Information Center. 2016. https://deathpenaltyinfo.org/state-and-federal-info /state-by-state/florida.

221 **Language for incarcerated people:** The words used to refer to a person involved in the justice system have quite a range, and some of them, like *convict*, are seen as very pejorative. According to the Marshall Project, the three terms preferred by people in prisons are *incarcerated person*, *inmate*, and *prisoner*. I have used these words based on that research. Hickman, Blair. 2015. "Inmate. Prisoner. Other. Discussed." The Marshall Project (April 3). https://www .themarshallproject.org/2015/04/03/inmate-prisoner-other-discussed.

221 **About UCI:** Serial murderer Ted Bundy was held and executed there, but not before managing to sire a child while incarcerated. There have been women on Florida's death row, but the women were held in a different facility in Broward County and only brought to Raiford for execution. "Union Correctional Institution." 2010. Florida Department of Corrections (July 24, 2010). https://web.archive.org /web/20100724221446/http://www.dc.state.fl.us/facilities/region2/213 .html.

222 **"perfect boring situation":** Oluwafemi, Funmilola A., Abdelbaki Rayan, James C.-Y. Lai, Jose G. Mora-Almanza, and Esther M. Afolayan. 2021. "A Review of Astronaut Mental Health in Manned Missions: Potential Interventions for Cognitive and Mental Health Challenges." *Life Sciences in Space Research* 28: 26–31.

222 **"abnormal pattern characteristic of stupor and delirium":** Grassian, Stuart. 2006. "Psychiatric Effects of Solitary Confinement." *Washington University Journal of Law & Policy* 22 (1): 327–80.

223 **5.3 million in nature-deprived settings:** Nadkarni, Nalini M., Patricia H. Hasbach, Tierney Thys, Emily Gaines Crockett, and Lance Schnacker. 2017. "Impacts of Nature Imagery on People in Severely Nature-Deprived Environments." *Frontiers in Ecology and the Environment* 15 (7): 395–403. doi:10.1002/fee.1518.

223 **100 million lack access to nature:** Children, non-white people, and those in lower income brackets are significantly and disproportionately more nature deprived than other Americans. "Access to Nature Is a Health and Human Rights Issue." 2022. The

Wilderness Society (February 24). https://www.wilderness.org /articles/blog/access-nature-health-and-human-rights-issue.

224 **"overwhelming feelings of sadness, hopelessness, and depression":** "'Pawns in a Failed Experiment': Testimony of Dr. Craig Haney on Solitary Confinement." 2011. *Solitary Watch* blog (September 1). https://solitarywatch.org/2011/09/01/pawns-in-a-failed-experiment -testimony-of-dr-craig-haney-on-solitary-confinement/.

224 **"Solitary confinement is like being stranded at sea":** "Pelican Bay: Solitary Confinement Is Pure Torture." 2013. *Mercury News* (September 20). https://www.mercurynews.com/2013/09/20 /pelican-bay-solitary-confinement-is-pure-torture/.

225 **Awe reduces aggression:** Thys's Blue Room experiment has since been followed up with research showing that awe reduces aggression via a sense of small-self and connectedness. Yang, Ying, Ziyan Yang, Taoxun Bao, Yunzhi Liu, and Holli-Anne Passmore. 2016. "Elicited Awe Decreases Aggression." *Journal of Pacific Rim Psychology* (January): 1–13. doi:10.1017/prp.2016.8.

226 **"a view of heaven from a seat in hell":** Callahan, Steven. 1999. *Adrift: Seventy Six Days Lost at Sea*, reprint ed. Boston: Mariner Books.

227 **"It's the training that provides":** John Leach, interview with author, 2021.

227 **"When people start to lose meaning in life":** Leach, interview.

228 **"striving to find meaning":** Frankl, *Man's Search for Meaning*.

228 **Intrinsic motivation helps manage trauma:** Kashdan, Todd B., and Paul J. Silvia. 2009. "Curiosity and Interest: The Benefits of Thriving on Novelty and Challenge." In *The Oxford Handbook of Positive Psychology*. Edited by Shane J. Lopez and C. R. Snyder, 366–74. Oxford: Oxford University Press. doi:10.1093 /oxfordhb/9780195187243.013.0034.

228 **Skylab strike:** Weick, Karl E. 1977. "Organization Design: Organizations as Self-Designing Systems." *Organizational Dynamics* 6 (2): 31–46.

228 **"to find their place amid these baffling . . . experiences":** Weick, "Organization Design."

229 **"there is no distinct dividing line":** Steven Callahan, communication with author, 2021.

229 **Percentage of threat-based awe:** Gordon, Amie M., Jennifer E. Stellar, Craig L. Anderson, Galen D. McNeil, Daniel Loew, and Dacher Keltner. 2017. "The Dark Side of the Sublime: Distinguishing

a Threat-Based Variant of Awe." *Journal of Personality and Social Psychology* 113 (2): 310–28. doi:10.1037/pspp0000120.

230 **"silver linings":** There are similarities between horror and awe, both being "schema incongruent" emotions, meaning they are both experiences that our brain struggles to comprehend. They do appear to be different, however, with the "silver linings" elements being a key differentiator. Taylor, Pamela Marie, and Yukiko Uchida. 2019. "Awe or Horror: Differentiating Two Emotional Responses to Schema Incongruence." *Cognition and Emotion* 33 (8): 1548–61. doi:10.1 080/02699931.2019.1578194.

230 **Threat-based awe and COVID-19:** Yang, Yikai, Ou Li, Xixian Peng, and Lei Wang. 2020. "Consumption Trends during the COVID-19 Crisis: How Awe, Coping, and Social Norms Drive Utilitarian Purchases." *Frontiers in Psychology* 11 (October): 1–10. doi:10.3389 /fpsyg.2020.588580.

230 **Awe ameliorates sense of loss:** Research shows that nature-induced awe also ameliorates the sense of loss in small ways, such as losing a precious heirloom or personal object. Koh, Alethea H. Q., Eddie M. W. Tong, and Alexander Y. L. Yuen. 2019. "The Buffering Effect of Awe on Negative Affect Towards Lost Possessions." *Journal of Positive Psychology* 14 (2): 156–65. doi:10.1080/17439760.2017.1388431.

231 **PTSD:** Xue, Chen, Yang Ge, Bihan Tang, Yuan Liu, Peng Kang, Meng Wang, and Lulu Zhang. 2015. "A Meta-Analysis of Risk Factors for Combat-Related PTSD Among Military Personnel and Veterans." Edited by Christian Schmahl. *PLoS ONE* 10 (3): e0120270. doi:10.1371 /journal.pone.0120270.

231 **White-water rafting PTSD experiment:** In the white-water rafting experiment, Anderson used the words *awe, amazed,* and *wonder* as synonyms for "awe." Beyond cortisol, they also tested other physiological markers, like proinflammatory cytokines. Other benefits beyond reduction in PTSD symptoms included an 8 percent boost in happiness, a 9 percent increase in life satisfaction, and a 10 percent improvement in social relationships. In this experiment their GoPro data is also incredibly cool research, supporting other findings that there is a typical "awe" face. Anderson, Craig L., Maria Monroy, and Dacher Keltner. 2018. "Awe in Nature Heals: Evidence from Military Veterans, At-Risk Youth, and College Students." *Emotion* 18 (8): 1195–1202. doi:10.1037/emo0000442.

232 **"We found that people":** Anwar, Yasmin. 2018. "Nature Is Proving to Be Awesome Medicine for PTSD." *Berkeley News* (July 12, 2018). https://news.berkeley.edu/2018/07/12/awe-nature-ptsd/.

232 **"It was curiosity":** Anwar, Yasmin, and Media Relations|. 2016. "Rush of Wild Nature Lowers PTSD in Veterans, At-Risk Teens." *Berkeley News* (May 31, 2016). https://news.berkeley.edu/2016/05/31 /awevswar/.

233 **PTSD and PTG can coexist:** Sometimes PTSD and PTG can exist at the same time. Cao, Chengqi, Li Wang, Jianhui Wu, Gen Li, Ruojiao Fang, Xing Cao, Ping Liu, Shu Luo, Brian J. Hall, and Jon D. Elhai. 2018. "Patterns of Posttraumatic Stress Disorder Symptoms and Posttraumatic Growth in an Epidemiological Sample of Chinese Earthquake Survivors: A Latent Profile Analysis." *Frontiers in Psychology* 9 (Aug). doi:10.3389/fpsyg.2018.01549.

233 **Hippocampal volume and PTSD:** Apfel, Brigitte A., Jessica Ross, Jennifer Hlavin, Dieter J. Meyerhoff, Thomas J. Metzler, Charles R. Marmar, Michael W. Weiner, Norbert Schuff, and Thomas C. Neylan. 2011. "Hippocampal Volume Differences in Gulf War Veterans with Current Versus Lifetime Posttraumatic Stress Disorder Symptoms." *Biological Psychiatry* 69 (6): 541–48. doi:10.1016/j .biopsych.2010.09.044.

234 **"We were taken into the hot zone":** Bojilova, Alia, and Anita Sands. 2021. "Resilience, Curiosity and Belonging: The Drivers of Successful Change." Thoughtworks (January 12). 51:38. https://www .thoughtworks.com/en-ec/insights/podcasts/pragmatism-in-practice /resilience-curiosity-and-belonging-the-drivers-of-successful-change.

235 **"finding a way to have a conversation with your adversary":** Breakthrough Co. 2019. "Psychologist, Alia Bojilova on Surviving Being Kidnapped in Syria, Leadership, and Diversity." 2019. www .youtube.com (September 10). 55:35. https://www.youtube.com /watch?v=yL1LkQsOOpY.

235 **Curiosity and PTG:** Kashdan, Todd B., Paul Rose, and Frank D. Fincham. 2004. "Curiosity and Exploration: Facilitating Positive Subjective Experiences and Personal Growth Opportunities." *Journal of Personality Assessment* 82 (3): 291–305. doi:10.1207 /s15327752jpa8203_05.

235 **"Facilitating curiosity can build":** Kashdan, "Curiosity and Interest."

235 **"People don't make decisions under immediate threat":** John Leach, interview with author, 2021.

236 **Openness to experience and stress:** Williams, Paula G., Holly K. Rau, Matthew R. Cribbet, and Heather E. Gunn. 2009. "Openness to Experience and Stress Regulation." *Journal of Research in Personality* 43 (5): 777–84. doi:10.1016/j.jrp.2009.06.003.

236 **"'awe junkie'":** Scott Barry Kaufman, communication with author, 2021.

Chapter 14: Religion

239 **Spiritual but not religious:** Lipka, Michael, and Claire Gecewicz. 2017. "More Americans Now Say They're Spiritual but Not Religious." Pew Research Center (September 6, 2017). https://www.pewresearch .org/fact-tank/2017/09/06/more-americans-now-say-theyre-spiritual -but-not-religious/.

239 **Awe and religion:** Keltner and Haidt described awe as a "spiritual emotion" but not necessarily a religious one.

239 **Pew religion and wonder study:** Jehovah's Witnesses, Buddhists, and Muslims report feeling wonder the most, but only marginally. However, those who reported no religious affiliation experienced wonder as often as Orthodox Christians, with both groups still reporting a high frequency of wonder compared with other religions. And people who experienced wonder once a week were almost equally likely to use common sense as their means for deciding right and wrong as using religious tenets. "Religious Landscape Study." 2014. Pew Research Center's Religion & Public Life Project. https://www.pewforum.org/religious-landscape-study /frequency-of-feeling-wonder-about-the-universe/.

240 **Universal religion:** Smith, John E. 1965. "The Structure of Religion." *Religious Studies* 1 (1): 63–73. doi:10.1017/S003441250000233X.

240 **"[It] is more than an emotion":** Heschel, Abraham Joshua. 1966. *God in Search of Man: A Philosophy of Judaism.* New York: Harper Torchbooks.

240 **"Religion is the domain par excellence":** Meyer, Birgit. 2016. "How to capture the 'wow': RR Marett's notion of awe and the study of religion." *Journal of the Royal Anthropological Institute* 22 (1): 7–26.

241 **Structure of religion:** Smith, "The Structure of Religion."

242 **Belief in God and awe:** Krause, Neal, and R. David Hayward. 2015. "Assessing Whether Practical Wisdom and Awe of God Are Associated with Life Satisfaction." *Psychology of Religion and Spirituality* 7 (1): 51–9. doi:10.1037/a0037694.

242 **P'an Ku:** "Pan Gu | Chinese Mythology." 2016. *Encyclopædia Britannica.* https://www.britannica.com/topic/Pan-Gu.

243 **"is the sense of wonder and humility":** Heschel, *God in Search of Man.*

243 **Wonder of God and life satisfaction:** Krause and Hayward, "Assessing

Whether Practical Wisdom and Awe of God Are Associated with Life Satisfaction."

243 **Spiritual transformation and positive outlook:** Cohen, Adam B., June Gruber, and Dacher Keltner. 2010. "Comparing Spiritual Transformations and Experiences of Profound Beauty." *Psychology of Religion and Spirituality* 2 (3): 127–35. doi:10.1037/a0019126.

243 **More charitable on Sundays:** Malhotra, Deepak K. 2008. "(When) Are Religious People Nicer? Religious Salience and the 'Sunday Effect' on Pro-Social Behavior." *Harvard Business School NOM Working Paper* 09-066 (November 6).

243 **Less porn on Sundays:** Edelman, B. G. 2009. "Red Light States: Who Buys Online Adult Entertainment?" *Journal of Economic Perspectives* 23, 209–220. doi:10.1257/jep.23.1.209.

244 **Awe, religion, and oneness:** Bai, Yang, Laura A. Maruskin, Serena Chen, Amie M. Gordon, Jennifer E. Stellar, Galen D. McNeil, Kaiping Peng, and Dacher Keltner. 2017. "Awe, the Diminished Self, and Collective Engagement: Universals and Cultural Variations in the Small Self." *Journal of Personality and Social Psychology* 113 (2): 185–209. doi:10.1037/pspa0000087.

244 **Leaderless movements:** Mandela, Gandhi, MLK. Some names are so synonymous with a movement that it's almost impossible to define it without them. But it's interesting to consider that the past decade has seen the emergence of several leaderless social movements, such as the Arab Spring, Brazil's June Journeys, Occupy Wall Street, France's Gilet Jaunes, and Hong Kong's Umbrella Protests. Research of past movements would suggest that leaderless movements are not sustainable past the protest stage, but we may be seeing the transition to a higher-order type of wonder-based leadership structure. Perhaps various charismatics, virtually connected to followers, can ignite a movement while also supporting a more diffuse leadership structure (what one organizer called a "leader-full" movement) that hedges against the dangers and weaknesses of cult-of-personality movements. Keating, Joshua. 2020. "The George Floyd Protests Show Leaderless Movements Are the Future of Politics." *Slate* (June 9). https://slate.com/news-and-politics/2020/06/george-floyd-global-leaderless-movements.html.

244 **Civil religion:** Bellah, Robert N. 1967. "Civil Religion in America." *Daedalus* 96 (1): 1–21.

244 **Jonestown background:** "Alternative Considerations of Jonestown & Peoples Temple." 2019. Department of Religious Studies at Sand Diego State University. http://jonestown.sdsu.edu.

245 **Jonestown children:** Krause, Charles A. 1978. "Survivor: 'They Started with the Babies.'" *Washington Post* (November 21). https://www.washingtonpost.com/archive/politics/1978/11/21 /survivor-they-started-with-the-babies/ec559372-be60-4355-a5fc -f5e306370992/?noredirect=on&utm_term=.9de22dd61a5c.

245 **Jonestown deaths:** "Alternative Considerations of Jonestown & Peoples Temple."

245 **Wonder and cults:** Stancato, Daniel M., and Dacher Keltner. 2021. "Awe, Ideological Conviction, and Perceptions of Ideological Opponents." *Emotion* 21 (1): 61.

246 **"divine magnetism":** Wallis, Arthur, Duncan Campbell, and Edward England. 2010. *In the Day of Thy Power: The Scriptural Principles of Revival.* Fort Washington, PA: CLC Publications.

246 **Charisma as a divine gift:** 1 Peter 4:10 (NIV).

246 **History of charisma:** Potts, John. "Charisma Eclipsed." 2009. *A History of Charisma:* 51–83. London: Palgrave Macmillan.

247 **"of the body and spirit":** Weber, Max. 1968. *On Charisma and Institution Building.* Chicago: University of Chicago Press.

247 **"[Weber] said the person":** Szelényi, Iván. 2011. "19. Weber on Charismatic Authority." YaleCourses (March 5). 49:25. https://www .youtube.com/watch?v=wvnamo2sRjU.

248 ***Vergemeinschaftung:*** Weber, Max, and Guenther Roth. 2013. *Economy and Society: An Outline of Interpretive Sociology.* Berkeley: University of California Press.

248 **"In a way, charismatic":** Szelényi, "19. Weber on Charismatic Authority."

249 **Surprise and worship:** Keltner and Haidt observed that accommodation without vastness (the wow moment) could be surprise, and vastness without accommodation (the whoa moment) could be worship or reverence. Allen, Summer. 2018. "The Science of Awe." Greater Good Science Center. https://ggsc.berkeley.edu /images/uploads/GGSC-JTF_White_Paper-Awe_FINAL.pdf.

249 **"Radicalisation occurs when this need for certainty":** "A Scientist's Opinion: Interview with Professor Arie Kruglanski About Our Need for Cognitive Closure during COVID-19." 2021. European Science-Media Hub (April 14). https://sciencemediahub.eu/2021/04/14/a -scientists-opinion-interview-with-professor-arie-kruglanski-about -our-need-for-cognitive-closure-during-covid-19/.

249 **"One is struck with awe":** Quinn, Philip L. 1997. "Religious Awe, Aesthetic Awe." *Midwest Studies in Philosophy* 21 (1): 290–5. doi:10.1111 /j.1475-4975.1997.tb00529.x.

250 **"I ate the tiny Host"**: Smith, Norman. 2011. *Out of the Norm.* United States: Dog Ear.

250 **"The most beautiful emotion"**: Einstein, Albert, and Etienne Delessert (1931). 1985. *Living Philosophies.* Mankato, MN: Creative Education.

251 **"No one can stand"**: Darwin, Charles, E. J. Browne, and Michael Neve (1839). 1989. *Voyage of the Beagle: Charles Darwin's Journal of Researches.* London, New York: Penguin Books.

251 **"the notion that science"**: Druyan, Ann, and Carl Sagan. 1997. *The Demon-Haunted World: Science as a Candle in the Dark.* London: Ballantine Books.

251 **"I have often said"**: Goleman, Daniel, Bstan-'dzin-Rgya-Mtsho, 14th Dalai Lama XIV, and Mind & Life Institute. 2003. *Destructive Emotions and How We Can Overcome Them: A Dialogue with the Dalai Lama.* London: Bloomsbury.

252 **"There is a God-shaped vacuum"**: Pascal, Blaise, and A. J. Krailsheimer (1670). 1995. *Pensées.* London, New York: Penguin Books.

Chapter 15: Slow Thought

254 **"We are enslaved by speed"**: "The Slow Food Manifesto." n.d. https:// vf63g1zsy1jqfwy46tx5qk6i-wpengine.netdna-ssl.com/wp-content /uploads/slow-food-manifesto.pdf.

254 **"The slow simmer approach to living"**: Kirk Schneider, interview with author, 2021.

255 **Meditation market size:** LaRosa, John. 2019. "$1.2 Billion U.S. Meditation Market Growing Strongly as It Becomes More Mainstream." MarketResearch.com (October 16). https://blog .marketresearch.com/1.2-billion-u.s.-meditation-market-growing -strongly-as-it-becomes-more-mainstream.

255 **Calm revenue:** Curry, David. 2020. "Calm Revenue and Usage Statistics (2020)." Business of Apps (August 20). https://www .businessofapps.com/data/calm-statistics/.

255 **Meditation market statistics:** Zuckerman, Arthur. 2020. "46 Meditation Statistics: 2020/2021 Benefits, Market Value & Trends." CompareCamp.com (May 20). https://comparecamp.com /meditation-statistics/.

255 **Kabat-Zinn background:** Kabat-Zinn, Jon, and Bhikkhu Anālayo. 2020. "Jon Kabat-Zinn & Ven. Anālayo Discuss Mindfulness & Health." 2020. The Wisdom Experience. https://wisdomexperience .org/wisdom-article/kabat-zinn-analayo-mindfulness-health/.

255 **STEs and postoperative pain:** Recent studies have shown that experiencing a mindfulness-based self-transcendent experience predicts better postoperative clinical outcomes, including improved healing and pain management, similar to Ulrich's findings vis-à-vis nature. Hanley, Adam W., and Eric L. Garland. 2022. "Self-Transcendence Predicts Better Pre-and Postoperative Outcomes in Two Randomized Clinical Trials of Brief Mindfulness-Based Interventions." *Mindfulness* 13 (6): 1–12. doi:10.1007/s12671-022-01896-6.

256 **Breadth of meditation traditions:** Millière Raphaël, Robin L. Carhart-Harris, Leor Roseman, Fynn-Mathis Trautwein, and Aviva Berkovich-Ohana. 2018. "Psychedelics, Meditation, and Self-Consciousness." *Frontiers in Psychology* 9 (September). doi:10.3389/fpsyg.2018.01475.

256 **"tsunami of meditation research":** Goleman, Daniel, and Richard J. Davidson. 2018. *The Science of Meditation: How to Change Your Brain, Mind and Body.* London: Penguin Life.

256 **Four primary styles of meditation:** Millière et al., "Psychedelics, Meditation, and Self-Consciousness."

257 **Deep versus wide meditative practice:** Goleman and Davidson, *The Science of Meditation.*

257 **Challenge with studying yogis:** Even researching these yogis is difficult. Some are quite literally in caves at the top of mountains. You can find in Goleman and Richardson's book an excellent story of the trials and tribulations of some intrepid researchers who first attempted to bring EEG equipment up to the yogis in their remote, rugged environs. Suffice to say, researchers now bring the yogis to the lab, not the other way around. Goleman and Davidson, *The Science of Meditation.*

257 **"that what gets practiced gets improved":** Goleman and Davidson, *The Science of Meditation.*

259 **"all forms of meditation share a common core":** Goleman and Davidson, *The Science of Meditation.*

259 **Meditation intensity matters:** Goleman and Davidson, *The Science of Meditation.*

259 **"quite similar, if not indistinguishable":** Barrett, Frederick. 2015. "Psilocybin, Meditation, Mystical Experiences, and the Brain." Horizons 2015. 20:37. https://www.youtube.com/watch?v=X5E2LVQNknI.

259 **Similarities between meditation and psychedelics:** Millière et al., "Psychedelics, Meditation, and Self-Consciousness."

260 **Meditation's original purpose:** Goleman and Davidson, *The Science of Meditation.*

260 **Meditation benefits even beginners:** Creswell, J. David, Adrienne A. Taren, Emily K. Lindsay, Carol M. Greco, Peter J. Gianaros, April Fairgrieve, Anna L. Marsland, et al. 2016. "Alterations in Resting-State Functional Connectivity Link Mindfulness Meditation with Reduced Interleukin 6: A Randomized Controlled Trial." *Biological Psychiatry* 80 (1): 53–61.

260 **the "dark night":** There is a phenomenon called "the dark night," in which, just like a bad trip, some people have had negative results from meditation. This phenomenon is rare but not unheard of. Hunt, Harry T. 2007. "'Dark Nights of the Soul': Phenomenology and Neurocognition of Spiritual Suffering in Mysticism and Psychosis." *Review of General Psychology* 11 (3): 209–34. doi:10.1037/1089-2680.11.3.209.

260 **Meditation supports wonder elements:** Millière et al., "Psychedelics, Meditation, and Self-Consciousness."

260 **Meditators have lower "attention interference":** Hodgins, Holley S., and Kathryn C. Adair. 2010. "Attentional Processes and Meditation." *Consciousness and Cognition* 19 (4): 872–8. doi:10.1016/j.concog.2010.04.002.

261 **Meditation and repetition suppression:** Kasamatsu, Akira, and Tomio Hirai. 1966. "An Electroencephalographic Study on the Zen Meditation (Zazen)." *Psychiatry and Clinical Neurosciences* 20 (4): 315–36. doi:10.1111/j.1440-1819.1966.tb02646.x.

261 **Mindfulness increases openness to experience:** Barner, Charlotte P., and Robert W. Barner. 2011. *Mindfulness, Openness to Experience, and Transformational Learning.* Oxford Handbooks Online. Oxford University Press. doi:10.1093/oxfordhb/9780199736300.013.0087.

261 **Yogis exhibit trait-level changes:** Lutz, Antoine, Lawrence L. Greischar, Nancy B. Rawlings, Matthieu Ricard, and Richard J. Davidson. 2004. "Long-Term Meditators Self-Induce High-Amplitude Gamma Synchrony During Mental Practice." *Proceedings of the National Academy of Sciences* 101 (46): 16369–73.

261 **Novice meditators and bias:** Empathy and openness both decrease bias. Research shows that compassion meditation can be an effective method to reap this benefit, as it can negate previously held biases in as little as sixteen hours of practice. Kang, Yoona, Jeremy R. Gray, and John F. Dovidio. 2014. "The Nondiscriminating Heart: Lovingkindness Meditation Training Decreases Implicit Intergroup Bias." *Journal of Experimental Psychology: General* 143 (3): 1306.

262 **Cortical thickness:** Grant, Joshua A., Emma G. Duerden, Jérôme Courtemanche, Mariya Cherkasova, Gary H. Duncan, and Pierre Rainville. 2013. "Cortical Thickness, Mental Absorption and Meditative Practice: Possible Implications for Disorders of Attention." *Biological Psychology* 92 (2): 275–81. doi:10.1016/j .biopsycho.2012.09.007.

262 **Oceanic breath and vagal activity:** Gerritsen, Roderik J. S., and Guido P. H. Band. 2018. "Breath of Life: The Respiratory Vagal Stimulation Model of Contemplative Activity." *Frontiers in Human Neuroscience* 12 (October). doi:10.3389/fnhum.2018.00397.

262 **Meditation and proinflammatory cytokines:** Rosenkranz, Melissa A., Antoine Lutz, David M. Perlman, David RW Bachhuber, Brianna S. Schuyler, Donal G. MacCoon, and Richard J. Davidson. 2016. "Reduced Stress and Inflammatory Responsiveness in Experienced Meditators Compared to a Matched Healthy Control Group." *Psychoneuroendocrinology* 68: 117–25. doi:10.1016/j .psyneuen.2016.02.013.

263 **"We find gratitude journaling":** "Robert Emmons: Awe and Gratitude." 2010. Greater Good (November 24). 2:42. https://www .youtube.com/watch?v=Ck6IgrlDhBo.

263 **Gratitude and lower depression:** Studies show gratitude leads to lower depression and higher levels of social support while making one less likely to consider suicide. Wood, Alex M., John Maltby, Raphael Gillett, P. Alex Linley, and Stephen Joseph. 2008. "The Role of Gratitude in the Development of Social Support, Stress, and Depression: Two Longitudinal Studies." *Journal of Research in Personality* 42 (4): 854–71. doi:10.1016/j.jrp.2007.11.003.

263 **Gratitude and cardiovascular health:** Research conducted at Massachusetts General Hospital found the presence of gratitude in a patient "may independently predict superior cardiovascular health." Huffman, Jeff C., Eleanor E. Beale, Scott R. Beach, Christopher M. Celano, Arianna M. Belcher, Shannon V. Moore, Laura Suarez, et al. 2015. "Design and Baseline Data from the Gratitude Research in Acute Coronary Events (GRACE) Study." *Contemporary Clinical Trials* 44 (September): 11–9. doi:10.1016/j.cct.2015.07.002; "Discovering the Health and Wellness Benefits of Gratitude." n.d. Wharton Health Care Management Alumni Association. https://www .whartonhealthcare.org/discovering_the_health.

263 **Gratitude and physical activity, inflammation:** Other studies show that gratitude increases physical activity and therefore the speed of recovery for heart patients while reducing their inflammatory biomarkers. Mills, Paul J., Laura Redwine, Kathleen Wilson,

Meredith A. Pung, Kelly Chinh, Barry H. Greenberg, Ottar Lunde, et al. 2015. "The Role of Gratitude in Spiritual Well-Being in Asymptomatic Heart Failure Patients." *Spirituality in Clinical Practice* 2 (1): 5–17. doi:10.1037/scp0000050.

263 **Gratitude and sleep:** Another study found regularly focusing on gratitude and thankfulness improved both the quality and duration of sleep, and people who keep gratitude journals "reported fewer health complaints, more time exercising, and fewer symptoms of physical illness." Emmons, Robert A., and Michael E. McCullough. 2003. "Counting Blessings Versus Burdens: An Experimental Investigation of Gratitude and Subjective Well-Being in Daily Life." *Journal of Personality and Social Psychology* 84 (2): 377–89. doi:10.1037/0022-3514.84.2.377.

263 **Benefits of gratitude:** Van Cappellen, Patty, and Bernard Rimé. 2013. "Positive Emotions and Self-Transcendence." In *Religion, Personality, and Social Behavior.* Edited by Vassilis Saroglou, 133–56. London: Psychology Press.

263 **Gratitude and well-being:** Emmons, Robert A., Michael E. McCullough, and Jo-Ann Tsang. 2003. "The Assessment of Gratitude." *Positive Psychological Assessment: A Handbook of Models and Measures.* Edited by Shane J. Lopez and C. R. Snyder, 327–41. Washington, DC: American Psychological Association.

263 **Gratitude and prosocial behavior:** Stellar, Jennifer E., Amie Gordon, Craig L. Anderson, Paul K. Piff, Galen D. McNeil, and Dacher Keltner. 2018. "Awe and Humility." *Journal of Personality and Social Psychology* 114 (2): 258–69. doi:10.1037/pspi0000109.

263 **Openness, curiosity and gratitude:** Szcześniak, Małgorzata, Wojciech Rodzeń, Agnieszka Malinowska, and Zdzisław Kroplewski. 2020. "Big Five Personality Traits and Gratitude: The Role of Emotional Intelligence." *Psychology Research and Behavior Management* 13 (November): 977–88. doi:10.2147/prbm.s268643.

264 **Gratitude and small-self:** Piff, Paul K., Pia Dietze, Matthew Feinberg, Daniel M. Stancato, and Dacher Keltner. 2015. "Awe, the Small Self, and Prosocial Behavior." *Journal of Personality and Social Psychology* 108 (6): 883–99. doi:10.1037/pspi0000018.

264 **Gratitude and leadership:** According to a Wharton study, grateful leaders "motivated employees to become more productive [because] when employees feel valued, they have high job satisfaction, engage in productive relationships, are motivated to do their best, and work toward achieving the company's goals." "Discovering the Health and Wellness Benefits of Gratitude."

264 **Gratitude lowers aggression:** DeWall, C. Nathan, Nathaniel M. Lambert, Richard S. Pond, Todd B. Kashdan, and Frank D. Fincham. 2012. "A Grateful Heart Is a Nonviolent Heart: Cross-Sectional, Experience Sampling, Longitudinal, and Experimental Evidence." *Social Psychological and Personality Science* 3 (2): 232–40. doi:10.1177/1948550611416675.

264 **Ingrouping, bias, and gratitude:** Rambaud, Stéphanie, Julie Collange, Jean Louis Tavani, and Franck Zenasni. 2021. "Positive Intergroup Interdependence, Prejudice, Outgroup Stereotype and Helping Behaviors: The Role of Group-Based Gratitude." *International Review of Social Psychology* 34 (1). doi:10.5334/irsp.433.

264 **Meditative prayer:** Poloma, Margaret M., and Brian F. Pendleton. 1991. "The Effects of Prayer and Prayer Experiences on Measures of General Well-Being." *Journal of Psychology and Theology* 19 (1): 71–83. doi:10.1177/009164719101900107.

265 **The impact of stories is universal:** Dehghani, Morteza, Reihane Boghrati, Kingson Man, Joe Hoover, Sarah I. Gimbel, Ashish Vaswani, Jason D. Zevin, et al. 2017. "Decoding the Neural Representation of Story Meanings Across Languages." *Human Brain Mapping* 38 (12): 6096–106. doi:10.1002/hbm.23814.

265 **"reverse engineer what it all means":** Michelle Shiota, interview with author, 2021.

266 **Journaling and empathy:** Outlaw, Kerri, and Deborah S. Rushing. 2018. "Increasing Empathy in Mental Health Nursing Using Simulation and Reflective Journaling." *Journal of Nursing Education* 57 (12): 766–66. doi:10.3928/01484834-20181119-13.

266 **Journaling prompts and awe:** Piff et al., "Awe, the Small Self, and Prosocial Behavior."

266 **Benefits of nostalgia:** Routledge, Clay, Jamie Arndt, Tim Wildschut, Constantine Sedikides, Claire M. Hart, Jacob Juhl, Ad J. J. M. Vingerhoets, and Wolff Schlotz. 2011. "The Past Makes the Present Meaningful: Nostalgia as an Existential Resource." *Journal of Personality and Social Psychology* 101 (3): 638–52. doi:10.1037/a0024292.

267 **"People who score high":** Mineo, Liz, and Harvard staff. 2022. "That Feeling You Get When Listening to Sad Music? It's Humanity." *Harvard Gazette* (May 11). https://news.harvard.edu/gazette /story/2022/05/that-feeling-you-get-when-listening-to-sad-music -its-humanity/.

267 **Mixed emotions support resiliency:** Larsen, J. T., S. H. Hemenover, C. J. Norris, and J. T. Cacioppo. 2003. "Turning Adversity to Advantage: On the Virtues of the Coactivation of Positive and

Negative Emotions." Edited by L. G. Aspinwall and U. M. Staudinger, *A Psychology of Human Strengths: Perspectives on an Emerging Field*, 211–26. Washington, DC: American Psychological Association.

267 **Mixed emotions support grief recovery:** Bauer, Jack J., and George A. Bonanno. 2001. "Continuity amid Discontinuity: Bridging One's Past and Present in Stories of Conjugal Bereavement." *Narrative Inquiry* 11 (1): 123. doi:10.1075/ni.11.1.06bau.

268 **Mixed emotions increase task accuracy:** Rees, L., N. B. Rothman, R. Lehavy, and J. Sanchez-Burks. 2013. "The Ambivalent Mind Can Be a Wise Mind: Emotional Ambivalence Increases Judgment Accuracy." *Journal of Experimental Social Psychology* 49: 360–7.

269 **"I was the only person of color":** Azizi Seixas, interview with author, 2021.

269 **"Sleep helps from a mechanical standpoint":** Seixas, interview.

269 **Stress inhibits mixed emotions:** Reich, John W., Alex J. Zautra, and Mary Davis. 2003. "Dimensions of Affect Relationships: Models and Their Integrative Implications." *Review of General Psychology* 7 (1): 66–83. doi:10.1037/1089-2680.7.1.66.

270 **"I thought about shift workers":** Dayna Johnson, interview with author, 2021.

270 **Gratitude and sleep:** Emmons and McCullough, "Counting Blessings Versus Burdens."

271 **Patience in world religions:** "Patience as a Virtue: Religious and Psychological Perspectives." 2007. *Research in the Social Scientific Study of Religion* 18 (January): 177–207. doi:10.1163/ej.9789004158511.i-301.69.

271 **Well-being benefits of patience:** Schnitker, Sarah A. 2012. "An Examination of Patience and Well-Being." *Journal of Positive Psychology* 7 (4): 263–80.

271 **Mindfulness reduces rumination:** Deyo, Mary, Kimberly A. Wilson, Jason Ong, and Cheryl Koopman. 2009. "Mindfulness and Rumination: Does Mindfulness Training Lead to Reductions in the Ruminative Thinking Associated with Depression?" *Explore* 5 (5) 265–71.

Chapter 16: Psychedelics

273 **"When is it going to come back?":** Sakuda, Pam. 2012. "Pam Sakuda Speaks on Psilocybin Ability to Ease Anxiety for Cancer Patients Facing Death." www.youtube.com (May 3). 8:43. https://www.youtube.com/watch?v=uCdzoJ4QRpk.

274 **"There's my Pammy":** "Can Psychedelic Drugs Treat Depression?"
    2017. MAPS. https://maps.org/news/multimedia-library/2211-can
    -psychedelic-drugs-treat-depression1.

275 **Existential depression and psychedelics:** Based on results found at
    the six-month follow-up. Griffiths, Roland R., Matthew W. Johnson,
    Michael A. Carducci, Annie Umbricht, William A. Richards, Brian
    D. Richards, Mary P. Cosimano, and Margaret A Klinedinst. 2016.
    "Psilocybin Produces Substantial and Sustained Decreases in
    Depression and Anxiety in Patients with Life-Threatening Cancer:
    A Randomized Double-Blind Trial." *Journal of Psychopharmacology* 30
    (12): 1181–97. doi:10.1177/0269881116675513.

276 **"I had great difficulty in speaking clearly":** "Bicycle Day Revisited."
    2018. Mike Jay (December 31). https://mikejay.net/bicycle-day
    -revisited/.

277 **Hofmann's hope for the social change potential of LSD:** Albert
    Hofmann saw therapeutic potential in psychedelics from early in
    the development of LSD, but it was the potential of psychedelics to
    support social issues that most inspired him. Just prior to his death
    in 2008 at age 101, Albert Hofmann wrote, "Alienation from nature
    and the loss of the experience of being part of the living creation
    is the greatest tragedy of our materialistic era. It is the causative
    reason for ecological devastation and climate change. Therefore I
    attribute absolute highest importance to consciousness change. I
    regard psychedelics as catalyzers for this." Bache, Christopher M.
    2019. *LSD and the Mind of the Universe: Diamonds from Heaven.* New York:
    Simon and Schuster.

278 **"therefore it is political":** David Nutt, interview with author, 2021.

279 **Equasy:** Nutt, D. J. 2009. "Equasy—an Overlooked Addiction with
    Implications for the Current Debate on Drug Harms." *Journal of
    Psychopharmacology* 23 (1): 3–5. doi:10.1177/0269881108099672.

279 **"Most drug experts believe":** "Sacked—for Telling the Truth About
    Drugs." 2009. *The Independent* (October). https://www.independent
    .co.uk/life-style/health-and-families/health-news/sacked-ndash-for-
    telling-the-truth-about-drugs-1812255.html.

279 **"a bad day for science":** "Sacked—for Telling the Truth About Drugs."

279 **"My view is policy":** "Sacked—for Telling the Truth About Drugs."

279 **"people have realized they've been lied to":** David Nutt, interview
    with author, 2021.

280 **"classic psychedelics are a class of hallucinogens":** Davis, Alan
    K., Sara So, Rafael Lancelotta, Joseph P. Barsuglia, and Roland R.
    Griffiths. 2019. "5-Methoxy-N,N-Dimethyltryptamine (5-MeO-

DMT) Used in a Naturalistic Group Setting Is Associated with Unintended Improvements in Depression and Anxiety." *American Journal of Drug and Alcohol Abuse* 45 (2): 161–9. doi:10.1080/00952990.20 18.1545024.

281 **"acute destabilization of brain networks":** Johnson, Matthew W., and Roland R. Griffiths. 2017. "Potential Therapeutic Effects of Psilocybin." *Neurotherapeutics* 14 (3): 734–40. doi:10.1007/s13311-017-0542-y.

281 **Psychedelic destabilization prompts pliability:** Johnson and Griffiths, "Potential Therapeutic Effects of Psilocybin."

281 **"therapeutic window":** Nutt, David, and Robin Carhart-Harris. 2021. "The Current Status of Psychedelics in Psychiatry." *JAMA Psychiatry* 78 (2): 121–22. doi:10.1001/jamapsychiatry.2020.2171.

281 **Psychedelics increase oxytocin and bonding:** Schmid, Yasmin, Florian Enzler, Peter Gasser, Eric Grouzmann, Katrin H. Preller, Franz X. Vollenweider, Rudolf Brenneisen, Felix Müller, Stefan Borgwardt, and Matthias E. Liechti. 2015. "Acute Effects of Lysergic Acid Diethylamide in Healthy Subjects." *Biological Psychiatry* 78 (8): 544–53. doi:10.1016/j.biopsych.2014.11.015.

281 **"MKUltra tried that":** David Nutt, interview with author, 2021.

282 **MKUltra:** Kinzer, Stephen. 2019. *Poisoner in Chief: Sidney Gottlieb and the CIA Search for Mind Control.* New York: Henry Holt and Company.

283 **"this is like a baby's brain":** David Nutt, interview with author, 2021.

283 **"It's hard and energy expensive":** Nutt, interview.

284 **Osmond and psychedelics:** Kaplan, Robert M. 2016. "Humphry Fortescue Osmond (1917-2004), a Radical and Conventional Psychiatrist: The Transcendent Years." *Journal of Medical Biography* 24 (1): 115–24. doi:10.1177/0967772013479520.

284 **"There is a heightened political lens":** Peter Hendricks, interview with author, 2021.

285 **Alcoholism symptom improvement:** Johnson and Griffiths, "Potential Therapeutic Effects of Psilocybin."

285 **Bill Wilson and psychedelics:** Lattin, Don. 2012. *Distilled Spirits: Getting High, Then Sober, with a Famous Writer, a Forgotten Philosopher, and a Hopeless Drunk.* Berkeley: University of California Press.

285 **Cost of smoking addiction:** "Burden of Tobacco Use in the U.S." 2019. Centers for Disease Control and Prevention (January 23). https://www.cdc.gov/tobacco/campaign/tips/resources/data /cigarette-smoking-in-united-states.html.

285 **Efficacy of smoking-cessation drug:** Study reflected psychedelics

as compared to the drug Chantix at a one-year follow-up. Baker, Timothy B., Megan E. Piper, James H. Stein, Stevens S. Smith, Daniel M. Bolt, David L. Fraser, and Michael C. Fiore. 2016. "Effects of Nicotine Patch vs Varenicline vs Combination Nicotine Replacement Therapy on Smoking Cessation at 26 Weeks: A Randomized Clinical Trial." *JAMA* 315 (4): 371–9. doi:10.1001/jama.2015.19284.

285 **Psychedelics and smoking cessation:** Johnson and Griffiths, "Potential Therapeutic Effects of Psilocybin."

288 **Percentage of sudden death:** Lewis, Mary Elizabeth, Feng-Chang Lin, Parin Nanavati, Neil Mehta, Louisa Mounsey, Anthony Nwosu, Irion Pursell, Eugene H. Chung, J. Paul Mounsey, and Ross J. Simpson. 2016. "Estimated Incidence and Risk Factors of Sudden Unexpected Death." *Open Heart* 3 (1): e000321. doi:10.1136/openhrt-2015-000321.

289 **Life-threatening cancer diagnoses:** Andersen, Kristoffer A. A., Robin Carhart-Harris, David J. Nutt, and David Erritzoe. 2021. "Therapeutic Effects of Classic Serotonergic Psychedelics: A Systematic Review of Modern-era Clinical Studies." *Acta Psychiatrica Scandinavica* 143 (2): 101–18. doi:10.1111/acps.13249.

290 **Dosage effects psychedelic study:** Griffiths, Roland R., Matthew W. Johnson, Michael A. Carducci, Annie Umbricht, William A. Richards, Brian D. Richards, Mary P. Cosimano, and Margaret A. Klinedinst. 2016. "Psilocybin Produces Substantial and Sustained Decreases in Depression and Anxiety in Patients with Life-Threatening Cancer: A Randomized Double-Blind Trial." *Journal of Psychopharmacology* 30 (12): 1181–97. doi:10.1177/0269881116675513.

290 **OCD and psychedelics:** Andersen, Kristoffer A. A., Robin Carhart-Harris, David J. Nutt, and David Erritzoe. 2021. "Therapeutic Effects of Classic Serotonergic Psychedelics: A Systematic Review of Modern-era Clinical Studies."

290 **Psychedelics and color blindness:** There have been self-reported cases of recreational psychedelic use improving color blindness. Anthony, J. E. C., A. Winstock, J. A. Ferris, and D. J. Nutt. 2020. "Improved Colour Blindness Symptoms Associated with Recreational Psychedelic Use: Results from the Global Drug Survey 2017." *Drug Science, Policy and Law* 6: 1–6. doi:10.1177/2050324520942345.

290 **Psychedelics as anti-inflammatory drug:** Khan, Shariq Mansoor, Gregory T. Carter, Sunil K. Aggarwal, and Julie Holland. 2021. "Psychedelics for Brain Injury: A Mini-Review." *Frontiers in Neurology* 12 (July). doi:10.3389/fneur.2021.685085.

291 **Magnitude of mystical experience predictive of outcomes:** Johnson and Griffiths, "Potential Therapeutic Effects of Psilocybin."

291 **Microdosing:** Despite its popularity, especially in Silicon Valley, microdosing—taking very small, sub-perceptual amounts of a psychedelic, typically LSD—doesn't offer a verifiable effect, according to recent research. While self-reporting showed results of enhanced creativity and performance, a large, randomized study of microdosing did not find those results. There was a study with mice that indicated microdosing might lower anxiety and improve mood, so perhaps further study is required to fully understand the impact, if any. If taking a microdose makes you feel more focused, relaxed, creative, etc., great, but the evidence suggests that groovy feeling is, according to David Nutt, "a very sophisticated placebo." But Nutt is also keen to remind us that placebo effects are still effects. Nutt, interview.

291 **Quantum of academic papers about psilocybin:** After the UN Convention on Psychotropic Substances of 1971, psychedelic studies came to an effective standstill, and while some did continue quietly, they were within a very limited scope. Even today, despite current restrictions, there have still been more than 13,000 academic papers published about psilocybin in the past ten years alone. You can find that info on Google Scholar: https://scholar.google.com /scholar?hl=en&as_sdt=0,5&as_ylo=2012&as_yhi=2022&q=psilocybin.

292 **"It's the negative emotional experiences":** Nutt, interview.

293 **"psychedelics . . . the only real game in town":** David Yaden, interview with author, 2021.

293 **"if we just want to make the claim":** Michelle Shiota, interview with author, 2021.

294 **"shows the power of the mind":** Nutt, interview.

295 **"That's why we don't see much parapsychology":** "David Luke, Ph.D: Synesthesia, Shared Hallucinations, and Telepathy with DMT." 2020. *Third Wave* (May 3). 1:05:07. https://thethirdwave.co/podcast/episode -80-synesthesia-shared-hallucinations-telepathy-with-dmt/.

295 **Bias against more "mysterious" branches of science:** This is not uncommon among scientists. Science reporter Steve Paulson once wrote, "I've interviewed a number of prominent scientists who are quite hostile to the very idea of mystery, which they think is an invitation to obfuscation, mumbo jumbo—trying to sneak religion in through the back door." It's no surprise then that bias against certain ideas in academic publishing is also a well-documented phenomenon. Academic Alena Drieschová wrote in a paper exploring this issue, "Publications are crucial for determining who

gets to transmit knowledge (and therefore what kind of knowledge) onto students. . . . In short, beyond individual academics' life stories, these publications matter for how our societies are run." Drieschová believes that this kind of idea blockade has real-life consequences, even if the ideas don't seem that consequential when they are being studied. Drieschová, Alena. 2020. "Failure, Persistence, Luck and Bias in Academic Publishing." *New Perspectives* 28 (2): 145–49. doi:10.1177/2336825X20911792; Paulson, Steve, Lisa Sideris, Jennifer Stellar, and Piercarlo Valdesolo. 2021. "Beyond Oneself: The Ethics and Psychology of Awe." *Annals of the New York Academy of Sciences* 1501 (1): 30–47. doi:10.1111/nyas.14323.

296 **Huxley received LSD at death:** Schimmel, Nina, Joost J. Breeksema, Sanne Y. Smith-Apeldoorn, Jolien Veraart, Wim van den Brink, and Robert A. Schoevers. 2022. "Psychedelics for the Treatment of Depression, Anxiety, and Existential Distress in Patients with a Terminal Illness: A Systematic Review." *Psychopharmacology* 239 (1): 15–33. doi:10.1007/s00213-021-06027-y.

296 **"psychedelics break down your brain":** Nutt, interview.

296 **Psychedelic experience is most meaningful moment:** Yaden, David Bryce, Jonathan Haidt, Ralph W. Hood, David R. Vago, and Andrew B. Newberg. 2017. "The Varieties of Self-Transcendent Experience." *Review of General Psychology* 21 (2): 143–60. doi:10.1037 /gpr0000102.

296 **"one of the most important figures":** Nutt, interview.

296 **"You go deep enough or far out enough":** Pollan, Michael. 2019. *How to Change Your Mind: The New Science of Psychedelics*. London: Penguin Books.

297 **"These drugs facilitate":** Nutt, interview.

297 **Loosening psychedelic regulations:** "Psychedelics Legalization & Decriminalization Tracker." n.d. *Psilocybin Alpha*. https:// psilocybinalpha.com/data/psychedelic-laws.

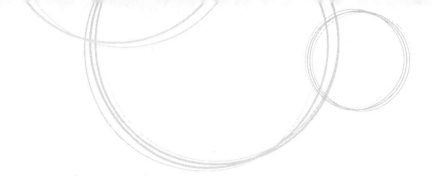

Index

Page numbers in *italics* refer to figures and tables.

About the Author

A world-renowned speaker, writer, and authority on the future of work, **Monica C. Parker** has spent decades helping people discover how to lead and live wonderfully. The founder of global human analytics and change consultancy HATCH, whose clients include blue-chip companies such as LinkedIn, Google, Prudential, and LEGO, Parker challenges corporate systems to advocate for more meaningful work lives. In addition to her extensive advocacy work, she has been an opera singer, a museum exhibition designer, a policy director, a chamber of commerce CEO, and a homicide investigator defending death-row inmates. A lover of the arts, literature, and Mexican food, Parker and her family split their time between Atlanta, London, and Nice. Her wonderbringers include travel, fellowship with friends, and Trey Anastasio's guitar.

www.monica-parker.com

Ready for Wonder?

Want to start developing your wonder mindset and begin enjoying the benefits of a life steeped in wonder?

Take the Wonderprone Quiz now at:
Monica-Parker.com/wonderprone

- Discover how wonderprone you are.

- Learn where you sit on the spectrum of each of the wonder elements of openness, curiosity, absorption, and awe.

- Identify your wonder strengths so you can start developing your own wonder practice today.

- Then, when you're ready, invite a friend to take the test themselves—wonder shared is wonder multiplied!

Visit Monica-Parker.com for the Wonderprone Quiz, other wonder resources, and to share in *The Power of Wonder* together.